MW01138113

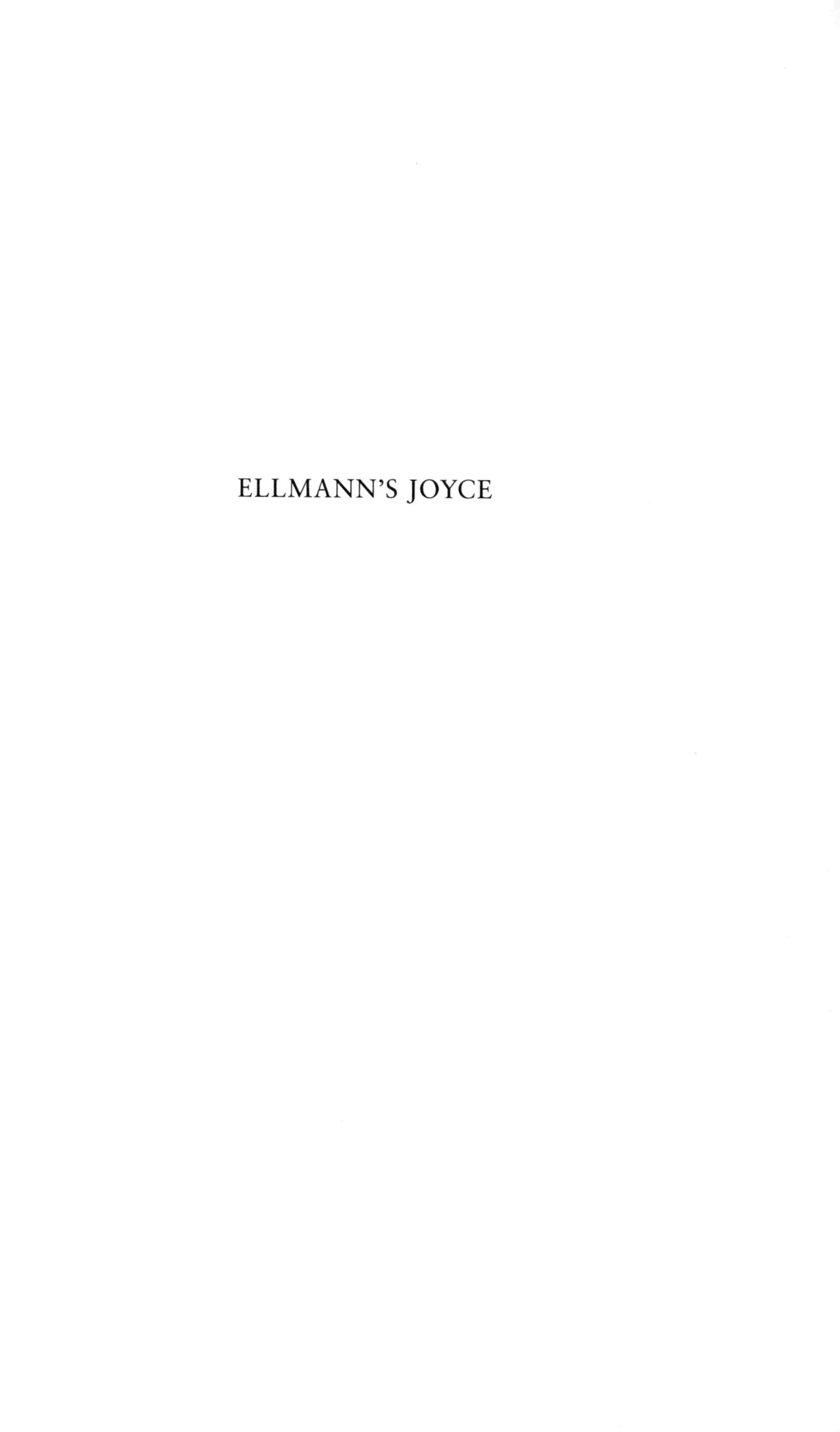

ELLMANN'S JOYCE

ALSO BY ZACHARY LEADER

Reading Blake's Songs

Writer's Block

Revision and Romantic Authorship

The Life of Kingsley Amis

The Life of Saul Bellow: To Fame and Fortune, 1915–1964

The Life of Saul Bellow: Love and Strife, 1964–2005

EDITED BY ZACHARY LEADER

Romantic Period Writings: 1798–1832: An Anthology (with Ian Haywood)

The Letters of Kingsley Amis

On Modern British Fiction

Percy Bysshe Shelley: The Major Works (with Michael O'Neill)

The Movement Reconsidered: Essays on Larkin, Amis, Gunn, Davie, and Their Contemporaries

On Life-Writing

ELLMANN'S JOYCE

THE BIOGRAPHY OF A MASTERPIECE AND ITS MAKER

ZACHARY LEADER

THE BELKNAP PRESS OF HARVARD UNIVERSITY PRESS
Cambridge, Massachusetts & London, England
2025

Printed in the United States of America

First printing

Library of Congress Cataloging-in-Publication Data

Names: Leader, Zachary, author.
Title: Ellmann's Joyce : the biography of a masterpiece and its maker / Zachary Leader.
Description: Cambridge, Massachusetts : The Belknap Press of Harvard University Press, 2025. | Includes bibliographical references and index.
Identifiers: LCCN 2024042498 (print) | LCCN 2024042499 (ebook) | ISBN 9780674248397 (cloth) | ISBN 9780674300446 (pdf) | ISBN 9780674300453 (epub)
Subjects: LCSH: Ellmann, Richard, 1918–1987. James Joyce. | Ellmann, Richard, 1918–1987. | Joyce, James, 1882–1941. | Biographers—United States—Biography. | Critics—United States—Biography. | Novelists, Irish—20th century—Biography. | Biography as a literary form. | LCGFT: Biographies.
Classification: LCC PR6019.O9 Z533235 2025 (print) | LCC PR6019.O9 (ebook) | DDC 823 / .912 [B]—dc23 / eng / 20240923
LC record available at https://lccn.loc.gov/2024042498
LC ebook record available at https://lccn.loc.gov/2024042499

To the memory of my wife
ALICE LEADER
(1947–2023)

CONTENTS

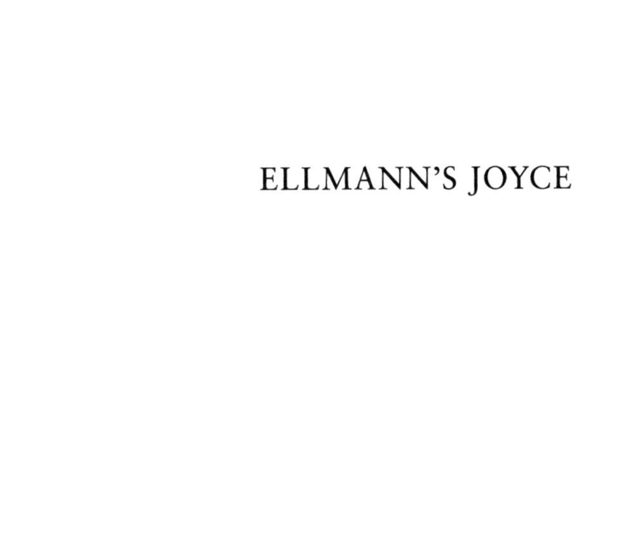

ELLMANN'S JOYCE

Introduction

RICHARD ELLMANN'S *James Joyce* has been called "the greatest literary biography of the twentieth century."[1] On the eve of its publication in 1959, Sheldon Meyer, Ellmann's editor at Oxford University Press, reported "the most ecstatic reaction I have seen to any book I have known anything about."[2] It was reviewed on the front page of the *New York Times Book Review* and won the National Book Award in the United States. In Britain, Frank Kermode wrote in the *Spectator* that he thought the biography would "fix Joyce's image for a generation," a prediction that was, if anything, too cautious.[3] Five decades later, Joseph Brooker, a literary academic and author of a reception history of Joyce's writings, described Ellmann's book as "the central scholarly work in Joyce studies, present in the bibliography of literally every work published on Joyce."[4] When the revised and expanded second edition was published, the *New York Times Book Review* again featured it on its front page, a rare honor for a second edition. In Britain it won the James Tait Black Prize and the Duff Cooper Prize.

This book tells the story of the making of *James Joyce* and of its maker. It is neither a conventional biography nor a conventional analytic study. Part I, "The Biographer," takes Ellmann up to 1952, the year he began to work seriously on the biography. The chapters in this part of the book proceed for the most part chronologically, in the manner of Ellmann's own biographies. Part II, "The Biography," is structured by topic rather than chronology, with chapters devoted to different aspects of the biography's making. In broad terms, the book shows how and why Ellmann became a biographer and what skills he brought to the task; how he chose Joyce as a subject; how he won the cooperation of the Joyce estate and of Joyce's family (and at what cost, in terms of what he felt he owed to them or could reveal); how he collected or gained access to Joyce's scattered papers; how he chose interviewees and conducted interviews; how he placated publishers and thwarted competitors; how he determined the biography's themes and structure, including the problem of balancing narrative with literary analysis; how and why he produced a second edition; and how the biography has influenced Joyce studies and Joyce's readers up to the present day.

Although aspects of the biography's making have been discussed in scholarly articles by Amanda Sigler, John McCourt, and others, the larger story has never been told in book form.[5] Nor has anyone considered how Ellmann himself balanced the rival claims of life and art—what Yeats called the writer's "choice."[6] In what follows, I discuss the claims of Ellmann's family life and those of his research and writing. I will also discuss his teaching and administrative duties, and the reasons he moved from Harvard, where he taught from 1946 to 1951, to Northwestern University, where he taught for seventeen years despite a steady stream of offers from Ivy League and other universities. He worked all the time, according to his daughters, but he was also a social being, a lover of gossip and parties.

According to Gabriel Garcia Marquez, "everyone has three lives, a public life, a private life, and a secret life."[7] Ellmann's public life was richly rewarded; his private life was admirable, though not without troubles; and his secret life, a late development, was startling. He was a good man, and goodness, I shall argue, like happiness, need not, as Henry de Montherlant put it, write in "white ink on a white page."[8]

How *James Joyce* came about is amply documented in the Richard Ellmann Papers at the University of Tulsa, a collection of some 450 boxes of correspondence, manuscripts, photographs, published articles, drafts, sound recordings, lectures, lecture notes, and galley and page proofs. Ellmann kept everything. So did his parents and his brothers. The family was extremely close, and all its members were voluminous correspondents. That Ellmann chose to place his papers at Tulsa was partly due to the university's provost, Thomas F. Staley, professor of English and founding editor of *Joyce Studies: An Annual* and the *James Joyce Quarterly*. Staley would become director of the Harry Ransom Humanities Research Center at the University of Texas at Austin, gobbling up modern British literary manuscripts to the dismay of Philip Larkin and other cultural nationalists.[9]

Ellmann was born in the Midwest, in the city of Highland Park, Michigan, today an enclave of Detroit, on March 15, 1918, and died in Oxford on May 13, 1987. He wrote what most people think of as two other biographies: *Yeats: The Man and the Masks* (1948) and *Oscar Wilde* (1988). The Yeats book, his first, was published when Ellmann was thirty. It was his PhD thesis, minimally revised, and had begun life as a study of Yeats's intellectual development. *Oscar Wilde,* his last book, was finished two months before his death at the age of sixty-nine and published posthumously. In the United States it won the Pulitzer Prize and the National Book Critics Circle Award.

Of the eighteen other books Ellmann published in his lifetime—books of criticism, scholarly editions, collections of biographical essays, and anthologies—the most obviously influential were two anthologies: *The Modern Tradition: Backgrounds of Modern Literature* (1965), coedited with Charles J. Feidelson Jr., and *The Norton Anthology of Modern Poetry* (1973), coedited with Robert O'Clair. Both became staples in American university courses. In a 2014 British Academy memoir of Ellmann, Nicholas Barker described *The Modern Tradition* as "a manifesto for a branch of study, remote twenty-five years earlier, that had become a new orthodoxy."[10] This orthodoxy Ellmann spread in person as well as in print, as a teacher at Harvard, Northwestern, Yale, and Oxford, forwarding the careers of many loyal students. "The power you wield!" his friend and fellow Joycean Ellsworth Mason once told him. "God save us you never take over the Mafia!"[11]

Ellmann's private life, in particular his life as a husband and father, revolved around strong, clever women. His wife, Mary Donahue Ellmann, was the author of *Thinking about Women* (1968), a fiercely witty "feminist classic," according to Virago Press, which reissued it in 1979. Like her husband, Mary had a PhD in English from Yale—her dissertation was on Tennyson—and taught at university level. The oldest of the three Ellmann children, Stephen Ellmann, much admired his father but believed, "It was my mother who was the genius." "I would go along with that," his sister Lucy has said, "as I think my father would have too."[12] After Ellmann's death, his daughter Maud, a literary academic, went on to become a professor of English at the University of Chicago and chair of the department, having previously taught at Cambridge, Notre Dame, and Southampton University. She, too, has written on Joyce, and on modernism more generally, and lists her areas of specialization as critical theory, feminism, and psychoanalysis. Her father had little time for critical theory, either as a teacher or as a writer, although Maud believes he was "certainly a Freudian" and also a feminist. "He knew I needed to take another direction" is how she describes his attitude to her work. When she had doubts and worries, "he tried to keep me going."[13] Lucy, the youngest, was writing her first novel, with Ellmann's encouragement, when he died; her most recent novel, *Ducks, Newburyport,* was shortlisted for the 2019 Booker Prize and won the 2019 Goldsmiths Prize, awarded for a work that "breaks the mould or extends the possibilities of fiction." Feminist in intent, the novel consists of a single sentence of more than a thousand pages, interspersed with short episodes of a story involving a lioness and her lost cubs.

Ellmann's friends and admirers portray him variously as tolerant, well-mannered, genial, gentle, and level-headed. But this is not the whole picture. He was also driven, competitive, exacting, and sometimes frightening. To write a PhD dissertation on Yeats, a modern poet, was daring for a graduate student at Yale in the 1940s, when no modern writers were taught there; for some, to write a biography of Yeats, even an intellectual biography, was doubly so. The old-fashioned professors in the department might not disapprove, but the younger faculty might well, influenced as they were by the New Criticism, with its emphasis on close reading over historical or biographical analysis. In 1947, the year Ellmann submitted his dissertation, Yale hired Cleanth Brooks, a prominent New Critic, author of what became one of the movement's best-known books, *The Well-Wrought Urn,* published the same year. One of Brooks's first PhD students at Yale was Hugh Kenner, whose 1950 dissertation on Joyce became *Dublin's Joyce* (1956), and who consistently disparaged biographical approaches to literature and Ellmann's biography of Joyce in particular.

The nature and status of biography, literary biography in particular, remain vexed topics to this day. To general readers, including most writers, biography is thought of as a lesser literary form. When *James Joyce* won the National Book Award in 1960, Ellmann was photographed between the winners of the poetry and fiction prizes. The winner of the poetry prize was Robert Lowell; the winner of the fiction prize was Philip Roth. Both have had many books and articles written about them; Ellmann has not. Yet Ellmann was as productive as they were, and as acclaimed in his field.

Biography is thought to be restricted to fact or history. Saul Bellow thought of biographers as lesser figures than novelists, not because they deal in fact—novelists also deal in fact—but because they lack imaginative power and distrust it. "I'm a bird, not an ornithologist," he liked to say. For Bellow, "The fact is a wire through which one sends a current." Without this current, the writer cannot "do full justice" to fact or history, cannot bring it alive.[14] But is it true that biographers are necessarily earthbound? The literary biographer Claire Tomalin does not think so. For her, biography "can be as interesting as fiction." When Tomalin was asked if she had a theory of biography, she answered: "I know some writers have a theoretical objection to biography, but that seems to me a bit like having a theoretical objection to fiction: there is good and bad fiction, good and bad biography, crude biography and subtle biography. It can't be argued about in general."[15]

Others take a more complicated view, especially about the relations between fact and fiction. "Someone complained that I put a 'real' restaurant in it," Kingsley Amis once said of a review of one of his novels, "but once it's in the novel, even if it's a real place, it isn't real anymore. Not quite." On another occasion, Amis told Andrew Davies, who adapted Amis's novel *The Old Devils* for television, that "a good source of material and a salutary exercise was to take an aspect of his own character he wasn't particularly proud of, push it to the limit (in fictional form, of course), and see what happens." This salutary exercise offers literary biographers a salutary warning, one Amis contradicts in his *Memoirs,* where he claims to have "already written an account of myself in twenty or more volumes, most of them called novels."[16]

Joyce wrote close to the life. He was like Shem the Penman in *Finnegans Wake,* who wrote the book of himself over the skin of his body.[17] How Ellmann dealt with the dangers of reading the life through the works is a source of controversy and will be defended in the pages that follow. He is not embarrassed to identify real-life characters and incidents in the fiction. That on occasion differences or discrepancies are noted only lends credence to a predominating certainty about such sources, one that contemporary literary critics and scholars mostly question or deplore.

Today's academics distrust literary biography for other reasons besides its tendency to see the life in the writing. To some academics, literary works can be understood only in relation to a detailed historical background, or in relation to some theory of writing or language (the sort of theory Tomalin distrusts, as did Ellmann), or in comparison with the works of dozens of other writers, including writers known only to specialists. A focus on the individual life distracts from or crowds out such considerations. There is also a widespread belief among literary academics that focusing on individual lives is old-fashioned—and in the case of Joyce, disrespectful. Joyce's fiction challenges person-centered notions of identity, on the one hand, and narrative continuity or development, on the other, both of which are staples of literary biography, or at least staples of the sort of literary biography that aims to attract general readers. *James Joyce* aims to attract general readers, but it also aims to attract specialists. In seeking a general audience, Ellmann was encouraged by his family but also by his publisher, who warned him against writing for his colleagues exclusively:

> I've looked at four new literary biographies to appear in the last eight or nine months, and every last one of them is so dedicated to his own MLA section to be heart-breaking. . . . This is a plea for general reader interest then, and as protest against telling not the life story but the conflict of scholarship. Authentic it should be, but that's not enough.[18]

Ellmann replied reassuringly: "Whether I will succeed in hitting the level you would want in my Joyce biography I'm not sure, but believe me that I want very much to have a popular success."[19] For the most part the book was acclaimed by Joyceans and non-Joyceans alike.

In discussing the virtues of *James Joyce* and its maker I stress the importance of sympathy and psychological acuity, virtues derived in part from Ellmann's freedom from doctrine or schematization. In a discussion of "legendary" mid-twentieth-century literary biographers, Hermione Lee distinguishes Ellmann from Leon Edel and George Painter, whose lives of Henry James and Marcel Proust "now seem skewed by their psychoanalytical bias."[20] It is likely that Lee is drawing here from Ellmann himself, in "Literary Biography" (1971), his inaugural lecture as Goldsmiths' Professor of English Literature at Oxford, in which he questioned what he saw as the doctrinaire Freudianism of both biographers.[21] Another virtue of *James Joyce* is its complex treatment of the way events in Joyce's life find their way into the work and "shape again the experiences which have shaped him." It is the literary biographer's job, Ellmann writes, "to measure in each moment this participation of the artist in two simultaneous processes."[22]

The depth of Ellmann's digging partly accounts for the book's length—842 pages. Early on, a sentence reads: "A little of his history as a businessman may be traced in old deeds" (p. 10). These deeds refer not to those of Joyce himself, who entered into several business ventures, nor to his father or his grandfather, but to his *great* grandfather. The attention Ellmann pays to seemingly "undistinguished" moments in Joyce's life also contributes to the book's length. The evidence of such moments, as Ellmann puts it, "accumulates along with the evidence of distinguished moments; small particulars begin to define when they appeared only to multiply, traits become reiterative, a central energy seems to evoke rather than to compile them, and within that energy artist and man rule each other. Respect, which Joyce elicits at once, converges with growing affection" (p. 1).

Here, as elsewhere, Ellmann admits to a growing identification with his subject. Joyce, too, of course, saw value in documenting seemingly undistinguished moments in the lives of his characters. That these characters are themselves "undistinguished" reflects what Ellmann calls "the initial and determining act of judgment in [Joyce's] work . . . the justification of the commonplace" (p. 3), a view that by no means was the consensus before *James Joyce*. Of Joyce's attitude to his protagonists, Ellmann writes: "It is hard to like them, harder to admire them. . . . Unequivocal sympathy would be romancing. He denudes man of what we are accustomed to respect, then summons us to sympathize" (p. 4). The same is true, I will argue, of Ellmann's own depiction of Joyce.

Winners of the 1960 National Book Awards: Robert Lowell, Richard Ellmann, Philip Roth.

PART I

The Biographer

To dwell, as a biographer today would dwell, upon the influence of Lichfield on Dr. Johnson, would not be Boswellian; to deal with Johnson's relations with his parents as something central, rather than as something to be got over to reach the adult Johnson—the finished product—without too much delay, would also seem to Boswell gratuitous. More than anything else we want in modern biography to see the character forming, its peculiarities taking shape.

—RICHARD ELLMANN, "LITERARY BIOGRAPHY" (1971)

CHAPTER ONE

Family

IN 1959, the year *James Joyce* was published, the received image of the author of *Ulysses,* according to Richard Ellmann, was that of "the impersonal artist, cold and aloof." This view Ellmann attributed to, among others, the Harvard professor Harry Levin, whom he described in the book's preface as having "laid the foundation of Joyce scholarship."[1] For Ellmann, in contrast, Joyce was a man devoted to his family as well as his work, a view he derived from many sources, including Joyce's children. Joyce also valued the idea of family. Maria Jolas, Joyce's patron and publisher, told Ellmann that what Joyce admired about the Jews was their "family attachment." Joyce had also told Jolas that he thought of Homer's Odysseus as "a kind of family man."[2]

The theme of Joyce as family man is declared on the first page of *James Joyce,* with an allusion to *A Portrait of the Artist as a Young Man:* "Stephen Dedalus said the family was a net which he would fly past, but James Joyce chose rather to entangle himself and his works in it." It is heard also in the biography's closing sentences: "In whatever he did, his two profound interests—his family and his writings—kept their place. These passions never dwindled. The intensity of the first gave his work sympathy and humanity; the intensity of the second raised his life to dignity and high dedication."

Hence the detail-packed pages that open the biography—about parents, grandparents, great-grandparents—as well as many pages involving Joyce's uncles, aunts, siblings, and children. In this chapter, the very different family Ellmann was born into will be treated more briefly, but its influence on his life and writing is clear, a source of his own sympathy and humanity—perhaps, also, of his depictions of Joyce as family man and of Joyce's Bloom as family man.

Four generations of the Joyce family. James with his son George [Giorgio] and grandson Stephen beneath the portrait of Joyce's father by Patrick Tuohy. Photograph by Gisèle Freund, 1938.

* * *

Richard David Ellmann was born on March 15, 1918, in Highland Park, Michigan, which at the time was a small town six miles north of Detroit and is now part of Metro Detroit. Between 1910 and 1920, thanks to the growth of the automobile industry, the town's population swelled from 4,120 to 46,449. Highland Park was the home not just of a large Ford Motor plant, opened in 1909, but also of the Chrysler Corporation, founded there in 1925.

The Ellmann family was comfortably upper-middle-class. Dick (as he will mostly remain in this chapter, with its many other Ellmanns) was the second of three sons of James Isaac Ellmann and Jeannette (Jean) Ellmann, née Barsook. His older brother Erwin was born in 1915, his younger brother Bill in 1921. The family lived at 55 Connecticut Street, just off Woodward Avenue, known as "Detroit's Main Street," in a large house (five bedrooms, three baths) on a small lot. They had a maid and a buzzer beneath the dining room table with which to summon her. They had a modest summer cottage on a lake, and in the mid-1920s mother and sons wintered in southern California, in part for health reasons. For most of the 1930s the family had few money worries. The sons went to the local high school, and though Dick won scholarships to Yale, he could have attended without them.[3]

The family's bourgeois comforts were the product of remarkable immigrant parents. James Isaac Ellmann was born in 1887 in Galatz, a port on the Danube in eastern Romania, and emigrated to the United States at sixteen, in 1904, just before war broke out between Russia and Japan. James was not the first member of his family to emigrate. In 1910, according to a census report, he was living in Brooklyn in a house occupied by his mother, two older brothers, and a younger sister (his father, Isaac, a tailor, had died in Galatz). How many Ellmann family members were in New York when James arrived in 1904 is not clear, though an older brother, Samuel, eleven years his senior, had been in America long enough to become a lawyer and a Republican. James's son Erwin described Samuel in later life as "a short, jaunty, would-be Jewish boulevardier, a small-scale political *macher.*"[4]

James followed his older brother by studying law at night at NYU and working during the day, first on Wall Street taking telephone quotations on the stock market, then as an assistant export clerk at the American Express Company. Fiorello LaGuardia, later mayor of New York, was one of James's

Ellmann family in 1926. Left to right: Richard, James, Jean, William, Erwin.

fellow law students at NYU. In 1910 James received his LLB degree, passed the bar exam, moved to Highland Park, eventually married Jean, and after only eight years as a practicing attorney was elected a municipal court judge.

At thirty James became "one of the youngest judicial officers in Michigan and one of the few Jewish men of the country who has attained such a high position at his age." These words come from an article of April 11, 1919, in the *Detroit Jewish News,* one of hundreds of stories in the *News* and the *Detroit Jewish Chronicle* in which James I. Ellmann figures. In 1925, after retiring as a judge, he returned full-time to private practice, specializing in arbitration and conciliation. Eventually he set up offices on the eighteenth floor of the Penobscot Building, the tallest and grandest office building in Detroit's financial district. In 1933 he was appointed assistant attorney general of the State of Michigan, a year after unsuccessfully running for mayor of Highland Park. The 1932 mayoral campaign was neither his first nor his last; he had run and lost ten years earlier and would run again in 1936.

The 1932 campaign was especially noteworthy. The year before, the Michigan branch of the Black Legion, an offshoot of the Ku Klux Klan, was founded by a Highland Park resident named Arthur Lupp, an official of the Detroit Board of Health. The Legion, like the Klan, was a secret vigilante group opposed to Blacks, Jews, Catholics, immigrants, and Communists. In Highland Park in 1932, Black Legion members included the town's chief of police, a city councilman, and James Ellmann's opponent in the mayoral race, N. Ray Markland.

Markland and his fellow Black Legion members objected to Ellmann not only because he was a Jew and an immigrant, but because he was known for defending the rights of immigrants, aided in part by an ability with languages (in addition to English, he could converse in Romanian, Yiddish, French, Spanish, and German). James was a Democrat, unlike his older brother Samuel. For a time he was counsel for the Detroit branch of the American Civil Liberties Union. In campaign material, he stressed his judicial independence. "I have no axes to grind; I carry no chips on my shoulders; I bear no ill-will to any man or group of men or women" he declared in a campaign circular from the 1922 race. "If I am elected, Highland Park will be obligated to no one for anything I do."

During the 1932 race, according to an article of June 26, 1936, in the *Detroit Jewish News,* Markland was quoted as saying that "it was necessary to knock a chip off the Jew Ellmann's nose." Threats were issued both to Ellmann and to his supporter Arthur L. Kingsley, the Catholic editor and publisher of the local newspaper, the *Highland Parker,* and attempts were made on Kingsley's life, with weapons supplied by Markland. On election eve, robed and hooded Legionnaires marched past 55 Connecticut Street, jeering and shouting antisemitic abuse. In the center of the city, the marchers tore down posters and flyers from shop windows and poles, threw them on a bonfire, and danced around the blaze. Ellmann lost the election by 400 votes. Undaunted, he ran again in 1936, in an election manipulated directly by Henry Ford, who threatened local Ford plant workers with dismissal if they were found to have supported Ellmann. This time Ellmann lost ten of fourteen districts. Some months later, Markland was one of forty-eight Black Legion members indicted for murder and conspiracy to murder.

Among the Legion's supposed victims was a Baptist lay preacher named Earl Little, a Black man from Detroit whose son Malcolm would become Malcolm X.[5]

With his electoral ambitions blocked, James Ellmann focused his energies on Jewish causes. While heading a flourishing law practice, he became president of the Jewish Community Council of Detroit, which he helped to found, and of the Zionist Organization of Detroit. He was director of the Detroit Roundtable of Catholics, Jews, and Protestants. In addition to being an active member of Temple Beth El, a Reform synagogue, the oldest Jewish congregation in Michigan, he became president of Knollwood Country Club, the local Jewish golf club. Two hundred friends gathered at Knollwood in 1937 to celebrate James's fiftieth birthday. The Jewish newspapers reported all his activities: convening conferences, giving addresses, organizing roundtables, chairing meetings and talks, soliciting funds for worthy causes. Michael Ellmann, Erwin's son, particularly remembers James's "energy, drive, and zealous cultivation of contacts," qualities he saw also in his uncle Dick.

* * *

These qualities were as evident in Ellmann's mother as in his father, as can be seen in her memoir, "From Door to Door," an unpublished work of 440 typed pages and the source of many of the quotations that follow. The memoir's length is characteristic. Jean Ellmann wrote voluminously throughout her life: thousands of single-spaced typed letters to family and friends (son Erwin, newly arrived in college, had to discourage her from writing daily, and from expecting daily replies);[6] hundreds of poems ("embarrassingly bad," according to Ellmann's daughter Lucy);[7] dozens of articles, reviews, including music and opera reviews for the local Jewish papers, as well as talks for the National Council of Jewish Women, Hadassah, Temple Beth El's Sisterhood, and the Zionist Organization of Detroit. Jean was proud of her writing, often sending articles and poems to her sons for comment. "That was an excellent article, Mom, really very good," writes seventeen-year-old Dick Ellmann, newly arrived at Yale. "If you had signed my name to it I wouldn't have objected at all."

Jean Barsook Ellmann was born in Kiev in 1889 (some sources say 1887) and came with her Russian Jewish parents to America as an infant.[8] Her four younger siblings, three brothers and a sister, were born in the United

States. The family settled in College Point, New York, a small town near Flushing Meadows, which at the time was a largely Catholic immigrant community. Jean recalled her childhood as idyllic. When she was eleven, however, at the turn of the century, the family moved to Manhattan in search of advancement. The years in College Point may have been idyllic for Jean, but for her ambitious parents they brought "no revolution in our circumstances."[9]

The title of Jean's memoir, "From Door to Door," is apt. In Manhattan the family lived first in a top-floor apartment on Third Avenue; then in an apartment in the South Bronx, near Crotona Park; then in the lower floor of a two-family house on the edge of Bronx Park. In none of these locations did their circumstances improve. From the Bronx, they moved to Williamsburg in Brooklyn, then to nearby Seaside, Rockaway Beach, then to a farm in New Jersey. When Jean was in her early twenties, the family moved further afield, to Omaha, Nebraska, where they had relatives, then finally to Detroit, which had impressed them when they passed through on their way to Omaha. After almost two decades on the move ("a family of gypsies" is how James Ellmann's mother described them), in 1910 the Barsooks at last "staked out a claim and put roots down to stay" (p. 270).[10]

Detroit was on the rise in 1910, an industrial town on the brink of becoming, in Jean's words, "one of the richest spots not only in this country but all the world." At the same time, it "still retained an atmosphere of domestic tranquillity" (p. 270). Jean's father Emil had little trouble finding work and opportunities in Detroit. He was clever, industrious, an inventor of sorts (though poor at securing patents), and a talented mechanic and handyman. Whether working in factories or shops, farming, or starting businesses, Emil Barsook always managed to provide food and shelter for his family. What he previously had not been able to provide for the family was a house of their own or an automobile. In Detroit, he provided both, turning a successful box-lunch business across the street from the Ford plant into "a principal source of plant meals for the automobile workers."[11]

Emil's wife, Sophie, Jean's mother, is described in the memoir as indomitable, uncomplaining, and certain that her husband was destined for better things. She did all the housework and organized the family's many moves. Her life, her daughter writes, was "one long inarticulate hymn to work" (p. 66). Like Emil, Sophie was committed to what Jean calls "Americanism" (p. 132), but she also made sure the family retained Old Country or Jewish habits. Yiddish and Russian were spoken at home, Kosher was observed, as was Shabbat (recalled for "clean clothes, good food and merriment" [p. 69]). Despite being anchored in the home, she was neither insular nor isolated, being "a serious extrovert" (p. 70) and for the most part living in communities where "everybody came from somewhere else and nobody was prejudiced against outlanders" (p. 84).

The religious upbringing Ellmann's mother received was unorthodox in several senses. On the one hand, she describes herself as "rejoicingly Jewish." On the other hand, she wrote that she "had never seen or entered a synagogue. I was a religious illiterate." A similar doubleness seems to have marked the Jewish upbringing she and James passed on to their sons. Few parents could have been more active in Jewish affairs, including the affairs of their synagogue, than James and Jean Ellmann, yet neither Dick nor his brothers received a bar mitzvah. If the sons had resisted, or if they were given a say in the matter, is not known. Nothing is said about this aspect of her children's upbringing in Jean's memoir or in the surviving correspondence, nor do her grandchildren remember being told about the matter.[12]

The Barsooks did not think of themselves as Zionists. They thought of themselves as Jews who wished to be Americans, though "Palestine was always accepted as the Jewish homeland, and everybody shared the Messianic dream of a rooted nation" (p. 91). Jean's interest in Zionism, like that of her husband, began, she writes, in 1933 (the year Hitler was appointed chancellor of Germany, also a year after James's defeat in the bitter 1932 mayoral race). In 1935 the Ellmanns traveled to Switzerland to attend the World Zionist Congress in Lucerne, then to Palestine "to see for [ourselves] the progress there" (p. 423). It was Hitler's rise to power, James admitted in a speech in 1936, that led him at last to commit fully to Zionist causes.[13]

Judging by his mother's memoir, the Jewish identity Richard Ellmann inherited from his parents was less a matter of faith or ritual than of culture and values. There was also an element of insecurity about it. While away at university, the Ellmann sons were urged by their parents to observe the high holidays. "You must arrange to come in for the holiday," Jean writes to Erwin in a letter of October 8, 1935. "It is not so much for the Jews as for the Christians, who have more respect for us if we insist on observing our Holy Days." In a letter of May 15, 1938, to her "Dearest Boys," Jean writes of being invited to the home of Christian acquaintances. At dinner ("a delicatessen meal . . . maybe they thought that would be a treat"), the hosts complain of the idleness of their grown sons. Jean attributes the sons' failings to the mother. Not only had the mother long been the family breadwinner, but she earned her income by working outside the home, "and that is how those two boys grew up—rather alone and by themselves." Later in the letter she confesses: "You know, boys, I used to think that some of the undesirable traits of our own people were so disgusting and disappointing that they could never be matched by the Christians." After encountering women like her hostess, "I no longer think all the virtues on the Christian side."

* * *

A second inheritance for Ellmann and his brothers derived from their mother's love of books and learning. This love, she writes, began the moment she opened the dictionary and "was instantly and gloriously enslaved." An excellent student, she skipped three grades in five months in the equivalent of junior high school, despite having to switch schools whenever the family moved. "My extra reading set me ahead" (p. 154). By her early teens she had read "many of Scott's novels," as well as Kipling, Stevenson, Shakespeare, and Victor Hugo (p. 155). At Girls High School in Brooklyn, English was her favorite subject. She and her friends memorized "pages and pages of Shakespeare, Wordsworth, Coleridge, Keats, Shelley and Byron." She chose Latin and Greek as her foreign languages, to read the classical authors in the original. "My love was school, and my greatest hope was to do well in my examinations" (p. 169), a hope she would later invest in her sons. "I'm glad you are breathing easier as to marks," she writes to Dick, in a letter of November 19, 1935. "Is your roommate far ahead?"

At the end of her junior year in high school, Jean's ambitions suffered a terrible blow. Her mother decided that she should leave school, missing her senior year. Her mother made this decision primarily because she believed that "educational advantages were the preserve of men only, and woman's duty . . . was to concentrate on living fully, which meant being a wife, mother and homemaker." Although Jean's father had always encouraged her "mental aspirations," he went along with the decision, as "my mother was stronger-willed." In the memoir, Jean says little of her disappointment. After describing herself as a supporter of "women's vote and rights," she quickly adds that she was also always "glad to be a girl." "Now older and wiser, the scheme of creation seems quite perfect, and I know I have gotten a very fair deal from all the men in my life" (p. 222).

At seventeen, without a high school diploma, Jean enrolled in the Long Island Business College in Brooklyn, to learn typing and shorthand. Here, too, she proved an excellent student, so much so that before completing her course she was invited to teach on it, an invitation she described as having "important consequences for me" (p. 197). In the evenings, the college rented its auditorium to a discussion group, the Brooklyn Philosophical Society. The society attracted young men and women, many of whom were the children of Jewish immigrants and, in Jean's words, eager for "information, facts, theories and abstract ideas—the meat of reality and the wine of philosophy" (p. 208). Discussion topics in philosophy included "the materialism of Marx, Kantian philosophy, and Bergsonism." Other sessions were devoted to economics, politics, psychology, music, and literature.

The society served a social as well as an educational or intellectual function for its members. Many of them, Jean included, spent Sunday afternoons together, attending improving talks at the Felix Adler Society for Ethical Culture at Carnegie Hall. These talks, organized by Theodore Schroeder, the writer and free speech advocate, were given by well-known speakers. Jean recalls hearing talks by Emma Goldman and Charles Whitman, attorney general of the State of New York, later governor of New York. "It was exhilarating to those of us who were culturally undernourished and sensitively searching." "Naturally all this helped to free me from more of my small-town limitations where I was drilled in the veneration for duty, where hard work was the elixir of life" (p. 218). After lectures, Jean and her friends would continue their discussions at one another's homes. The liberating influence these discussions had on Jean is described in unliberating terms: "It was not considered unrefined for the girls to argue down the boys, even if they remained unconvinced and charmingly unreformed" (p. 220).

At one such "lecture postmortem," held at the Barsook home in Brooklyn, someone had brought along a young law student recently arrived from Romania. It was James Ellmann. That evening James "read to us an essay he had written on socialism. He said well what he had to say and we were the right audience at the right time. It was a remarkable performance for one in this country but a short time and I was impressed, and I was not a little in love with him too."[14] Soon James and Jean began going out together, "and every meeting whetted my desire for more of his company" (p. 221). He quickly established himself, she wrote, in "our circle," and with several other young men he started an offshoot discussion group, the

Websterian Oratorical Society, which flourished for several years and was revived decades later in the form of annual reunions. The speech James gave in 1936 when he ran for mayor, quoted earlier, was delivered at one such reunion. When Richard Ellmann and his brothers entered high school, they carried on their parents' interest in public speaking, winning prizes in debate and oratory, skills of obvious use for future lawyers like Erwin and Bill, and for a university professor like Dick.

Eight years passed before James and Jean married. When Jean's family moved to Omaha, she stayed behind in Brooklyn. She had work, a circle of friends, and relatives to stay with. But she soon missed her parents and siblings. James worked all day to earn money and all evening to become a lawyer. In addition, there was little encouragement from the families. For Jean's family, marriage was out of the question until James could prove himself "a good provider." For James's mother, what Jean calls the "indifferent social position" of the Barsooks "was no asset for the advancement of a young professional" (p. 278). Jean's longing to see her family led the young couple to decide "that a separation would be a test as to whether our future was together and help us to determine if it was an authentic love that bound us" (p. 252).

* * *

Four years later, in 1910, James graduated from law school, passed the bar exam, and began work in his older brother Sam's law practice in New York. This was not a happy time for him. According to his son Erwin, "one year of practicing law with Sam in New York's Jewish neighborhood proved more than enough." Erwin suspects his father was put off by Sam's "imperious manner," as well as by the "unpromising" mix of legal cases handled by Sam's practice.[15] What Jean writes of this moment is that "my friend in New York was not getting far in the law in that city. It was very difficult in a highly competitive and overcrowded field" (p. 277). She uses a biblical analogy to describe his situation: "He must have begun to feel like Jacob who waited seven years for Rachel" (p. 278).

Unlike Rachel, Jean was making good money. After securing her parents' reluctant consent, she advanced James bus fare to Detroit, to try his hand as a lawyer in the Motor City. "To this day," she writes, "he repeats that he had to work a whole lifetime to pay it back to me!" (p. 278). It took another four years for James to become a good provider (at some point paying $300 for an engagement ring, not far off $8,000 in today's money). In 1914 the couple finally married, "without fuss. I simply gathered up my books and sewing machine, which constituted my dowry, put on a new blue dress, with something old and borrowed added" (p. 279). Jean's mother's advice was thoroughly Old Country: "Don't get angry if he does the opposite thing to what you tell him; husbands want their unquestioned ways. . . . You made good on all your jobs; now make good on your marriage" (p. 280).

Jean had little problem with this advice, describing James as belonging to "that gentle school of kindly-tyrant husband who rules his wife without her even finding it out" (p. 282). James's other virtues she lists as being "inspired by pressure . . . a man of bold initiative, swift decisions, forcefulness and energy," yet also "methodical, rigidly scheduling himself by the hour, and as I always complained, unfair to disorganized labor (like mine)." Bored by what Jean calls "the dry bones of the law," James specialized in "keeping people out of court." He was public-spirited, believing "that if one lives and thrives in a community, one owes to it an obligation not only in allegiance but in actual service." Hence his entry into politics in 1918, the year of Dick's birth, when James ran successfully for the judgeship. Jean approved James's political ambitions, while also worrying that in becoming "a community asset" he would end up "a near stranger to his wife and children" (p. 299).

Jean's worry proved unfounded. Her autobiography is largely cloudless. Throughout their marriage, James was "a life companion both intellectual and understanding" (p. 282). As a father, although formal and demanding, he was loving. "Kiss the two boys," he writes to Jean from New York, in a letter of January 29, 1933, "though I cannot excuse their failure to drop a few words." Jean describes herself as the disciplinarian in the family, in some cases given to Old Country methods. Lucy Ellmann was told by her father that when he wet the bed as a child, his sheets were hung outside so that the neighbors could see, as a form of public humiliation.

In her early years with the boys, Jean was "immured" in motherhood, with "no time for outside activities. On reflection now, I consider my sacrifice was extravagant, fanatical and unnecessary" (p. 293). With Erwin, "I talked to him a great deal as if he understood everything and treated him from infancy like an adult" (p. 289). With all the sons, "we liked them to know why something was one way and not another and encouraged them in argument to tell their side." It was important for the boys to be articulate and imaginative as well as disciplined, tantrums and showing off were "absolutely forbidden" (p. 306).

* * *

Literature took center stage in the boys' education. Early on, Jean recited simple poems to them: "Emerson's 'Rhodora,' 'Forbearance,' Wilcox's 'Creeds,' so that they would get the music if not the thought of entire poems. By picking poems apart we got to figures of speech, learned about the simile, metaphor, personification or hyperbole." Reading was treated as a serious business, "no hammock and bonbon activity. . . . We always marked parts we wanted to be sure to reread. (This habit resulted in their keeping résumés and favorite quotations from books useful through their college years)" (pp. 312–13). In summer, Jean and the boys stayed in the family's lakeside cottage, while James worked in town, joining them on the weekend. To keep their father abreast of their activities, Jean encouraged the boys to produce a family newspaper, "News from Lake Mandon" (p. 314), for which they wrote poems as well as articles. The books she chose to read to them, or to have them read for themselves, were by "Dumas, Hugo, Dickens, Scott, Stevenson, Kipling, Twain, all so rewarding" (p. 352). What Erwin remembers of these books, as of the poems Jean read to them, is that they "were often scarcely comprehended. But we never acknowledged that we did not understand or were bored or impatient. 'I got something out of it,' I would assure her even if it was only an incantatory lull."[16]

In describing Dick's character as a child, Jean stresses his love of "papers" (which became a lifetime preoccupation for Ellmann, never more so than when he was at work on Joyce). "His earnestness about them was almost pathetic. His father would bring home a portfolio. Dick would ask, 'Are these important papers?'" "He was in his glory when he was up to his chin in important papers. He would fondle them and arrange them, and all that mattered was that they were important, long before he could even pronounce the word" (p. 315).[17] He was also always in search of things, often to collect: "tops, marbles, a string or rope, a fishhook or something else quite as precious." Later he took up stamp collecting as a hobby "for many years" (p. 403). The other childhood trait Jean recalls, aside from collecting, was Dick's obsession with reading, "gobbling all signs and wrappers to learn to read. He slept on his reader and as soon as it was light he began reading" (p. 353). At the "early age of seven or eight Dick had a trick of memory for reproducing the entire contents of a book. We did not know whether we should encourage this memorizing" (p. 403).

Dick adored his older brother Erwin, described by Jean as "fiery, articulate and at the controls" (p. 315). Erwin was "Dick's oracle," and Dick followed his lead and his advice. Doubtless, Dick's eagerness to read owed something to Erwin's example. In California, Erwin's intensity impressed the local librarian: "He seemed to want to devour the whole library every time he came in" (p. 353). Given their reading mania, the sons soon "found themselves far ahead of their schoolmates," a position their mother sought to maintain. "I supervised their work at home and stressed arduous preparation of homework" (p. 382). How Erwin and Dick reacted to their mother's vigilance she does not say, but given her descriptions of their characters, one can guess. Erwin she describes as "handicapped by his natural ability which could easily foster idleness." Dick, in contrast, was "more gently introspective and dependable, and a born plugger" (p. 317). Dick was chubby and awkward as a child, less outgoing than Erwin, but he had what his mother describes as a "beguiling" manner and smile. "Children like him should be patented and put into every home!" (p. 363) declared one of the family's housekeepers. Dick was "more patient and indulgent" (p. 363) than Erwin with their younger brother Bill; Erwin could be "a tormentor, not so tender-hearted as Dick" (p. 364).

* * *

Jean's memoir has relatively little to say about Dick and his brothers once they leave home for university, and the evidence from the correspondence complicates and darkens the picture she offers in the memoir. Letters, of course, can be as rose-tinted, as unreliable as memoirs, but they can also be as revealing, as Ellmann makes clear at the beginning of the introduction to his 1966 edition of *Letters of James Joyce,* volumes 2 and 3: "Letter-writing imposes its small ceremonies . . . even a perfunctory message discloses a little with what candour, modesty, or self-esteem its writer ranks himself in the world [or the family]. Some accompanying hint of his appraisal of that world is bound to appear in the way he asserts or beseeches a tie with his correspondent, the degree of familiarity he takes for granted, the extent to which he solicits action or approbation, the alacrity and tenacity with which he joins issue." In Dick's case, as we shall see, the frequency or infrequency with which he responds can also be telling.

When Erwin went off to the University of Southern California (USC) as a freshman in 1932, spurred by memories of warm winters in southern California, Dick, aged fourteen, was a sophomore at Highland Park High School, a short walk from Connecticut Street. Erwin's letters to Dick report his own doings, but also offer advice, about teachers, extracurricular activities, what to read, and girls. On September 4, 1932, Erwin asks, "What are you writing in the Spec [the school newspaper] and when do I get it?" He suggests that they write twice a week. His letters to Dick and family are open, funny, only occasionally condescending, and long. As Erwin's son Michael puts it, in reference to his father's legal work as well as his correspondence, "My Dad could crank." His written output, including some twenty volumes of "frequently eloquent" legal briefs, was "well-nigh Trollopian. . . . In his way, he was as productive as Dick."

Dick's letters to Erwin in this period are relaxed, friendly, and undeferential. A letter of March 17, 1933, in response to a letter from Erwin that discusses Pascal, ends: "Oui, je désire à écriver en français, et, quand j'ai le temps, j'écriverai à California de cette façon. Vous avez fait beaucoup de fautes dans votre lettre." In a letter of October 10, 1933, Erwin informs Dick that someone has just come into his dorm with "a bunch of new books. One of Guy de Maupassant, Point Counter Point, and the works of Nietzsche." In a letter of November 4, he admits to having trouble with Baudelaire, notwithstanding the poet's reputation as "the progenitor of Wilde, Swinburne . . . Pater, and the whole school, including Maupassant and Balzac."

Here, as elsewhere, Erwin presumes a shared interest and knowledge. In a letter of October 8, 1935, Joyce's name appears for the first time in correspondence. "Last night, as I say, I heard James Stephens, the Irish bard, mentioned by Joyce once in a while, of whom you have probably never heard." In Dick's junior year at Yale, Erwin writes again of Joyce, in a letter of October 12, 1937: "Hear Joyce's Work in Progress comes out this week along with his verse." Dick's own poetry is often mentioned in the correspondence. In a 1933 letter jokily dated "May 12 (for the sake of posterity)," Erwin comments on a poem Dick has written as a junior in high school, commending its "iambic pentameter and the interesting treatment of the strophe form. The first two verses I thought were drivelish without being funny but the rest wasn't bad. Byron wrote some stuff even worse—and I almost have."

The mention of Byron leads Erwin to a confession: "My erotics have been decidedly limited of late." As for Dick's erotics, we learn from the early correspondence that he received several letters from a girl he knew in high school (nickname "Willis"), who writes flirtatiously, also a bit like an older sister, from Ann Arbor, where she is now a freshman at the University of Michigan. Of another girl, Hilda, Erwin comments, "I have no prejudices, but it is alright that she is Joosh."[18] Dick's own references to girls are frequently adolescent, also jokey: "The trouble with you, Erv," he writes in 1933 in an undated letter, "is that you not only read this Newman girl like a book, but that you try to use the Braille system while doing it."

Scattered through the correspondence from Dick's years as an undergraduate at Yale are letters from spirited "good girls," often written in elaborate cursive on girlish stationery. Jean would approve. At the beginning of his senior year at Yale, in a letter posted on November 2, 1938, Dick writes home about a recent weekend in New York. He spent Sunday afternoon helping "my old pal Madeline decorate a Hallowe'en party and in the course of the afternoon both she and her mother virtually proposed to me," news that prompts an immediate response from his mother. It begins: "I know the rest of the family will join me in an overwhelming interest in Madeline Goldberg. Who is she and what does she do and who is her father and who is her mother and how much money have they got? This questionnaire must accompany all bids on our Dick. With a Yale degree . . ."[19]

A joke, perhaps, but revealing. Other letters are revealing about Jean's ambitions for Dick's career at Yale. Shortly after his arrival in New Haven, Dick visited old friends of his parents from Brooklyn, who were now living in New Haven. "They have three lovely boys," Jean writes in a letter of October 10, 1935, "and their records are enviable ones. But I know you will do well too, Dick." The name of this family is Rostow, and when Dick shows up at their home, "Mr. Rostow, as soon as he saw me, said I looked just like my father. That was in 1910 that he saw you last, I guess."[20] Victor Rostow, a Russian-Jewish immigrant, came to the United States at the age of eighteen in 1904, the same year as James Ellmann. A metallurgist, he was educated at the Pratt Institute in Brooklyn. His wife, Lillian, also a Russian-Jewish immigrant, was a census taker in the 1910 census, "to ensure that Jews and other Communists were counted."[21] Whether the Rostows met the Ellmanns at the Brooklyn Philosophical Society is not known, but they sound very much like Society types. Victor and Lillian met on a train when she was seventeen. She was reading Spinoza.[22] The "three lovely boys" produced by the Rostows were named after great Americans: Walt Whitman Rostow, Eugene Victor Debs Rostow (after the American socialist, political activist, and trade unionist Eugene V. Debs), and Ralph Waldo Emerson Rostow.

The eldest Rostow brothers had excelled at Yale. Eugene, born in 1913, entered the university at sixteen with examination scores so high that the *New York Times* called him the first "perfect freshman."[23] He won a Henry Fellowship to Cambridge, then returned to Yale Law School, where he edited the *Yale Law Journal*. Walt, born in 1916, entered Yale at fifteen, graduated at nineteen, went to Oxford on a Rhodes Scholarship, and returned to Yale for a PhD in economics, which he was awarded when he was twenty-four. Both went on to glittering, if controversial, careers.[24] On October 7, 1935, newly arrived at Yale, Dick wrote to his father to describe his first visit to the Rostows: "They gave me a nice meal, and when I subtly let them know that I was here on scholarship, they seemed to respect me much more." The oldest son, Eugene, was said to be particularly bright: "his brother Walt, whom I met, is dumb. He only got an average of 92!" Walt, two years above Dick at Yale, later invited him for lunch at Pierson College, and Dick concluded: "They are the most intelligent people I have met with around here." He was not alone in this opinion, nor in enjoying the Rostows' hospitality. According to their grandson Victor, son of Eugene, from the time the Rostows moved to New Haven in the mid-1920s, their home on Orange Street "was a refuge for all Jews at Yale."[25]

* * *

In the spring of 1938, toward the end of his junior year, Dick concocted a plan to spend the summer on a solo walking tour through Europe. When his father expressed concern, he (Dick) enlisted the help of his older brother Erwin, who was about to graduate as a law student from the University of Michigan. Erwin agreed to accompany Dick on the tour, though he was skeptical about the walking part. As he wrote in a letter of May 11, 1938, "I can hardly imagine you lasting for long with nothing but a knapsack and a copy of 'Walden.'"[26] On May 23, 1938, their father wrote again. "My Dear Dick," his letter begins, "You created quite a problem for your mother and me by your suggestion of a trip." His concerns now were with Erwin and finances. Erwin was due to take the law exams in September and "a trip will bar him of any serious preparation. Besides, there will be involved an expense of approximately $350.00 for each of you." Instead, James suggested an idea volunteered by a lawyer from his firm: that Dick drive a Buick from Detroit to California, with all expenses paid plus a per diem of "$20.00"; that in Los Angeles he contact a friend of the lawyer, an ex-Detroit resident who knew all about "the excellent opportunities to take many tramp steamer trips with excellent accommodations. It would cost you approximately $80.00 for three months, going to South America, Japan, Hawaii, etc."

As the point of the trip for Dick was to tour Europe, the tramp steamer suggestion was quickly rejected. In the May 23 letter, James had been careful not to rule Europe out completely: "If your heart is set on a European trip rather than the other journey we just mentioned, there is still a possibility that Erwin may be able to join you." Erwin could reschedule taking the law exam, though he would be "much more likely to succeed if he prepares." James then outlines four options: "1. To go alone. 2. To go with Erwin. 3. To go by way of California. 4. Not to go this season." The letter ends: "It is mighty sweet of you to suggest to assist Erwin with whatever share of money he might require." When Dick sticks to his guns about the trip, James yields, and a way is found for Erwin to accompany Dick and for James to accept his accompanying him. The objections of Dick's mother Jean, in a separate letter of May 23, had also to be overcome. That the trip would now include bicycling filled her "with terror." When she was in London in 1935, she learned that "an appalling number of people are killed yearly" on bicycles. She also worried about Dick's preparations for his senior year at Yale: "Will this make much difference in the work you mapped out for the summer?" Like her husband, however, she did not insist: "If you have set your heart on it I hate to tell you not to go. . . . Maybe a fellow should go when he gets the bug and trust to luck for the rest, so I hate to discourage you myself."[27]

In a letter of June 1, 1938, written to James A. Pierson of the Union Guardian Trust Company, James Ellmann explains (perhaps as much to himself as to Pierson) the reasons for the trip. Sons Dick and Erwin will spend the summer touring England and France "with a view to extending their educational outlook," a description only half accurate. Erwin had literary interests, but his "educational outlook" was legal rather than literary. It was Dick, an English major, whose educational outlook would be extended. "He will visit on his journey many of the places and schools [he means Oxford and Cambridge] which, as I stated, will broaden and intensify his educational background—necessary in the work in which he is specializing." As for money, during his first three years at Yale, Dick "succeeded in doing it on complete or partial scholarship. I personally supplemented his requirement without his touching his estate. He now requires the sum of $500.00 for the purpose of travelling and preparing for his trip, which I would like to recommend to you to pay him."[28]

* * *

Without rancor, threat, or tantrum, at least according to surviving correspondence, Dick got his way, a tribute in part to his parents' commitment to dialogue, in part to the persuasive powers that would serve him throughout his life. With the trip approved and financed, Dick took care of the details. In an undated letter written just after he had finished his last law exams, Erwin reported to his younger brother that he had received "all your cards and will faithfully comply with the directions," adding that he had "definitely abandoned taking a tux. . . . I doubt if it is the season for them, even on shipboard, and am not overly anxious to crash first class if there are wenches below." The brothers set sail from New York on the SS *Volendam,* a ship on the Holland America line, and arrived in Plymouth, England, on June 26, 1938.[29]

From Plymouth they traveled directly to London, where they could call on friends of their parents. In a letter of June 3, James offered Dick advice about contacts: "Keep a book or card in which these addresses and details pertaining to the individuals might be recorded. . . . In my own journey I found that I missed seeing some people because I had so many addresses that I did not connect them together at the right time." The letter also contained advice about money: extravagant purchases should be left till the end, "when you are quite sure of what your needs will be." Only a few letters survive from their time in London, but the brothers seem to have taken their father's advice to heart in respect to contacts: "Saw the Bennetts last night and I am going to a party at the daughter's studio," writes Erwin. "Tomorrow we are with the Taubes. Life is very hectic for us trying to cram much into a little time." Among cultural highlights, Erwin lists *The Tempest* with Philip Merivale, the Ballet Russe, and Covent Garden. He describes the English as "cool but interesting" and London as expensive and "full of rain."

Erwin Ellmann, early 1940s.

In London the boys bought three-speed bicycles for a trip south to Cornwall, from where Dick sent an undated letter reassuring his mother that "everything has gone well. We are learning how to use the bikes and Erwin no longer uses the wall as a brake." Dick also reports that they have bought her a present in Polperro, a Cornish fishing village, and that they "made a wish while eating our first strawberries of the season, an old Cornish custom." The only bit of adventure Dick recounts concerns a policeman who stopped them on the road: "Two cyclists had stolen something at a nearby town. Our American accent saved us." As for oddities, he mentions "a Cockney boy yesterday . . . who was absolutely incomprehensible" and "a place in Cornwall where they sing their words." With his mother's fears in mind, Dick says nothing of what Erwin much later told his son Michael: that while bicycling they sometimes grabbed on to a passing truck or tractor to save having to pedal.

The French leg of the trip was spent in Paris and Brittany. In an undated letter written in late August, Dick describes their travels as "progressively more enjoyable." He mentions visits to Mont Saint-Michel, Saint-Malo, and a train trip to Chartres, but takes most pleasure in improving his French. "We met two boys a few days ago, one of whom spoke only French . . . and we were with them for two days, speaking nothing but French. . . . We have now gotten to the point where we can express ourselves comprehensively if not correctly in French, and we have long conversations frequently." When Erwin takes over the letter, Dick is having just such a conversation, "with an attractive Parisienne, telling her about the intricacies of the classics dept. of Yale." Erwin is the racier of the brothers and has even tried to grow a goatee (which Dick persuaded him to ditch before returning home). He describes a visit to Montmartre, where "we luckily found a real Frenchman who was most obliging and who took us to all the real dives not usually seen by the tourists and assiduously kept us away from all the high-priced places." Erwin writes on a sunny Sunday ("the only summer heat we have seen"), lying under a tree outside the inn where they are staying. He has been talking about Proust with a "Polish gal." From inside the common room, "filled with French gals and a couple of fellows," he can hear music. "France will be harder to leave than England," he declares, "no one is too worried about work here; women and wine and good talk is the best part of the day."

Dick has less to say about French girls than Erwin, except to mention that he and his brother are constantly being approached by foreigners (Swiss, Belgians, an Argentine), "all of whom would like to show us the 'naked girls,' as well as steal all our money." While later correspondence with friends suggests that he had had romantic encounters, in the letters he writes to his parents it is high culture that absorbs him. On July 5 he writes from Paris to describe a second day's visit to the Louvre, to "that huge room where they have most of the world's famous pictures, the Italian room with three of Leonardo's works, etc. We decided that Pater was right about the Mona Lisa, despite the cries of blarney which have been uttered against him." What Pater was right about is found in a passage in *Studies in the History of the Renaissance* (1873), though it is likely that Dick knew the passage through Yeats, who used it, controversially, as the first "poem" in his 1936 edition of *The Oxford Book of Modern Verse:*

> She is older than the rocks among which she sits; like the vampire, she has been dead many times, and learned the secrets of the grave; and has been a diver in deep seas, and keeps their fallen day about her; and trafficked for strange webs with Eastern merchants, and, as Leda, was the mother of Helen of Troy, and, as Saint Anne, the mother of Mary; and all this has been to her but as the sound of lyres and flutes, and lives only in the delicacy with which it has moulded the changing lineaments, and tinged the eyelids and the hands.

Thirty years after approving these sentences, Ellmann invokes them in an essay titled "Overtures to 'Salome'" (1968), by way of distinguishing Pater from Ruskin. In giving birth to Helen and Mary, the Mona Lisa embodies "exactly the indiscriminateness, as well as the fecundity, which Ruskin condemned . . . she combines sacred and profane."[30]

Having defended "Saint Walter" (as he is called in "Overture to 'Salome'"), the brothers spend the rest of their afternoon browsing bookstalls on the banks of the Seine, picking up books "for a franc apiece." Here and elsewhere, Dick is at pains to show his parents how careful he is with money. This care he exhibited throughout his life, though he could also be generous, as in offering to pay Erwin's way. His letters often list expenses and complain of or commend prices. Bed and full board at the inn, he writes in the undated late August letter, costs seventeen and a half francs or fifty-two and a half cents. "Our money supply is not what it was," he confesses in the July 5 letter, "though we have been faithful to economy in our fashion. . . . [W]e will probably have to draw on the extra $100."

* * *

Only once is the political situation in Europe referred to in surviving letters from the brothers, and then only briefly and indirectly. In the late August letter, Erwin writes of meeting "several non-Jewish Austrian refugees." There are no references to fascism, German belligerence, or antisemitism. The next summer, however, when Dick again toured Europe, this time with younger brother Bill, the political situation was unavoidable, especially toward the end of the tour. The idea for this second trip, to Scandinavia, Russia, and France, was broached by Dick to his parents as early as February 1939, and their initial objections were again financial. Dick was in his senior year, and while considering whether to become a writer rather than a university teacher, he had applied to graduate programs in English at Yale and Michigan. To keep his options open, he also considered spending a year at the Sorbonne. What concerned his father was whether the graduate schools Dick was applying to would offer him a fellowship. Without financial aid, "every penny that you save will be that much more useful to you later on when the need might be greater." As for a year at the Sorbonne: "I do not know what practical advantages it will bring to you personally. You can convince me, of course, but I would like to be convinced."

The idea of Bill accompanying Dick also concerned his father. Bill was a senior at Highland Park High School and destined to attend university in southern California, at Occidental College. His interests at the time were not especially literary or cultural and he was not as academic as his brothers. A trip to Europe "would mature him considerably," the father agreed, but it would also involve his spending "approximately $500.00." "He could get almost as much [maturing, that is] by tramping through Michigan with other boys, which he has in mind doing." Only a handful of Bill's letters survive from this period and they tell us nothing about his hopes for the trip. The first, to an unnamed girlfriend, is more openly romantic than anything his brothers might have written. Undated, it begins: "Come, please! Let me hold you once again before you have gone. It may be a long time before we meet again, dear, so come let us say our farewells early. But then I don't suppose it interests you—this indiscretion on my part. But to me it is a lot." On an accompanying sheet, Bill writes: "Destroy at *once*." A second letter, written after the trip, was addressed to Dick, and will figure later in this chapter.

On April Fool's Day 1939, the University of Michigan turned Dick down for a fellowship, though later that month he was offered one by Yale. This offer he accepted. With financial concerns addressed, the trip was on, though Dick also admitted in an undated letter to his father, written in April or early May, "that you are probably right about cutting out the Russian excursion. It will probably be safer to stay in northeastern Europe anyway." As in 1938, Dick handled all the details. In the undated letter, he suggests to his father "that you go and see Pierson now [of Union Guardian Trust] and find out how much dough he's got—I am not anticipating its costing more than $400 apiece, and hope it will be less." He also raises the possibility of money from a prize, though "it looks pretty likely that the prize won't be announced till commencement, and I don't want to count on it

William Ellmann, mid-1940s.

anyway." In fact, he did win a prize, as he had in each of his previous years at Yale, this time for having written the best essay by an English major in his senior year.

Bill was visiting Dick in New Haven at the time of the undated letter, presumably on Easter break from high school. In anticipation of their trip, the two brothers went to see the professor of Norwegian at Yale. The professor, Dick writes, "knew almost nothing about the country, amazingly enough; having only been there once, as far as I could tell, and then for a short time." The single piece of advice he could offer them was that only a light coat would be needed for July and August in Norway, even in the mountains. On a separate sheet, Dick then listed all the items of clothing Bill would need for the trip, from pairs of socks (five or six) to numbers of ties (two or three). "We plan to see the Swedish prof next."

Only four letters among the Ellmann Papers in Tulsa—two of them fragments, one barely legible and unlikely to have been intended for parents—

survive from the tour. One of the fragments, written on a single sheet of stationery from a hotel in Olden in Norway, was in fact composed in Trondheim, "Norway's ancient capital where its kings are crowned" and where "we have even seen the Norwegian Army, three or four hundred strong, greet Prince Olaf, newly returned from America." Dick was not impressed with Norway, or so the fragment suggests, "with its immense mountains and small towns." He might have agreed with Thomas Hardy, who mostly considered landscape "unimportant beside the wear of a threshold, or the print of a hand."[31] Of Norway's inhabitants, he says only that they complain about taxes and think the Social-Democratic Party in danger of being defeated.

In the second fragment, Dick writes from Bergen, which made an even less favorable impression upon him than Trondheim, certainly in respect to cuisine. "Carl Sandburg wrote a poem about Chicago and Vachel Lindsay wrote one about Springfield, but I think I will write one about Bergen. Bergen is a town in Norway where I shouldn't like to live but if I had to starve I should want to starve in Bergen. In Bergen you can starve on hills, you can take the cable railway up to Floyen [one of seven mountains surrounding the city] and starve there." In Bergen, he adds, "the girls are used to the sailors who get off the Norway America Line boats. And provide satisfaction at decent prices." It is hard to imagine this passage intended for Dick's mother.

The two completed letters, written to the Ellmann parents on July 15 and 21, are signed "Love, Dick and Bill," and written in Dick's hand. The first is from Bergen, which is now described as "a very pleasant little town." Its sights and population are noted and there is a bit about the political situation. "Against Germany the feeling runs very high and almost unanimous," Dick writes. "They want to stay neutral, but don't expect to be able to." As for the opposite sex, he wrote that, upon debarking, "we must have met half Bergen's feminine population [no mention is made of what they provide] and one came down to see us off today. The girls are very pretty and most of them speak a little English or German." The second completed letter is written from a youth hostel in Trondheim. In it Dick expresses disappointment with their fellow tourists. Of the Americans, one is going around the world but "has no interest in art or in anything, except 'seeing the country,' a phrase which seems to have some far-reaching symbolism for him." Another, from Oregon, declares "that everything is lovely, but we can do better in Oregon." The letter is perfunctory, closing with talk about youth hostel prices.

There are no surviving letters from Dick about Sweden or Helsinki, which they visited on a side trip from Stockholm. In Sweden Bill was impressed by the King's Palace, Tivoli, and the many pretty girls. Bill's son Robert remembers hearing only a single story from his father about the Scandinavian trip, concerning an act of derring-do outside a German embassy (which German embassy he does not recall): "They waited till it was dark. It was the Swastika flag of the Nazis. My Dad took it down or pulled it down or ripped it down. I can't remember how. And he did it with Uncle Dick. Then they ran or biked away because they were scared of being caught."[32]

The brothers arrived in Paris on August 15, where they found a letter from their mother full of advice about what to see, including the Folies Bergère, "for that is part of seeing Paris, I guess." She asks pointedly if they have picked up their mail at Oslo, Stockholm, and Copenhagen. A couple of weeks later, Dick received a letter from his father, dated August 25, two days after the signing of the Nazi-Soviet Pact:

> My Dear Dick:
> For the last three days the world has changed a good deal, and your good friends, the Communists, have run the full dictatorial gauntlet, as you can see. . . . A Dad should not tell his son "I told you so," especially while you are on the firing line in France. I am rather sorry that I was far more correct than wrong. I wish I had been wrong in matters of this sort. I recognize the numerous implications that youth who had ideal concepts must grovel in the capitalistic and democratic period with the rest of us—stupid liberals.

Dick's politics in the 1930s, such as they were, are hard to square with his father's "I told you so." When he was asked in 1936 by the editor of the *Yale Literary Magazine* what his political views were, he wrote, "I told him I had no fixed political views, which satisfied him."[33] In a letter of May 21–22, 1939, addressed to an unnamed girl ("My Dear"), Dick writes of a friend having given him a pamphlet by Trotsky: "It's propaganda—the Trotskyites, it appears, are endeavoring to prevent us from going into war; but when it comes, they will enter in wholeheartedly, get decorated for bravery, wait till the morale of the troops begins to break, then circulate propaganda to the effect that 'the Germans are our brethren; our enemies are our officers.' The next step is to shoot the officers and the world revolution is on. Their methods don't appeal to me much."

These are hardly the views of a good friend of Communists. Ellsworth Mason, a Yale classmate and friend, recalled that their generation was "thoroughly infected by the powerful propaganda of the peace movement. . . . [W]e were convinced that Europe's great powers were a bunch of thugs who should be allowed to bash each other's brains out without our getting involved in it at all," a view which "tended to slow down the perception in this country of the extreme brutality of the Nazi regime." As Mason remembered it, "Ellmann participated in these general attitudes,"[34] which were presumably seen by his father as pro-Communist. The father's chiding in the August 25 letter gives way in the next paragraph to concern, a hope that all has gone well, that the trip has brought "lots of fun," "great value," and that Bill is "now on the high seas." When, he asks, will Dick return? Given that "the American government has asked all citizens to leave France. . . . I feel satisfied that you will use common horse sense in deciding whether or not you should stay or leave." It is important that Dick respond to letters from home. "These are dangerous days, and we certainly ought to keep in touch with each other more closely."

In fact, Dick would not write back for almost three weeks. On September 13 he sent a cable from La Baule, a seaside resort in Brittany. The cable reads: "BIEN ADDRESSEZ POSTE RESTANTE LA BAULE ATTENDANT PASSAGE TRANQUILLE. DICK." That same day, having received this cable, James wrote to say that he had been in correspondence with Cordell Hull, the US secretary of state, in reply to a cable Hull had sent. It seems that at some point James had asked the government to help locate Dick. Bill, meanwhile, having sailed on the *Empress of Australia,* a Canadian liner, landed in Quebec on September 2. Dick was not with him, Bill later told his son Douglas, because, in Douglas's words, "there was only one ticket available, and like a good big brother, he sent my Dad. According to my father, the boat was monitored by a German U-boat and under threat of a torpedo attack" (a year later it was sunk by just such an attack). It was overcrowded, jammed with Canadians and Americans, and there was a blackout during its dangerous passage. By the time of Dick's cable from La Baule, Bill was already "comfortably situated" at Occidental College, according to James's letter of September 13. The letter ends: "Needless to tell you, mother was very happy to hear from you and so was Erwin. At least we have your address."

They would not hear from Dick again until October 2, in a cable from New York that read "Arriving Friday." During this period Dick received a letter from his mother, written on September 18: "Every day we hope there will be some word from you." On September 20, Erwin wrote, complaining that "we have little or no idea what is happening to you." Both Erwin and his father encouraged Dick to keep a record of his adventures in France. "I trust you are making the best you possibly can of your opportunities to preserve your impressions," James wrote in the September 13 letter, "after all, you are a 'writin' man' and these things are the tools of your trade." Erwin imagines Dick's experiences "ought to produce a book at least."[35] Bill, too, wrote, reporting that he has gone out for the football team, that the weather is "swell," and that Eagle Rock, where Occidental is located, is a "fine little town." The letter ends: "Why the hell didn't you write the folks?"

* * *

It was odd for a hitherto "dependable," "indulgent," "patient" son not to write. One thing it suggests, in addition to the difficulty of correspondence in wartime and the run-up to war, is that by the date of the 1939 trip, Dick was irritated with his parents and seeking distance from their needs and expectations. Nowhere is the distance he sought clearer than in two letters written on either side of the trip, both unlike any others among the Ellmann papers from this period. The first was written around mid-January 1939 and concerns what Erwin called his "erotics." Erwin had transferred from USC to the University of Michigan at the end of his freshman year, graduating with a BA from Michigan in 1936. In 1938 he took his JD degree, again at Michigan. He then spent a year clerking for a Michigan Supreme Court justice, before moving to Washington, DC, "to find a job in the New Deal." In 1936, his last year as an undergraduate, he began dating Steffani Fedoryshyn, a lively eighteen-year-old girl. Eventually, after an interval even longer than his parents had waited, Erwin and Steffani married.

Steffani was the daughter of Catholic immigrants from the Ukraine, whose circumstances, to quote her son Michael, were "modest in the extreme."[36] Steffani's father worked as a skilled laborer at the Ford plant in Dearborn, Michigan; her mother was, in grandson Michael's words, "an illiterate housewife." That Steffani was neither Jewish nor from a "good" family counted against her in the eyes of both Ellmann parents, but especially in Jean's. Erwin had met her at a dance, at a time when she already had a boyfriend. In a letter of May 28, 1937, the first to refer to Steffani, Erwin writes to Dick that she has met their mother, in response "more or less to a deliberate challenge." Steffani herself writes to Dick on October 26, 1937, teasing him about his love life. Erwin has shown her a letter in which Dick describes what she calls his "so called progress" with a young lady. This progress she deems "sadly pathetic in its passivity." Unless Dick manages "a few vigorous extra-curricular activities," she (Steffani) will be "saddened into a kind of Slavonic melancholia."

The first sign of parental disfavor appears in a letter of January 10, 1938, in which Erwin asks Dick if he knows anything about "the parental attitude that regards Steff as somewhat of a fait accompli?" This attitude, Erwin admits, is not at all how he regards their relationship, "even were I it were otherwise." A year later, on April 23, 1939, Jean writes to Dick in full assault: "Aunt Rose was greatly disappointed when she met Stephanie [*sic*] recently when Erwin brought her over. . . . She drank more than anyone and became very gay and free and seems to have made a poor impression on the entire group. I think she [Aunt Rose] means to tell Erwin too when she can." On May 9 Jean elaborates. In addition to drinking too much, Steffani "acted up to all the other boys so that all their girlfriends were displeased. . . . Aunt Rose sized S up as a nice girl who would get places because she has a pleasant voice and a good personality, but she told him she was not the girl for him. She told him she was too sexy for him to keep [her] satisfied. . . . She is desired by the rich and the wise and the important, for he has recounted to me all the men who want her, and yet there she sticks to little Erwin. . . . Aunt Rose told him that she would leave him the minute it was advantageous to her to do so, and that vows would not bind her."

In the same letter, Jean describes another occasion on which Steffani behaved badly. On most weekends Erwin traveled to Dearborn from Ann Arbor to visit Steffani. When he arrived "last Saturday," he discovered she was out with another man. She had been posing for the artist David Fredenthal, who introduced her to "his friend, a wealthy Grosse Pointer by the name of Cook" (presumably George Cooke, most likely the man she was dating when she met Erwin, according to Michael Ellmann).[37] "She did not even think to call Erwin on the phone and prevent him from taking the long ride out to her place. . . . Any girl who will do that can hardly be trusted in the larger things. She holds him for a sucker. . . . I have been boiling about this injustice, and I trust he is putting two and two together for himself." It was Erwin who told his mother about this "injustice," something "he does not ordinarily do," although he also told her that Steffani had explained the situation satisfactorily, which "he took, and it went down smoothly."

Several weeks later, in a letter of May 22, Erwin writes to Dick of their parents' "keen resentment of Steffani and my interest in her and what she represents." This resentment he relates to a "tart observation" his mother had made about a Polish caddy at the Knollwood Golf Club who had been caught stealing: "You can't expect anything else from Polish boys." "I suppose I should have let that pass," Erwin writes, "as you would have done in discretion but I had to indicate that it is reasoning like that which produces fascism and anti-Semitism at a glance. There is a Polish thief; q.e.d. all Poles are thieves. And the Jews in the next breath become highly resentful when the same sort of logic is applied to them."

Sometime between this letter and the end of the year, most likely after the trip to Europe in the summer, Erwin writes to Dick of having received a letter from their father. The letter makes it clear that father and mother were united in disapproving of Steffani, or rather of Erwin's relationship with Steffani. "For three years apparently he has harbored secret apprehensions about me and my interests in Steffani, only to write me his feelings when he writes three thousand miles away. (Incidentally, I was surprised to see how decently and effectively he presented them.) I could not expect him to know that confidence is not given when it is not inspired."

When Dick learned of the father's letter, he challenged his parents' attitudes directly. Among the Ellmann papers is the second page of a typed letter Dick wrote to his father, subsequently dated, "abt 1/15/39." It seems to have been written from Yale, after Christmas vacation in Highland Park:[38]

> I presume Erwin won't be home when this comes, so I'll tell you what I think of the situation. You wonder that "he seems mad at us all the time, and exceedingly displeased about something." Frankly, I can't understand how it would be otherwise. Ever since he has gone with Steffani he has been forced by parental disapproval to meet her half secretly and half openly. He can hardly be unaware of how Billy's mind has been turned

against her by constant reiteration of this disapproval. He can hardly be so obtuse as not to recognize the attempts to have him meet other girls for what they are—definite attempts to get him away from her. He knows that every time he says he is going to Dearborn you talk about it behind his back; I shouldn't wonder if he had a persecution complex by this time.

As to whether she should be accepted as his friend or fiancé, the very question seems to me a ridiculous one. If you can't tell that he is in love, you certainly don't know anything about Erwin. And likewise, if you think he is going to marry before he knows definitely that it will work out, you don't know Erwin. The whole question of whether she should come to the house or not is an academic one—it is based entirely on certain external concepts and a blindness to the individuals concerned. Of course she should come to the house—and of course you should tell Erwin, if you feel that way, that you don't think marriage with a Gentile is the wisest thing but that his happiness is a great deal more important than any abstract principle, and that you want to accept Steffani into the family, and are willing to accept her as a daughter-in-law whenever he thinks it's wise.

If you don't agree with me on philosophic grounds it makes absolutely no difference. You're confronted with the status quo, or better, the fait accompli, and simple opportunism and the fact that they have been going together now for three years, that Erwin has had plenty of time to learn to know her, and that if he continues with her it is because he sincerely feels it is best for him. Personally, I am far from sure that it isn't, and I don't understand at all how you can have any degree of certitude about it. I think you should take her in as soon as possible . . . you will forgive my speaking so strongly but it seems to me that this persecution of my brother should stop, whether you think it's for his own good or not.

Love,
Dick

Despite its toughness, the letter remains respectful, its criticisms licensed by the parents' commitment to argument. For Dick, an eventual biographer, "abstract principles," "external concepts," and "philosophic grounds" not only take second place to "the individuals concerned" but "blind" the parents to those individuals' true qualities—in Erwin's case, to the complexity and uncertainty of his feelings for Steffani, whom he loves but does not yet "think it's wise" to marry. The tangle of Erwin's feelings is neatly captured when Dick considers whether it is "best for him" to continue the relationship: "Personally, I am far from sure that it isn't, and I don't understand at all how you can have any degree of certitude about it." That Dick's letter was written in mid-January 1939 and his mother's campaign against Steffani continued through the spring suggests that his father never showed it to his wife. The strength of Dick's feelings and his mother's continued hostility may help to explain the infrequency and reserve of surviving correspondence.

In his 1997 memoir, Erwin describes his mother as having "a profound and overpowering influence on me and my brothers." In moving to Washington, DC, in late 1939 to find a job in the New Deal, he may have been motivated in part by a desire to escape this influence. His father's keenness for him to join his law practice may also have been a factor. Within a year of the move, in October 1940, Steffani married George Cooke. Erwin spent the war years first in the Department of Labor, where, among other issues, he worked on child labor law, then in 1943 in the Department of the Interior, helping to improve working conditions for coal miners. Steffani's marriage to Cooke lasted almost four and a half years, until February 1945. Within a year of her divorce, on October 10, 1945, she and Erwin married in Alexandria, Virginia. The next year Erwin and his new bride moved back to Michigan and he joined his father's law firm, which became Ellmann and Ellmann. In 1951, after the birth of their children, Michael and Barbara, he and Steffani moved from Dearborn to a house within a mile of 55 Connecticut Avenue. In 1967, for a variety of reasons, Erwin left Ellmann and Ellmann to join a rival law firm in Detroit. In addition to continued tensions between Steffani and Erwin's parents ("a frosty cordiality" is how Michael Ellmann characterized their relations), there were tensions between Erwin and Bill, who had joined the firm in 1951. Dick, however, remained on good terms with both brothers throughout his life. The marriage between Erwin and Steffani lasted sixty years, until Steffani's death in 2006.

The second strong letter from Dick to be discussed in this chapter is if anything more outspoken than the letter about Steffani and Erwin. It concerns Bill and his future, was addressed to both parents, and was written from Yale early in 1940, after another Christmas vacation in Highland

Erwin and Steffani Ellmann, undated photo.

Park.[39] What prompted it was a letter his father had written to Bill, which he (the father) subsequently showed to Dick.

> Your letter to Billy shocked me considerably, Dad. It had never occurred to me that you would choose such an obvious way of exerting pressure upon him; "it seems you may be doomed to take up law." Why should he be doomed! What conceivable relation is there between Erwin's decision not to live in Detroit and your insistence upon Billy's going into law?
>
> I think I know what the connection is. You say that it's wrong for Rosin to take over the firm. Why is it wrong? It is wrong because you want to perpetuate yourself, because you had expected Erwin to carry your work on, and, now that he has quit, you want to make Bill do it. This desire to perpetuate oneself is very strong in everybody, and I am not blaming it as such; but in this case you have allowed your emotions to interfere completely with your own theories of bringing up your children.
>
> This is what I mean: you have always had an influence on both Erwin and me, and a very good influence, not by insisting in our following in a

> certain pattern or obeying your suggestions, but by emphasizing our freedom of choice and then by hints and suggestions bringing us around. Your letter to Bill is a complete departure from this, and distressed me profoundly.

Dick criticizes his father not just for breaking with his principles, but also for failing to acknowledge and respect Bill's individuality, the charge he leveled against his parents in the letter about Erwin and Steffani. As Dick sees it,

> If there is anything important for Bill at this moment, it is the idea that he is an independent person, independent of his friends and of his family. You yourself admitted to me over Christmas vacation that it was possible that he listened to you too much. . . . You have a boy very sensitive to the opinions of others, particularly of his father, and you abuse the fact. Don't you see how important it is that Billy think he is making up his own mind! Don't you see what a terrifying thing it will be for him to go through life with the realization that he is doing it because his father strongly advised it.
>
> You will say that you are merely helping him along, that he is in a state of indecision, and that you don't mean this as final. But you are concealing your own motives if you say so: you cannot bear the idea of the office dying with you (very natural, I repeat), and you know that you can influence Billy in whatever direction you wish.
>
> If you think this is merely psychological theorizing, impractical, and so forth, let me put it another way. If there is such a thing as human personality, then the choice of a career is one place where it should be exercised. There are problems where the personality is not important, but this is certainly not one of them. Billy must not feel he is doing what he is told by someone who has dominated him throughout his high school career. I am not sure you realize what a dangerous thing it is that you can control him as easily as you do.

The intensity of Dick's concern for Bill's independence, and of his criticism of what he saw as his father's abuse of his influence, seems likely to reflect his feelings about his own life choices. According to Lucy Ellmann, Dick's parents had not been pleased when he chose to go to Yale rather than to Michigan, for all their later pride in having an Ivy League son. James may also have been disappointed at Dick's choosing to become a professor rather than a lawyer, though there is no support for this speculation in correspondence. When Dick considered abandoning an academic career "to write" (in part the rationale behind his considering applying to the Sorbonne), beneath his father's acceptance was understandable concern. This concern was not new, it was voiced also at the beginning of Dick's senior year at Yale when Dick proposed changing courses to further his ambitions as a writer. "With regard to your sudden determination," the father writes on October 24, 1938, "it is no surprise to either of us." He is not opposed to Dick becoming a writer, will even send under separate cover "a book which mother has read with much interest, and so have I. I am sure you will like it because it will give you some practical ideas on writing, so long as you are inclined to make up your mind along those lines." But he also advises caution about the proposed change in courses:

> Just as you have suddenly made up your mind in that direction, you may find in the course of some time that you will want to retrace your steps. Do not therefore burn all your bridges behind you. If, by reason of the proposed change, you desire to emphasize certain subjects, well and good, but you need not tell yourself that you are quite definite that one rather than another course is to be followed. Your mind is still in the process of gestation, and it may evolve new ideas from contacts that you are yet to make rather than from those already made.
>
> Neither mother nor I is upset about your proposed change, and we feel that if you should find it necessary to pursue the new course completely, it is probably for your best interest.

Dick's decision to accept the Yale graduate fellowship six months later left him feeling ashamed. In the letter of May 21–22, 1939, addressed to an unnamed "My Dear," he quotes T. S. Eliot: "I am not Hamlet, nor was meant to be, Am an attendant lord, one that will do To swell a progress, start a scene or two, Advise the prince. . . ." At least it looks that way, because I have accepted a fellowship to Yale's graduate school out of pure greed, despise [*sic*] all my contrary inclinations. The only glimmer of relief is that I may not last out the year." It is hard not to read "despise" here (for the intended "despite") as revealing, hard also not to attribute the intensity of the letter to Dick's sense of his own susceptibility to his father's influence. Ellsworth Mason quotes lines from a poem Dick sent him in June 1944 titled "In Dispraise of Parents," which hints at the strength of such influence:

In the clutch, in the blow,
Power lies, but truly lies
In the tickle, the scratch,
Using the Christian name,
Jollying to weakness.[40]

Ellmann explains to Mason in a letter of August 18, 1944: "The proposition is that parents control us not by their strength (clutches, blows) but by their insinuations. A favorite method is to call up ancestors, traditions, etc., which thus weakens us into conforming with the pattern (which by the way is false, because our ancestors were pioneers not conformers)." He cites as an example the myth of Zeus castrating Kronos in order to get to the throne: "My point is that he really had to kill his mother (Rhea) too—she is the tickle / weakness, Kronos the blow / strength, in this context. 'The mother wells up in his breast' is an allusion to Lear's 'O how the mother wells up in my breast,' which means something like 'there's a lump in my throat'—the mother is an Elizabethan word for emotions."

To return to the letter about Bill, it concludes with a mix of feelings:

> I am extremely doubtful as to whether law is the best thing for him; this question does not seem to have bothered you; and that is what I am complaining of. Let us start with Bill; he is this kind of person, with these interests, with this background; since we cannot possibly know yet whether he is built for law or not, let us keep our hands off; let us encourage him to think about a career. . . .
>
> I wrote a much stronger letter on this subject which I have decided not to send; I hope that the fact that I have discussed it here rather mildly will not disguise the fact that I consider you are bringing on a crisis in Bill's life before he has any equipment to meet it, and that I heartily disapprove of your letter to him and hope you will remedy it.
>
> Love über alles,
> *Dick*

In fact, law seems to have been the right choice for Bill. After a year at Occidental College, he spent four years in the Army Air Corps, finished his undergraduate degree at the University of Michigan, got his JD from Wayne State University, and joined Ellmann and Ellmann, where he remained throughout his career. In 1967 he was elected president of the Michigan

Bar Association, and over the course of his career he was almost as active in Jewish causes and organizations as his father had been.[41] Throughout his life, Dick was closer to Erwin than to Bill—closer in character and in interests—but they maintained good relations.

* * *

The desire to become a writer was difficult for Dick to drop. Around the time of his letter to his parents about Bill—that is, midway through his first year in graduate school—he wrote again to his father, to ask about possible job contacts in New York. In a letter of February 5, 1940, his father wrote back with the name of David Bernstein, "one of the foremost officials in the American Jewish Committee of New York." Bernstein "writes a little bit" and is "familiar with literary problems and knows a good many of the publishing houses." The father also reminds Dick, "Mother and I, of course, are strongly of the belief that the degree will be of utmost value to you later on." In addition, perhaps under the influence of Dick's letter about Bill, the father admits not only that "we may not be correct in this," but that "your own best interests are of utmost importance, and your parents' prejudices should not count in that."

A week or so later, in a letter of February 13, 1940, Erwin writes to Dick about Dick's letter concerning Bill (everyone in the family knows everyone else's business), a letter about which, he writes, he is "in hearty accord." He then discusses their relations with their parents in general. He found the tone of Dick's letter "cheering," but he was not "particularly taken in by the camaraderie of revolt." Dick was "suffering the same reactions from the paternal shade that I have felt myself." In revolting against this shade, or against parental influence more widely, he writes, "we are, of course, not too well equipped. . . . The life into which we have been bred, and its attendant habituations, do not go to sharpen self-reliance and individual courage." In a later letter of February 25, Erwin writes of a conversation he has just had with their parents: "Dad and Mom spoke to me long distance today, apparently trying to make sure that everything that was said about Bill was meant in good clean fun. It is very difficult to fight with such decent people."

This difficulty—or ambivalence—Ellmann and his brothers negotiated throughout their lives. In Dick's case, it shaped his understanding of the role of family not only in his own life and work but also in the life and work of Joyce. Consider, to take a single example, his account of Joyce's decision in 1902 to give up medical school in Dublin and move to Paris, ostensibly to study medicine but in fact to write. This decision, described in *James Joyce* with a mixture of wit and admiration, was made by Joyce at the exact age at which Ellmann himself contemplated giving up academic study to write, in a plan also involving a move to Paris, ostensibly to study at the Sorbonne.[42] It is hard not to see Ellmann's account of this moment in Joyce's life as shaped by his own quite different decision at a comparable moment, a decision partly taken under the influence of parental fear, prudence, and fair-mindedness. On March 7, 1940, in the wake of the Bill letter, Ellmann's father had news to report: "Billy writes again in the last few days about the possibility of coming to the University of Michigan. Within a few days I shall write him a long letter and give him the basic reasons that he might use in coming to a determination of what he might and might not do. I hope I shall have the time to prepare such a letter, in which case I will very likely send you a copy."

Ellmann's parents, Jean and James Ellmann, early 1960s.

CHAPTER TWO

Yale

ELLMANN GRADUATED from Highland Park High School in 1935, fourth in a class of 326, with an average school grade of 98 out of 100. The number of colleges he applied to is unclear, but in a letter of August 1 to an admissions officer at Brown University, he writes of having unexpectedly received a scholarship from Yale, one he "felt obliged to accept due to the larger stipend it makes available." That he may also have applied to the University of Michigan is suggested in a letter of September 17, written to his parents from New Haven, "one of the most wonderful places you can imagine. Ann Arbor is nothing compared to it."[1]

Less wonderful was his freshman roommate, who "hauls a lot of Jews into the room all the time."[2] That this roommate was Jewish was no accident. In addition to a quota system limiting Jewish enrollment to 10 percent, housing at Yale automatically segregated Christians and Jews.[3] A story told by a later Yale roommate, the critic Charles J. Feidelson Jr., also a Jew, is recounted by his son John. Ellmann persuaded Feidelson "to participate in a fraternity rush despite my Dad's hesitation, knowing in advance the outcome. In the end they were not tapped. I have an image from that conversation of the two men standing alone in the Old Campus after the final draw. My father laughed at the absurdity of it all. The chance of selection was slim; they were Jews after all."

One fraternity Ellmann did join, in his junior year, was Chi Delta Theta, a literary society founded in 1821, the second oldest university Greek society in the United States (the oldest, Phi Beta Kappa, which Ellmann joined on graduation, was also originally founded to discuss and debate literature). Ellmann was invited to join Chi Delta Theta in his junior year, when he was also elected to the executive editorial board of the *Yale Literary Magazine* (known as the *Yale Lit* and the *Lit*) along with, among others, Louis S. Auchincloss, later a novelist of old-money WASP society.[4] Ellmann had been contributing poems and essays to the *Lit* since freshman year. He was also admitted as a freshman to Advanced English, whose fellow students, he wrote to his parents, were "smarter than I ever saw before, with few exceptions."[5]

One of Ellmann's contributions to the *Yale Lit* was an unsigned editorial of April 1938 titled "Yale's English."[6] The editorial begins by declaring that "on the basis of the reputations of its instructors," Yale was "as good a place as any to study English." In undergraduate teaching, however, it had its weaknesses. Chief among these weaknesses was a failure to provide undergraduates with a sense of the purpose of literary study and of the essential or defining features of literature. It is not enough to give students a sense of the ideas of William Shakespeare or Henry James if no reason is given "why the communication of those ideas comes under the heading of literature," or if no attempt is made to find these ideas in the writings, as opposed to "extraneous facts of biography."[7] When on occasion a teacher does focus on "the real stuff of literature—*the writing,*" he is "recognized by the stigma of 'poor scholar'" (p. 6).

Executive editorial board, *Yale Literary Magazine,* 1939, Ellmann in front row, far right.

These complaints reflect the influence of the New Criticism, soon to produce what Paul H. Fry, a Yale English professor, describes in a brief online history as one of "the most notable (or notorious) epochs in the history of Yale's fabled department."[8] The New Critics sparked ambitious young English students like Ellmann by challenging the view of criticism that prevailed at that time among academics as unserious, subjective, soft, or easy in comparison to scholarship and philology ("creating editions, compiling lore and information, tracing the development of languages"). By advancing a theory of literature grounded in philosophy and/or psychology, as well as offering a systematic methodology for its study, they sought to bring intellectual respectability to criticism.

The movement's originating ideas came from England, drawn principally from T. S. Eliot's essays, I. A. Richards's *The Principles of Literary Criticism* (1924) and *Practical Criticism* (1929), as well as influential collaborations with the philosopher C. K. Ogden, in particular *Foundations of Aesthetics* (1922) and *The Meaning of Meaning* (1923), and William Empson's *Seven Types of Ambiguity* (1930). In 1938, the year of the "Yale's English" editorial, John Crowe Ransom, a poet/critic from Vanderbilt University, published *The World's Body,* described by Fry as the "first great manifesto" of New Criticism. Also in 1938, Ransom's fellow southerners Cleanth Brooks and Robert Penn Warren published *Understanding Poetry,* a much-reprinted textbook and poetry anthology in which students were encouraged to approach poems without reference to historical or biographical details. Three years later, in 1941, Ransom published *The New Criticism,* from which the movement took its name. That summer Ellmann enrolled in a course co-taught by Ransom and Theodore Greene, the Princeton philosopher, at the Bread Loaf School of English in Vermont. The course was titled "Critical and Philosophical Approaches to Literature."

That Ellmann, at the time of his "Yale's English" editorial, was familiar with the writings of Ransom and Richards is suggested not only by the editorial's echoes from their writings,[9] but by correspondence with Feidelson, perhaps his closest friend not only at Yale but throughout his life. Like Ellmann, Feidelson was born in 1918, but he entered Yale a year earlier than Ellmann, at sixteen. Ellsworth Mason, their fellow student, describes him as "probably the most deeply intelligent mind of us all."[10] In 1947 Feidelson was the first Jew to join Yale's English Department, where he taught for thirty-five years and chaired its American Studies program. The most important of Feidelson's publications, *Symbolism and American Literature* (1953), cites Richards, Eliot, and Ransom, as well as a number of European philosophers. Its introduction ends: "I have tried to let the materials speak for themselves as much as possible; and my end is not pure theory but practical criticism."[11]

In 1938 Feidelson graduated at the top of his class and won a Henry Fellowship to study English at Cambridge, where he arranged to be supervised by I. A. Richards. In a letter of November 4, 1938, he writes to Ellmann in a way that assumes his friend's knowledge of and interest in Richards's writings, which he describes as "only a pale reflection of his brilliance." "Richards gives you an inferiority complex. . . . He's an ugly little man, very mild-mannered but quite conceited. I'm reading rather widely in psychology proper [with philosophy, the discipline upon which Richards grounded his theories], before going into the special aspects in which I am interested, and I go to see him once a week to talk over what I have read. He strips you naked with questions."

At the time of this letter, Ellmann was agonizing over whether to pursue a career in academic English. Feidelson thought it would be a mistake not to do so, partly for reasons like those of Ellmann's parents. "My God," he writes in the letter's first paragraph, "what are you going to do if you don't go into English?"

> Let me tell you, son, I've gone through similar, if not equally porcine, wallowings in the slough of despond—even I. Turn your face to the stars, have a band play "Onward Christian Soldiers," and try to look Aryan. Seriously, you know, I think one ought to be very sure of what he is doing before he gives up anything in which he has made progress. I mean, to start on something relatively new, the attraction of which may be entirely due to novelty, and to give up something partially mastered, the distaste for which may be entirely due to a temporary surfeit—that's a risky business under any circumstances.

Feidelson sounds a similarly prudential concern in a letter of January 30, 1939: "What kind of job do you have in mind for support while you are enjoying the 'world?'"[12]

At the end of the November 4 letter, Feidelson returns to his friend's "wallowings," offering something more positive than prudence as a reason for continuing with English. "Let me know what you do decide on. And a word in your ear, sirrah—the study of English will be taking on a new life when I return to the States (I have many revolutionary ideas); and if you remain faithful you may reap the benefits." That these ideas were sparked by Richards and Ransom and the philosophical works they drew on is hinted at by a joke addendum to the letter. Feidelson transcribes a passage from an article in the Oxford philosophy journal *Mind,* which he describes as "an expert opinion." The title of the article is "Voluntary Action," and after a passage beginning "Prolonged and repeated indecision is highly detrimental to the general conduct of life," he adds an exclamation mark.[13]

* * *

The highest academic rank at Yale was Sterling Professor, the equivalent of university professor at other universities. The Sterling Professor of English Literature during Ellmann's undergraduate years at Yale, and the department's presiding spirit, was Chauncey Brewster Tinker (1876–1963), described by Fry as "a great scholar and charismatic teacher." Tinker was an outspoken opponent of the New Critics, whom he accused of "whoring after I. A. Richards." He began his career as a student of Old English before moving into eighteenth-century studies. In 1936, in his sophomore year, Ellmann took Tinker's course "English Poets of the Nineteenth Century" and received the only low grade of his undergraduate career: "a horrible 75, my worst mark."[14] That he deserved this mark is unlikely, given that all his other marks were in the 90s. Perhaps Tinker detected the influence of Richards, Eliot, or Empson in Ellmann's essays. He may also have taken exception to what Ellsworth Mason describes as Ellmann's propensity to "slip into any conversation information about contemporary poetry" (p. 4), which was not a field of study at Yale until 1947. It is also possible that Tinker took against Ellmann because he was Jewish. "He did genuinely not believe that a Jew could be understanding of the English literary tradition," recalled a Yale contemporary, George Pierson, professor of history. When, on the eve of World War II, the English Department considered hiring Lionel Trilling from Columbia, Tinker vetoed the idea.[15]

Feidelson was appointed Sterling Professor in 1947, two years after Tinker's retirement. That he was a southerner rather than a New Yorker (he was born in Savannah, Georgia, and raised in Birmingham, Alabama) may have helped his candidacy. One of his students, David Bromwich (Sterling Professor of English Literature at Yale since 2006) remembers Feidelson as "dignified, thoughtful, impressive," with an "appealing, pretty thick

Southern drawl." Jewishness, it seemed to Bromwich, was "an incidental fact about him (as it was not with e.g. [Geoffrey] Hartman and [Harold] Bloom)," an observation that might also have been made of Ellmann. In the opinion of Feidelson's first wife, Kathryn, however, the Jewishness of the two friends "should not be ignored. The Yale Department of English for many years was knee-deep in WASP rites and culture, perhaps more than any other Yale entity. When both men were students, they were told that in their future they would not be playing a part in that culture."[16] Even after Feidelson joined the department, he was made to feel something of an outsider. Fry tells the story of when, after the war, Trilling was finally invited to New Haven to give a talk. Feidelson was chosen to meet him at the train station "because they would understand each other."

* * *

Aside from "Poets of the Nineteenth Century" and "Advanced Freshman English," the English courses Ellmann took as an undergraduate were "Chaucer and His Century," "Shakespeare and His Contemporaries," "Milton and His Contemporaries," and in senior year a required "Honors English" discussion course "designed primarily to assist students in their preparation for the departmental examination."[17] The aim of these undergraduate courses was to give students a sense of the major literary historical periods, arranged, according to Ellmann's "Yale's English" editorial, "in such a way that laid end to end they pretty much cover any three hundred years of English literature" (p. 6). Ellmann quickly paraded his knowledge of this history in two seriocomic contributions to the *Lit,* one about the Devil ("Speak of the Devil," February 1937), whose "biography" he traces from biblical times to the present, the other about Love ("Love—Brocaded and Streamlined," December 1937), in which he attributes popular support for Edward VIII's abdication to "a modern epidemic of love-sickness," a twentieth-century equivalent of courtly love extremes "under Richard I, in the last days of the twelfth century" (p. 7), an extreme he then anatomizes.[18]

One aspect of undergraduate English Ellmann praised in his "Yale's English" editorial was the way courses were scheduled. With the exception of honors English, all courses met three times a week for a total of three hours. The first two of these hours usually took the form of lectures, "the third hour course, a brilliant idea, was designed originally to bring down to the student in a preferably informal group, the main outlines which had been suggested in the lecture. . . . As a matter of practice, they have become completely distinct from the main portion of the course" (pp. 6–7). In Ellmann's senior year, one such third-hour seminar helped to determine the direction of his career. A fellow senior in English, Henry V. Jaffa, later a professor of government and a follower of the political philosopher Leo Strauss, "dragged" Ellmann to a seminar taught by Andrews Wanning, a young instructor recently returned from Cambridge. Like Feidelson, Wanning had been influenced by I. A. Richards. The textbook he used for the seminar was Brooks and Warren's *Understanding Poetry.* In the seminar, students were presented with unidentified and undated poems to discuss, in the manner of a "Practical Criticism" session. One of these poems, Yeats's "The Cold Heaven," powerfully affected Ellmann. After learning its author's identity, he set out to read everything Yeats had written, then everything written about him. Three years later, as a second-year graduate student, he proposed Yeats as the subject of his PhD dissertation.[19]

Earlier that same year, Ellmann set out to win the Henry H. Strong American Literature Prize. For all his ambivalence about academic English, he remained an ambitious student. Initially he considered writing about Poe. Feidelson, in the November 4, 1938, letter, suggested that he write about Thomas Wolfe instead. "He's contemporary, so that you should be satisfied, and he is dead, so that the English department should be satisfied." Eventually Ellmann settled on Edward Arlington Robinson, a "very good" choice Feidelson wrote on January 30, 1939, "and a lot more useful afterwards than a piece of lumber on Poe."[20] Once Ellmann decided on Robinson, everyone in the family pitched in, keen to encourage his rekindled interest in English study. "I guess you and Erwin will have lots to discuss about the Robinson situation," writes his father, on December 15, 1938. "I tried to understand what you were driving at but it is over my small head." The next day his mother wrote: "Erwin is still doing Robinson for you and is looking forward to your arrival so we can all dig into him. Look in the periodical index to find all criticisms on him, in Modern Language Association bulletins or whatever they are, for the libraries here may be incomplete. . . . A biography was recently done by Hagedorn that might be worth glimpsing."

Ellmann reviewed the Hagedorn biography in the January 1939 issue of the *Lit* and found it wanting in several respects. To begin with, it "fails to make any real inroads upon the poet's mind, as if from fear of invading his privacy." "This is good etiquette, but for a biographer it isn't cricket.

Occasionally he indicates the *rapport* between an incident in Robinson's life and one of the poems, but this is as far as he will go, and he chooses to consider the gap between as biographically unbridgeable." Nowhere is Hagedorn's reticence or timidity clearer than in the biography's treatment of Robinson's later poems.

> Mr. Hagedorn is content to explain the failure of a number of the later long poems solely on the ground of haste, neglecting the evidence of psychoses to be found in them with such persistency as to suggest that they are largely autobiographic. Such mental limitations must be frankly admitted and dealt with. In other words, now that the chorus of posthumous eulogy has died down [Robinson died in 1935] [he] must be treated as a Sphinx whose secret is not impenetrable, and the careful biographer need not (as Mr. Hagedorn may have feared) level his subject by revealing it. (p. 24)

The "impenetrable" riddle of the Sphinx in the Oedipus story is "What goes on four feet in the morning, two feet at noon, and three feet in the evening?" The answer is "man." Ellmann is suggesting that Hagedorn's reluctance to "level his subject" (to admit weaknesses on Robinson's part) is a reluctance to see him as fallibly human, a man.

To obtain a PhD in English at Yale, students entering graduate study in 1939 were required to take two-plus years of graduate courses, meet three language requirements (two modern, one ancient), and pass a daunting pre-PhD oral examination. In his first year, the courses Ellmann took were "Old English," "The Romantic Movement," and "The Augustan Age," plus a course in French titled "Poetry of the Nineteenth Century: The Romantic Period." In his second year, he took two English courses, "Spenser and His Age" and "Carlyle and Matthew Arnold," plus a "Special Course in Old French." At the end of this second year, Ellmann was awarded an MA for a thesis ("The Social Philosophy of Thomas Carlyle") that grew out of the course on Carlyle and Matthew Arnold. The course was taught by the Old English specialist Karl Young, "who has a wide reputation as a scholar."[21] In his third year Ellmann took "Victorian Poets," the sole graduate course in English in which Yeats might figure, if only in terms of the time period. This course was taught by William Clyde DeVane, newly appointed dean of Yale College, a post he would hold for twenty-five years. DeVane encouraged Ellmann's interest in Yeats and would go on to serve as nominal supervisor of his dissertation.[22]

Ellmann, class photo, Yale, 1939.

Of Ellmann's other instructors, the most eminent was Frederick Pottle (1897–1987), the great Boswell scholar, an example to Ellmann in several respects. In his brief "History of the Department," Fry describes Pottle as "in many ways the backbone and mediator of the department during the epoch of the New Criticism." Harold Bloom, whose dissertation Pottle supervised, called him "the best mind in my profession in my lifetime."[23] Pottle had been a graduate student at Yale in the early 1920s. He published his first book, *Shelley and Browning* (1923), before he received his PhD. Like Ellmann, he wrote poems while in graduate school, winning honors in the Cook Poetry Prize competition. Tinker turned Pottle into an eighteenth-century scholar, suggesting that he undertake a bibliographical study of Boswell for his doctoral dissertation. This dissertation, which Tinker supervised, won the John Addison Porter Prize for the best doctoral thesis of 1925, a prize Ellmann would win in 1947 for his Yeats dissertation (Pottle being one of the prize's three judges, with Maynard Mack and Eugene Waith). In 1925 Pottle was also appointed to an instructorship in English. A year later he was promoted to assistant professor and in 1946 he succeeded Tinker as Sterling Professor of English Literature.

Pottle shared a number of Tinker's objections to the New Criticism, and in *The Idiom of Poetry* (1941), originally the Messenger Lectures delivered that spring at Cornell, a year after Ellmann took his graduate seminar on "The Romantic Period," he mounted a powerful defense of the need for students of literature to attend to shifts of sensibility from period to period. The history of literature, Pottle argued, was one of discontinuity rather than of unchanging forms or elements, and it was the reader's job not only to recognize differences in period but to keep them in mind when assessing a work's value and meaning. In mounting this argument, Pottle, whose interests, nonliterary as well as literary, were wide, drew on science as well as philosophy, in particular on relativity theory (he called his book a "relativist" account of the history of taste in English poetry).[24] Pottle also took issue with the anti-Romantic bias of some New Critics and their sources, for whom Shelley was a particular bugbear.[25] In explaining his choice of explanatory illustrations in the book's introduction, he admits that "there ought to be more illustration from contemporary poetry: less Wordsworth and more Yeats. But a man who speaks to be understood [Pottle is thinking here of his Cornell audience] cannot always use the illustrations he would prefer. He can assume that an academic audience is a group of high intellectual capacity, but he cannot assume that it is widely read in contemporary poetry."[26] Whatever Ellmann the graduate student thought of Pottle's "relativist" reservations about the New Criticism, he would have approved these and other respectful references in *The Idiom of Poetry* to Yeats, Joyce, and contemporary poetry.[27]

Pottle was a biographer as well as an editor and a theorist of poetry. In his biographical writings, he was no Hagedorn when it came to his subject's failings, whether those of Boswell himself or of revered Boswellians. Consider his account in *Pride and Negligence: The History of the Boswell Papers* (1982) of the moment in which Tinker, Pottle's mentor, was confronted with a huge suitcase full of Boswell manuscripts from Malahide Castle, obtained by the collector Colonel Ralph Isham.

> Tinker, though very much a man of good will, too often allowed himself to act the prima donna. . . . He was himself a collector of Boswell and could not see these treasures in another's hands without exquisite pain. He was upset to see spread before him so many texts that ought to have been in his own edition of Boswell's letters. He was temperamentally unfit to work under direction, especially under Isham's. It pained him to see

> the attractive image of Boswell he himself had created now threatened by masses of new evidence that could be used by new Macaulays. He was, in fact, beginning to regret that Boswell's private papers had ever been recovered, a feeling that grew stronger after he had read the journals.[28]

Two other virtues of Pottle as scholar and biographer are visible in this passage, aside from a willingness to admit flaws or weaknesses in his subject. The first is his commitment to evidence, however overwhelming or contradictory; the second is his excellent prose style. How the biographer deals with evidence is discussed in Pottle's introduction to *The Literary Career of James Boswell, Esq.* (1929), a much-revised version of his dissertation. The biographer begins "with a trial impression of the personality he is attempting to reconstruct. He then collects his facts with this tentative reconstruction always in mind. If the facts fit, he uses them to fill in the picture; if they won't fit, he must modify his conception until they do. But he always builds up on this imaginative core; he does not simply collect facts and wait for something to quicken the chaos." When motives or incidents or narrative connections are missing, conjecture is permissible, so long as it is identified as such; a balance must be drawn between the amorphous accumulation of facts, on the one hand, and an overly selective portrait, on the other.[29] I will argue in the chapters that follow that this was how Ellmann wrote his own biographies.

The other virtue of the passage about Tinker and Colonel Isham is how well written it is—in this case how elegantly it combines tact and truthfulness. David Bromwich describes Pottle as "the most gifted writer" in the English Department. In 1929, the year Pottle published *The Literary Career of James Boswell, Esq.*, the first volume of a projected two-volume biography, he also published a memoir, *Stretchers: The Story of a Hospital Unit on the Western Front*, an account of his experiences in World War I working as a surgical assistant in an evacuation hospital in France. Pottle's aim in the memoir, he writes in its introduction, was to give "an exact and detailed description of the whole process of the surgical care of battle casualties." One of his tasks in helping to provide this care was "holding the hands of badly wounded soldiers as they were anaesthetized, describing in precise anatomical detail how they were mutilated and what had been done for them, and separating the living from the dead during the course of twelve-hour shifts." What makes these experiences worth recounting, Pottle believes, is that "few people have ever heard of an evacuation hospital or have any kind of notion of the work it did. Dressing stations, field hospitals, and base hospitals are well known, at least by name, because of their appearance in popular fiction, but the evacuation hospital or casualty clearing station has as yet received no such attention."[30] As this passage suggests, the memoir combines close and moving descriptive writing with originality, the scholarly imperative to contribute to knowledge or understanding. The audience Pottle sought, like the audience Ellmann sought in his biographies, was general as well as academic.

Pottle was director of graduate studies during Ellmann's student years at Yale, and relations between student and professor seem to have been formal and business-like. Ellmann rarely refers to Pottle in correspondence. The two men were different in character. Ellmann was easy, approachable, funny; Pottle, according to an admiring profile by Bruce Redford, was "omniscient, venerable, invulnerable, detached." Bromwich remembers Pottle as "a solitary . . . without being anti-social."[31] Alvin Kernan tells a much-repeated story about Pottle's pre-PhD oral examination at Yale, an ordeal in which candidates "were expected to answer accurately questions on any English book or author from the past fifteen hundred years." Pottle did so well on the examination "that all his examiners filed out at the end to congratulate him. Everyone shook his hand and said what a fine job he had done, and then, in the manner of academics, stood around with nothing to say until Pottle spoke up: 'Well, anybody going to the library?'"[32] Ellmann received a note from Pottle at the end of his oral examination in 1941, congratulating him on how well he had done. Pottle was no mentor to Ellmann, in the sense that Tinker was Pottle's mentor; Ellmann did not have mentors, at Yale or elsewhere. What Pottle offered, in addition to crucial academic and wartime references, was a standard of excellence. He seems also to have been free of Yale snobbery and prejudice. By 1950, according to correspondence, "Mr. Ellmann" had become "Richard" then "Dick," and "Mr. Pottle" became "Fred." Pottle even asked "Dick" to look over something he'd written about literary biography.[33]

* * *

Students rather than professors figure most prominently in Ellmann's correspondence during his graduate years at Yale, although most of these students became professors. Feidelson, of course, but also two British students—Eric Bentley, who would become an influential theater critic and a professor at Columbia, and Arnold Kettle, a Commonwealth Fellow from Cambridge who became a prominent Marxist literary academic. Ellmann was also associated with three precocious undergraduates: James J. Angleton, John Pauker, and Reed Whittemore, poets and founding editors of *Furioso,* a student literary magazine whose contributors included major contemporary poets. "With his graciousness and charm," Mason recalls, Ellmann developed many acquaintances: "He was always visible, always companionable, and full of delights from off the beaten track" (p. 4).

These delights Ellmann shared not only in classes and informally, but in a small discussion group formed in 1939, precursor to the *Finnegans Wake* reading group he formed at Northwestern University in the 1950s. Ellmann, as Mason puts it, "instilled the proper enthusiasm" into the group. "[It] met in the large lounge area in [William K.] Wimsatt's suite in Silliman College which he made accessible to us once a week. I can remember all of us poking in a crude way at the first three lines of 'Ash Wednesday' for an hour at a time, week after week, in the spring of 1941, with no success. They constitute a total of eight words, and at this distance it is hard to realize how remote they were from our reading experience. The second world war was to change all that" (p. 5). Mason's memoir of Ellmann begins with their meeting in 1939 as English graduate students. He describes him as one of "three remarkable graduate students," the other two, both considerably older, being Wimsatt (1907–1975), who seems not to have joined the discussion group, and Norman Pearson (1909–1975), who did.[34] Like Feidelson, both went on to join the Yale English Department. Wimsatt came to graduate school late, having spent several years after obtaining his BA from Georgetown teaching English and Latin at prep schools. What connected him to Ellmann and his circle was an interest in theories of literature, in particular the theories of the New Critics and their sources. Like Pottle, Wimsatt wrote a dissertation under Tinker (on Samuel Johnson's prose style, the subject of his first book), joined the English Department as soon as he received his PhD, stayed at Yale for the rest of his life, and published extensively on eighteenth-century topics. The best-known of his writings, however, were essays written in collaboration with the philosopher Monroe K. Beardsley: "The Intentional Fallacy" (1947) and "The Affective Fallacy" (1949), works as influential in the spread of New Critical practices as Cleanth Brooks's *The Well-Wrought Urn* (1947) or the Brooks and

Warren textbook *Understanding Poetry*. In person, Wimsatt was Pottle-like: reserved, formidably learned, yet patient with students and assistants. He was also very tall: six foot ten.

Norman Pearson, the third of Mason's "three remarkable graduate students," had full WASP credentials (Wimsatt was Catholic, hence Georgetown). Well-connected and sociable, he attended Phillips Andover Academy, then Yale (class of '32), then Oxford, where he obtained a second BA in 1934, returning to Yale in 1935 for a doctorate. It took him a while to become a PhD—he called himself "the oldest *living* graduate student" (Mason, p. 4)—in part because of illness, tuberculosis of the hip, in part because of editing jobs ancillary to his dissertation. In 1937 he edited the Modern Library edition of Hawthorne's novels and selected tales. In 1938 he coedited *The Oxford Anthology of American Literature* (1938) with the poet and editor William Rose Benet, brother of the poet Stephen Vincent Benet. Two years after taking his PhD in 1941 with a dissertation on Hawthorne and joining the Yale faculty, he and W. H. Auden coedited the first of five volumes of *Poets of the English Language*. Mason remembers Pearson as "warm and interested in people, even graduate students," but not always around, living outside the Hall of Graduate Students, where Ellmann roomed with Feidelson for a period (p. 4). Pearson not only shared Ellmann's interest in contemporary verse, but had close personal ties with influential poets, including Ezra Pound, Archibald MacLeish, Marianne Moore, and H.D. (Hilda Doolittle), as well as Auden. In later years he would play a key role in Ellmann's life, as in the lives of other Yale students in Ellmann's circle, including the *Furioso* editor James J. Angleton.

* * *

The first issue of *Furioso* came out in June 1939, the year Ellmann began graduate school. In addition to student contributions, the magazine published poems by Pound, Wallace Stevens, William Carlos Williams, Marianne Moore, E. E. Cummings, and John Ashbery. Prose contributions again mixed student pieces with essays by such well-known writers as Edmund Wilson, William Empson, and Irving Howe. Ellmann's first contributions appeared in the Summer 1941 issue, alongside poems by Stevens, MacLeish, Auden, Moore, Tambimutti, Cummings, and Lawrence Durrell. Reviewers in the issue included Andrews Wanning, who had taught Ellmann, Richard Eberhart, and John Crowe Ransom. The issue also contained the first printing of a lecture by

I. A. Richards. "Looks like I'll burst into print this month," Ellmann wrote to his parents that spring, in an undated postcard. "I'll be in good company."

The four Ellmann poems printed in the Summer 1941 issue of *Furioso* are worth examining, not only because they shed light on Ellmann's poetic preoccupations, but also because they attracted the attention of publishers, agents, and established poets, encouraging his hopes of becoming a writer rather than an academic. What marks the poems also marks the poetry out of which they grew—difficulty, a quality sometimes complained of by Ellmann's brother Erwin, who read and commented on most of the poems his brother wrote at Yale.[35] The hardest of the poems to interpret is probably "The Simplified Future," one of three poems written in rhymed quatrains. These poems (couplets aside) betray the influence of the quatrain poems in T. S. Eliot's 1920 collection, several of which are almost comically unintelligible. Here are the first three of the six quatrains of Ellmann's poem:

Crisis without denouement and expense
Of spirit in a waste of sense
Till priests default on holy writ
For conscience will not cover it

Law is glad that gun has shot her
Beds with sins begin to totter
Mind tries every kind of trick
To keep the body politic.

Commonplace until the end,
The sequacious tables bend,
Manifesting no concern,
Suddenly the tables turn.

The allusion to Shakespeare's Sonnet 129 in the first quatrain ("The expense of spirit in a waste of shame") gives Ellmann's poem its theme and starting point. That Shakespeare's sonnets consist of three quatrains and a closing couplet offers a formal connection as well. The "simplified future" the poem imagines, and toward which its attitude is fashionably mixed, is one in which sexual desire is no longer denigrated or stigmatized, as it is in Sonnet 129, where "Lust" is called "a bliss in proof and proved, a very woe," "a heaven that leads men to this hell." In Ellmann's poem, as I read it, lust's "denouement" results in neither "expense of spirit" nor "woe" nor "hell," nor even "a waste of sense" ("shame" having been dispensed with). In the first quatrain, "priests default on holy writ" after "conscience will not cover it" (that is, uphold religious sanction), nor, the second quatrain suggests, do law, morality, or mind object or intervene.[36]

"Unless I am misreading," Erwin writes to his brother in a letter of January 12, 1940, in relation to a different poem, "I do not think it is very obscure; certainly reader effort is the prerequisite of the day, it seems." This view of contemporary poetry Erwin shared with Frederick Pottle, for whom the distinguishing feature of contemporary poetry was "its obscurity: its urgent suggestion that you add something to the poem without telling you what that something is. . . . The great difference between obscure poetry of our day and that of the past is that the modern poet goes much further in employing private experience or ideas than would formerly have been thought legitimate. Milton's *Paradise Lost* is one of the most allusive poems ever written . . . but Milton planned to keep the allusions within the range of the cultivated English reader of his day."[37]

In "The Simplified Future," the third quatrain requires most "reader effort" (though the first quatrain is no stroll in the park). What is meant by "sequaceous tables bend"? The several definitions of "sequacious" ("intellectually servile," "tractable," "ductile," "pliable," "flexible") offer little help. Only after reading "tables" as "tablets," as in "tablets of stone" or the Ten Commandments (routinely called "tables," as in the 1897 Yeats essay "the Tables of the Law"), does the quatrain make sense. "Tables turned" means the Mosaic law overturned. Ellmann chooses "tables" over "tablets" to produce "Tables turned," but also, I suspect, because it requires more reader effort. The quatrain's difficulty recalls the obscurity of the most infuriating of Eliot's quatrain poems, "Mr. Eliot's Sunday Morning Service," which Eliot also wrote in his twenties.[38] Here are the Eliot poem's opening quatrains:

> Polyphiloprogenitive
> The sapient sutlers of the Lord
> Drift across the window-pains.
> In the beginning was the Word.
>
> In the beginning was the Word.
> Superfetation of *το ἕν*,
> And at the mensual turn of time
> Produced enervate Origen,

No notes accompany this poem, such as those Eliot provided two years later for *The Waste Land.* (Ellmann provided notes for at least one of his poems, which in a letter of February 25, 1940, Erwin described as "supererogatory," since "the difficulties do not arise where you explain them.") The obscurity of "Mr. Eliot's Sunday Morning Service" is on the order of *Finnegans Wake,* but indirection, allusion, and ambiguity mark the poetry and criticism of even the most plain-speaking of modernist poets. Among the *Furioso* papers at Yale is a letter of March 5, 1939, from William Carlos Williams to the editors, Angleton and Whittemore: "What you do, to my thinking, and you both do it, is to restate things by trying to be too explicit. All you have to do is *TOUCH* the meaning, you don't have to hammer it down with a maul. . . . Tell me to go to hell if you want to. I don't care."

Craig Raine thinks Ellmann draws on Yeats as well as Eliot in "The Simplified Future," citing "Under Ben Bulben" (1938), written the year before Yeats's death, as the model for the poem's catalectic tetrameter trochees ("catalectic" means lacking a final unstressed syllable).[39] In the simplified future, according to the poem's penultimate quatrain, "Plato, More, and Bacon walk / Bearing torches as they talk," a couplet that reminds Raine of the quatrain that opens "Under Ben Bulben":

> Swear by what the sages spoke
> Round the Mareotic Lake
> That the Witch of Atlas knew,
> Spoke and set the cocks a-crow.

Ellmann, of course, had been preoccupied with Yeats since at least 1939, the year of the Wanning seminar. Mason remembers him spending much of his allowance as a graduate student buying Yeats first editions. Soon after passing his pre-PhD oral examination, on October 1, 1941, Ellmann submitted his proposal for the dissertation on Yeats, the first dissertation ever approved by the Yale English Department on a twentieth-century topic. The proposal was approved in part because Ellmann was approved, in part because his choice of a contemporary poet could have been worse. Although Yeats was not Auden, described by Mason as "front and center for those brave souls willing to wade into poetry they could not read," neither was he Pound or Eliot. "Much of his poetry was hard to read," Mason explains, but "not all of it was. Besides, by 1939 he was properly dead, an essential condition to be considered literature at the time" (p. 6).

Raine's final judgment on the *Furioso* poems is that they are "sophisticated, academic five-finger exercises . . . try-outs," but lack "the force of personal experience." This judgment he applies even to "Admonition," a poem about repression, an implicit theme in "The Simplified Future" and "Your Loveliness, I Say," the shortest, perhaps also the slightest, of the poems.[40] In "Admonition," the repression that matters is self-repression, which can be related to Ellmann's agonizings over his career ("wallowings," to Feidelson). Here are the first two of the poem's six quatrains:

Our senseless bodies have their little rooms
Where senses claw and caw, and, never tame,
The bestial heart snorts madly up and down
To shake the galling bridle of the frame.

The aviary and stable have been built
To keep the horse and birds from working free,
Or thieves from plundering; both dangers here
To ordinary folk like you and me.

This locking up of the "senses," we learn in the poem's fifth or penultimate quatrain, is the work of "our enemies," but it is also "our" fault: "By such appeasements of our enemies/We hope for safety." In the final quatrain the result is desolating:

When that day comes, the solid flesh is frail,
The doors will crack, the iron hinges yield,
The senses claw their hearts out, and the heart
Survey with hungry eyes an arid field.

The speaker's shame at "appeasing" his enemies "for safety" recalls Ellmann's shame at taking on ("appeasing") his parents' fears about giving up his studies "to write," a decision taken around the time the poem was written. The title of the poem is thus double, referring both to an admonition appeased *in* the poem ("our" internalizing of external prohibitions) and to the poem *as* admonition (not to end up as the speaker does, surveying "an arid field"). Read biographically, the poem can thus be said to derive from "personal experience" as well as literary convention. Whether it possesses "force" is another matter.

* * *

The best of the poems, "Tarzan—Winter Prospect," is printed first and although no less academic than its companion poems, is wittier, topical, and politically revealing. Its starting point is Tennyson's "Ulysses," described by Eliot as "a perfect poem."[41] (In William Clyde DeVane's Victorian poetry class Ellmann would write a paper on Tennyson's influence on Yeats, Robinson, and Eliot.) The poem is worth quoting in full:

Deep in his den the aged Tarzan sits
Dictating memoirs, though his time is short.
Life in the jungle has made sharp his wits,
Besides enabling him to lead in sport.

His memoirs grow apace, that glorious story
Of lowly nurture in the darksome wood,
Of how a savage turned into a Tory,
Although the tribes had doubted that he could.

And then in fifty fascinating pages
The medals were discussed and reproduced,
Which England had awarded as his wages
For many shrewd reforms he introduced:

As building churches, subjugating natives,
Amassing a considerable lot of funds:
As saving English girls from arrant caitiffs,
And paying ten per cent on British bonds.

And now poised in the best society,
Tarzan is old and somewhat musclebound,
Respected for his riches and his piety,-
Disused to struggle now,- and he has found

Leisure in which to tell the reading world
How it was saved from chaos by his hand,
How every javelin his strong hand hurled
Warded an unseen danger from the land.

Death may come soon, but Tarzan's ready for it,
Whether it come in form like to a tigress,
Jaguar, or elephant—he does not fear it,
But will die fighting as he lived for progress.

The irony here is uncomplicated and may extend even to the "doubting Tribes" at the end of the second quatrain, who could be British as well as African. The poem is political in intent, its anti-imperialist and anti-British sentiments being of the moment. In Ellmann's circle the prevailing view of the war in Europe was that it was being waged on both sides by "thugs," an equivalence made possible in the period 1939–1941 by a lack of evidence, or relative lack of evidence, of Nazi atrocities.[42] "Despite the superb heroism of the British people in fending off all alone the Nazi air force in 1940," Ellsworth Mason recalls, "we still suspected that somehow that tiny country might have some imperial motives hovering around in the background" (p. 7). These suspicions were voiced by Ellmann's brother Erwin in a letter of December 10, 1940, to their younger brother Bill: "Most of the leading interventionists today piped the same tune in 1917. I would like to see Hitler beaten, none the less, but I think that any war we fight against him will have nothing to do with fascism from abroad and everything to do with sheer imperialism and fascism from within right here. The British Empire, as it has persisted for the last hundred years, is beyond salvage regardless of what happens in the war." Although neither Erwin nor Ellmann was a Trotskyist, as their father at times claimed, theirs was the Trotskyist line: the war was not a "conflict between democracy and fascism, but a struggle of two imperialisms for the redivision of the world."[43]

To hold such a view brought Ellmann and Erwin into uncomfortable alliance with supporters of America First, a movement begun at Yale. In 1939 a group of Yale Law students (among them Gerald Ford; Potter Stewart, later a Supreme Court justice; and Kingman Brewster, later president of Yale) formed College Men for Defense First, which a year later became the Committee to Defend America First and eventually had 800,000 members (the group disbanded three days after Pearl Harbor). According to the Yale historian Robin Winks, the America First students were opposed by an "equally vocal group of undergraduates led by McGeorge Bundy, '40, and many faculty." Prominent among these faculty was a newly appointed instructor in English, Norman Holmes Pearson, who described himself as "150 percent interventionist."[44]

James I. Ellmann was also 150 percent interventionist and determined to bring his left-isolationist sons to their senses. In dozens of letters, some as long as ten single-spaced typed pages, James laid out the case for entry into the war. How could they possibly equate the British under Churchill with the Nazis under Hitler? "I get ripping mad to hear some upstart take a poke at [Roosevelt] and his wife," James writes to Dick in a mammoth letter of April 13, 1941, "and I listen every day to men and women who have suffered from all the agonies of Hitler in Europe and have come here." He likens the alliance of left and right isolationists to the Hitler-Stalin pact, characterizing "many of the so-called proposals for peace" as "vague" and "meaningless."

Ellmann replies to these criticisms in a letter of April 24:

> In regards to your letter, Dad, it seems to me that you confuse the issue by assuming that to be against Roosevelt is to support the party line. I don't say that setting forth the peace aims is an easy job, but that doesn't make it unnecessary to try. It seems to me there are two things to be done: 1) prevent Germany from winning or at least from complete victory; 2) insure that at least part of the world will be able to show enough spiritual superiority (I use the word advisedly) to offset Germany's technical superiority and make democracy look appealing. I think you probably agree with both aims but think the second can be postponed: I, on the contrary, think they must go together, and that either without the other is valueless.

James replies that it would be bad for Britain to be defeated. "Even you seem to want to make that sort of concession, and I suppose Erwin too might reluctantly admit this. What neither of you fully admit is the tragic implications of the defeat of Britain not to Britain alone but to the hopes of half a billion people." The debate between father and son pretty much stops at this point, partly, one suspects, because Ellmann was always less interested in politics than in literature (whether this lack of interest limits *James Joyce* is a matter of dispute, as we shall see), partly because he may have been put off by the heat of his father's letters. By 1941, it is worth noting, his increasing involvement with Yeats and the history of Irish independence may also have affected his views. In an undated postcard to his parents early in the year, he defends Ireland's neutrality as a matter of history: "They won't expose themselves for the sake of the old enemy."

* * *

The impact of the *Furioso* poems on Ellmann's ambitions as a writer was immediate, as evidenced by his experiences in the summer of 1941 at the

Bread Loaf School of English, where he and Feidelson had also been the previous summer. Bread Loaf's name comes from Bread Loaf Mountain, also Bread Loaf Village, in western Vermont. The school was founded in 1920 as a section of Middlebury College's summer session. It offered residential courses for credit or audit to mature students "interested professionally in the study and teaching of English," drawing applicants from all over the United States. The student enrollment in 1941 was 231, a record, with a six-to-one ratio of women to men. Course instructors and scholarship students were drawn mostly from Ivy League colleges; contact between students and teachers was advertised as "friendly and informal." In addition to academics, the school offered a variety of leisure activities: hiking, horseback riding, swimming, tennis, games (croquet, badminton, archery). There were also concerts, plays, art exhibitions, and informal lectures and readings given by visiting writers and critics. Students were offered "an opportunity to meet the visiting lecturers personally and to seek from them counsel in their work."[45]

Courses began on July 1 and ended on August 12. On August 18 a separate two-week Writers' Conference took place, with more guest lecturers. Among writers who visited Bread Loaf in the summer of 1941 were Robert Frost, Edmund Wilson, Louis Untermeyer, William Carlos Williams, Theodore Roethke, the Irish poet Padraic Colum, the Irish critic Mary Colum, and Edward Weeks, editor of the *Atlantic Monthly*. Ellmann took two courses for credit at Bread Loaf: "The Transcendental Movement" (taught by Daniel Aaron of Smith College, later of Harvard), and "Critical and Philosophical Approaches to Literature" (taught by Ransom and Theodore Greene of Princeton). He delivered a paper on Whitman for Aaron's seminar and one on "precision and obscurity" for Ransom and Greene. In both courses he received top marks. An early issue of "The Crumb" (the school newsletter) advised students that "copies of the summer issue of the Yale poetry magazine, *Furioso,* may be purchased in the Bookstore. This issue contains poems by MacLeish and Auden, a critical essay by Mr. Ransom, and poems by Richard Ellmann of our student body." At the Writers' Conference, which Ellmann also attended, he was one of only three students who were chosen to read their poems. He appears, very suntanned, in an official photograph of visiting poets, along with Frost, Roethke, Williams, Untermeyer, and Ted Morrison, director not only of the Writers' Conference but of writing courses at Harvard.

Bread Loaf Writers' Conference, summer 1941. *Left to right, back row:* Edward Weismiller, Theodore Roethke, William Carlos Williams, Louis Untermeyer, Robert Frost, and Theodore Morrison; *front row:* Ellmann in the middle, flanked by Charles Edward Eaton, later a professor of English and poet, and Cedric Whitman, later a professor of classics at Harvard.

The opening day of the 1941 Bread Loaf School of English was July 1, but Ellmann and other scholarship students arrived early, to ready the campus for the coming session. Ellmann's tasks included raking the grass, widening and clearing a ditch, weeding, painting, and carrying chairs. "I look surprisingly healthy," he wrote his parents on July 1, "having been out in the sun for most of the last ten days." Once the session began, he and the other scholarship students had jobs waiting table (they were known collectively as "Hoi Polloi," though most were from Ivy League colleges). Three of the students he mentions in the July 1 letter were fellow scholarship winners: Larry Spingarn, younger brother of the critic J. E. Spingarn; Danny Lerner, younger brother of the syndicated columnist Max Lerner; and Robie Macauley, a pupil of Ford Madox Ford and John Crowe Ransom. All went on to have careers as writers: Spingarn as a poet, Lerner as a social and economic theorist, and Macauley as a publisher and also novelist and critic. Spingarn, Ellmann reported to his parents, is "full of stories about old families and old houses, to which he has a particular fondness, though his politics are red"; Lerner "drinks regularly"; and Macaulay is editor of the Kenyon College magazine, *Nike,* soon to become the *Kenyon Review.* In the same letter Ellmann reports that he is reading Yeats's *Autobiographies* and that he has met Frost and Untermeyer at Morrison's farm. Untermeyer, whom he calls "Louis," "has seen Furioso already" and "urged me to find him a beautiful girl to play tennis with."

Three weeks later, on July 21, Ellmann apologizes to his parents for having been out of touch. No excuse, just "general lassitude. The days roll by here with a lot of sun and swimming and beer drinking and very little done." In a week, however, he is scheduled to deliver his paper on "precision and obscurity" to the Ransom and Greene seminar, "and I'm trying to sort out my objections to Ransom's method."[46] His other news is that he has been "courting a very beautiful girl from Baltimore, mostly because she's the most beautiful one hereabouts."[47] His friends Kettle and Whittemore have come from New Haven for a visit: "Kettle relieved at the fact that he can now support Britain," Germany having invaded the USSR. During the Writers' Conference, Erwin and a friend from Washington also came to visit. Theodore Roethke took a shine to Ellmann at the Conference and in a letter of September 20 invited him out west: "I'll feed you as best I can and fill you with Scotch." He also urged Ellmann to get his *Furioso* friends to review his latest book of poems.

Ellmann's *Furioso* poems were praised at Bread Loaf not only by Roethke, Untermeyer, and Frost but by Elizabeth A. Drew, who for sixteen summers taught the school's modern poetry course and was the author of *Directions in Modern Poetry* (1940), a well-regarded introduction to the field. Like "everyone," Ellmann reported to his parents in the letter of July 21, she liked "Tarzan—Winter Prospect" and "Admonition" best. As for the other student poets, one "is apparently a slightly adolescent romantic with escapist stuff, which Morrison likes better than more modern work; he seems to be wild about the boy's work though the members of the writing course tell me it's really not good. I hope this isn't entirely spleen on my part." Later Ellmann would claim he benefited from hearing the poems of the other student poets, "because I can better understand now the distinctness of my own style and approach. I find my subjects and intentions more ambitious than most, which is a good sign."

Soon after the end of the Writers' Conference, Harcourt Brace wrote to Ellmann to express interest in publishing a volume of his poems (later he was approached by Dodd, Meads). His answer to the Harcourt inquiry, according to an undated postcard to his parents, was that "there were too many bad first books already, and they wrote me a very nice answer agreeing with me and reiterating that they would like to see anything I had when I do feel it up to scratch." In an earlier letter to his parents, written on September 1, the day after his arrival back at Yale, he writes jokily about his prospects: "As Erwin probably told you, Harcourt Brace is publishing my first book of poems and the Atlantic Monthly Press is publishing my first novel (neither in the immediate future, of course, if I may be pardoned an anticlimax); Untermeyer will have me in his anthology six years from now; and, in general, I have all the contacts and need now only to write something." After a talk given by Untermeyer ("How to Hate Poetry") and a brief conversation in which Untermeyer was "very funny and pleasant as ever," Ellmann's only wish was that "I had more poems to show him." He would not produce these poems upon return to Yale. In the undated postcard, after describing his exchange with Harcourt, he adds that he is "reading four Shakespeare plays a day now," in preparation for pre-PhD orals.

* * *

The "general lassitude" letter of July 21 ends with reference to "the girl downstairs, Jean Douglas, who did a black and white study of me two days ago." Ellmann thinks this study "very subtle and intelligent." Daniel Aaron thinks it "wonderful." A month later, on August 22, Larry Spingarn, who did not stay on for the Writers' Conference, wrote to Ellmann to ask how it had gone. He ends his letter: "Regards to Jean." By this date, the Writers' Conference having finished, Jean and Ellmann were writing to each other almost every other day, he from Detroit, then New Haven, she from Westfield, Massachusetts, her family home. Jean was the daughter of a doctor, and like Ellmann she was born in 1918. After attending Northfield School for Girls, she went on to Smith (class of '40), where she was taught by Daniel Aaron (though not, apparently, Elizabeth Drew). She met Ellmann one early morning at Bread Loaf "when you stopped sweeping the steps at Brick [an abbreviation for Burdick Cottage, a residence] and suggested that I drop Victorian Poetry and take Elizabeth Drew."

At Bread Loaf, Jean had an exhibition of her drawings, which an art critic from the *New York Times* liked, offering to help get her into art school. But she was also literary, and much of her correspondence with Ellmann takes the form of an exchange of funny and flirty poems. Ellmann kept her letters but none of his survive; neither his daughters nor any of their five children had heard of their romance. Early in September Jean wrote to say she was off to New York "to look at the Art Students League" (what she should do now, after graduation, is a recurring topic in the correspondence): "How about a beer between trains? I keep finding myself in imaginary conversations with you" (September 9, 1941). Three days later she invites him to Westfield for the weekend. A visit he seems to have made. On September 23 she admits:

> I can't write sentimental letters—they always sound just that. I seem to write you a special type of letter tho, rather different from the way in which I address the common horde.
>
> Which may
> or may not
> be
> to your advantage.
>
> *J*

On October 7, 1941, as pre-PhD orals loom, she writes to buck Ellmann up: "Good luck! You did it at Bread Loaf, boy—ad astra per aspera."

How far advanced the relationship is at this point is hard to tell. In a letter of October 26, before a visit to Yale, she writes: "If you can still locate some chaste nook for me, I'll arrive in N.H. this Saturday." When the visit had to be canceled, however, she expressed her regret, having "anticipated a gay gamble in N.H. avec tu et les sept pêches mortel [je suis un linguiste!]." The October 7 letter ends with her contribution to a joint poem:

> Your couplet is charming. In reply:
>
> So man has held, since first the Word was said,
> And so shall hold, till steel and gold are lead.
>
> This not only rounds off our opus, but also gives the alpha and omega of obscurity the one-two. I'm expecting you to set tone and meter for a new series.

On November 11, weeks after a successful Yale visit but no letters from Ellmann, she writes:

> Thou who hast loved me one whole day and night
> Art silent now,
> And cold as winter light
>
> Thou who wouldst love me by the year's twelfth part
> Art silent now,
> And cold doth wrap my heart.

In the same letter, Jean complains of a poetry reading by Paul Engle, from the Iowa Writers' Workshop: "He commits a damning crime in my opinion by over-working inversion. I grew rather unsympathetic to men who were starting out 'the land to farm, the wheat to grind,' etc. What do you think of this Younger Poet?"

Back in Jean's good books, Ellmann has her running Yeats errands. From a letter of December 5: "My dear—here am I, surrounded by books on Ireland and acquiring the letters of Yeats and D[orothy] Wellesley in a secondhand bookstore. . . . Sometimes I am amazed by the extent to which you have directed me." In the autumn and winter of 1941, with Ellmann preparing for his orals and deep into Yeats, "duty" and "desire" figure prominently in their correspondence and poetry, with Jean chiding Ellmann for paying too much attention to his work and not enough attention to her. In a letter of December 15, Jean offers "Lines to a gentleman who practically conceives of duty":

> Drop the bar across the gate,
> Guard the lowering sky;
> Irish tweed a coat of mail
> Bathed in duty's rite.
>
> Butter in a lordly plate,
> Blackbirds in a pie—
> Love's hot color quenches pale
> Mouthed in duty's night.

On December 21, Jean writes to thank Ellmann for a present: a copy of *Ulysses*, which she finds "much more comprehensible than you had led me to believe." She also explains her poem: "I was not putting forth my beliefs re duty, kidlet, simply amused by something you said at the R.R. station. I believe that duty circumscribes personal love. Would you synchronize duty with the highest personal ideal?" The letter ends: "Happy holidays! Don't keep to your scholastic schedule too rigorously."

Sometime in the New Year, Jean writes from New York where she has been job hunting. In a letter that suggests they have begun sleeping together, she offers to "whip up to N.H. on the 4:35. OK? Sad, but our unmentionable desires may be curbed—you with pneumonia [Ellmann's health had suffered from overwork] and me likely toting a quart of Lydia Pinkham [for menstrual pains]." A number of letters at this time contain poems involving a Lady, sometimes like Guinevere, sometimes like Rapunzel, sometimes like Griselda, who has been left by her Lord (he cannot tell "the white ash from the snow"), or who needs rescuing from a fire-breathing dragon. "I'm working on another version of our dragon theme," she informs Ellmann on January 6, 1942, perhaps in reference to a poem titled "Fidelity" that she includes in an undated letter from around this time: "My hair turned white as driven snow / When I was one and twenty, / The gold was beat out in the glow / Of saint's desire, / And dragon's fire." Here are carbons of two undated dragon poems from Ellmann's papers of this period, presumably collaborations:

"THE LADY AND THE DRAGON"

O dragon, dragon, put on shoes
Cover up your claws
If you would my body use,
And venerate the laws.

O dragon, dragon, sheer your horns,
They cut me to the quick.
Parental admonition warns
That horns like these may stick.

O dragon, dragon, dim that flame
Since it may melt my heart,
And I'd not have you take the blame
For damaging that part.

"LAMENT FOR CAUTION"

It's true I told you, "Pare your claws,"
But never thought that you would next
Pull every
tooth out of your jaws
And quietly grow undersexed.
Because
I deprecated force
You've
left your sulfur at the forge.
I loved you scaly, fierce and coarse,
But now I think I'll take St. George.

On January 10, 1942, Jean reports to Ellmann about a bit of Yeats research. She has been tasked with finding out about the Steinach operation to increase sexual potency, which a surgeon performed on Yeats in 1934 when he was sixty-nine. "The success of the operation is most dubious, the greatest success would probably result from the psychological factor—the man believing himself to be rejuvenated." At this point Ellmann is working on Yeats feverishly, in several senses, both hard at work and in the infirmary with pneumonia. Jean writes on January 29, sorry that she can only "hold your fevered head in mind." On February 3, Jean is "glad to hear that you are agin feeling fit," signing off "Yrs w. becoming chastity, J." Two days later there's an exchange about endearments: she promises to "strike out 'kidlet' on condition that 'Jeannie-weenie' be forever banished. A deal?"

All this time Jean is interviewing for jobs—with magazines (*Time, Life, Mademoiselle*), the USO (United Services Organization), Naval Intelligence ("Unless the government, in checking my past, digs up my career with the ASU [American Student Association] or as a distributor for socialist propaganda"[48]), the Boston Museum of Fine Arts, the New York office of the Washington Immigration Bureau, and Smith College (as a possible visiting lecturer). From December 7 onward, Ellmann was in a comparable limbo. On the one hand, he could be said to be riding high: his poems were attracting attention; he had been commended on his orals; his thesis topic had been approved; he was deeply absorbed in Yeats research; and he had an intelligent, talented, and charming girlfriend. On the other hand, the draft loomed, as did a range of unappealing and/or unlikely alternatives (government positions of varying degrees of unsuitability). Try as he might to focus on his writing and on Yeats, the war and its demands would soon take over his life.

Jean Douglas, early 1940s.

CHAPTER THREE

The War Years

SEVEN MONTHS BEFORE Pearl Harbor, Ellmann was summoned for a medical by the Highland Park draft board and classified 1-B, "available for the draft but fit only for limited military service." The reason for the 1-B classification was his eyesight. At twenty-two he was slim, fit, able-bodied, and almost blind without his glasses. He could, however, still be drafted. As Erwin reported in a letter of January 22, 1942, writing from Washington, DC, "Hershey [General Lewis Hershey, director of the Selective Service System] has just announced that 1-Bs and 4-Fs may be drafted for clerical work in the Army." Erwin advised Dick that "if you came down here for a week and looked around you might be able to find something more to your liking." He had a specific lead in mind: Archibald MacLeish—the poet and librarian of Congress, head of the Research and Analysis branch of the recently formed Office of the Coordinator of Information (COI), precursor to the Office of Strategic Services (OSS), itself precursor to the Central Intelligence Agency (CIA)—"is taking over large numbers of the literati who never held paying jobs before. I think you would have a strong chance if you came down pretty well recommended." Several weeks later, in a letter of February 13, Erwin reported that there were also lots of jobs "in a number of propaganda agencies."

After passing his PhD orals in October 1941, Ellmann was hard at work on his Yeats dissertation, so hard that by mid-February he ended up in the Yale infirmary for a week, unable to shake off a series of persistent colds. As soon as he was released from the infirmary, he took Erwin's advice and headed for Washington. On February 23, Frederick Pottle sent identical letters of reference to MacLeish and Wilmarth Sheldon ("Lefty") Lewis, the head of a branch of the COI office known as X-2. Its function was to gather information from the FBI and Army and Naval Intelligence, for counterintelligence purposes. Like MacLeish, Lewis was a Yale man, literary, a member of the Skull and Bones society, and rich (richer even than MacLeish, whose father was the founder of the Chicago department store Carson Pirie Scott). Lewis's father had been the president of a California oil company, his mother was heiress to a great cattle corporation, and his wife was the granddaughter of one of the founders of Standard Oil. He lived in an elegant house in Farmington, Connecticut, that held a library of eighteenth-century books and papers, including his collection of the letters of Horace Walpole. As an independent scholar, Lewis edited Walpole's correspondence for Yale University Press.

Pottle's letter recommending Ellmann was short but effective:

> He had a brilliant academic record as an undergraduate, and has for the third year enjoyed a Yale College Fellowship in the Graduate School. He is one of the very ablest students we have, perhaps the ablest of all. Besides a very solid fund of erudition, he possesses unusual powers of style and an original and vigorous critical faculty. His dissertation is on the poetical theory of Yeats.
>
> Mr. Ellmann has tried in vain to enlist and wishes some civilian appointment in which he can feel he is of more direct service to his country. . . . The Yale Graduate School could not furnish an abler man.

Within a month Ellmann reported to his parents in a letter of March 17, 1942, that Wilmarth Lewis had hired him at a salary of $2,600, principally to replace Archibald MacLeish's son, who was planning to enlist in the Army or Navy. This news Ellmann learned from Lewis himself, whom he found "very nice." Lewis also revealed the extent of Pottle's efforts on his behalf. Pottle "not only sent Lewis a wonderful letter of introduction about me—done in formal style—but wrote him an informal letter saying that he really meant all those things. It's a kindness I had hardly expected from him, because he appears quite cold."

Lewis had a specific job in mind for Ellmann: to index the intelligence gathered by the X-2 section, which involved "revising procedures for analyzing and classifying confidential and secret documents received from Military and Naval Intelligence, Federal Bureau of Investigation, British Secret Service, British Ministry of Economic Warfare, and other intelligence sources."[1] At twenty-four, Ellmann was to head a team of ten. In addition to devising and producing the index, he oversaw the writing of digests of information to be issued to the chiefs of sections of the OSS (which supplanted the office of the Coordinator of Information on June 13, 1942, by presidential order). One of the most challenging difficulties Ellmann faced in devising the index was to find a way to safeguard information classified variously as "CONFIDENTIAL," "SECRET," and "MOST SECRET," while also making it available to those who needed to see it.

Ellmann was proud of his work on the index and interested in it, writing to his parents in an undated letter in June 1942 that it was now being used by "both military intelligence (G-2) and our Special Activities Branch." As for the information itself, he wrote to his friend Ellsworth Mason on April 20, 1942, although it was not always "terribly secret . . . it gives you a comfortable feeling to know you are being trusted with stuff that the newspapermen, for example, could not get to see." In addition to problems of access and secrecy, Ellmann was much preoccupied with categorization, specifically how to determine "categories which will fit the material and yet not be so large as to prevent one from finding a document quickly." "At the present time we can locate any of our nearly 20,000 documents within ten minutes with the barest indication of its subject matter—and usually we can get them within a few seconds. . . . Our index is becoming increasingly popular, and I hope I can stay long enough to see it fully accepted."[2]

This hope was realized, despite Ellmann's receiving a second letter from the draft board on April 26, 1942, shortly after beginning work at X-2. In replying to this letter, an undated draft suggests, he began by stressing, as Pottle had in his letter of reference, his conviction that "each of us should try to make a maximum contribution to the war effort." Hence his decision to abandon work on his doctoral degree at Yale and to take up a position in the office of the Coordinator of Information. The importance of the COI's office to the war effort, according to FDR's presidential order, was "second only to that of the armed forces; it has a governmental priority rating of Group 2." In addition, he wrote, "even if present Army requirements with respect to eyesight were further liberalized, [I] should be eligible only for non-combatant or clerical work which could hardly exceed in importance the job I am doing now." The effect of these arguments, assuming they were sent in a fair copy reply, was mixed. On May 1, 1942, the Highland Park draft board reclassified him 1-A, while allowing him to continue working in the office of the COI.

Learning to organize masses of "important papers," keeping their existence secret, while at the same time ensuring that the right people had access to them, would prove to be useful skills for Ellmann the biographer, as for Ellmann the editor and critic. In a study of the relation between intelligence agencies and universities, Yale historian Robin Winks distinguishes between the Research and Analysis and X-2 wings of the OSS and the "action-oriented, operational wings." The research wings called for academic types, "men and women who were patient, methodical, curious, able as if almost by instinct to see relationships between the parts and the whole. . . . They understood the function of trivia, of miscellaneous information, and understanding it could both remember an enormous range of data and assimilate that data into a coherent pattern that others might miss," precisely the qualities readers and reviewers were to praise in *James Joyce.*[3]

No less useful to Ellmann the biographer were the people skills required of him in X-2, especially as a unit head. "It is essential that I learn the elementals three times faster than the rest did," he writes to his parents at the start of the job, in an undated postcard. "The situation is rather complicated and I have to be tactful to avoid hurting anyone's feelings." As his father wrote on April 20, Ellmann was learning for the first time "what it means to do a job and find out while trying to do it how political considerations may prevent adequate performance. . . . I am very glad therefore that you are cautious and that patience on your part enables you to take a hold of the job." Away from the job, Ellmann made clear his frustration with the petty jealousies and turf wars of office life. "I come home every evening with Indexschmerz," he wrote to Ellsworth Mason on April 20, not because of the index itself, but because "the office situation is very complicated. . . . The personnel problem is very trying."

There was also a problem with Lewis, who proved rather less "nice" than he had at first seemed, though, characteristically, Ellmann managed to remain on good terms with him throughout his time in Washington. In an entry of February 23, 1943, in a notebook journal he kept sporadically during the mid-1940s, Ellmann describes Lewis as having "the temperament of a dissolute Roman emperor—love of sycophants—vanity—cruelty when roused—malice." After Ellmann left X-2, he received a letter from Larry Hall, a colleague who had joined the unit with naive hopes of reform. "I am working overtime to bring about the end of the inefficiency and injustice with which people in this division have been handled," he wrote to Ellmann on October 7, 1942. "I really regret that you won't be around for the kill if there is one." The letter ends with a handwritten PS: "Your absence has been a terrible blow to me spiritually and culturally." Within three months Lewis fired Hall, just as he had earlier fired Ellmann's friend and fellow Yale English graduate student Bill O'Donnell, who would himself become a distinguished Yeats scholar. As O'Donnell reported to Ellmann in a letter of September 4, 1942, Lewis fired him "on the grounds that I was conceited and also a *prima donna,*" charges hard to square with the modesty and generosity of his correspondence with Ellmann.[4]

O'Donnell was one of a number of Yale friends and acquaintances in Washington during the early years of the war, many in spy agencies. According to Winks, "From Yale's class of 1943 alone, at least forty-two young men entered intelligence work, largely in the OSS, many to remain on after the war to form the core of the new CIA."[5] Those who were in Washington at this time included the two older Rostow boys (Walt in the OSS, Gene in the Land-Lease Administration, later the State Department, eventually as assistant to Dean Acheson), Norman Pearson, Henry Jaffa, Paul Pickrel (who would return to Yale to edit the *Yale Review* and to teach in the English Department for twenty-five years), and Mason, who arrived in Washington in June 1942 to work at the Board of Economic Warfare. As Mason remembers it, "I saw Ellmann frequently at lunch or dinner, often with other Yale friends, and conversation would divide equally between twentieth-century poetry and the antics of Washington."[6] Erwin, at the Department of Labor, got to know these Yale friends and was especially close to Jaffa. He was also close to Larry Spingarn, Ellmann's friend from Bread Loaf, who worked under MacLeish as a special assistant.

As Erwin got to know Ellmann's Yale friends, Ellmann got to know Erwin's Washington circle, which, judging from Erwin's correspondence, involved lots of informal parties and dinners and almost as many women as men. That Ellmann wrote relatively few letters during this time in Washington can be easily explained: he was working "three times harder" than anyone else in X-2; his evenings and weekends seem to have been spent socializing; he was suffering from a form of low-grade depression ("I no longer correspond with anybody except the family," he wrote to his father in an undated letter of early 1943: "You have no idea of the apathy which took hold of me in Washington, from which I have not yet recovered"); and the letters he did write were to Jean Douglas, his girlfriend from Bread Loaf, who did not keep them.

From March 1942 through the summer, Jean wrote to Ellmann at least two or three times a week, often to complain about not hearing from him. "Your silence," she claims on April 2, "[almost] resigned me to the thought that you had transferred your affections to another." On April 15 she sends a poem teasing him about not writing.[7] On April 30 she asks him to fill out a mock multiple-choice questionnaire:

> I am . . .
> bursting with energy
> having things done with my lungs
> horsing around in the office, and/or engaging in activities confidential
> Well?

"*Ave,* o lad of few words," begins a letter of May 13. "My long silent one, how are you?" opens a letter of June 28. There are also complaints about Ellmann's taciturnity on weekends together (rare weekends, given the number of six-day weeks for X-2 staff). An undated letter written late in the summer begins: "Darling—I wished you talked to me more when you are with me—or wrote more. Have I made your life less complicated?—I recall hearing you condemn simplicity."

When not complaining about his silences, Jean's letters are bright and funny, full of jokey endearments, work gossip, and job-hunt gossip (in New York, Boston, and Washington). The letters often include witty and sometimes risqué poems, as well as comments on Ellmann's poems. "I like your poem," she writes on May 19, "it has a certain early-Joyce quality." Having borrowed Ellmann's limerick collection, she scouts out possible additions. "Nothing new," she writes on April 21, "with the possible exception of '. . . the young man named Cyril/Who was had in the wood by a squirrel./He found it so good/That he stayed in the wood/As long as the squirrel was vyril,'"

Jean Douglas's letters are all that survive of her relationship with Ellmann. I have found no surviving witnesses or firsthand accounts. When, therefore, in a letter of October 11, 1942, she announces that she has begun to fall out of love with him, the announcement comes as something of a surprise.

Dick, my dear—
I'm driving up to the Whip City [New York] tomorrow aft. to bring back the essentials for my new abode. If I'm to live there, I may as well be equipped with frying pan and coffee cup.

You have meant and mean a good deal to me. As you know, I enjoy being with you. But if you insist on an ultimatum of "all or nothing," I must take the latter. I feel rather defeated by your attitude; you, I presume, baffled by mine. Chalk it up to N.E. conscience. I have relied on you to a greater extent than you know. I don't want a "root and branch" job now. Nor a middle way which is simply an annoyance to you. It seems silly that we can't have a relationship which, to me at least, is both most pleasant and constructive. Is that impossible?

I am honest with you when I say that you mean much to me. If I do not have the same passion of a few months ago, it is thru no fault of yours, and in myself I do not understand. But I hope you may understand what I have been saying.

In my strange way, I suppose I shall love you always.

J.

What caused the waning of Jean's "passion . . . of a few months ago" is unknown. Also unknown is the nature of Ellmann's "ultimatum of 'all or nothing,'" his "'root and branch' job." Jean's reference to her "N.E. conscience" suggests the ultimatum might have concerned sex, but her references to Lydia Pinkham (the menstrual cramps medicine) and "unmentionable desires" suggest that they had slept together. Perhaps Ellmann was demanding that she live with him before marriage, giving up her apartment in New York. Perhaps he wanted more from her emotionally, to mean more to her than "a good deal" or "much." In the weeks following the October 11 letter, Jean invited Ellmann to Thanksgiving dinner with her family, an effort, presumably, to establish or retain a relationship "both most pleasant and constructive." Ellmann declined the invitation.[8] Only three more letters from Jean survive, from the fall and winter of 1942–1943. On December 19, in a note addressed to "Dick, old thing," she reports that she has returned all the library books he has taken out for her. Ten days later she writes a letter that ends: "I am more glad than you can know that you do not regret your love for me. As I've said before, you have given me a great deal which I have no desire to regret. You're honest, Dick, and I do love you for many things. J."

Ellmann's feelings at this point are hard to read. He took up with several women after the breakup, women he had met before Jean's letter of October 11. The next to last letter Jean wrote to him, however, does suggest that the parting was painful. Undated, it was written sometime in January 1943:

> Dear Dick—There seems to me no reason why I should be writing any letter of explanation. When a caller insults my guest, it hardly follows that I do the apologizing. I shall not ask an apology from you, as it is a bit late for that, but I shall point out that you are considerably off side.
>
> *Jean*

If Jean's guest was male, that might account for Ellmann's uncharacteristic behavior, not just his insult but asking for a letter of explanation. Although the relationship between Jean and Ellmann lasted only a year and three months, and was mostly conducted through correspondence, it was the first important romantic relationship of Ellmann's life, certainly the first for which there is evidence. That he was drawn to and could attract such an attractive woman makes one wonder what went wrong.

* * *

When Ellmann received the October 11 letter from Jean, he no longer lived in Washington, having left X-2 in late August. He had not been drafted, but his draft status had changed. On August 19 he was called to Fort Myer in Washington for a second Army physical; his 1-A classification was changed to 4-F, or so he was told. (According to the report on the physical, at twenty-four he was 5 foot 9 inches tall, weighed 153 pounds, with vison of 4/20, corrected to 20/20 with lenses.) News of his reclassification came to him after a visit to Bread Loaf earlier in the summer, where the poet Ted Morrison, who not only ran the Bread Loaf Writers' Conference but was a lecturer in English at Harvard, offered him a job. Morrison administered Harvard's freshman composition course, English A, and the job he offered Ellmann was to teach one section of English A to Radcliffe students and two sections to Harvard students. Ellmann's decision to leave X-2 after six months he explained to his parents in an undated letter of late August or early September:

> I have decided to accept the Harvard job because my work here is tiresome and I may have perfected the methods sufficiently so that it is mainly routine.

> I spoke to Lewis about it, and he said he could think of some reasons against it, but wouldn't advance them. My own feeling is that I will probably be taken [by the draft] before another year or so anyway, and that at least I'll be able to say I had taught at Harvard. . . . [Andrews, "Andy" to friends] Wanning is teaching up there, which ought to make it even better.

Ellmann's father approved of his son's decision. Once Ellmann had mastered teaching, he wrote, in a letter of September 14, "the increased leisure will make you produce. And as one of the boys of Harvard your product [the Yeats dissertation, his nonacademic writing] should be of greater value than before." As soon as they heard of the appointment, Ellmann's parents reported it to the wider family. Various cousins and aunts wrote to congratulate him. Cousin Alice Silberstein, an English major at Wellesley, could "think of nothing nicer than having a Harvard professor do my homework." She promised to introduce Ellmann to "some very spiffy young ladies with all the charm, beauty and brains (if I can find 'em) a Harvard professor would require."[9]

On October 1 Ellmann taught his first Radcliffe section. The next day he taught two Harvard sections (the sections met three times a week: Mondays, Wednesdays, and Fridays for Radcliffe students; Tuesdays, Thursdays, and Saturdays for Harvard students). His classes seem to have gone well, he wrote to his parents on October 4, despite one Harvard student asking to change sections "because his section man knew too much and mentioned people he never heard of" (Morrison told the boy "that he was in college now and must accustom himself," but Ellmann admitted that the boy had a point: "because I had an ulterior motive of impressing them with my erudition on that first day"). After a week's classes Ellmann concluded that the Radcliffe students were "much easier to teach . . . because they grasp things quickly and don't question much, whereas the Harvard boys continually try to upset me and sometimes nearly do." In addition, he reported, "Radcliffe girls are for the most part not pretty, though there are exceptions. You will laugh at me, but I have the feeling that the whole class is in love with me."

Ellmann wrote this letter from a room in the Brattle Inn, "which costs too much for what I am getting." He was still plagued by colds, "though in less serious form," and over the weekend would begin looking for an apartment, since the "very ancient" women who run the Brattle Inn "look through my bureau every day and through my keyhole every night." He instructs his parents to write to him at Warren House, the home of the English Department, where he shares an office with a teaching assistant on the third floor. He likes this teaching assistant, who is "very decent and at least has the proper sentiments, since he's secretary of the local Teachers' Union." Two weeks later, on October 18, a week after Jean Douglas wrote of her desire for a new relationship, Ellmann wrote to his parents that Morrison's secretary was "pursuing me hotly."

In addition to teaching his classes, Ellmann wrote in the October 18 letter, he spent the week conducting twenty-minute conferences with each of his students, all of whom received the same advice: "to write specifically, not in generalities, and to use lots of examples." For the first of their weekly writing assignments, they had been asked to produce brief autobiographies. Ellmann was tough on this first assignment, warning that their marks would only improve if they "stopped trying to write 'beautifully,' which I suppose is the first step toward writing well." For the second assignment, the students were asked to write about "a problem in [their] home town or a prejudice." His assignment for week three was to have them write a speech by Hitler justifying the failure to take Stalingrad. This speech was to be written "as cleverly and convincingly as possible. The girls were somewhat shocked at the idea, but the Harvard boys took it without a murmur."

Ellmann was interested in his teaching and in his students. It was the marking that got him down. "Seventy-six themes a week can go a long way toward submerging me," he wrote to his parents on October 24. "They're sort of fun in one respect, but they seem ever-present and that takes some of the enjoyment away." He had similarly mixed feelings about his pastoral duties, an important part of the job as an instructor in English A. In a letter to his parents of November 9, he writes of his most recent conference with a student "who has shown considerable intelligence but little skill in writing." Previously uncommunicative, the boy confessed that his father's stellar record at Harvard had intimidated him, so much so that he had seriously contemplated quitting. This revelation, Ellmann reports to his parents, "clearly called for a sermon":

> So I gave it to him in as secular a way as possible; at the end he assured me that he wouldn't give up, but said he would probably lapse into an unambitious C student. The idea was, as I made him admit, that if he didn't try and got C's, he would feel allright, but if he did try and got C's

his confidence in himself would be shaken. I of course stood up for the competitive instinct; it probably didn't do any harm to talk boy scout to him; yet I feel a little ashamed of my duties as arbiter juventis.

Ellmann was more comfortable treating his students as adults or encouraging them to see themselves as adults than he was giving them sermons. When confronted with a Radcliffe student who had been advised that D. H. Lawrence's *Sons and Lovers* "was not something young girls should read," he asked: "'You don't consider yourself a young girl, do you?' And she said, 'No.'" Another Radcliffe student wrote in a journal assignment about reacting angrily to a crude pass made at her at a dance. "A year ago I probably would have just giggled or looked shocked or something equally naïve." Ellmann's marginal comment was: "A year from now you'll probably answer politely and in detail."[10]

Ellmann wanted to be liked by his students. In a letter of November 6, he reported to his parents that one student "told me how my criticisms helped him a good deal, though he thought my marks were tough. It is always hard to find out what one's students think of you, and I can only hope that his is the general view." Another student also wrote to thank Ellmann for being tough: "I needed all the scolding you gave the day after our awful 'autobiographies.'"[11] In the November 6 letter, Ellmann describes himself as "competent" as a lecturer but lacking "enough eccentricities to convince them that I'm a great man." Although wry about pedagogical peacocking, he was unironic about the importance of the liberal arts. Writing to his parents on December 24, he deplores "the implications of this military assertion that literature, history, and the rest of the humanities are peacetime luxuries." On January 17, 1943, again to his parents, he reports: "I gave my students a final lecture on a comparison of literature and science, to the disadvantage of science, and a comparison of literature and fascism to the disadvantage of fascism. The dangers of private fascism—which I defined as oversimplification and irrationality—were brought home to them in a manner worthy of Demosthenes."

* * *

Teaching made Ellmann think hard about questions of literary form and function. In a letter of February 7, 1943, he tells his parents about a class in which he asked his students to compare "a sentimental religious poem" (found in I. A. Richards's *Practical Criticism*) with "a poem by e. e. cummings that has in it the words 'puke' and 'vomit.' They will probably say that the first one is good and the second awful, whereas the opposite is true." This teaching exercise prompted a notebook reflection of February 15: "It seems to me now, this partly in connection with Cummings's poem, 'A Man Who Had Fallen Among Thieves,' that I am trying to teach them about *evil.* To that end I am helping them to generalize about the age—something that most of them have not done."

In some instances the thoughts provoked by his experiences as a teacher informed Ellmann's later work on Joyce. In a notebook entry of February 3, 1943, he wonders whether "the best way to teach poetry is to pretend that it's prose—condensed prose—condensed so far that words assume tremulous connotations. These connotations may almost overcome the literal significances of the words, so that they produce an effect quite apart from the denotations." Four days later, in the February 7 letter to his parents, he writes of "trying to teach poetry in a hard-boiled way by assigning short stories and poems on related subjects together. Several instructors have borrowed the idea from me, but I've not taught enough to know whether or not it's working." Joyce, too, had mulled over the differences between poems and stories, and at roughly the same age. In Paris in 1902, taking up Baudelaire's challenge to produce "prose poétique," a challenge Baudelaire himself felt unequal to, Joyce composed a series of paragraph-length passages that he labeled "epiphanies."[12] In these passages, meaning is often elusive and unfixed, sometimes in the way Ellmann identifies in his February 3 notebook entry as "poetic," in which connotations "almost overcome" denotations, as they were to do increasingly in Joyce's writings. Ellmann himself, as we shall see, had a go at "prose poétique," also in Paris, also under the influence of a French poet.

Ellmann's social life at Harvard revolved around Ted and Kathleen Morrison, Andy and Pat Wanning, and his fellow English A instructors. In a letter of October 24 to his parents he mentions an outing to Lexington and Concord "with a few of the new members of the English A staff." After a Christmas Eve party at the Morrisons, Ellmann walked home with Robert Frost, who invited him up for a drink.

> He loves to talk, loves to talk to young men to win their awe. His technique is in fact very well developed; he knows how often to let the other

> person talk, he flattered me by asking what I was writing and what my compositional methods were. We got to talking about Untermeyer, whom he called a great man. . . . We spoke of Yeats a little; he disliked him personally but always read him. . . . Frost said that people are talking about Yeats now as if he were profound; which he isn't.
>
> I asked him if he decided to write about New England because it seemed to him that the field of regional verse had been neglected. He denied it, said it wasn't a conscious decision at all; that he suspected Ezra Pound of having done that, of having looked for someplace to piss in where nobody had pissed before. Of Pound he said that Pound's learning was probably exaggerated; his translations were all made with the help of trots ["cribs," literal translations, often used illicitly]. . . . Yeats treated Pound like a walking encyclopedia but Frost was suspicious of him.[13]

In a later undated letter to his parents, Ellmann reported that he was "still dodging Morrison's secretary, who spends her time offering me juice squeezers, glasses, assistance in fixing up my apartment, her car, etc. I'm becoming a more successful evader now." Sometime in October, Henry Wells, a friend of Ellmann's from Yale, was assigned to a five-month Harvard training course for Naval ensigns. Wells was engaged to Lucy Dimock, the sister of Connie Dimock, the wife of another Yale classmate, Frank Ellis. Ellmann invited Wells to room with him in Cambridge and Wells and the Dimock sisters brought a bit of Yale social life with them (and also a bit from Vassar, where Connie taught). A party was arranged on the weekend of the Yale-Harvard football game, when Ellmann had a brief fling or flirtation with a woman named Fran Alexander (who later wrote: "I had a beautiful time, and I hope to God you accept that at its face value. It doesn't mean that I think a new world is dawning").[14] There are also vaguely flirtatious letters from two recently married friends, one whom Ellmann had met with Erwin on the ship to Europe, another from the daughter of a family friend from Detroit.

* * *

All this time, notwithstanding his 4-F classification, the threat of the draft loomed, leading Ellmann to seek advice from friends and colleagues about future postings. On October 18, 1942, he had reported to his parents that he had written to the Navy "asking whether my eyes meet their requirement for the Japanese course." Charles Feidelson wrote from Maryland, on Army "Ordnance School" stationery, that he had no information about intelligence and language schools.[15] He recommends that Ellmann let himself be drafted, "because doing otherwise involves so much reasoning, constantly renewed. . . . I'm all for the simple and uncomplicated, in life if not in art." Ellmann was not yet ready to accept this advice, and sometime in January 1943 he inquired about the Army school of Russian. He had been teaching himself Spanish and dabbling with Portuguese for several years, believing that a facility with languages would prove useful in an academic career and in the military.

Robie Macauley, Ellmann's friend from Bread Loaf, now in the Army Counterintelligence Corps (CIC), also offered advice. In an undated letter he outlined what Ellmann should do when called for interview after induction: "The more outrageously you lie, the better. There is no check. Tell them you were assistant head of the WPB [War Production Board] in Washington or head of the Harvard English Dept. Anyway, exaggerate favorably on everything you've ever done. Tell them you speak French, Spanish and German. And, as for preference in Army jobs, be sure to ask for the Adjutant General's Office. Intelligence is next to impossible for a draftee to get into. AGO is the personnel section of the Army, where good jobs and high ratings abound." Ellmann's mother, who took to exaggeration naturally, also offered advice, describing her son's command of languages in a letter of January 14, 1943, as "Latin, some Greek, Spanish, Portuguese, French, German, and a smattering of English—quite an imposing list."[16]

As the draft's "Democlean sword" hung over Ellmann, the possibility arose that he might be able to continue teaching at Harvard, not in English A but in the sort of course Henry Wells was taking.[17] On April 23, 1943, he wrote to the Highland Park draft board to make a case for such a possibility:

> As you know the armed services are planning to return a large number of men to colleges for advance training. By July 1 Harvard expects to have about a thousand of these Army and Navy enlisted men. Almost all will be required to take the test in Basic E, sections of which Professor Morrison has asked me to teach. . . . My education and experience have prepared me for this kind of war work, and I think I can best serve the war effort in this way. I want to make clear, however, that if you decide that I can be of more use in the armed forces than in teaching soldiers and navy men, I am anxious to follow your directions.

This letter was accompanied by a supporting letter from Morrison, whom Ellmann described, in the spirit of Macauley, as "head of department."

Ellmann was of two minds about the case he was making. As early as March 29, 1943, he admitted to his parents that he was "far from at ease" about continuing to teach at Harvard. On the one hand, whichever branch of the military drafted him, his duties, given his eyesight, were likely to be confined to what Macauley described as "limited service" (light or office work) rather than "general service" (combat). As his father put it, "If you have the choice of teaching at Harvard and the draft board is willing, you are doing essential war work. . . . For any bit of interesting work in the army you have to give up much time to routine. It can't be much better than teaching soldiers at Harvard." On the other hand, "you will not belong to that caste which the military will develop now and after the war. You may have a sense of discomfort . . . as a very real possibility later on."[18]

At the end of June 1943 Ellmann received a letter from the Highland Park draft board ordering him to attend another physical, which he took "to be preliminary to redrafting." "You will have to determine for yourself," wrote his father on July 1, "whether it is not better to have some military association, however brief, back of you rather than feel you had not joined." By July 2 Ellmann had decided: "I have refused to permit the University officials to appeal your decision, as they wished to do," he wrote to the draft board, "and I want to appeal for immediate induction in Cambridge—will you kindly inform me what steps need to be taken." By the end of the month he was drafted into the Navy, undergoing four weeks of basic training (boot camp) ("both better and worse than I expected").[19] In August, after volunteering for General Services in the hope of a foreign posting, he was assigned to the US Navy Construction Battalions ("Seabees," or CBs), stationed in Camp Peary, Virginia, near Williamsburg. The mission of the Seabees was to build and maintain airstrips and related military facilities in the Pacific. According to Ellsworth Mason, "Of all the incongruities of the war none was greater than Richard Ellmann in the US Navy Construction Battalions."[20] Three weeks later Mason himself was inducted into the Navy and joined Ellmann at Camp Peary.

* * *

Ellmann had been inducted as a yeoman third class, equivalent to the lowest grade of army sergeant. Mason calls this rating a "stroke of luck," but yeoman third class is still an enlisted rating and Ellmann "always felt demeaned by his non-officer status throughout the war," a feeling Mason seems not to have shared.[21] Mason had been contemplating writing a PhD on Joyce and Vico, and he and Ellmann would go on to work together on Joyce, both formally and informally, throughout their lives. But they were different in character. In a letter of July 30, 1957, introducing Mason to Harriet Weaver, Joyce's literary executor, Ellmann describes him as having been "equally unfitted" for the Seabees. Unlike Ellmann, however, Mason made no effort to change postings. Instead, Ellmann writes, "he decided to become an expert on the starting motors of trucks and cars, and eventually became indispensable at this highly technical job. He was sent to the Marshall Islands, and in his off hours collected a great many rare and beautiful shells which are now in the Peabody Museum at Yale."

Ellmann's campaign to transfer out of the Seabees began almost as soon as he finished basic training. In a letter of August 13, 1943, to his parents, he reported that the assistant regimental commander, Lt. Cooper, had taken an interest in him and had arranged to have him transferred from Yeoman's School into Ship's Company, made up of "the personnel permanently stationed here" (considering Camp Peary the Seabees' "ship"). In Ship's Company, Cooper told Ellmann, "I would be much closer to things . . . than if I were sent to Yeoman's school. I said I could probably do more good in Intelligence—and he said that ship's company would be easier to transfer from and that he would be glad to help me as much as possible." Ellmann has a theory about why Cooper was so helpful: "He's a quiet fellow and I think my unaggressive manner helped me. Though, Mother, to quiet your fears, I wasn't excessively modest." The letter ends with Ellmann reassuring his parents that "so far I've been very well treated—everyone seems to be trying to figure out ways of getting me ahead."

By September, however, Ellmann was complaining to his parents of "the monotony and teleological inadequacy" of his work. His hours were 7:30 to 17:30 and they were filled with administrative and clerical duties, including filing, making sure the offices were cleaned each morning by a work detail, logging men in and out when they were coming back from or going away for leave, and saluting every time an officer entered the room. Despite "many efforts" to change his occupation, none had so far been successful. He therefore planned to travel to Washington "to work on [Wilmath] Lewis" and to make further inquiries about the Navy's Japanese school.

"While everyone is on to him," he writes of Lewis, "he's still in the good graces of Wild Bill [Donovan, head of the OSS], and may be able to do something yet." Five days later he reports to his parents that Lewis was "very cordial, called me 'Dick' instead of 'Mr. Ellmann.'" and that he (Ellmann) "went all over the agency seeing people I knew and set up a chain of people who will remind other people which ought to be efficacious."[22]

Eventually there were rays of hope from within Camp Peary itself. In October Ellmann was offered the job of lecturing to new CB recruits. The Navy Bureau of Personnel then visited Ellmann's office to see if any of the men in Ship's Company should be placed elsewhere. "My classifier was impressed," Ellmann reports, and "started to recommend me for Intelligence when it occurred to us that my parents weren't born in this country—hence no Intelligence." Three days later "an obliging young ensign" (Yale '36, "needless to say") called to offer Ellmann a job in the Navy Bureau of Personnel, "as one of the classifiers." This job Ellmann turned down on several counts: "1) I want to be near Washington [classifiers traveled "all round the country"]; 2) I'd like to try lecturing for a bit; 3) a lecturer's job may do me more good in trying for officer's bars."[23] The lecturing Ellmann was assigned, however, was unpromising. "The subjects are very dull, and little freedom of treatment is allowed, but it will be better than this office."[24]

Ellmann's relations with his fellow Seabees at Camp Peary were mostly friendly, but he did have one disturbing moment, described in a letter to his parents of December 30:

> We had quite a little squabble this morning—some chief (a particularly stupid one) yelled out, "Where's that Jew?" meaning me. Another Jew told me of it. I went up and told him how I didn't like it—he persisted in repeating it—so I grabbed him, swore if he said it again I'd hit him. Somebody pulled me away—I was trembling with rage—and later on Chief Gray gave me hell for my violence—you see, I could be given a summary court martial for hitting my superior (a chief petty officer). . . . He also took me aside and reminded me of what a dope the chief was.
>
> But the heartening thing about the incident is the way several of the boys took up my side, offered, if I wanted to press charges, to back me up, and in general half-apologized for the way the chief had acted.

After recounting this incident, Ellmann was at pains to reassure his parents that he had done nothing either to antagonize the officer or to lower himself: "I've made an effort to be one of the boys in the barracks, but have always acted as decently as possible."

Ellmann's "little squabble" with the chief petty officer was hardly his first experience of antisemitism, but it was a rare instance of the sort of overt antisemitism encountered by Leopold Bloom in the "Cyclops" episode of *Ulysses*. Like Ellmann, Bloom seeks a balance between not antagonizing the Cyclops-like Citizen and his drinking companions in Barney Kiernan's pub and acting "decently," which in this context means countering both the crudity and violence of the Citizen's nationalism and his antisemitism. With "timorous dark pride," Bloom recounts to Stephen how he stood up to the Citizen: "He called me a jew in a heated fashion offensively. So I without deviating from plain facts in the least told him his God, I mean Christ, was a jew too" (*Ulysses:* 16, 1082–1984). In *James Joyce,* Ellmann argues for Bloom's nobility, despite his flaws and weaknesses.[25] Bloom may not be as intelligent as Ulysses or a great warrior, but he retains what Joyce considered the Homeric hero's "primary qualities," summarized by Ellmann as "prudence, intelligence, sensitivity and good will" (*JJ,* p. 360). This idea, which is argued in the biography, challenged the prevailing view, that of Pound, Eliot, and Harry Levin, in which Bloom is a debased or mock-heroic figure, a symbol of decline. In *James Joyce,* Ellmann also claims that the two characteristics of Jews that most interested Joyce were "their chosen isolation, and the close family ties which were perhaps the result of it. These characteristics [Joyce] saw in himself as well, and they gave him a sense of affinity. A great deal of his own experience became Bloom's" (*JJ,* pp. 373–74). A similar point might be made about the part Ellmann's experience played in his affinity both to Bloom and to Bloom's creator.

* * *

At the time of his confrontation with the chief petty officer, Ellmann was involved with a girl he had met in Washington, DC, about whom he writes to his parents. "I've taken out President Taft's granddaughter, the Senator's niece, a couple of times. She's a splendid gal, I think, though Erwin is probably right in saying that she's self-conscious about her ancestry. She rooms with Doris Bernstein whom I knew at Radcliffe last year through Ira Marden of Yale."[26] Doris Bernstein was an economics graduate student at Radcliffe. as was her roommate, twenty-one-year-old Helen Taft Manning, who in addition to being a president's granddaughter was the daughter of the dean of Bryn Mawr College, Helen Herron Taft Manning, a professor of history, and of Frederick J. Manning, a professor of history at Swarthmore. At the time, Helen worked in Washington at the Board of Economic Warfare. Soon she and Ellmann became seriously involved.

Like Jean Douglas, Helen Manning was clever, attractive, and self-possessed, but she was unliterary and was open or uncomplicated about her feelings. It did not take her long to confess not only that she was in love with Ellmann but that she was surprised to discover herself subject to the traditional love-struck emotions, beginning with a desire to tell everyone she met how wonderful he was. "According to all the books and Smith girls [Helen, like Jean, had been an undergraduate at Smith], I shouldn't tell you so, but as I'm not much given to coyness. . . . I see no point in not telling you again that you may consider Helen Taft Manning as your property." At the end of the letter, Helen adds that she would "very much like to have you meet my parents. . . . I expect that you will approve of each other."[27]

Sometime after receiving this letter, Ellmann asked Erwin to invite Helen over to his apartment on Saturday night, when he would be in Washington, "since I'd already promised to see her and Mother might like to meet her."[28] The result of this meeting was a ten-page letter from Ellmann's father addressed to both Dick and Erwin. What precipitated the letter was not only "Dick's deep interest in a lovely young lady" but "Erwin's note to Bill some time ago that in matters of the heart advice should be given sparingly by others." Erwin's point about advice was quickly dismissed on the grounds that it did not apply to parents. As to Dick and Helen, "Mother assures me that she is a most lovely girl of class and quality. . . . I can easily understand the temptation of a Jew boy stemming from such humble beginnings to admire and fall in love with so lovely a girl who does not take her forebears too seriously, and yet can bring into the life of a young man so many of the things that are essential on the road to happiness and comfort and pleasant work. A Taft or a Manning will certainly be an open sesame to a thousand places otherwise shut tight in your face."

But there will be problems. According to his father, Helen Manning as prospective partner was bound to tempt Ellmann to hide or lose his identity, by which is meant principally his identity as a Jew. He gives detailed examples of friends who have married outside the faith: "emotionally, socially, psychologically, they just don't belong." "To ask Helen to abandon her own faith and that of her fathers is utterly unfair. To think that you can leave such a problem alone is I fear quite nonsensical." He intimates that his own standing in the Jewish community would be damaged by such a marriage: "I should not like to hold on to a job which requires me to show some appreciation for Jewish values and concerns while my sons desire to take a different turn to life."[29]

Ellmann's response to his father's letter was brief and high-minded. "I know of no personal problem so difficult that it can't be solved by a little rationality without . . . the humiliations you speak of as inevitable. I have always, with non-Jews, emphasized that I was a Jew and I don't intend to stop for any reason. That other individuals have sacrificed self for social prestige seems to me irrelevant. Nor do added difficulties deter me in this respect any more than they would you in others. I appreciate your arguments, but with youthful folly believe they have little to do with this particular case." He then reminds his father that "it will be some years" before he is out of the Navy and in a position to make any decision.[30] Helen's reaction to the father's letter was to consider it "irrelevant," and to regret that questions of religion were "brought up so soon." "It's undoubtedly something to which we'll have to adjust sooner or later, as we are both attached to our families, but at the moment it seems to me that we should concentrate on Dick and Helen as individuals instead of Dick and Helen as Jew and Gentile."

Helen also took issue with the father's assumptions about the sorts of people they were:

> After having been the family "red" for the last ten years, and having denounced and deliberately ignored the aristocrats of the Main Line as well as the R. A. Tafts, it's a little hard to be characterized as the gently-born wife who will lead you to social success. I think it highly unlikely that we should ever be able to move in any circles into which you could not get yourself on your own merits. What's more, I don't want to move in them, and neither do you, I'm sure. I am also very hurt for you—because of the aspersions cast on your own integrity. If it were not obvious to me that they are unjustified, I should never have fallen in love with you. . . . One more point—I have always had the greatest contempt for people who deny their backgrounds and ancestry—one of your attractions is that you didn't.[31]

In a later letter of March 13, Helen reports to Ellmann, "I'm writing my mother to expect us this weekend," adding that though she has taken to thinking of herself as having "achieved self-sufficiency I find myself amazingly bound by parental ties still. I don't like to do anything, anything important, that is, without telling them. Not because I want their advice, but because of mutual affection. So with your permission (I mean that not as an empty phrase) I'd like to tell them all about us. I won't be really comfortable until I have."

From the correspondence it is not clear when Ellmann met the Mannings, but in a letter of March 25 his father suggests that the meeting had its awkwardnesses.[32] In a letter to Ellmann of April 5, Helen writes that she and he have "(as usual) come to the same conclusions about our parents' arguments. You don't have to convince me that my mother's ambitious plans are likely to lead to regrets—that was quite obvious." On April 11, in explaining an intemperate letter he had written to his father, Ellmann confesses that he had been "enraged, no doubt, by how correct what you said about the Mannings' reaction was."

Ellmann's intemperate letter followed a meeting between Helen and his father, itself quickly followed by one of the father's mammoth letters, seven single-spaced pages. The meeting took place in New York when James Ellmann was there on business, presumably for the Jewish Council. He "could easily understand" why Helen's "abundantly good qualities should appeal to you at this stage of your life." On the plus side, "she has sureness; has fine nurture; is, as I have already said, a thorobred. Her good forebears guarantee that. She will do no violence to them. She's good to look at. And will be a striking lady in a salon." On the deficit side, "she's a bit tough minded, while you are tender minded. . . . More practical while you are less. More sure while you are more shy. Able to influence your thoughts more than you could influence hers. . . . No matter what the influence we may have exercised, hers will be hereafter a more powerful one."

He then turns to Helen's parents. "Her Dad's marriage to a Taft was something of a social comedown for the family. Helen Taft, the daughter of a president, married a mere history instructor, and even the Ellmanns are not awed or too much impressed by an instructor." Helen's "expressed resentment" of the richer and more aristocratic branches of her family is "an effort to find some compensation." "You must, of course, remember that a girl like Helen is no doubt apple of their eye. And you come along, modest, quiet, unlionized, and still unoriented, and sans epaulets, how do you expect to make much of an impression upon anyone other than Helen herself."

If Helen refuses to give Ellmann up, deciding "to brave the storm of home, she must offer some appeasement at an early date," he writes. "What could that be, Dick? It must be that you would be willing to give up your own identity and merge with theirs; become like them; share their type of existence; and finally allow your children to cling to them ["as opposed to us," he means]. Helen has such right. You have no right to deny her this. Her promise that she will not insist is not a reliable one." Again the father emphasizes the son's mildness: "Your more fragile nature (which is not necessarily a faulty one) is bound to be on the yielding end. Hers on the receiving end. And now, you, Jew-boy, come along, and a Manning, in an effort to prevent a further descent, is very likely to find you quite inadequate, if not undesirable." As for relations between the two sets of parents, "We shall not be the friends of the Mannings. You they will indulge from sheer tolerance, rather than love or respect." The Mannings "certainly are civilized, but on this sort of an issue they will not be civilized in the long run. This is how the human animal acts and reacts."

In response to these arguments, Ellmann loses his patience. "Your letter arrived last night, Dad," begins his half-page reply, impertinent in its brevity. "I appreciate your expressing your opinion. I have, however, no desire to make my personal life a matter of controversy. I am not such a dolt as not to have thought of things you mention." As for his father's disapproval of the relationship between Erwin and Steffani, about which the father's letter devotes several pages, "I have slowly come to realize in the last few years that whether you were right or wrong it was your duty to stay out of that business. And by staying out I mean avoiding implied as well as overt pressure." The letter concludes: "I believe strongly in the right of every individual to make his own bed and lie in it. I consider this my own business. I am old enough and rational enough to undermine myself without your assistance. You had a right to express your opinion, but I don't want to hear anything more about it. Nor do I want to hear anything more about not hearing anything more about it. Love, Dick."[33]

Ellmann's letter infuriated his father, who waited a week before replying:

> All I can say now is that whatever may have inspired the contents of your recent "directive," I have for the life of me been unable to identify my

> son in it. And you can readily imagine my difficulties in trying to formulate some thoughts to someone who suddenly out of a clear blue sky tells you, "your concerns are total strangers to me" [the exact opposite of what Ellmann wrote]. I was foolish enough to talk to you, as I have always talked to you. I talked simply, fully, sincerely. That I had no such right to do this I was not aware. That I must never again refer to these matters I fully realize now. That you should have your wish fulfilled is the only course I can follow from now on.

The letter ends: "Men usually deserve the things they receive. We must have earned just this. Wishing you well in everything you do. Affectionately. Dad"[34]

At this point in the correspondence, Ellmann backs down, distraught at his father's obvious anger and upset. "Dear Dad, your letter just arrived and made me very wretched, as I fully deserved. I had been very upset at not hearing from you, not realizing how bad my letter must have sounded. . . . [Here he adds the bit about how "enraged" he was in having to acknowledge the rightness of his father's predictions.] Needless to say, if I had been indifferent to your attitude I shouldn't have brought Helen to New York at all." The letter concludes: "You must understand that it is not pleasant to have one's fondest hopes attacked in the most convincing way. I feel rotten to think that my thoughtlessness of the moment should have caused you any pain. You have always been the best of fathers to me, and I'm only sorry that I haven't been as good a son. Please forgive me. You will do me a great wrong if you attach any lasting importance to what was the reaction of a moment." The emotion here strikes me as genuine. The influence of the family bond, the bond to the father in particular, was for Ellmann inescapable. His depiction of this bond in *James Joyce* as similarly inescapable he amply documents, as he does Joyce's own depiction of the hold of family and fatherhood.

A month after Ellmann sent his letter of apology he received a letter from Helen. Ellmann had sent her "a confusing poem about dragons" ("not likely to stir confidence!" suggests Lucy Ellmann)[35] that resulted in her being forced "to come clean (with myself as well as you) on one point—I'm afraid it's no go for us on a permanent basis. This is not only a matter of family—although I'm afraid that's part of it. It's also because I found that my earlier reactions were correct—there are basic differences between our points of view which would make an already difficult union impossible. . . . I think you know what I am talking about as much as I do." Like Jean Douglas, Helen ends her letter with a confession that "strange as it may seem, I still love you." How upset Ellmann was about this is hard to tell; Helen did not keep his letters. He clearly was serious about her, but in his letters to his father he several times suggests that speculation about marriage was premature. It is also true that he and Helen had different interests. Judging by her letters, Helen's were finance, office politics, and the viola. How their "points of view" differed the letters do not reveal.

* * *

When Ellmann received Helen's breakup letter, he was no longer at Camp Peary. In his last months at the camp he had been given a new job, teaching illiterate Seabees to read and write. "I have 2 Mexicans, 2 Navajo Indians, some southerners, and one Maine man. Most of them are learning pretty rapidly and are terribly grateful for it." Within a month, however, it was announced that 40 percent of the lecturers at Camp Peary would soon be moved out.[36] Ellmann expected, rightly, to be of their number, but in his case the move took four months.[37] In May 1944 he was sent to the headquarters of the Sixth Naval District in Charleston, South Carolina, a posting he described to Mason as "a couple of steps closer to dementia praecox or psychoneurosis than Peary" (p. 9). He was assigned to work in the headquarters personnel office preparing correspondence, work no more absorbing than the clerical and administrative jobs he had been given at Camp Peary.

Charleston itself, and the Deep South more generally, he found engrossing, certainly more engrossing than Williamsburg. "I had never expected to be so interested in a town before," he wrote to his parents, "but Charleston is fascinating in many ways."[38] In a notebook he kept at the time, there are entries on a range of themes and issues connected to the South: thoughts on John Crowe Ransom and the Southern Agrarians; quotations from books about slavery, plantation life, the Gullah dialect, Southern customs. Several entries comment on Southern hospitality. "Charleston differs from Williamsburg," reads an early entry, "in that Williamsburg is a reproduction. Charleston retains its charm, its people their integrity. Nowhere have people a better sense of good manners and good living." An acquaintance who once taught at Winthrop College in nearby Rock Hill,

Ellmann in naval uniform, 1945.

South Carolina, "told me that Charlestonians are like Chinese—they eat rice, speak a foreign language, and worship their ancestors." In another entry, Ellmann quotes an unnamed authority for whom "being a Southerner is like being a Jew," a comparison unlikely to please either group.

James Ellmann might well have been one of those not pleased, warning his son that he was unlikely to "find many of our people in Charleston."[39] In fact, Ellmann quickly made contact with an active Jewish community in the city. On April 7, before receiving his father's angry letter of April 9, he reported to his parents that he was going to a Seder held by a rabbi at the headquarters. This rabbi he describes as "cold and indifferent, overly afraid of offending the Gentiles by asking for things for the Jewish boys. Consequently, many prefer to go to the non-Jewish chaplains, who as a result get mostly the begging type and are therefore prejudiced." Then, with a dig: "It will gratify you, at least, to learn that I've not yet announced my conversion to high Episcopalianism."

Before receiving Helen's breakup letter, Ellmann writes of having "happened onto" a discussion group at the Jewish USO (United Service Organization). The subject discussed was whether *The Merchant of Venice* should be taught in secondary schools. Ellmann thought not, and the rabbi, impressed by his comments, invited him to dinner. At a second discussion, on a topic Ellmann does not name, he reports having made two observations: "that Jews were ordinary people and like everyone else" and that "the plight of the Jew was improvable on a large scale not by Jewish action but by social action," observations clearly related to recent exchanges with his father over Helen.[40]

The kindness of the rabbi, "a fairly intelligent man," led Ellmann not only to continue attending discussion sessions but to attend synagogue services and a dance put on by the Jewish USO. In all discussion sessions, antisemitism took center stage, regardless of topic. It was a "mass obsession," "downright masochism . . . as if the Catholics were to discuss nothing but what the Protestants think of them."[41] In this and other respects, the Charleston Jews were "amazingly like Detroiters." Ellmann writes of meeting two "prize specimens" of the community at the rabbi's house, one of whom irritated him by claiming to be interested in people rather than culture, "as if the people were independent of the culture. It's bad enough being uncultivated without attempting to justify it." The next night, however, at another discussion meeting, Ellmann "at long last" met someone with whom he could converse. The rabbi had made a remark about logic and was amused to discover there was a philosopher in the crowd, "just as the night he had spoken about Shylock there was an English teacher in the crowd."[42]

The philosopher was Frank Trager, who turned out not only to know Ellmann's father but to have been in the Ellmann house on Connecticut Street; he remembered Jean Ellmann's cooking fondly. Trager had taught philosophy at Johns Hopkins, worked for a period as a research assistant to Arthur Lovejoy, "who's very important in the history of ideas in English literature," and went on to become "one of the three top men in the American Jewish Committee," which is how he came to know James Ellmann and visit the Ellmann home.[43] Ellmann's father called him the Committee's "best man . . . in analyzing anti-Semitism and how to meet and combat it."[44] When Ellmann met him he was serving as a private in the Army Air Force.

Trager shared Ellmann's interest in the South, and the two men visited historic sites, not only in Charleston but in Savannah. He also sparked in Ellmann a short-term interest in architecture, "and to some extent even in furniture, and I hope to do some reading in them soon."[45] In addition, they discussed the local Jewish community. To Ellmann, the isolation of the Jews of Charleston was like that of the city's Black population. "I hadn't noticed much anti-Semitism, and there isn't much," he writes in a letter to an unidentifiable girl ("My Dear"), "because the Jews like the negroes know their place. They have accepted and even favored a ghetto condition, in which not only is there no assimilation, but no feeling of participation in the community life. . . . I told the rabbi that he should make the Jews Charlestonians first and then influence their religious convictions."[46] To his friend Bill O'Donnell he writes of the kindness of the rabbi but finds him "preoccupied with moving from orthodoxy to conservatism, a diversion that seems to me of little importance. And the Jewish girls here are unusually dull. I prefer elevator girls."[47]

Ellmann's decision to immerse himself in the Jewish culture of Charleston can be related to the breakup with Helen and his father's fears that his son would lose or discard his identity as a Jew. For all the warmth of the welcome he received, what most struck Ellmann about the Jews of Charleston was their parochialism and insularity. That these are the same limitations or dangers Joyce saw in notions of Irish cultural identity is amply documented in *James Joyce,* though, as we shall see, critics argue that Ellmann underplays the Irishness of Joyce's writing as well as his interest in and knowledge of Irish politics.

* * *

On August 19, 1944, after less than three months in Charleston, Ellmann was transferred to Washington, DC. He had at last managed to obtain a position that would send him abroad: a six-month posting to the Office of the CNO (Chief Naval Officer) in the Office of Naval Intelligence, to be followed by a further transfer to duty "beyond the Continental limits of the U.S."[48] "All this came about as a result of my letter to the Bureau of Naval Personnel," he wrote to his parents, despite "the rule in Naval Intelligence that only third generation Americans can work there."[49] In Washington he attended a sort of intelligence school, which he found "fascinating," despite not liking several of its minor instructors. The school was held in the building that housed the OSS, which meant that at lunch he kept running into old Yale and COI friends in the cafeteria.[50]

Three weeks after his return to Washington, Ellmann learned, or so he recalled to a friend, "that Admiral Kirk's flag secretary was looking for a

Yeoman who spoke French, and I was able to convince him that he need look no farther." Two days later he was en route to Paris. From New York, after being delayed by a hurricane, he flew to Newfoundland, then to Ireland, "thus preserving my naval virginity so far as being on a naval vessel is concerned. . . . I am what the French call a marin de l'eau douce." From Ireland, after the briefest of stopovers, he spent a few days in London, where he looked up "people I used to know, most of them occupied in super-secret stuff for my old agency."[51]

Chief among these people were Norman Pearson, now head of the London office of the OSS, and James J. Angleton, chief of the Italian desk. Pearson, as usual, was "ostentatiously au courant."[52] Angleton was doing work "both good and important, an enviable combination these days."[53] Angleton was "delighted" to see Ellmann, took him to lunch, and gave him a book on the Gobelins tapestries to "'whet his appetite'" for Paris.[54] Writing to his parents, Ellmann described London as "badly knocked up, of course, but the people are very cheerful and don't mind talking about the very worst days. They're very friendly towards us, much more so, I think, than in 1938. As for the women, there is a respectability imposed by London which even a large number of floozies can't destroy." In addition to looking up old friends, Ellmann traced Yeats's footsteps in London and further afield, news that pleased his father.[55]

Admiral Alan G. Kirk, the director of the Office of Naval Intelligence, was also Commander of Naval Forces in Europe and had been the Senior US Naval Commander during the Normandy landing of June 6, 1944. Ellmann was excited to join his staff, having been posted to the Office as a translator. As he explained to his parents, this was "the best assignment I could possibly [have] as an enlisted man. . . . I hope I'll be able to carry it off allright. The officers are very decent, one of them being an old Yale man [McGeorge Bundy] whom I knew slightly before." Soon it became clear, however, that Ellmann was to be less a translator than a "factotum."[56] His immediate boss was Commander Donald J. Macdonald, the Plans Officer, whom he described to Ellsworth Mason as "the most bemedaled man in the Navy," also "a very good guy." Macdonald had been commander of the USS *O'Bannon,* a destroyer involved in the heaviest sea battles in World War II. One of Ellmann's jobs was to provide Macdonald with a draft of the foreword he was meant to write for a book about his experiences as a naval commander (the book was titled *Action Tonight,* written by James

Horan). "The last two pages are mostly mine," he wrote to Mason of the foreword, "the first page entirely his; he wisely removed some of my grandiloquence, which I had inserted I suppose to compensate for my complete ignorance of battle. There is a description of colors of battle, which I made up out of my own little head, and which seems to have been sufficiently exact to be left in."[57] By January, in addition to "factotum" duties, Ellmann was asked to provide French lessons on a formal basis to eight sailors, "while Mac Bundy, the admiral's Aide, took 10 more." The sessions were held from 8:15 to 9 in the morning every day except Sunday.[58]

Ellmann and the other enlisted men in the Office of Naval Intelligence were at first housed in private rooms in hotels. Then they were moved to the Château Louveciennes, in the western suburbs of Paris, some twelve miles from the city center. Ellmann was given a bed above the château garage. After a freezing winter, he and the other staffers were returned to the city, sleeping in bunks a mere 18 inches apart from each other. Still, "the city remains Paris . . . [so] these are hardly complaints."[59] Nor, for the same reason, were there many complaints when his superiors treated him as "office boy, chief file boy, ear banger extraordinaire."[60] Although the war had not yet ended, there is no indication from his correspondence that he found his work in the Office of Naval Intelligence to be of much use or interest.

Paris, however, was everything he had hoped for. In his first letter to his parents, written on September 29, he praised the friendliness of the people, though "I arrived too late for the orgies of kissing, unfortunately." His initial days were spent "visiting Mme. Monnier's bookshop, talking to as many Frenchmen as possible, being kind to French enfants." At Mme. Monnier's shop, La Maison des Amis des Livres, he inquired about Sylvia Beach, whose own bookshop, Shakespeare and Company, had closed during the Occupation. Beach interested Ellmann because she had published Joyce, but then so too had Monnier, in her journal *Le Navire d'Argent*. At Monnier's shop Ellmann met a Sorbonne student who took him to the Café de Flore and pointed out "a former French film producer, named, I think Prévert [Jacques Prévert, screenwriter and poet], and then told me Hemingway had been there only 2 weeks before."[61] When in October Ellmann finally met Sylvia Beach, he found her "very interested to hear about the new developments particularly in Joyce criticism," a subject Ellmann knew about because of his many conversations with Ellsworth Mason, who was soon to embark on his PhD on Joyce and Vico. "Her story about Joyce," Ellmann recounted to his parents, "was that someone had lifted the winding sheet at his funeral and he had opened one eye and said 'One world at a time! One world at a time!' Apparently a favorite expression."[62]

In the autumn of 1944, Paris was "swarming with GI's," and Ellmann counted himself lucky to have escaped requests for gum or cigarettes. Dealings on the black market were "assez commun," but chief among the deprivations he listed in correspondence were coal, newspapers (published only "irregularly"), and books (barely published at all—"because of the paper shortage"). He had remarkably little to say about the war ("too serious to write about") or current politics, except in respect to collaborators, who "can best be described as petulant, and not in the least defiant." On the Champs-Élysées, his "usual haunt," he falls into conversation with a man who tells him that during the Occupation "nobody starved" and that "there had been more Lumière, mais on ne vivait pas. Maintenant, on n'a rien, mais on vive encore." In the same letter to his parents, he reports that "cleavages" between rich and poor are "becoming more apparent, but "there's as yet no evidence that they're serious in the sense of portending future trouble."[63]

Ellmann's love life was complicated in this period. Shortly before Helen Manning's breakup letter of August 9, he had begun corresponding with a young woman named Julie Smith, whom he met late in the summer and who wrote to him on Vassar stationery (he may have met her through Connie Ellis, who taught English at Vassar).[64] At the end of August, Helen had second thoughts about the breakup and resumed corresponding with Ellmann. As usual, her letters were affectionate but bland, also nonliterary. Julie's letters are arch and extravagant and often about poetry. Ellmann wrote to them both in a mixture of French and English, teasing Julie but not Helen about possible "amorous successes." In an October 8 letter to Julie, he recounts a night "with the haut monde in a very lovely apartment on the Seine's rt bk with a couple of large Poussin canvases and the divorced wife of the former French naval attaché to Berlin." Also present on this occasion were "two charmantes daughters and a young poet of the resistance." They lend him "some Paul Claudel so I could find out why Auden says, 'And we will pardon Paul Claudel,/Pardon him for writing well.'"[65] To Helen, in a letter of October 11, he reports on the politics discussed that evening: "We drank Moët champagne and talked about Pétain, whom she and her friends are particularly anxious to defend, not because he did right, but because he's such a nice old man. But, though they say he was wrong, it is fairly obvious that they are très content that things have gone as they have and that French resistance has not resulted in the destruction of their proprieties." A few nights later, Ellmann continues, he attended a party given by Jewish organizations in honor of American servicemen. "The effect of the occupation was written plainer there than anywhere else in the city; the people were very poorly dressed, had horrible stories to tell of dispossession, kidnapping of children and parents and so forth. . . . The soldiers had contributed their week's rations to the Jewish children of the city."

The move to the Château Louveciennes in mid-October made evening engagements difficult, though it seems not to have cut down their number, judging by correspondence. When he discovered that Charles Feidelson had been in Paris for some time (in Army Ordnance, as a first lieutenant), Ellmann took him "to a nice party on the Seine's right bank, held by Liszt's great granddaughter (illegitimate), who is also great grandniece of Wagner."[66] Days later he writes of "a big party at the home of a man who owns the Salon de France—with champagne, pastries, and even ice cream. Through a lady I met there I'm to visit the niece of Marcel Proust, and possibly a member of the French Academy."[67] On another occasion he meets a woman who "got in touch with Paul Valéry, whom I was anxious to meet, and arranged for me to meet him this afternoon at the home of a friend who lives near us."[68] There was a mix-up about dates and Valéry did not appear. The friend, however, turned out to be Mlle. Jeanne Baudot, one of Renoir's pupils and models, "and the house in which she lived used to be Renoir's atelier." Ellmann meets Mlle. Baudot's nephew there, who was secretary to de Gaulle, as well as a French lady, head of the Alliance Française, who is a good friend of de Gaulle "and will soon go to London on a mission for him." Visits to the Rodin Museum were spent with its chief curator, Marcel Aubert, "who was at Yale much of the time I was there."[69] This was all rather different from USO dances in Charleston.

For a young man with Ellmann's interests, Paris post-Occupation was a cultural paradise, even in freezing winter:

> Art and literature thrive; Picasso had a whole room full of 74 paintings and 5 pieces of sculpture at the Salon d'Automne, which people thronged to see; someone tried to cut them up, fortunately without success, because of the presence of about 20 gendarmes.

> The book stalls still stand on the left bank; Notre Dame is intact though the windows have been removed; the Louvre is still minus most of its paintings, but in general, despite much mourning and many privations, the city has a festive air.[70]

The most memorable, if not the most comfortable, of Ellmann's social engagements was dinner with Mme. Suzanne Adrienne Mante, Proust's niece, who lived in a great stone house in the sixteenth arrondissement.[71] Mme. Mante was very rich. "The cloak room is larger than your living room," he reported to Helen. "We had some amontillado in a great salon with silk-covered fauteuils, elaborate tapestries, Italian primitives, and Oriental rugs; she introduced me to her two filles and one fils; the latter immediately informed me that he had no interest in literature. The daughters were 15 and 12 ½, the 12 ½ remarkably developed as a tight sweater made me aware (I mention this lest the evening seem too literary)." There are descriptions of a comparably lavish dining room on the next floor, "where we were served a very light, smooth consommé followed by poulet brought from the country and some chicory and lettuce, here very rare (the first salade since I came to France)." The party then ascended to the library, with its portrait of Proust, "and in a closet all his manuscripts . . . written in a gracefully casual hand, with many corrections, many of them long. The notebooks were of the same type but each had a name for a color, as in Cahier Bleu etc."[72] The papers are described with as much relish as the dinner.

Why Mme. Mante invited Ellmann to dinner he was not sure, aside from the fact that the Alliance Française woman "had spoken to her of me." In the letter to Helen he describes Mme. Mante as "a very striking woman with a slightly and delicately hooked nose not altogether unlike Proust's." "As the evening wore on I felt more and more that this was a salon of the de Guermantes and that I didn't know the code." Mme. Mante seemed to him "hospitable out of duty, as I perceived from the rather impassive look she wore even when seeming very interested. On the whole it was a relief to depart du côté de chez Mante."

Helen was impressed by "the high literary circles" Ellmann was moving in, though she remarked, "I don't know that I envy you—you may remember my views about Proust" (they were disapproving, as were her views on Baudelaire).[73] Shortly after that evening, Ellmann learned that Mme. Mante had been "a collaborationiste" and that her millionaire husband was in hiding, having profited handsomely during the Occupation. Ellmann reported to his parents that the Alliance Française woman thought Mme. Mante's interest in Americans "seemed to be an attempt to excuse herself," which is why she rarely sent any to her, "but because of my interest in Proust she had made an exception." "Just how she [Mme. Mante] and her husband reconciled their attitude with her at least partially semitic ancestry I have no idea."[74]

* * *

The most important of the literary contacts Ellmann made in Paris was with the Belgian-born poet and artist Henri Michaux (1899–1984), whose poems he would introduce and translate for New Directions in 1951. On his first visit to La Maison des Amis des Livres, Ellmann asked Adrienne Monnier and the writer and critic Maurice Saillet, her assistant, for something new to read: "Both proposed Michaux. When I learned that he was not only the author of *L'Espace du Dedans* [1944] but a painter as well, I went to see his work at the Galerie de la Rive Gauche. There, while I was examining paintings with headless torsos, or mouseheads for heads, or *têtes de monstres,* the artist came in and startled me by having a human head, indeed a Roman, a senatorial head, framing legislation undreamt of by Cato."[75] Writing to his parents of this first meeting, Ellmann described how "a rather thin, rather ineffectual, rather lost human being came in, and the proprietor said to me sotto voce that it was Michaux! I introduced myself and we left together; he invited me for a drink and then to his house, but I had another appointment. He was very genial, very unaffected, and told me that he had never been translated into English. So I'm going to write and ask him if he wants to be."[76]

Throughout his career, Ellmann's boldness, as well as his ability to attract and hold the trust of people he had just met, proved invaluable. "I introduced myself and we left together." "So I'm going to write and ask him." A week later Ellmann reported to his parents that he had made his request and that Michaux "immediately agreed." Michaux then introduced Ellmann to René Bertelé, the newly appointed editor of the French literary review *Confluences*.[77] Also immediately impressed, Bertelé asked Ellmann to write an article for *Confluences* on the state of American letters, "which I'm doing. These jobs require all my spare time, needless to say."[78] The next day Ellmann met with Michaux and his wife at an exhibition of paintings

Henri Michaux.

by Henri Rousseau (many of them fake, according Michaux's wife). He then accompanied Michaux and his wife and several friends to the Café de Flore, which was even more jammed with writers than usual, "since it's warm enough so that they can do their work there; and in cold weather like this, their homes are unbearably cold. So you see people with manuscripts all over the place."[79]

That Michaux wrote poems in prose as well as verse, taking on Baudelaire's challenge of "prose poétique," was part of his attraction for Ellmann, as it was to the French avant-garde. By 1944 his fame as poet seemed to Ellmann equivalent to that of Sartre as dramatist and Camus as novelist. He was "the most representative-of-our-time poet I have read," "the favorite of the French literary avant-garde." His fame, however, was relatively recent. Although his poems had been known and admired by a small group since about 1926, he only gained what Ellmann called "official recognition" in 1940, when André Gide was stopped by the Nazis from delivering a lecture about him, then published an expanded version of the lecture as a small book, *Découvrons Henri Michaux* (1941).[80]

The strangeness of Michaux's poems, how hard they are to describe or interpret, intrigued Ellmann, who was always drawn to difficulty. In attempting to explain them, he stressed Michaux's "habit of casting psychological insights into physical instead of mental terms, or into a system of images which at first appear arbitrary."[81] In one sense Michaux could be described as an allegorical writer, "in that he finds the internal world more important than the external one," but unlike most allegorical writers he was "unable or unwilling to keep the two separate. They merge disconcertingly." The dreamlike quality of Michaux's poems "comes upon the reader unawares," their surreal or phantasmagoric quality can be likened to sections of *Ulysses* (the "Circe" chapter in particular) or *Finnegans Wake,* though they are written in a style as clear and concrete as possible, quite unlike the styles of late Joyce. As Ellmann puts it: "His words are as severely constricted in their meaning as his pictures in their detail. . . . For all his stylistic freedom, he rigidly disavows those metaphorical connotations and allusions that most contemporary poets insist upon. With Michaux, the poetry is not in the metaphor of words, but of situations. The statement itself is prosaic, but the tensions created are ultimately equivalent to those created by poems."

The writer to whom Ellmann most frequently compares Michaux is Kafka. Michaux might not be as "profound" as Kafka but he is more "subtle." The themes and mannerisms they share include "the poker face," "the use of spatial images to describe parts of the personality," a "casual way of describing the preposterous which is, after all, not so preposterous," the frequency of "the unexpected," the way "unknown or scarcely known forces dominate helplessly resisting or unresisting characters," the "veneer of logicality," and "the steady light of a sardonic humor, which restores a kind of equilibrium, a kind of normalcy, imparts detachment, and in the end suggests that man is more than a creature thrown into a mine without tools, flashlight, or map."[82] Other Kafka-like qualities Ellmann might have mentioned are the obscure locations in which the poems are set, the unreality of real locations, the prevalence of monsters and dangers, and the fragility or weakness of those they threaten.

Where Michaux differs from Kafka, according to Ellmann, is in "implying no general guilt; he posits no god or devil to explain what is going on in the world. Instead he clearly and clinically presents the algebra of suffering; in spare, almost antiseptic terms, he works out the equation: man being man, here is what happens."[83] The suffering in question is sometimes depicted as a product of external forces, as in Kafka ("It began when I was a child," announces Michaux. "There was a big adult in the way"), but it is also internal in origin, a product of the self's instability. What makes the external world threatening derives ultimately from this instability. In Ellmann's words, when the "fluid, elastic self attempts to come to grips with the world of objects, it is necessarily incapable of dominating them; they slip away. The attitude of the poems is one of non-acceptance of the world, of constant struggle against disintegration by the world."[84] This sense of the self's fragility or disunity, with resulting "extreme states of consciousness and perceptual disorder," connects Michaux to French predecessors, listed by Malcolm Bowie as Nerval, Corbière, Lautréamont, Rimbaud, "and a multitude of lesser solitaries."[85]

Michaux the man was as intriguing to Ellmann as Michaux the poet. When Michaux met Ellmann, he described Joyce as "the most *fermé* [closed off], disconnected from humanity, of men" (*JJ*, 574). Michaux's disconnection from humanity was less a matter of being closed up than of an unworldly otherness or oddity. Ellmann recalled a remark Michaux made at an art exhibition they both attended (Michaux was "suffering as usual from a thousand and one maladies"),[86] an exhibition sponsored by Gertrude Stein. Like Ellmann, Michaux had attended the exhibition out of curiosity about Miss Stein rather than about the English painter she was sponsoring. "She did not disappoint him," writes Ellmann, "but the exhibition did." When asked by another of the exhibition's sponsors what his opinion was of the English painter, Michaux replied politely: "It's very hard for me to say, because you see I suffer from daltonism, which prevents my distinguishing between his reds and his greens. But I can make out his blues, and they seem to me very fine." When this response was relayed to Ellmann, it opened "a chink" into the poet's consciousness, "with its fanatical interest in diseases, its refusal to play any predictable role, least of all that of objective critic, its transformation of both art and art-observer into the aimless, preposterous, inane and yet sensuous games of children."[87]

An example of Michaux's "prose poétique"—one that Ellmann, in his first excitement after reading and meeting the poet, sent to both Helen and Julie—is "Nuit de Noces." He sent it in French, calling it "helpful advice for all nubile ladies" (in the letter to Julie) and "interesting advice" (in the letter to Helen).[88] Here it is in Ellmann's English translation:

BRIDAL NIGHT

If on your marriage day, returning home, you set your wife in a well to soak for the night, she will be dumbfounded. No comfort to her now that she has always had a vague uneasiness . . .

"There now!" she will say, "so that's what it is then, marriage. That's why they keep the manner of it so secret. I've let myself be taken in."

But being vexed, she will say nothing. That is why you will be able to dip her for long periods and many times, without causing any scandal in the neighborhood.

If she has not understood the first time, she has little likelihood of understanding later, and you will have a great many occasions to continue without incident (bronchitis excepted), if that still interests you.

As for me, as I suffer even more in others' bodies than my own, I have had to give it up quickly.

To Helen, he also sent the second section of a poem called "Magie" ("Magic"):

As soon as I saw her I wanted her.

And first, to seduce her, I spread out plains and plains. The plains which emerged from my look lay out full length, soft, pleasant, reassuring.

The idea of plains went forth to meet her, and without knowing it, she walked about on them, and was content there.

When I had sufficiently reassured her, I possessed her.

That done, and after some rest and relaxation, resuming my natural manner, I allowed my spears, my rags, my precipices to reappear.

She felt a sudden chill and that she had been completely taken in by me.

She went off with a hollow and defeated look, as if somebody had robbed her.

Sometime shortly after receiving these poems, in an undated letter, Helen wrote to Ellmann "to reemphasize my former doubts": "There have been special circumstances: the war, and the fact that we were both lonely, and our naturally excitable temperaments, which have made it hard to see clearly. In thinking things over, I'm not at all sure we're a good match, partly because I can't see in either of us the great romantic figure which I think you tend to create. . . . I'd rather not get into a lengthy discussion of this through the Transatlantic Mail, but I do want to keep you from constructing in your mind what is really a highly unlikely future. Sorry." Ellmann's response, written on Christmas Day, offers a glimpse of the "excitable temperament" Helen attributes to them both, though there is little evidence of such temperament elsewhere in his correspondence. After agreeing that she is "perfectly right and that our incompatibilities are superabundant and that we would never hit it off," he "objects mildly" to being called a romantic, "since though I romanticize I am not in the least (as you surely must realize at times even in that oversimplified universe of yours where I have felt completely at home) a romanticist." The objection is Michaux-like in its depiction of mental states in physical terms, in its sudden or unexpected admission of weakness ("where I have felt completely at home"), and in its sardonic irony. The letter ends, however, with a blow: "The tepidity of your letters I could excuse, but not the dullness." It is signed: "Your loving—Richard."

* * *

It was Sylvia Beach who had paved the way with Michaux. Ellmann recounted that at his first encounter with the poet, "I told him I knew Sylvia Beach and he said she had mentioned me to him."[89] Soon, though, there were problems. On March 21, 1945, Ellmann reports to his parents that he had seen Sylvia Beach the night before, that she described his translations as "wonderful," also complimenting him (as had Michaux) on his article in *Confluences* on American literature.[90] She then proceeded to point out errors in his translations, mentioning the fact that someone else was translating Michaux as well. What worried Beach, Ellmann decides, was "that Michaux's personal liking for me would enable me to get hold of all the rights; something which had not occurred to me." To Julie Smith, two days later, Ellmann complains of how complicated "the Michaux business" was becoming, "not from the point of view of translation but of my relations with le monde littéraire, and especially Sylvia Beach, who is trying to cut in on me by translating him herself, after telling me my translations were wonderful. She seems to have pretty complete control over the French literary world."[91] Writing to his parents on March 29, he reports that his translations of Michaux "have somehow engaged me in a first class literary squabble with Sylvia Beach, who has decided she wants to discover him herself, and is a very sharp tradeswoman."

What was required was for Ellmann to reassure Beach that his intentions in translating Michaux were purely literary. Once he provided Beach with this reassurance, good relations resumed, which was a matter of some importance in later years, given the crucial role Beach had played in Joyce's life, most clearly in publishing *Ulysses*. Between 1946 and the publication in 1951 of Ellmann's translations as *L'Espace du Dedans: The Space Within: Selected Writings,* Ellmann shaped the volume's reception by placing translations of individual poems in influential American periodicals: *Partisan Review, Kenyon Review, Sewanee Review, Poetry,* and *Furioso*. James Laughlin, founding editor of New Directions, the volume's publisher, wrote that "it was Dick's book which made Michaux in this country, by its sensitive translations and perhaps even more by the long introduction which so brilliantly analysed Michaux's writing in terms of his life, personality and literary background."[92]

* * *

One final episode from Ellmann's time in Paris is worth recounting. On the night of March 9, 1945, six days before his twenty-seventh birthday, the Stage Door Canteen in Paris had its grand opening.[93] Among the notables attending the opening were General Pierre Koenig, commander of the Free French at the Normandy landings and military advisor to General De Gaulle; Duff Cooper, the British ambassador; Lady Diana Cooper; "and all the colonels and brigadier generals in the various armies and their wives." One of these commanders was Ellmann's boss, Admiral Kirk. On the afternoon of the opening, Ellmann and a fellow staffer from Naval Intelligence were passing the canteen, and when Ellmann remarked "that it was a pity we couldn't go," the staffer revealed that before the war he had worked at the Stage Door Canteen in New York and that he still had his employee's identification card. "So we pushed our way past a lot of forbidding-looking guards to the office of the manager, the Vicomte somebody or other, and demanded an invitation; he said there would be no table for us, since all were already taken, but we could 'circuler.' We gladly agreed."

Ellmann and the staffer, Lou Myers, who was later a cartoonist for the *New Yorker,* arrived early and watched the celebrity guests file in. They then did their best to find a table, despite the manager's warnings. As Ellmann described it, passing near the stage he "noticed three soldiers, sitting as close as possible to it. I said 'How did you get here?' And they explained that

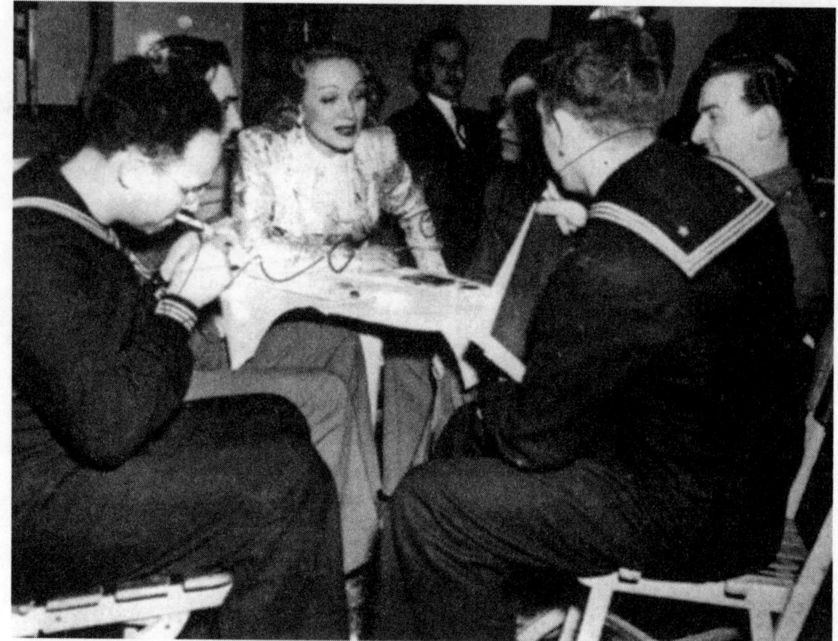

Ellmann (left) with Marlene Dietrich, Noel Coward, and Lou Myers at the opening of the Stage Door Canteen, Paris, March 9, 1945.

they were working the microphone system; hearing that we had no table they invited us to join them." Ellmann bribed a French attendant to find them some chairs, "and we were soon installed in the best seats in the house." Shortly afterward, Admiral Kirk walked in and was given a table "not nearly so close as we were." Ellmann describes the glance he got from the admiral as "stupefied and slightly piercing."

The evening's entertainers were Noel Coward and Maurice Chevalier. Before the war Myers had been a graphic artist and caricaturist. He drew a caricature of Coward, which he asked him to sign. Coward signed: "May God forgive you. Noel Coward." On stage, Coward sang "Mad Dogs and Englishmen," "Nina from Argentina," and ended "with something in French on France." The surprise of the evening was Marlene Dietrich, recently returned from the front. "She sang several of her old standbys, 'I've been in love before' (though not the German ones, of course) and some new ones in that peculiarly sensual, throaty voice of hers." Then Chevalier came on "and brought the house down."

The photographers at the opening included several from American publications and news agencies, including the Associated Press and *Life* magazine. A request was made for photos of Dietrich with some GIs. "We were the only GIs there, so she sat down at the table, held somebody's hand, the pictures were taken; she said 'Who will dance with me?' I offered myself up and that is the way I came to dance with Marlene Dietrich."[94] To Frank Ellis, in a newsy letter of April 15, 1945, Ellmann reported, "My own activities have been limited to making myself famous, which I achieved in my usual quiet way by grabbing the first dance with Marlene Dietrich at the vernissage of the Paris Stage Door Canteen, thus spattering my picture all over America."

Within a month the war in Europe was over.

CHAPTER FOUR

Yeats

For all his love of Paris, by the spring of 1945 Ellmann was ready for a change. Bored with his work at the Office of Naval Intelligence, he began agitating for a transfer and a commission. "The Navy is very wearing," he writes on April 15 to a friend in North Carolina, "and unless I get a commission soon, I shall feel a complete galley slave. The commission is a possibility because the Admiral recommended me, but I haven't much faith in my naval star."[1] Admiral Kirk's recommendation was unsurprising, given his reaction to "a little light verse poem" Ellmann had written requesting leave for the office "crew." "He liked it so much he distributed it around the command and also at a big dinner party he had."[2]

The poem, "Plea of the Gobs among the Gobelins" ("Gob" is a slang term for sailor), is worth quoting for the affectionate fun it pokes at both Paris and London. "Zigzig" in the first quatrain means sexual intercourse (what "TD" means in the last quatrain is unclear[3]):

"PLEA OF THE GOBS AMONG THE GOBELINS"

We are weary of zigzig and cognac
        And Paris and Louveciennes,
We long for the sound of the buzz bombs,
        And the daughters of Englishmen.

The champagne has lost its savor,
        The folies no longer enthrall,
We long for the 'alf and 'alf flavor,
        The toffs and the tarts of Pall Mall,

The hacks and the haitches of Limehouse,
        The clubs and the pubs of Soho,
We are weary of 'je ne comprends pas,'
        And women who never say no.

So far from the arms of our loved ones,
        So distant from kippers and gin,
With the gloomier prospect before us
        Of guttural sounds in Berlin,

We hereby request, Mr. Cragg, you
        Indulge these poor lads of the sea,
Who've nothing at all for amusement
        But two demoiselles on each knee.

And send us in pairs, in a series,
        To the hops and the ha'pence and haze,
For TD (not VD) to London
        For a year or a month or ten days.

In addition to this verse plea, Ellmann enlisted the help of his friend Norman Pearson in getting a move to London. At a chance meeting with Pearson and James Angleton in Paris, Ellmann made clear his dissatisfaction with his work at the Office of Naval Intelligence. When Pearson sought to have him transferred to his X-2 division of the London office of the OSS, Ellmann wrote to thank him, adding, "It is possible that a request from OSS would even help the commission along, provided it was made clear that the work required officer competence." Neither Pearson's request nor the admiral's letter succeeded in getting Ellmann a commission, "again on the grounds of eyesight."[4] But Pearson did succeed eventually in bringing him to London. On May 13, 1945, Ellmann wrote to his parents with the news: "Though I like Paris better, the fact that I will escape from typewriter and filing cabinet and that I will not have to think of an evening as a method of compensation for a day's ignominy and pettiness is all-important."

There are few details of Ellmann's work in London. In later years he played it down as "very secret and very dull."[5] In an article on literary espionage in the *New York Times,* Eliot Weinberger listed Ellmann as one of the literary types recruited by Pearson and Angleton. The article appeared in 1992, three years after Ellmann's death, and when Erwin Ellmann read it, he wrote to the *Times* describing it as "a confection of fact and fancy." "So far as I am aware," Erwin writes of his brother, "he never undertook an intelligence mission in or outside Britain, never collaborated with a bona fide agent, and never served as more than an insignificant rather helpless cog in a bureaucratic agency."[6]

A somewhat different view is offered by Robin Winks, in *Cloak and Gown: Scholars in the Secret War, 1939–1961,* who writes that in his time in London, "Dick was put in charge of investigating an English agent who took a French mistress after parachuting into France, and he also had to investigate an American agent who took up with the same mistress."[7] Winks provides no source, and there is no reference to these investigations among Ellmann's papers. There are, however, references in his correspondence to the importance of the work he was doing in London. To Feidelson, Ellmann described his job as "very interesting and not menial." To brother Bill he described it as "most interesting, involving all my language qualifications and some mental effort as well; and you can imagine how it feels not to have to type or file or draw rations for somebody else."[8] When in July 1945 the columnist Arthur Krock wrote an opinion piece in the *Times* favorable to the OSS, Ellmann described the article to his parents as "probably induced by his [Krock's] affection for the big businessmen Congress is said to be attacking." Conceding that some personnel "might have been picked more wisely, in expectation of this criticism," Ellmann went on to defend the OSS, which had "done pretty well notwithstanding."[9]

One task Ellmann was given amused him. Pearson decided that he was the only person in X-2 who knew how to spell and that therefore he should have the job of writing out citations for bronze and silver stars. What made this job difficult was that nothing about what had earned the citations could be revealed. As Winks puts it, with the bias of an academic historian, "they had to consist of elaborated boilerplate, which required the skills of a literary critic." After writing more than a hundred citations, Ellmann was ordered by Pearson "to write one up for himself" ("For unusual skill in the accomplishment of a difficult task in the European Theater"), an order he described in a letter to Julie Smith as "a reductio ad absurdum" of the "awards and decorations racket": "It's the last irony and therefore I accepted it more in jollity than pride. I'm convinced it would have been better for me had I never learned how to spell, since spelling is undoubtedly the virtue which earned me this job. I expect now to do rather more essential work, but chiefly to relax for a while."[10]

This expectation seems to have been met. On September 6, in a letter to his parents, Ellmann describes his new work as "very interesting with much greater responsibility."[11] That he does not disclose its nature is not surprising. Ellmann's habitual discretion and reserve were reinforced in the OSS and in the office of the Coordinator of Information (COI). They were also crucial to his career as a biographer, as we shall see. To give a single example: when in 1956 he gained access to the papers of Joyce's brother Stanislaus, a protracted business involving many interested parties, Ellmann wrote to his friend Ellsworth Mason that it was "absolutely essential that the secret of their contents be guarded. I will be able to make this clearer shortly. I begin to talk as if I were an intelligence agent. But please don't write any library or Joyceans about the stuff for the present."[12] Mason's response was: "The OSS has you in its thrall."[13] Ellmann was serious, though, begging Mason to "indulge my OSS mentality for a few weeks longer."[14] What made Stanislaus's papers so important was that Stanislaus "undoubtedly came closer to writing Joyce's books than anybody except Joyce."[15] To his publishers, with the Stanislaus papers chiefly in mind, he reported that he had come away from Europe "overladen with secrets of all descriptions."[16]

* * *

Ellmann spent five months in the London office of the OSS, from the end of May until mid-October 1945. One great perk of the job was that he was no longer required to wear a uniform, "The point of the mufti," he wrote to his parents on June 19, 1945, "is that I have a fairly responsible job and no one would listen to me were I obviously an enlisted man." To brother Bill, a week later, he admitted, "It's a great relief to me, since my contempt for those above me has just about gone off the deep end." This contempt for superiors figures also in Ellmann's observations about British politicians, the general election in July being "the big news here." In Marylebone, where he lodged, Ellmann attended all the hustings, reporting in his letters on the local candidates. The Tory incumbent, Alec Cunningham-Reid, he wrote to Julie Smith on July 3, missed a thousand out of twelve hundred divisions (votes) during the last session; was involved in an adulterous affair with the billionaire tobacco heiress Doris Duke; fled to Hawaii once the war started; was expelled from the Conservative Party; and was now running as an Independent Conservative. The "official" Conservative, Sir William Wavell Wakefield, "can't answer any questions, even the easy ones—tries to bulldoze the crowd—and if he gets in will owe it all to the Conservative Party machine and more particularly to Churchill." Only the Labour candidate, a doctor named Elizabeth Jacobs, impressed him. Although "not especially personable as a speaker [she] is loved by thousands of people whom she has helped with free medical care." Sir William, the official Tory candidate, won the seat, though Labour, described by Ellmann as "more serious" than the other parties, won the election. In a letter of June 26, written to brother Bill ten days before the elections, Ellmann described Churchill as having fought "a dirty campaign, accusing the laborites of wanting to bring to England a Gestapo, referring to the false charge that [Harold] Laski advocated overthrow of the govt by violence." Laski was chair of the Labour Party and Jewish. After the election, on a trip to the Lake District, Ellmann found himself in the company of a Tory colonel who "kept referring to Laski as 'those foreigners—as I like to call them.'" In recounting this anecdote in a later letter to Smith, Ellmann observed that "the interesting thing about the British upper classes is that they actually act just as their caricaturists say."[17]

In addition to attending hustings, Ellmann often spent evenings at the theater. He saw Gielgud's *Hamlet, The Merchant of Venice* ("the tendency to sentimentalize Shylock, which Henry Irving started, persists"), *A Doll's House, Rosmersholm, The Alchemist, She Stoops to Conquer,* Shaw's *Getting Married,* and a rare production of Joyce's *Exiles.* On weekends he went on trips, not only to the Lake District, but to Stratford, where he saw *Antony and Cleopatra,* and to Buckinghamshire, where he cycled around historic churches, visited the Quaker meeting house where William Penn was buried, and met "some English girls, one of them an Amazon, and a Communist, who practically wore me out bicycling up hill and down dale."[18] On a trip to Cambridge he visited Hersch Lauterpacht, later Sir Hersch Lauterpacht, Whewell Professor of International Law at Cambridge, who would assist in the prosecution of Nazi defendants at Nuremberg and would play a crucial role in establishing the legal status of the concepts of genocide and crimes against humanity.

It was James Ellmann's secretary in Detroit, a relative of Lauterpacht's wife, who suggested that Ellmann contact him. In Cambridge, Ellmann also looked up G. M. Trevelyan, master of Trinity College, who invited him to breakfast (an invitation that astonished Lauterpacht, a Trinity fellow). The introduction to Trevelyan had been arranged by the English Speaking Union (ESU), an educational organization set up in 1918 to which Ellmann belonged. Its headquarters were at Dartmouth House, a grand eighteenth-century building in Mayfair not far from the offices of X-2. Ellmann also belonged to the Churchill Club in Westminster, a social club set up for American servicemen. Between them, both institutions, "run by wealthy old ladies," offered welcome amenities: lectures, concerts, cheap meals, cheap drinks, the use of libraries, and introductions (to Trevelyan, but also to the colonel in the Lake District who spoke of "those foreigners"). At the Churchill Club, Ellmann was "roped into" leading a discussion on American poetry.[19] The only other literary event he reports on from this period was a memorial ceremony for Paul Valéry, to which he was taken by Pearson, "my boss." Speakers included T. S. Eliot, C. Day Lewis, and the Anglo-French writer and critic Denis Saurat. "It reminded me of how the old man [Valéry], when he found out I wrote verse, addressed me several times as 'mon jeune collègue.'"[20]

Although Ellmann complained that there were fewer talks and readings in London than in Paris, he had no complaints about the literary background of his bosses and colleagues at the offices of X-2 (located in St. James, at 14 Ryder Street, in a building shared with MI6). Pearson's literary circle included T. S. Eliot, the Sitwells, Graham Greene, Elizabeth Bowen, E. M. Forster, Norman Douglas, Compton Mackenzie, and the imagist poet H.D. and her cousin/companion Bryher (the pen name of Winifred Ellerman). Angleton, a founding editor of *Furioso,* listed Ellmann as one of his four closest literary friends at Yale (the others were E. Reed Whittemore, Andrews Wanning, and Eugene O'Neill Jr.). In London, Angleton lunched with his MI6 friend Kim Philby, drank with William Empson, and dined with T. S. Eliot.[21] Angleton's secretary was H.D.'s daughter Perdita. Angleton's later description of counterintelligence as "a wilderness of mirrors" comes from Eliot's poem "Gerontion." His connection with Eliot and with other literary figures in London owed much to Ezra Pound, whom he had visited in Rapallo as an undergraduate. In 1939, the year *Furioso* was launched, Pound visited New Haven, where he advised Angleton and his *Furioso* coeditor Whittemore about the magazine's contents and helped to secure several of its best-known contributors.[22]

About a month before his time in London came to an end, Ellmann asked Pearson for a week's leave, his first leave in over a year. The war in Europe had ended four months earlier and neutral Ireland had relaxed its entry restrictions on American servicemen. Ellmann wanted the leave to go to Dublin to meet Yeats's widow. Pearson told him to take two weeks. Ellmann's request for leave was prudent: with the war ended, it was not clear what would happen to the London office of X-2 (there were rumors that it would be disbanded). In addition, Ellmann's chances of a Navy discharge were "fairly remote," at least according to the Navy's points system for demobilization. He might end up back in uniform, "which would be hard to bear."[23] It made sense to visit Ireland while he was still in London.

* * *

Mrs. Yeats (Georgie Hyde-Lees, "George" to her husband, whom Yeats had married in 1917, when she was twenty-five and he fifty-two) was a notoriously poor correspondent, something Ellmann had not known when he wrote to her, but she answered his letter, agreeing to see him in Dublin. In explaining his good fortune, Ellmann guessed that his "must have been the first letter from a serviceman and an American that she had received since the war was over." (That George Yeats was English rather than Irish may also have worked in his favor, he later speculated.)[24] Their first meeting was at the Royal Dublin Society exhibition, at her stall advertising the Cuala Press (set up in 1908 by Yeats and his sisters Elizabeth and Lily). At the exhibition, "she encouraged me to come to tea the next day at her home in the south Dublin suburb of Rathmines."[25] As Ellmann puts it in the preface to the 1979 reprint of *Yeats: The Man and the Masks* (1948), which was a minimally revised version of his Yale dissertation, the first sight of Mrs. Yeats's study, which had been her husband's, was amazing. "There in the bookcase was his working library, often heavily annotated, and in cabinets and file cases were all his manuscripts, arranged with care by the widow."[26] In an unpublished account of the visit he provides further details:

> It turned out that there were also all the manuscripts for Yeats's book, *A Vision,* in cupboards underneath some of the bookshelves. I told her I was interested in the Golden Dawn, and she then produced a crate full of Yeats's regalia, including ceremonial robes and talismans. It also

contained some of the rituals of the Order. She showed me some other papers which had to do with his earlier experiments in ritual, including a journal of his work at the Blavatsky Lodge in London. I copied as much as I could and returned several times in the course of the next two weeks. On my last visit I said I would like to come back and she said "I hope you will."[27]

Although meeting Mrs. Yeats was the main reason for Ellmann's visit to Dublin, she was by no means the only person he wished to interview. He wrote also to Yeats's younger brother Jack, the painter; to his sisters Elizabeth and Lily; to Maud Gonne MacBride, "a wonderful old lady of 80, with

Mrs. W. B. Yeats, at Ballylee, 1930.

a young voice and a sweetness and a simplicity that one does not expect in people of her age"; to Joseph Hone, "Yeats's biographer," who gave him "a lot of stuff" (perhaps because Ellmann described his work as "a thesis on W. B. Yeats and his intellectual background," as opposed to a biography);[28] to Richard Hayes, the director of the National Library of Ireland, who was a friend of Norman Pearson (and who lent him a typewriter during his stay); and to Douglas Hyde, the recently retired president of Ireland under Éamon de Valera, among other things a key figure in the Irish cultural revival. In his letter to Hyde, Ellmann wrote: "Since you played so outstanding a role in both literary and political life in Eire, it would be of inestimable value to me if you would grant me an interview."[29] Of the literary people Ellmann wrote to, the most forthcoming was the novelist Sean O'Faolain, one of several "astonishingly capable writers, who find their subject matter in the 'troubles' of the last 50 years."[30] "The only refusals," Ellmann wrote to his parents on August 29, "were from a sister [of Yeats], on the grounds that she's an invalid, which I guess is true, and from Douglas Hyde, who I'm told is in his second childhood, and who also pleaded invalidism." From other Dublin writers, described by Yeats as "fleas on other fleas' backs,'" Ellmann reported hearing "a whole stream of vicious anecdotes about W. B. and others."[31]

* * *

Shortly after his return to London on September 27, 1945, in an excited letter to his parents, Ellmann described the Dublin visit as "of great importance." Far from being "difficult to deal with," Mrs. Yeats "turned out to be a very intelligent and sympathetic woman." On the day before he left Dublin, she said to him: "'You know, you're the first person who's been here who has read Yeats.'" Ellmann took her to mean read Yeats extensively, but she replied, "'No, I mean understood him.' She explained that she had realized from my questions and comments that I had grasped what I had described to her as the central position of mysticism in his work, the point from which everything else came." Her approval gave Ellmann what he called "my thesis," a term that in this context means both main argument and dissertation.[32] For Ellmann in 1945, the mystical or occult aspects of Yeats's intellectual background mattered not only because they mattered to Yeats, being "the point from which everything else came," but because he would be the first scholar to explore them in detail, making his dissertation an original contribution to knowledge and thus worthy of a doctorate. And not only a doctorate. Mrs. Yeats's support raised a grander possibility: "In concrete terms, this meant that she showed me a wealth of material in manuscript that nobody else has ever seen, that she gave me leads that nobody else has had. And that, in short, she is giving me a chance to write the first definitive or semi-definitive book on him."[33]

* * *

The most important of the "materials in manuscript" Mrs. Yeats showed Ellmann was an unpublished preface Yeats wrote to his collection of essays, *Ideas of Good and Evil* (1903). Ellmann had asked her "if there was any truth to the story that when Joyce, then 20 years old, met Yeats, who was an established writer in his late thirties, Joyce said to him 'You are too old for me to help you.' Mrs. Yeats said, it's true that in later life both men denied that it happened, but look at this." She then showed Ellmann the unpublished preface, where Yeats had included the incident. Young Joyce's remark had a personal meaning for Ellmann, as he later recalled. "As all mild men must [be], I was delighted by this arrogance; it made me look into the several meetings that Joyce and Yeats had after that."[34] In the preface to the first edition of *James Joyce,* Ellmann went further: "My book had its origin at that time" (p. vii).

Ellmann held fast to his conviction that Yeats's unpublished preface confirmed that Joyce had made the debated remark, despite subsequent denials and powerful rival accounts. The extent to which Ellmann's "delight" in the remark derived from his claim of being a mild man is worth considering. "For all his mildness of manner," writes one observer, Ellmann was "one of the canniest literary detectives of any decade."[35] He was one of the most ambitious as well. In an essay on Ellmann, a student of his, Henry Hart, later a professor of English, described his "Buddha-like calm and compassion," but also stressed his "keen sense for rivalry. Like most ambitious men he was fiercely competitive, although he usually managed to hide his competitiveness under the aplomb of a gentleman." Hart recalls hearing Ellmann praise the young John McEnroe, a tennis player as arrogant as young Joyce. When, at a party, the critic Christopher Ricks beat Ellmann at table tennis, accusing him of "not having a piranha instinct," Ellmann's reaction, Hart recalls, was "to laugh in a way that indicated Ricks was wrong."[36] Gentle and courteous when corresponding with potential interviewees, Ellmann was also patient, persistent, and calculating. A newly hired junior colleague recalls Ellmann's explanation for appearing, unannounced, at one of his lectures (Ellmann claimed to be interested in the junior colleague's take on Wallace Stevens's "Sunday Morning," whose ending "I've never been entirely convinced by"). "Perfect Ellmann," the colleague writes, "diffidence and flattery as a way out of an awkward situation. Of course, he was checking on me, but it also struck me that he had a copy of my syllabus, so he knew where I was that day."[37]

These instances, easily multiplied, are from later periods in Ellmann's life, when he was much lionized. At the time of the Dublin visit, he had reason to see himself as a mild man, as opposed to a man with a mild manner. Choosing the safety of an academic career, New Haven over Paris, had felt like a surrender; the breakup with Helen Manning had been humiliating, in part because it seemed to prove his father right. Both episodes involved concessions to parental influence and authority. In the Navy and intelligence services, he spent his time catering to the needs of those above him, officers, heads of station.[38] The PhD he was at work on was meant to be original, but it also needed to meet the requirements of his examiners. In Dublin, he spent two weeks "proving to Mrs. Yeats that I was the brightest of the flock of young and old who have come to pick up old bones at the shrine" (where "flock" suggests pigeons or sheep).[39] In each of these areas of his life, instead of defying or challenging authority, as had young Joyce, Ellmann bent to it, or so he felt. To others, however, Ellmann's mildness, including in his early years, was on the surface. In an undated letter of reference, probably written in late 1946, Robert French, master of Jonathan Edwards College at Yale, recommended Ellmann in the following terms: "Thoughtful and quiet in his manners, he commands the respect and affection of those with whom he associates. In a remarkably brilliant group of friends he held a position of influence, to which his sound judgment of men contributed largely."[40]

How Yeats himself reacted to Joyce's remark is worth thinking about in this context. In *James Joyce* Ellmann claims Yeats was "pleased" with "this young man who talked back to him" (p. 101). In a letter of January 10, 1955, to Stanislaus Joyce, who disputed the remark's having been made, or made in the manner described in the unpublished preface to *Ideas of Good and Evil,* Ellmann writes of having been "steadily impressed by the number of stories I collected about [Yeats's] delight in young men who disagreed with him, patronized him, corrected him." This delight Ellmann attributes not to mildness but to its opposite: Yeats's "own rather intimidating manner and considerable reputation." As a result, "most people [were] too diffident in his presence, so that I feel sure he would have welcomed outspokenness." What complicates this account is that in *Yeats: The Man and the Masks,* Ellmann several times describes Yeats's "intimidating manner" as defensive, the product of underlying shyness and self-doubt, of a man who "hid his timidity under arrogance."[41] Had the Yeats book been a biography proper as opposed to a study of "intellectual background," Ellmann might well have included an anecdote he recorded from a July 14, 1946, interview with Frank O'Connor. Arriving at a crowded party at the Yeats's home in Rathmines, O'Connor was summoned by Mrs. Yeats to sit beside her. O'Connor's report: "'It was nice of you to pick me out,' I said, and she replied, 'I knew you were embarrassed because you put your hands through your hair the same way Willie does when he's shy.' Then I understood and I would watch for that gesture, which meant that he was putting the mask on to hide the fact that he was ill at ease."[42] By the date Ellmann recorded O'Connor's anecdote, on a second research trip to Dublin, the dissertation's main argument had altered. What constituted "the point from which everything else came" was no longer Yeats's occult interests per se, but what they revealed about the importance and ubiquity of masks and dual or divided personalities, not only in Yeats's life and work, but in the lives and works of many of his contemporaries. A detailed account of Yeats's spiritual or occult influences and enthusiasms would remain at the center of the dissertation but would now be woven into a larger pattern. How Ellmann came to recognize the importance of this pattern he explains in an unpublished recollection of a conversation with Mrs. Yeats:

> I remember talking with Mrs. Yeats about her husband's work, and asking her whether there was any specific model for Michael Robartes [a character in Yeats's early poems and stories], whom Maud Gonne had told me was to be identified with Mathers [MacGregor Mathers, a British occultist]. Mrs. Yeats said "Oh it's just self and anti-self." This idea took hold of me, and I began to see how Yeats's early novel, *John Sherman,* could also be seen as a similar battle. For Mrs. Yeats the battle could be denominated as that between the Pollexfen and the Yeats side of the family [Yeats's mother Susan was a Pollexfen, "silent, instinctive, deep-feeling";

> his father, J. B. Yeats, in contrast, was "affable, argumentative, opinionative"]. Michael Robartes was the mother's and Aherne [another character, Owen Aherne] the more conventional spirit, with the father's. What I did was to try to see this battle in Yeats. . . . I gradually realized that one could see Yeats working on various aspects of this antinomy, and in attempting to present it, I went backwards and forwards. . . . One could see, roughly, his occult activities as being on one side, and his Irish national activities as being on the other. But of course he tried to connect the two. . . . As I took hold of Yeats in this way, it seemed to me that I understood a good deal of how he was thinking.[43]

In terms of social or public manner, the mild Pollexfen side of Yeats's character was the side masked by the bolder or more assertive Yeatsian side. In Ellmann's case, the opposite could be said to be true, mildness of manner masked boldness.

* * *

On September 27, 1945, when Ellmann returned to London after his first trip to Dublin, it was to discover, as he had anticipated, that X-2 was undergoing "radical changes." The next day he reported to his parents that Norman Pearson, his "guardian angel," now in Washington, "has sent me a cable requesting my return. I expect to leave around October 11 and will go to Washington for duty. . . . I shall still be with this organization even though it may by that time have lost its name and be in some other department of the government."[44] Two days later Ellmann wrote to his parents asking a favor. "The people who wined and dined me in Dublin are all short of tea—I'm not sure if you can send some to them or not—but if so would you please send as much as you can (say, several pounds, if possible)." He lists Mrs. Yeats, Mr. and Ms. Joseph Hone, and Madame Maud Gonne MacBride, the most important of whom "by far" is Mrs. Yeats, who "also likes chocolates and American cigarettes."

Ellmann's parents were used to such requests. From the time he left Highland Park for New Haven, then Washington, Cambridge, Virginia, South Carolina, Paris, and London, they sent dozens of packages of all types both to him and to those he befriended, in particular to those he wanted to thank for help or hospitality. Among the items in these packages were candy, chocolate, sugar, tea, jam, cigarettes, cigars, soap, coffee, razor blades, hot water bottles, nylons, silk slips, and melon seeds (for Richard Hayes, the director of the National Library of Ireland). Always eager to forward her son's interests, Ellmann's mother occasionally had to be restrained. When Maud Gonne mentioned her difficulties in obtaining cocoa, "I wrote to my mother, and an avalanche of cocoa appeared, for which Maud Gonne wrote appreciative letters."[45] In an undated letter written sometime in December 1945, Ellmann wrote to his mother "troubled to hear that you have sent another package to MacBride. While she may receive it in the proper spirit, she may suspect she is being bribed or used. . . . Maybe I ought to make my position more clear: my relations with the Irish are extremely delicate: that's why I told Dad I thought it best to leave them alone and not insist upon an obligation by adding to it. . . . Could we then make it a rule not to send any packages or letters without first consulting me? Otherwise I may find myself in a very embarrassing situation; I am a little afraid that Mrs. Yeats may become very wary, for example."[46] Similar worries were to trouble Ellmann while at work on Joyce.

* * *

Ellmann returned to the United States on the *Queen Mary,* embarking on October 10, 1945. After visits to New Haven and Cambridge, he traveled to Washington, staying with Erwin and Steffani, who were now married (Steffani and George Cooke had divorced the previous February). As in his correspondence from London and Paris, Ellmann's letters reveal little about the nature of his work in Washington, although some letters were written on stationery headed "Department of State, Washington, D.C, Interim Research and Intelligence Service, Research and Analysis." To his parents, he describes his job as "nothing entrancing but fairly decent and working conditions are good."[47] His new boss, he writes in another letter, is "a woman who is writing a novel and doesn't bother me when I 'goof off' which is army slang for not working. I talk French a good deal with a Frenchwoman."[48] Part of what made this second spell in Washington tolerable, he wrote to his parents, was the knowledge that he would not be there for long. The Navy's points system had been reduced and with the war in the Pacific over, further reductions were promised.[49] In addition, living with Erwin and Steffani was no hardship, either for Ellmann, who was fond of

Steffani, or for the newlyweds, "since I am not at home much anyway—spending most of my evenings at the Library or in the theatre and many of my weekends in New York," often visiting Julie Smith.

* * *

On his visit to Cambridge, before reporting for duty in Washington, Ellmann met with Ted Morrison, who urged him to return to Harvard and English A "as soon as I can."[50] At Yale he met with Professors Pottle, French, DeVane, and Menner (Robert J. Menner, Lampson Professor of English at Yale, who had taught Ellmann Old English). Ellmann had applied for a Rockefeller Post-War Fellowship in the Humanities while in London, which during this visit the professors said they thought he had a good chance of winning. They also encouraged him to apply for a Sterling Fellowship at Yale, in case the Rockefeller fell through.[51] As he several times emphasized in letters to his parents, his overwhelming priority now was to finish his dissertation, which meant returning to the Yeats papers as soon as possible. Without a PhD, he wrote, "I cannot get a higher job than instructor. The prospect of correcting themes for English A is no longer as attractive as it was. . . . Meanwhile, there are too many other guys who might get over to Ireland too, and there would be some advantage in getting in on the ground floor and immediately."[52]

* * *

Ellmann's correspondence from this period contains accounts of the dissertation's evolving structure and aims. In a letter of December 23, 1945, he announces that it will consist of five chapters (three years later, *Yeats: The Man and the Masks,* the book it became, would contain nineteen chapters).[53] He provides summaries of these chapters, the first of which is worth quoting because it not only contains an early account of what would become the dissertation's main argument but also suggests how Yeats's occult interests serve the argument:

> Chapter 1 as I now plan it will be on Yeats' concealment of his mystical obsessions, the reasons for doing so, and on his conception of his own personality as revealed in two characters [Robartes and Aherne] about whom he wrote stories; these are supposed to represent his self and his anti-self. The concept of a divided personality is common enough in the

> 'nineties; there's Wilde, who said the only important thing in life was the pose, which was the artificial self created by the natural self but transcending it; and then there's the concept of the pseudonym, which was common among Yeats and his friends, beginning with [W. K.] Magee who called himself John Eglinton primarily for euphony, developing further in [George] Russell, who called himself AE to show his connection with aeons and the timeless; and culminating in William Sharp, who wrote half his works as Fiona Macleod in a different style than the other half.

The remaining chapters would show how Yeats's interest in the Golden Dawn grew out of three main sources (membership in the Hermetic Society in Dublin, the Blavatsky Lodge of the Theosophical Society, and the editing of Blake's poetry); how *A Vision* derives from the Golden Dawn and antecedents; and how a range of Yeats's poems can be explained in terms of his sources and the spiritual "system" they helped him to create. Little is said about Yeats's politics in the letter (though they are implied in the conflict between Robartes and Aherne) or about his personal life, in particular about his upbringing, although both topics are discussed in the finished work, if not always to the satisfaction of subsequent critics, especially Irish ones.

* * *

Early in January 1946, in Washington, Ellmann learned not only that he had been awarded a $2,500 Rockefeller Fellowship but that he was likely to be discharged from military service "about May 1 and conceivably before. . . . So I should be going over [to Ireland] in late spring or early summer."[54] Sometime before his discharge, he applied to Trinity College Dublin to be admitted to study for a BLitt, partly financed by the GI bill. The idea of studying at Trinity while at work on his Yale PhD came from Peter Allt, a friend of Mrs. Yeats. Allt had lectured in French and English at Trinity before the war and would go on to become a joint editor of the Variorum edition of Yeats's poems. Ellmann's Yale supervisor, William DeVane, approved the idea in May 1946, presumably having been assured that the required BLitt thesis could be taken from the Yale PhD. As Ellmann was later to recall, at Trinity "my curriculum consisted of going to have sherry about once a month with the professor (there was only one)."[55] This professor was H. O. White, a friendly and helpful man who "made many important introductions" and reassured Ellmann that "Yeats is still everywhere in this town."[56] In addition to suggesting that Ellmann apply to Trinity, Allt offered to find him a place to live, advising him to steer clear of college lodgings. Ellmann relates this news to his parents in a letter of March 19, 1946, in which he also writes of hearing from "Jack Sweeney, who is head of the Poetry Room at Harvard Library, who said he had some friends who would give me all the letters of introduction I need."

On Monday, May 6, 1946, Ellmann was discharged from the Navy. On May 31 he sailed to Ireland on the SS *Argentina,* an aging ship of the Cunard line unconverted from its wartime role as troop transporter. Before departure, Ellmann visited his parents in Highland Park, his first visit since returning to the States in October. Whether he met up with Julie Smith before leaving for Ireland is unclear. By May 1946 their relationship was pretty much over, partly because she had been seeing someone else, partly because when he returned, she several times missed or mistimed planned meetings. An undated letter she sent to Ellmann shortly before his departure for Dublin ends: "Can you forgive me and [leave] me without too much bitterness? Needless to say, I do love you darling."

* * *

Ellmann was accompanied on the SS *Argentina* by a recent acquaintance, John Kelleher, a junior fellow in the Society of Fellows at Harvard. Kelleher, who would spend his career at Harvard as its first professor of Irish Studies, came from an Irish family in Lawrence, Massachusetts ("the Immigrant City"). He had learned Irish from his grandmother, and after an undergraduate career at Dartmouth, where he "read every book of Irish interest in Baker Library," he arrived at Harvard in 1940 as a junior fellow (a three-year fellowship "to give scholars at an early stage of their scholarly careers an opportunity to pursue their studies in any department of the University, free from formal requirements").[57] In the fall of 1942, at the age of twenty-six, he was asked to deliver the Lowell Lectures at Harvard, on modern Irish literature. During the war he served in military intelligence at the Pentagon. He was two years older than Ellmann and this was his first trip to Ireland. In a letter of June 6, 1946, written on SS *Argentina* stationery, Ellmann described him to brother Bill as "a very nice Irishman with a tremendous fund of anecdote and a good head on his shoulders." The two young scholars bunked in a big cabin designed to house returning soldiers.

Each had a five-tiered bunk to himself, there being only six passengers in the cabin.

There were few stewards on the voyage and few compulsory activities. Those there were, Kelleher recalled, were organized "by a lively, bossy British Navy wife who was returning from five or six years in New Zealand." This woman Kelleher managed to offend, over a game of Twenty Questions, and when she complained to Ellmann, Kelleher recalled, Ellmann's response "soothed her. He listened smilingly and a little pensively, then began to chuckle softly—not at her, not at me, not at the questions, but at the situation. The things that people got themselves involved in. Presently she began to laugh too. By the next afternoon she had forgiven me almost fully, though for what I could never figure out. That was the first time I saw Dick's tact in operation. It was wholly personal, quite instinctive, and as far as I could observe it always worked" (p. 13). It was also well-practiced, thanks to dealings with demanding parents, Wilmarth "Lefty" Lewis, and the wealthy old ladies of the ESU and the Churchill Club.

* * *

Kelleher recalled that when the SS *Argentina* came to anchor off Cobh, a seaport on the south coast of Cork, "We were edified to see that the approaching tender was the *John Joyce* . . . even if it was unlikely that the craft was named for John Stanislaus, father of James" (p. 14). From Cork they traveled directly to Dublin, where Kelleher was impressed by how many acquaintances Ellmann had made on his trip the previous October. Kelleher had a stammer and "a stammerer's shyness," and, he said, Ellmann's ease on the telephone was "of great service to me, as was his practical gift for solving the problems that daily confront tourists." Relations between the two men were easy, helped by the fact that they had different but related research ambitions, Kelleher's being more general than Ellmann's: "to learn as much about Ireland as I could and possibly to meet some of the writers—Sean O'Faolain, Frank O'Connor, and Austin Clarke—in whose work I was then most interested" (p. 14). Twenty minutes after they checked into the Shelbourne Hotel on St. Stephen's Green, Ellmann made a telephone call to Niall Montgomery, the architect, poet, and literary critic, who invited them to dinner at his home the following night. The next day Ellmann took Kelleher to the Palace Bar on Fleet Street, "then a great haunt of Dublin litterateurs," where he introduced

Kelleher to Frank O'Connor and his wife. From the Palace Bar they went to Davy Byrne's pub on Duke Street, a haunt of Joyce and Bloom, where it did not take long for Kelleher to learn "that Irish writers were not all a band of brothers" (pp. 14–15).

Ellmann also took Kelleher to meet Mrs. Yeats, who was described by Kelleher as "a large woman with a hearty laugh and much kindness and humour" (p. 15). Within a week, at Ellmann's suggestion, they moved from the Shelbourne to the United Arts Club in Upper Fitzwilliam Street, much frequented by Jack Yeats. Each had a large comfortable room on the club's top floor where the maids brought them their breakfasts on trays. Early in their stay, Ellmann took Kelleher to meet Maud Gonne MacBride, warning him beforehand about what not to say, what subjects not to raise, warnings he had been given by Mrs. Yeats. Kelleher was happy to stay quiet, not only because he was shy but because his political views "were almost diametrically opposed to those of Madame MacBride." Kelleher noted that the questions Ellmann posed elicited answers drawn almost word for word from the relevant pages of her 1938 autobiography, *A Servant of the Queen*, with "few intervals for the insertion of further questions." "I thought her the vainest woman I had ever encountered." On the walk back to the Arts Club, he recalled, "I wondered if Dick thought he had got anything useful out of the interview, but he hadn't much to say except to agree that Yeats's luck had held when Maud had turned him down for the last time and he had married Georgie Hyde-Lees. It wasn't till much later that I realized that in these interviews he could perceive clearly many things, small significant traits of personality for instance, that I, with my all-too-ready judgments, might miss completely" (p. 17).

One of the things Ellmann clearly perceived was that for all her vanity, eighty-year-old Madame MacBride was still sharp. "That was an interesting letter," he wrote to his mother a year later (about a thank-you note she had received from Maud Gonne): "The old gal doesn't miss a trick and knew exactly what I thought of her."[58] What he may not have perceived at this time, or chose not to perceive, was her antisemitism. According to Roy Foster, in the second volume of his authoritative two-volume Yeats biography, "Years after the post-war revelations of genocide, [Gonne] was still saying that if she had been German, the only thing that would have stopped her becoming a Nazi was their exclusion of women from positions of power; she also boasted of telling Richard Ellmann ('a young American Jew') that, compared to Hiroshima and Nagasaki, Hitler's death-camps were 'quite small affairs.'"[59]

Few of what Kelleher describes as the "small significant traits" Ellmann noted in interviews found their way into the dissertation or *Yeats: The Man and the Masks.* Those singled out by the Yeats scholar Warwick Gould at the beginning of his introduction to an edition of Ellmann's 1946–1947 Dublin and London notebooks, are of several sorts:

> Does it matter that Yeats "detested parsnips"? That his old nurse would say of him "Master Willie's not the fool he looks," that Austin Clarke and an unnamed friend thought him a "ham"? That Yeats's view of Pound's "erudition" [in contrast to the view Frost attributed to him] was that "Ezra has learned how to make a little go a long way"? That the resentful view of Monday evenings in Woburn Buildings [in London, where Yeats took rooms in 1896 and where he held literary soirées] was that Pound had "set himself up as Yeats's best friend"? That George Moore "never went with a lady—he was always with a woman of his own class"? Or that Yeats "liked to be taken down," so that when protesting to L. A. G. Strong [English novelist, poet, and critic] and Frank O'Connor that "I shall die in her arms—on her white bosom—and what better way to die than on her white bosom," O'Connor interrupted and said "W. B, you're talking balls!" with Yeats expostulating, "O'Connor, you have no right to talk to me that way," whilst nevertheless looking "pleased"—[the Irish actor] Margaret Collis's being the bosom in question?
>
> To Ellmann such things mattered such that he wrote them down. His 1946–7 Dublin and London Notebooks are the quarry from which much of the real detail which informed his sense of Yeats's life is drawn. (p. 279)

Gould attributes the absence of such reminiscences in *Yeats: The Man and the Masks* to the fact that almost all of Ellmann's informants were alive in 1948, that Yeats had only died in 1939, and that "the candour of Yeats's own manuscripts and Dublin anecdote lay some way ahead in public taste" (p. 280). There was also the matter of private obligation, of debts incurred, particularly to Mrs. Yeats, a reason, presumably, for Ellmann's admission in the preface to the 1979 reprinting that "I did not feel at liberty in this book to discuss Yeats's late love affairs" (p. xxvi). Over the course of his 1946–1947 stay in Dublin, Ellmann had become "Dickie" to Mrs. Yeats (perhaps because, according to Lily Yeats, her sister-in-law, "he looked so young and full of health. He had the usual beautiful teeth").[60] At Christmas 1946, Mrs. Yeats presented him with Yeats's copy of *The Poetical Works of John Milton,* on the endpaper of which was a penciled draft of the poem "News for the Delphic Oracle." Mrs. Yeats enjoyed accompanying "Dickie" to the Abbey Theatre and dining in restaurants with him, sometimes also with Kelleher; she wrote a letter of support for the renewal of his Rockefeller fellowship; she provided him with introductions, including one of November 7, 1946, to T. S. Eliot, assuring him that "unlike many of the young men who are now writing about WBY Dickie Ellman [*sic*] seems to me to have a purpose which is neither gossipy paragraphs or the easy way to get a Ph.D."[61] Most importantly, she provided Ellmann with almost unrestricted access to Yeats's papers, allowing him to take manuscripts back with him to the Arts Club to copy out overnight or to have microfilmed.

In return, Ellmann offered George Yeats several sorts of assistance. Before he left for the States in July 1947, she asked him to find out what he could about Ezra Pound, who had been transferred from a maximum security ward in St. Elizabeths Psychiatric Hospital in Washington, DC, to a ward where he could read, write, and receive visitors. Ellmann sent her as many newspaper reports of Pound, and of Pound's wife, Dorothy, as he could find. Also at Mrs. Yeats's request, Ellmann made inquiries into the possibility of Yeats's son Michael studying at Yale. In November 1947, having heard that Mrs. Yeats was bedridden with bronchitis, he arranged for a *ton* of coal to be delivered to her house in Rathmines, "ensuring for the first time in six years a warm winter." The extravagance of this gift may have been inspired by John Kelleher, who had sent *two* tons of coal to Sean O'Faolain in May 1947.[62]

A final factor in accounting for the fact that many striking personal details found in Ellmann's 1946–1947 notebook are not mentioned in *Yeats: The Man and the Masks* is the fact that the book began its life not as a biography but as a Yale PhD dissertation, the aim of which was "to represent as fully as possible the development of Yeats's mind." When, for example, the relations between Yeats and his father are discussed in the book, the purpose is almost always to explain the poet's intellectual or poetical interests, such as his attraction to symbolism: "No doubt Yeats's frequent failures in argument with his father had something to do with his cultivation of his image-making faculty. . . . The use of symbols, then, was evasive.

He soon found that a picture, unlike a logical proposition, cannot be refuted" (p. 55). "I have written most of two chapters on the old man and his son," Ellmann writes to Ellsworth Mason on September 1, 1946, "trying to show what a difficult legacy of ideas he (the father) left him and how WBY made the best of the limitations of the legacy."

Ellmann's notes and correspondence make it clear, however, as does the preface to the 1979 reprint, that over the course of 1946–1947 he grew interested in Yeats the person as well as in his ideas. On a side trip from Dublin to London in 1946 (from November 13 to early December), Ellmann "saw about 20–25 people; very few had ever thought of Yeats's intellectual development. . . . But I was glad to bring down to earthly level the legendary figures who walk his verse and prose." He was disappointed to learn that the letters Yeats wrote to Maud Gonne and to her daughter, Iseult, were lost, "so that there are really no love letters at all." The loss mattered, he told his mother in a letter of October 10, 1946, because Yeats "only fully confided in women. I am not complaining, for I have too much stuff as it is, but in a way it's a pity not to have more of that side of his character." In an interview with Frank O'Connor of June 30, 1946 (this is the interview in which O'Connor told Ellmann the anecdote about Yeats's shyness), Ellmann began by complaining to O'Connor "that none of the people I talked to in Dublin saw Yeats as a human being." In an undated letter to his brother Erwin, he describes O'Connor as having done just that, which is "quite valuable to me, since my tendency is to turn him into an abstraction or idea machine."

Under the influence of O'Connor and other writers and Dublin literary types, Ellmann began to apply his theory of self and mask to Yeats's behavior as well as to his ideas. He also began to seek ways to spice up the narrative. On September 23 he reports to his parents that he has "found an excuse for putting in a lot about Yeats's sex life, which makes interesting reading." To his academic advisors and friends, however, he stressed the difficulty of making sense of Yeats's occult and psychic interests and his debts to philosophy and Eastern religion. "It has been a tough grind," he writes to Mason in a letter of October 27, 1946, "and what is to come will be tougher because more intellectualized and more intelligent. . . . I feel that I shall produce the definitive book on Yeats for many years to come; whether it will have the importance of The Road to Xanadu I know not, but should like to continue to hope." John Livingstone Lowes's *The Road to Xanadu: A Study in the Ways of the Imagination* (1927) traces the origins and antecedents of

Coleridge's "The Rime of the Ancient Mariner" and "Kubla Khan." It is a source study, not a biography.

* * *

In the almost five months of research and writing that followed this letter, the dissertation became something more than a study of intellectual influences. Hence its being frequently described in later years as a biography, or a critical biography. Ellmann himself on occasion referred to it as a biography. It proceeds chronologically, like most biographies, contains much information about Yeats's doings, and discusses Yeats's poems in relation to his life, both personal and intellectual, rather than as discrete literary artifacts. But important aspects of the life are missing or barely touched on in the book. Here, for example, is the book's single reference to Yeats as a father and to his children: "In 1922 he made several poems about the castle where with his family, which now included a son and a daughter, he lived" (p. 239). It is in a note from an interview with Mrs. Yeats (June 17, 1946) that one learns that "Yeats hardly spoke to his son. Once, after he refused to take Michael along somewhere, the boy burst into tears, and when he returned said, amid sobs, 'Who is that man?'"[63] Nor is much said in the book about material matters or reputation. After a detailed unweaving in chapter 15 of the occult or esoteric strands that make up *A Vision* (1926), chapter 16 opens with a declaration: "With this new burst of intellectual vigor came material success. When Yeats returned to his own country in the spring of 1922, after several years of residence chiefly in England, he found himself a famous man" (p. 240). Following directly upon the abstruse complications of chapter 15, these sentences appear as if out of nowhere. Throughout the book, in fact, Ellmann says very little about Yeats's standing as a poet or a public figure, or about the reception of his works. As one critic puts it, "following Mr. Ellmann through the mind of Yeats we frequently have no idea of where the poet's body was at a given time or how he managed to clothe it."[64] Also odd, or odd for a biography, is how little is said about the background of important figures in Yeats's life, including Lady Gregory and Maud Gonne herself. We are told almost nothing about where they have come from or what they were doing before they met Yeats. The reader is either expected to know about these matters or is thought not to need to know. In *James Joyce,* a better balance is struck between the needs of specialist and nonspecialist readers.

That more biographical detail needed to be included in the dissertation was also the view of Sean O'Faolain and Frank O'Connor, Ellmann's closest writer friends in Dublin.[65] Ellmann had given both writers a copy of the dissertation shortly after he submitted it to Yale, and in a letter of June 22, 1947, to his parents he reported that

> O'Faolain said, amid much favorable comment, that I ought to put in more of the novelist's art; if Yeats moves to Kensington, let's *see* it. He said it read like a detective story, and was the first good book on Yeats and so forth; but his criticism, if I adopt it, means far-reaching revision. . . . I'm anxious to have O'Connor's opinion, which will probably be on the same lines. O'Faolain also said that I had perhaps been over-discreet, which I don't think is so; and that some quotations might be shortened, and some proofs of my points abridged. . . . I begin to think that there are really two books in my head, one which I've written, the other a straight biography.[66]

What he might also have begun to have in his head was a sense that through biography he could be both an academic *and* a writer—that the alternatives he had agonized over in 1941, when deciding whether to go to graduate school or to Paris, were neither fixed nor mutually exclusive.

* * *

Ellmann submitted his dissertation to Yale in March 1947, at which point he began worrying about its unnamed examiners, particularly those with New Critical leanings. His friend Charles Feidelson did not help, describing the dissertation, which he otherwise admired, as "reactionary" in method.[67] "It has been clear [from] last summer," Mason wrote to Ellmann on January 27, 1948, "that you have been worried about the fact that Brooks and Warren criticism is fast hardening into dogma, and that you are bucking the current." This worry Mason rejected ("You underestimate Yale"), rightly as it proved. In a letter of June 3, 1947, Feidelson told Ellmann about a party at Yale given by Paul Pickerel, where Frederick Pottle told Feidelson that Ellmann's thesis had been read and much admired by its examiners, of whom he was one (the others were Eugene Waith and Maynard Mack, not New Critics exactly but influenced by them). "Pottle said he thought the thesis extraordinarily good," Feidelson informed Ellmann. "He thought you had done a splendid job of organizing, interpreting, and presenting.

He feels that it is quite publishable as it stands; will, indeed, be 'snapped up' by any publisher. . . . Pottle isn't a harsh critic, but he is a far from enthusiastic one. The thing that should give you most satisfaction is that he was really aroused by the book—as excited as he is capable of being."[68]

Pottle's enthusiasm was shared not only by the dissertation's other examiners but by the selection committee for the $500 John Addison Porter Prize, awarded to the best Yale PhD thesis "in any field in which it is possible, through original effort, to gather and relate facts and/or principles and to make the product of general human interest."[69] To Mason, what made the dissertation of general human interest had little to do with method. Mason had his criticisms of the dissertation, particularly of its readings of some of Yeats's later poems, but of Ellmann's powers as an author and scholar he was certain:

> The amazing thing about your own appraisal of *Triton* [the dissertation's title was "Triton among the Streams: A Study of the Life and Writings of William Butler Yeats"] is the fact that you base its merit on the apparatus you are using, and your position in literary history. Both of these things, it seems to me, are of extreme insignificance. What is important in the book, and what accounts for its merit, is your own ability, and I fail to understand what prompts you to look outside your own ability to justify your book. Whence these self-doubts, my lad? For Christ's sake, Dick, you're a brilliant man. The kinds of tools you choose to use is of very little significance, it is what you do with them that is important, and whatever tools you do choose to use you use to great advantage. It is not the biographical approach that has cleared Yeats from the mists, it is Ellmann. The reason why your book is so much better than what has been done before is first of all that you are using material that has not been used before, except by Hone (whom we can dismiss lightly, I presume), and the fact that you are better than anyone who has yet written on Yeats. If you had chosen to use Brooks and Warren you would not have fallen into the errors that some of that school have in their criticism of Yeats. And it is not B. and W. who have kept Yeats in a mist, such an implication is frivolous. Since when did an approach, or an attitude, hide the development of a mind as fascinating and important as Yeats's.[70]

When Ellmann received Feidelson's June 3 letter about the Yale examiners' approval, he was still in Dublin. Three months earlier his Trinity College

BLitt dissertation had been approved. Titled "William Butler Yeats: The Fountain Years," it consisted of the first five chapters of the Yale dissertation plus a brief conclusion. Its examiners were H. O. White, Ellmann's supervisor, and an "extern," who turned out to be Joseph Hone, who passed Ellmann but "didn't like what I said about Yeats and his father. Or in fact about any aspect of Yeats's psychology." As Ellmann explained to his parents in a letter of April 27, "since my first chapter deals with previous writings on Yeats as unsatisfactory, you can imagine that old Joe was not anxious to praise me."[71] On May 1, 1947, having spent four pounds on a BLitt hood ("rather a beautiful thing with blue and white border to dazzle American commencements with"), Ellmann received his degree and was photographed by several newspapers. The photographs made him look "like the hound of the Baskervilles."[72] They appeared in the papers because he was the only American at Trinity that year to take a degree "and the first to receive one under the GI bill." A month later, on June 18, while Ellmann was still in Ireland, the Yale degree was conferred on him in absentia, at a commencement ceremony in New Haven. On July 15, after conducting interviews in England (with James Stephens, Aleister Crowley, W. K. Magee, Gilbert Murray, and others), Ellmann sailed from Southampton to New York on the *Marine Falcon,* a government-owned "emergency class" passenger vessel operated by the United States Line. "When I arrive in New York," he wrote to his parents two days before departure, "I shall see some publishers regarding my book."

* * *

Pottle had been right about the interest of publishers. Before he sailed for New York, Ellmann sent a copy of the dissertation to the London office of Macmillan, "the obvious firm because they were Yeats's publishers."[73] Upon arrival in New York, he visited the separate New York office for Macmillan, which Frank O'Connor warned him was difficult to deal with.[74] Early in September he received acceptances from both offices. The New York office, however, offered substandard rates, which he refused to accept. He then submitted the dissertation to Houghton Mifflin, taking care to tell Macmillan's New York office what he had done. Some days later the New York office agreed to an improved offer, which Ellmann accepted on December 1, 1947.

The reader for the New York office was Horace Gregory, poet, critic, and professor of English at Sarah Lawrence College; the readers in London were Sir John Squire and Desmond McCarthy, "both of them very reputable critics."[75] On October 3 the London office wrote to tell Ellmann that it was of the opinion "that the book is long enough as it stands, and that no extensive additions should be made." They also encouraged him to cut back the book's footnotes, which they said were "too numerous and detailed for the general reader."[76]

* * *

The dissertation was published with only minor revisions or additions for two other reasons, aside from the wishes of Macmillan's London office. Ellmann had a rival, to whom Mrs. Yeats had also given access to unpublished material, as well as assistance in deciphering and interpreting manuscripts. This rival was A. Norman ("Derry") Jeffares, a young Irish scholar. On July 13, 1947, in the letter he wrote to his parents two days before he embarked from Southampton, Ellmann explained his need to contact American publishers about his dissertation as quickly as possible: "I must publish it before Jeffares, another fellow who used some of the same material, publishes his. Frank O'Connor says that there is no point in letting him spoil the material by publishing a bad book first." O'Connor was not alone in disparaging Jeffares's book. Mrs. Yeats herself seems to have had misgivings about it, despite having allowed Jeffares access to manuscript material. In an earlier letter to his parents, Ellmann reported about a letter Frank O'Connor wrote to Kelleher: "It seems that Mrs. Yeats called up O'Connor and urged him to urge Macmillan's to publish my book in a hurry—because my rival Jeffares is being published by Routledge—and the Yeats family feel that his book isn't so hot and wants mine to appear first. So I'm trying to rush ahead with mine."[77] The rush paid off: *Yeats: The Man and the Masks* was published two months ahead of Jeffares's *W. B. Yeats: Man and Poet* and received the lion's share of attention in both academic and nonacademic literary circles.

The differences between Ellmann and Jeffares and their books are worth considering. Jeffares was Dublin-born, two years younger than Ellmann, took his first degree at Trinity College Dublin, and like Ellmann was at work on a doctoral dissertation, at Oriel College, Oxford. According to Warwick Gould, a friend with whom Jeffares would go on to collaborate on a monumental edition of Yeats's poems (1989), the rivalry between the two men was over both approach and access. Jeffares thought Ellmann's book "overly schematic and over-psychologized." He also felt that Ellmann, in Gould's words, "was buying his way into [Mrs. Yeats's] affections . . . a young established American academic, who knew all sorts of famous people, Ellmann charmed his way into Mrs. Yeats's company." Jeffares was not alone in holding this view. The Irish critic and author Mary M. Colum, whom Ellmann had met at Bread Loaf in the summer of 1941, hints as much in the first paragraph of her review of *Yeats: The Man and the Masks:*

> The author, Richard Ellmann, an intelligent young man of about thirty, was given access by Mrs. Yeats to about fifty thousand pages of material, Yeats' literary remains, for which I may say some of the Yeats scholars and enthusiasts would have given years of their lives. But a young American naval man in the beginning of the war buys a volume of Yeats' poetry, reads it—one hopes aloud as Yeats wanted his poetry to be read—drops over to Dublin on leave, has tea with the poet's widow, who shows him the material, and finally allows him unrestricted access to it.

In the same paragraph Colum describes Ellmann's book as "extravagantly praised by the reviewers and with a certain amount of justice." She ends the review, after a fair bit of quibbling, by calling the book "an interesting and intelligent piece of research backed by a young man's enthusiasm for the work and career of a great man." Her main criticism of the book seems to be that it was written by an American: "What Yeats had from birth was rare in the modern world: the advantage of a national mythology and a racial inheritance, the richness of which was unexpected. The writer of *Yeats: The Man and the Masks* frequently goes astray when he tries to assess these two possessions."[78] This is a criticism made by other Irish reviewers, along with a Jeffares-like view of the book as overly schematic. In the words of the reviewer in the *Irish Independent,* the book "puts forward theories which many Irish readers may find difficult to accept."[79] In a review in the *New York Times,* James J. Sweeney, onetime editor of *transition* (a literary journal that came to figure prominently in *James Joyce*), praises the book while echoing Colum's reservations: "To write an excellent book about a great Irish poet without giving the reader the slightest sense of Ireland—the character of its people or the tradition of its literature—is a remarkable feat. Yet this is what Mr. Ellmann has done."[80] Presumably Sweeney was of Irish descent.

The most "extravagant" praise the book received in the United States appeared in the November 13, 1948, issue of the *Saturday Review of Literature,* an influential weekly. On the front cover of the magazine was a large photograph of Yeats, with a smaller photograph of Ellmann. The photograph of Ellmann appears again on the first page of the review itself, inside a boxed profile ("The Author") taking up a quarter of the page, remarkable publicity for a young first-time author and academic. The review begins by approving the book's main theme, which it describes as "the conflict between the self of everyday life and that of the imaginative life. . . . Mr. Ellmann's perceptive book on Yeats is a study of that dichotomy and the successive series of dramatizations which the mind of the poet gave it." Also approved is the book's scholarship and the manner of its presentation: "He is cool and detached; he sheds light not heat; he is at the same time full of his subject and yet detached from it. He has scaled detail wisely to interest and understanding. So clearly has he presented difficult backgrounds and related the poet and his work. . . . Surely this new life of Yeats is the most revealing and exciting yet to be written." At the end of the review, Horace Reynolds, an American, describes Ellmann's background admiringly: "A young man from Michigan, who graduated from Yale the year Yeats died and now teaches at Harvard, has dispelled much of the mist and haze that hovered around both Yeats the man and his work. From now on no one can study Yeats without studying Ellmann on Yeats." The truth of this last assertion is admitted even by those with reservations about the book. Gould, for example, an Australian Yeatsian long resident in Britain, takes issue with Ellmann's main argument along lines similar to those of Jeffares. Yet in his introduction to the 1946–1947 notebooks, he admits that "the grand simplicity of his project and the clarity of its outlines explain the survival of the book as a way into Yeats, and its dominance of the undergraduate reading lists for nearly sixty years" (p. 280).

The larger repercussions of this dominance, according to Ellmann's friend Ellsworth Mason, are attributable to the very feature of *Yeats: The Man and the Masks* that offended its Irish critics: its alleged undervaluing and/or misunderstanding of the Irish background. For Mason, Ellmann saw Yeats's development in relation to the development of modern poetry more generally, and this is what made his book "the first ambitious attempt to see a twentieth century poet in the twentieth century, and in the process . . .

to define our understanding of modernism."[81] The wider perspective Mason has in mind is exemplified in the first paragraph of chapter 5, "Combatting the 'Materialists'":

> While personal reasons impelled Yeats to depart further from his father's incredulity, he would hardly have turned to occult research had a movement in that direction not been under way. All over Europe and America young men dropped like him (and usually without his caution) into the treacherous currents of semi-mystical thought. They refused to accept the universe that their scientific, materialist, rationalist, and often hypocritically religious elders tried to hand to them. Science had disproved orthodox conceptions of the making of the world and of man and implied a threat to every traditional attitude. Darwin had husked the world of meaning, and few could share Bernard Shaw's confidence in Lamarck's contention that the giraffe had secured its long neck by willing it. Mathew Arnold's even-tempered but desperate assurances of the adaptability of Christianity aroused little zeal. (p. 56)

This international or "modernist" perspective would also trouble Irish critics of *James Joyce*, again for undervaluing what Colum calls the "advantages" of a rich national and racial inheritance. Behind this perspective, in both *Yeats: The Man and the Masks* and *James Joyce*, lies Ellmann's habitual resistance to parochialism, which he saw as defensive, a product of restriction or exclusion. One thinks of his reaction to the insularity of the Jews and African Americans of Charleston or his defiance of his parents' feelings about marrying outside the faith. Belief in the universal appeal of literature, a humanist or liberal humanist view, derives from a similar defiance.

* * *

One further feature of *Yeats: The Man and the Masks* is worth considering: what Reynolds calls its "detachment" or "balance," particularly in the treatment of Yeats's occult beliefs and practices. Ellmann seems not to have had a mystical bone in his body. When Mrs. Yeats asked him, "Do you not believe in ghosts at all?" he answered, "Only those inside me." "'That's the trouble with you,' she said with unexpected severity" (from the preface to the 1979 reprint, p. xxi). Privately, Ellmann held little back. When Mason embarked on a dissertation on Joyce's debt to Vico and other theorists of cycles, including Madame Blavatsky, Ellmann offered the following advice in a letter of February 12, 1947: "I'd make a brief summary of her doctrine and go on, because one could spend several years reading that fat old biddy without understanding any better than she did what she was talking about. Remember that anything that sounds good is probably a crib from Buddhism, Brahminism, Kabbalism, or at any rate some other doctrine."

In *Yeats: The Man and the Masks,* Ellmann is more detached. Here is how Madame Blavatsky is introduced, in a description of Yeats's first meeting with her, in London in May 1887:

> Madame Blavatsky had arrived a month before and within two weeks of her landing had founded Blavatsky Lodge. Yeats went to call on her with a letter of introduction from Charles Johnston soon after he came to London, and was immediately persuaded to dismiss his doubts and join the lodge. She exercised a peculiar fascination on her visitors, and Yeats, troubled as we have seen by his self-consciousness and lack of spontaneity, and filled with reverence for great personalities, was especially taken with her because she was so fully herself, so "unforeseen, illogical, incomprehensible." . . . [H]e saw in her a creature of myth who held in her head all the folklore of the world and much of its wisdom. The slender young Irishman with his enthusiasm and the fat Russian lady with her obsessions found common ground. (pp. 62–63)

A comparable restraint (fat-shaming notwithstanding) marks Ellmann's discussion of *A Vision,* especially of the Blakean complexity of its "system." Previously, as Ellmann puts it, Yeats saw life as "the opposition of two principles." In *A Vision* it becomes "a pitched battle fought by a whole cityful of faculties, gyres, phases, cycles, principles, spheres, spirits, and daimons, 'displaying the conflict in all its forms.' That the system appeared eccentric did not worry him overmuch, for he felt that it had enough tradition behind it" (p. 236). This judgment is characteristic, in that the system is seen, as is Madame Blavatsky, both from Yeats's perspective and from that of a nonbeliever or skeptic. It may be "eccentric," but it has "tradition behind it" (as chapter 15 makes clear), a balance Ellmann encourages us to see as Yeats's as well as his own. "He was proud of his accomplishment," Ellmann writes of *A Vision,* "and his half humorous description of himself in several poems of this period as Solomon is half serious too" (p. 236).

Even when Ellmann allows himself to poke fun at Yeats, there is sympathy, balance in one sense, though not in the sense of detachment. The different "lunar phases" of the system (twenty-eight in total) mark stages to and from what Yeats calls "Unity of Being." To some critics, among them Roy Foster, following these stages "requires the suspension not only of scepticism but of the faculty of rational analysis."[82] *A Vision,* Foster concludes, "represents a little of the best of WBY, and most of the worst." Although at moments it "retains the ability to make the esoteric and irrational at once universal and uniquely strange," mostly it is "ponderous, self-regarding, wildly didactic, inconsistent, and unconvincing."[83] Ellmann might share this view, but his manner in expressing it could hardly be more different. Here he is discussing the seventeenth lunar phase, just after the full moon, which Yeats says is "where Unity of Being is more possible than at any other phase." The seventeenth phase, Ellmann informs us, is where Yeats classified himself, "along with Dante, Shelley and Landor." Most of his acquaintances, Ellmann adds, "were consigned to less attractive phases of the moon." Ezra Pound is cited as an example of the unfixed nature of phases. Pound was originally consigned to "the highly subjective phase 12, but Yeats moved him among the humanitarians of the late objective phases after seeing him feed all the cats of Rapallo. So it went, with the dead as well as the living." The irony here and elsewhere in chapter 15 is balanced by assertions about the positive effect *A Vision* had on Yeats's creative powers. In addition to providing "a point of reference for all his thought and action" (p. 235), it was a great tonic psychologically. In Ellmann's words, "the power to classify is the power to control, and a new sense of strength comes into his writing" (pp. 236–37).

In his account of *A Vision,* Ellmann was no doubt inhibited by all that he owed to Mrs. Yeats, whom he presents, at times, as its coauthor (a claim Mary Colum derides in an admiring review of Jeffares's book, describing George's role as "overestimated . . . fantastically so by the author of a recent book," meaning Ellmann).[84] But the restrained nature of his criticisms of the book's system also owes something to a habitual bias in favor of the writers he admired. I have several times been told by former Ellmann students of the approach he urged them to take when faced with obscure or riddling lines in the poems of Yeats or Eliot or Wallace Stevens: "Let us take the poet's part." This bias Ellmann extended to the lives as well as the works of writers, partly by seeing them "as they saw themselves" as well as "as others saw them." To some critics, there are dangers in this approach. Ellmann's daughter Maud, who has written widely on Joyce, recalls her father's tendency to seek out "the best in people without sugar-coating their failings." In the case of "Joyce the person," this tendency, she believes, distracts the reader from Joyce's often terrible behavior, "his sponging, drunkenness, selfishness." In doing so it prevents Joyce from being "properly remembered."[85]

A similar objection can be made to Ellmann's depiction of Maud Gonne in *Yeats: The Man and the Masks,* not only to the absence of any mention of her antisemitism in the first printing, but to the single paragraph Ellmann devotes to the topic in his preface to the 1979 reprinting, in which Gonne's pro-Nazi sentiments are connected to her championing of Irish independence: "Her family and birthplace were English, yet she claimed Irishness, for reasons which, though creditable, remain puzzling. Her passion for her adopted country was in many ways admirable, but it was adulterated by a fanatical quality which led her from the time of the Dreyfus case to antisemitism, and from the time of Hitler to pro-Nazi sympathy. Hitler was to carry out the attack on Britain for which she had always longed" (p. xxv). Ellmann is hardly sugar-coating Gonne's pro-Nazi views here. He is explaining or contextualizing them. In the beautifully weighted passage that follows, he offers further criticism, plus a revealing picture of himself at the time of his first visits to Gonne in 1946: "Longevity brought its grandeur. Yeats had conferred upon her an immortality which she had perhaps not earned. Gradually young men, like those who had once adored her for her beauty, came as I did to visit because they adored Yeats's images of her; and she died, rather unwillingly, into his poems, which she had never greatly liked. John Sparrow told me he owned a copy of one of Yeats's books, inscribed to her by the poet, in which the only pages that she had troubled to cut were the ones that contained poems written to her" (p. xxv).

When Yeats's political views are criticized in *Yeats: The Man and the Masks,* the impulse to protect again comes into play. In 1907 Yeats toured Northern Italy with Lady Gregory and her son Robert. Before the tour, Lady Gregory read him Castiglione's *The Courtier,* with its idealized portrait of courtly values and virtues. On the tour itself, "the results of the patronage of artists by the great dukes were everywhere apparent." "It is in this period," Ellmann continues, "that Yeats makes ludicrous attempts to ally himself with the aristocracy" (p. 177), examples of which he provides. It is also in this period that Yeats's distaste for the "acquisitive, priest-ridden" middle classes, possessed "neither [of] family tradition nor a belief in anything beyond the material world," grows into "active hatred" (p. 177). Ellmann's disapproval of this hatred is followed within a page by the claim that Yeats was "secretly half-aware that he was overdoing his hatred," a claim Ellmann backs up by quoting the last lines of the poem "The People" (1915), in which Yeats looks back on his class hatred with shame: "After nine years, I sink my head abashed." A similar impulse to protect as well as reprove appears in Ellmann's brief account of Yeats's attraction to Mussolini: "Fortunately he did not go so far as to accept fascism explicitly,

Cover of the *Saturday Review* picturing Yeats and Ellmann.

but he came dangerously close. As a result of this perilous flirtation with authoritarianism, Yeats's political speeches of this period are not pleasant reading" (p. 244).

* * *

When Ellmann returned to the States in July 1947, it was to resume teaching at Harvard. Six months earlier, while still in Dublin, he had been offered a job at Yale as well, in literature as opposed to composition, but for less money. "I don't feel, in view of [Ted] Morrison's offer, that I need to play the suppliant with Yale," he wrote to his parents. A second point against Yale, aside from money, was the fact that Cleanth Brooks would be joining the Yale English Department in September, meaning that the field of modern verse, Ellmann's field, would be "more or less reserved" for Brooks, as Robert French, the department chair, warned Ellmann.[86] What sealed the decision to choose Harvard was a letter from Andrews Wanning, who wrote in May inviting Ellmann to teach on a new and experimental humanities course, Harvard's equivalent of the Great Books courses at the University of Chicago and Columbia. Wanning had "arranged with Ted to get me out of one class in English A," Ellmann reported to his parents in a letter of May 29. He also "explained that I should be in complete control of my own course, and pointed out that it might lead to something, whereas English A is usually a dead end. . . . Morrison sent a letter too—advising me to accept it, which was very nice of him. All in all next year is shaping up very well, and considering the number of offers pouring in I think if I stayed here [in Dublin] another few months I'd be offered the presidency of Harvard."

CHAPTER FIVE

Mary / Northwestern

AFTER THE EXCITEMENTS of Dublin, Harvard was a letdown. "Have been conferring with people all day," Ellmann writes to his parents from Cambridge, in an undated letter of late August 1947, "very dull and trying." Also "trying," as well as "time-consuming," was dinner with the master of Kirkland House, one of Harvard's twelve undergraduate residential houses. Ellmann's affiliation with Kirkland House, where he was a residential tutor, came with pastoral duties. "These are beginning to look rather appalling," he wrote in a second undated letter to his parents. "I'm not sure I'll be able to escape taking on a play-reading group which my predecessor started, though I really haven't time for it." In this same letter, written a day after having met his first classes, Ellmann describes his humanities students as "exceptionally intelligent, rather too intelligent for my tastes; the attitude of a bright sophomore is entirely distinct from that of a bright freshman; the latter can easily be cowed. As to my English A courses, they don't inspire me much; one class seems good, the other dull."

Ellmann's tone in these letters, unimpressed, a trifle impatient, can be attributed to several sources: a year's exposure to Dublin literary figures; anxieties about securing a fair contract for *Yeats: The Man and the Masks;* the rush to revise his dissertation into a book. Teaching on the humanities course, he felt, took up more time than he could afford, often involving texts and topics he had never taught before. More generally, he resented being an instructor, the academic equivalent of a noncommissioned officer. While at work on Yeats in Dublin, Ellmann had received a letter from George Sherburn, chair of the Harvard English Department. Sherburn had read a query from Ellmann in the October 12, 1946, issue of the *Times Literary Supplement* in which he described himself as "on leave from the faculty of Harvard University." "Technically," Sherburn reminded Ellmann, "teaching fellows and annual instructors are not 'members of the faculty.' No harm has been done, so far as I know; but clearly harm for you and your project may result from inaccurate accounts of your status."[1] When Ellsworth Mason, who was still at Yale, inquired about becoming an instructor at Harvard, Ellmann warned him off. Ted Morrison was "a very fine man" and the pay was decent, but the position "leads nowhere . . . one is pretty much sealed off from the English Dept. Students grudgingly appreciate the course but dislike it and have little respect for the instructor. . . . At any rate, I'm heartily weary of being an instructor, and don't intend to remain one."[2]

Ellmann was open about his weariness. Anxious to keep him, Morrison appealed to the English Department, which was willing to help up to a point. In February 1948, shortly after warning Mason off, Ellmann was offered a promotion, from instructor to "Briggs-Copeland Assistant Professor of English Composition." He was also offered the opportunity to teach a course in the English Department.[3] These offers Ellmann did not immediately accept. In a letter to his parents of March 5, he recounts that "[Morrison] called me in today and showed me a future press release, in which it says that Harvard has promoted two young poets, John Ciardi and me, to assistant professor; he didn't say I was committed to accepting it, and I didn't like to raise the issue; at any rate, the appointment has been passed by the Harvard Corporation, which is the governing board. . . . I like the idea of being labelled a poet, even if I don't deserve it."

The English Department's willingness to help Morrison retain Ellmann was a product of Ellmann's growing reputation as a scholar. The press reported his having been awarded the John Addison Porter Prize. He had a contract to publish a revised version of his PhD dissertation with Macmillan. Other universities were interested in hiring him, among them Yale. Most recently, at the end of December in New York, he had been one of three speakers to appear on a panel on Yeats at the sixty-second annual MLA meeting. The other speakers were W. H. Auden and Eric Bentley (Auden spoke on "Yeats as Poet," Bentley on "Yeats's Theatre in Theory and Practice," Ellmann on "Yeats: Responsibility and Evasion," a shortened and modified version of chapter 6 of his dissertation).[4] After the panel, John Crowe Ransom asked Ellmann if the *Kenyon Review* could publish his talk.

John Pawker, an editor at *Furioso,* also asked for the talk. William York Tyndall of Columbia, a specialist in contemporary British and Irish writing, and later a rival Joycean, approached Ellmann to praise his contribution. "My talk at the MLA went well," Ellmann reported to Mason on January 1, 1948: "I met Tyndall and was glad to hear that Macmillan had told him, when he offered to do a book on Yeats, that they already had one."

Ellmann's presence on the panel was the work of Eric Bentley, its organizer. Bentley, an Englishman who later became an American citizen, came from Oxford to Yale in September 1938 and gained his PhD in three years. His dissertation, which became his first book, won the 1941 John Addison Porter Prize.[5] He and Ellmann knew each other at Yale, and Ellmann occasionally refers to him in correspondence. After several years teaching at the experimental Black Mountain College in North Carolina, he became an assistant professor at the University of Minnesota and in 1946 published the book that made his name, *The Playwright as Thinker: A Study of Drama in Modern Times.* He also began writing about drama for prominent newspapers and periodicals. In 1953, after a move to Columbia, he became theater critic for the *New Republic.*

After the Yeats panel, Bentley tried to lure Ellmann to the University of Minnesota. Ellmann had already turned down feelers from Kenyon College and "something called Coe College, of which I had never heard."[6] In addition to these feelers, he told Mason in a letter of February 13, 1948, he expected "two more offers from the Middle West," one of which, presumably, was Minnesota's. Hence his hesitation in accepting the Harvard promotion. "I thought of writing to Minnesota that they better hurry up and make their offer," he confessed to his parents in the March 5 letter. What made an offer from Minnesota worth waiting for, aside from its coming from an English Department, was the strength of the Minnesota faculty. In addition to established scholars such as Joseph Warren Beach, Samuel Monk, and Henry Nash Smith, in 1942 it hired Robert Penn Warren from Louisiana State University. Warren, coauthor of several books with Cleanth Brooks, including the New Critical handbook, *Understanding Poetry,* had recently won the 1947 Pulitzer Prize in Fiction for *All the King's Men* (1946). Also at Minnesota was a young novelist from Chicago, Saul Bellow, an instructor in the humanities program, whose second novel, *The Victim,* had been published to enthusiastic reviews a month before the MLA meeting. Another faculty member worth noting was a first-year instructor in the English Department, a Yale PhD named Mary J. Donahue.

* * *

Whether Minnesota came through with an offer in 1948 is unclear. If it did, Ellmann rejected it. The Briggs-Copeland promotion had done its job. As for the second offer Ellmann expected from the Middle West, it took a year to materialize. In April 1949 the University of Iowa offered him a full professorship. Austin Warren, coauthor with René Wellek of *Theory of Literature* (1948), an influential study of literary theory, criticism, and history, was leaving Iowa to take up a post at the University of Michigan. Ellmann was being invited to succeed him. Warren was fifty-one in 1949, Ellmann was thirty-one, but he was a coming man. In addition to the success of *Yeats: The Man and the Masks,* his poems (also his translations of Michaux's poems) were appearing in *Partisan Review, Furioso,* and *Kenyon Review;* Alfred Kazin had mentioned his New Directions edition of Michaux's *Selected Writings* in the *New Yorker* ("Henri Michaux, or the Intent Traveller," May 28, 1949); and he had been awarded both a Guggenheim Fellowship for 1950 and a term's paid sabbatical leave from Harvard, to provide him a year off to write.

When Morrison heard of Iowa's offer, he wrote on April 15, 1949, to B. J. Whiting, now chair of Harvard's English Department. What alarmed Morrison was that "Iowa is anxious enough to get him so that they have even written him that he could begin his appointment with a year off to carry out the work for which he has received a Guggenheim Fellowship and a term's leave of absence with salary from Harvard." Morrison guessed that Iowa was offering a salary of $6,000. What could Harvard do to keep him? Perhaps "an immediate associate professorship," he suggested, adding "I suppose that would be an extravagant notion." Another possibility was "some fairly tangible encouragement, such as giving him the hope that he would be seriously considered for a joint appointment in General Education and the English Department at a not too distant period." Morrison asked Whiting to pass his letter on to Harry Levin, a supporter of Ellmann and a member of the English Department's Committee on Appointments and also Harvard's Committee on General Education.

Ellmann's father was clear that his son should stay at Harvard. "I feel that it is a good stepping stone for you in the next few years. During this time you may find a wife, you may publish one or two more books, you may continue to build up your reputation. New England is still by far [a] better place from which to venture forth during this formative few years than Iowa. An Iowa chance may not come again but I should be most surprised if it doesn't." He also had advice about the way Ellmann should let Harvard know that he had decided to reject Iowa: "If you could capitalize this offer from Iowa by saying to your superiors I have considered it fully and have decided against it, they will remember that you did not dilly dally with an offer but were courageous and clear cut and have confidence in Harvard."[7]

* * *

This advice may have played a part in Ellmann's decision to stay at Harvard, but the decision may also have been influenced by a factor Ellmann chose to keep from his father. In the summer of 1948, Mary J. Donahue moved from her instructorship in English at Minnesota to an instructorship in English at Wellesley College. Her name first appears in Ellmann's correspondence in a letter of February 4, 1949, to Yeats's widow, whom he seems to have kept apprised of his love life. "For all the glamour of loving my opposite, I feel I'm well out of the Julie Smith affair," he writes. "I've recently unearthed a renegade Catholic girl who teaches English at Wellesley and has the virtue—which seems most extraordinary after some months of J.S.—of keeping appointments. I'm regularly startled to find her on time. But I'm not yet sure whether or not she's my opposite." In a letter of October 10, 1947, to Mason, written before he met Mary, Ellmann had also spoken of his love life. He was almost thirty and worked all the time. "Alas, I am too old for toying." Marriage was on his mind not only because of remarks like his father's, but because of the number of his friends who were now married. Charles Feidelson had married earlier in the year and Ellmann had not heard from him for a long period. "Is the marriage bond so engrossing?" he asked Mason.[8]

There are several reasons Mary Donohue chose to move to Wellesley after only a year at Minnesota. Minneapolis was too cold for her, colder than the East Coast. She had begun an affair with another instructor in English, Robert Hivnor, also from Yale, a budding playwright who left her to marry someone else (an instructor in the Speech Department who happened also to be an elevator heiress). Mary told her daughter Lucy that she had been deeply in love with the instructor, whom she did not name, and when he suggested that they continue their affair "on the side," she was "disgusted."[9] Yet as correspondence suggests, Mary seems to have maintained cordial relations with Hivnor after his marriage. In June 1948, Hivnor, too, left Minnesota, and several years later taught at Reed College in Oregon and then Bard College in upstate New York. Another reason Mary decided to leave Minnesota is that she missed her family in Massachusetts, where she was born, brought up, and attended college. Pay was not an issue (her salary at Wellesley was $200 less than it would have been had she stayed on at Minnesota), nor does she seem to have been dissatisfied with her teaching or with others of her colleagues, several of whom became close friends.[10]

Family was important to Mary. She was born on January 5, 1921, in Newburyport, Massachusetts, a coastal town thirty-five miles northeast of Boston. The family home was a ground-floor apartment in a house just off the town's High Street. Her father, William Donahue, held different jobs, none very successfully, but always managed, if at times only just, to support his wife and children. At one point he owned a bakery, which failed in part because he gave all the bread away at the end of the day, so that eventually this became the only time customers turned up. He was a drinker, witty and sociable, and Mary disapproved of him and was reserved in his presence. Her mother, Nora Donahue (née Hanafan), with whom she was close, was a housewife. Both parents came from Irish Catholic stock, "possibly from Cork," their families having emigrated to the United States in the mid-nineteenth century at the time of the Irish potato famine.

Mary had an older brother, William Jr., known as Bill, and an older sister, Kathleen, known as Katty. Bill had been to university, trained as an accountant, and went on to teach accounting at the University of Bangor in Maine. When Katty reached college age, the family decided that it could not afford to send her to university (that she was a girl, Lucy Ellmann suggests, may have been a factor in this decision). Katty took on clerical and other jobs and as soon as she married left off work outside the home. That Mary was able to attend college was thanks to Bill, who covered her expenses with insurance money he had received after a car accident. Mary had always been a stellar student: valedictorian at Newburyport High School, cum laude from the University of Massachusetts, recipient of a full graduate fellowship in English at Yale, where she wrote a dissertation on Tennyson. In 1946, the year she was awarded her doctorate, she was hired by Minnesota.

Something of Mary's character and background at the time she met Ellmann is suggested by an unpublished novel she wrote in the late 1940s or early 1950s titled "The Sisters." These sisters, Agnes and Lily, are not Katty and Mary, nor are their situations exactly those of Katty and Mary, but they come from a small town outside of Boston, belong to a family not unlike the Donahues, and have a father who drinks too much and with whom one of the sisters, Agnes, the older one, does not get on. In the novel it is the younger sister, Lily, who goes to college, graduating cum laude. The older sister, Agnes, is sent out to work (there was no insurance windfall for her). The fortunes of the sisters are traced through their marriages and the births of their first children, a period in which their lives are closely entwined.

"The Sisters" is an intimate, straightforward account of 1950s womanhood, quietly sardonic and witty. In later years, according to Lucy, Mary "never spoke about it [the novel] except to dismiss it as no good." After receiving several rejection letters, she had put it away, but had she found the right editor it might well have been published.[11] It is narrated mostly from Agnes's point of view and details her attitude to the clerical and other jobs she takes on. "She did what was expected of her and nothing more, she performed her forty-five hours a week with cool, bored exactitude. On bad days she found the boredom sharpening into anger."[12] Unwilling to conform to female stereotype, Agnes is thought by her boss to be "too quiet," until "it slowly and scandalously reached him that she was not friendly. She was not afraid of him" (p. 8). When Lily enters the world of work, she, too, refuses to please or conform. "The men had the main work of the office, she and the other girls were doled out problems which they solved and returned to the men who made private and presumably significant uses of them" (pp. 35–36). Like Agnes, Lily keeps to herself, having almost as little to do with the other women in the office as with the men. These men she "openly" resents, "because they profited by its [the office's] double standard" (p. 91).

The men the sisters see outside work, the men they date, are coolly observed. At the start of the novel, Agnes has an amiable but feckless boyfriend, Benjy, with whom she sleeps. When Benjy tries to kiss her, she turns away: "Mustn't get mushy" (p. 19). Each sister vetoes one of the other's boyfriends. When Lily vetoes Benjy—"I don't mind lots of guys, but not this one" (p. 87)—Agnes drops him. The boyfriend of Lily's that Agnes vetoes, Andrew, has been married twice and has two sons. Agnes describes him as "middle-aged, paunchy and stupid," the sort of man who "overcame indifference or hostility by his slowness to comprehend it." Lily herself admits that "it was in some perverse agreement with boredom that she went home with him the first time" (p. 68). On the verge of marrying Andrew, Lily submits to Agnes's veto. Then both sisters resume meeting men at clubs and sometimes bringing them home for the night. When Lucy Ellmann read the novel, she was impressed by "the amount of pre-marital sex the women seem to be having. My mother never told me much about her early amours."[13]

Also impressive are the sisters' cultural interests. The room they share at home, before they rent an apartment together in Boston, contains cases holding books and records above which hang "two Cezanne prints and a Degas." On a blackboard are signed photographs of jazz musicians: "Red Allen, J. C. Higginbotham, Louis Armstrong and Jellyroll Morton." Agnes smokes like a chimney, likes a drink, and reads old copies of the *New Yorker.* The sisters frequent jazz clubs and take classes at night, including a course "on Mann, Joyce and Proust" (exactly the course Harry Levin taught at Harvard). When the course ends, they shift "to Russian lessons on Tuesday nights . . . and got as far as translating a Chekhov story." At the same time, they have domestic or "womanly" skills and interests. Agnes makes Lily a new dress. What Lily liked about Andrew, the boyfriend Agnes vetoed, was taking care of his children and home. When Agnes complains that all Andrew wants is "a housekeeper and a cook and a babysitter," Lily replies: "I'd just as soon cook and baby-sit. I think I'm pretty good at both" (p. 76). And she is, as were Katty and Mary. The novel pays respectful attention to what the sisters cook and eat, how they decorate their rooms, the details of childcare and daily routine, matters Mary Ellmann herself cared about in real life, in addition to her work as writer, critic, and academic.

When the sisters marry, it is to men neither as intelligent nor as sophisticated as they are. These are good men, but they are without humor or irony, which were staples for the sisters as for their creator. The man Lily marries is an engineer, Agnes's husband is a garage mechanic. There is nothing in either marriage of the playful joking and sparring that marked the Ellmann marriage, recalled by Craig Raine as "like affectionate warfare. She didn't let up. She took the fight to him. He covered up. She cornered him. She was a slugger. He responded with mildness, disarmed her with tolerance."[14] The husbands of Agnes and Lily, though quite different in background, share something of this disarming mildness. More importantly, they are reliable, quite unlike the sisters' father, or Mary's father.

Here and elsewhere, the novel offers hints about what drew Mary to Ellmann when first they met, beginning with his wit. It also suggests something of Mary's attitudes and preoccupations, both at the time of the meeting and beyond. That the author of "The Sisters" went on to write *Thinking about Women* (1969), described by Mary Poovey as the "earliest U.S. incarnation" of feminist literary criticism, is unsurprising.[15]

* * *

It was a "Mrs. Field" who brought the Ellmanns together. On October 5, 1947, Ellmann reports to his parents that "yesterday" he went out to Wellesley "and met that girl Mrs. Field had mentioned to me, who seemed quite nice." The next week he took the girl out on a date, reporting again to his parents that "she asked me to take her sister and a boy-friend back to Wellesley with me; the boy-friend turned out to be one of my freshman students, who got very embarrassed and thought the incident would lower his mark." The story Mary recalled to Lucy was that they met on a blind date with another couple, at the Copley Plaza, in Boston's Back Bay. On subsequent dates, they often went for drives, on one of which Ellmann's car broke down. It was summer, and when he got out of the car to check the engine, Mary said, she fell in love with him when she saw his legs. Mary also recalled dates in which they discussed Yeats, even edited proofs, while drifting in a small rowboat on the pond in the Boston Public Gardens.[16]

Almost all the surviving correspondence between the couple in the period of their courtship comes from the summers of 1948 and 1949 and the Christmas holiday between them. The earliest of Mary's letters is dated August 2, 1948. Ellmann is in Highland Park not having a good time; Mary is in Newburyport "sitting bleary and disheartened in front of Tennyson and the typewriter." Mary is sorry that things are not better for Ellmann at home: "The least families can do, when one has heaved oneself home to visit them, is to be cheerful." She writes of Katty's infant son Michael, her nephew, whom she has seen twice: "He screams incessantly [as does Agnes's infant son in "The Sisters"], he eats gravel, and while I was there Katty taught him how to throw water at me." The letter's final paragraph begins: "You will approve of me—I've been very industrious. I've fixed up the worst spots in the *Tithonus* thing, I think, and churned out another version of the political poem one. It rather surprised me—it's easy to clatter away with the stuff here."[17] On August 8 she reports that visits to Boston and New York mean "the week is swallowed up without any work done," which makes her feel guilty: "If you start any new work there I will feel estranged. It is very bad not to be self-sufficient, I know . . . but now I am lazy and impatient and quite insufficient without you." He must come back right away, though on second thought if he does so, she writes, "your parents would be annoyed and then you'd never have any chocolate-flavored cherries when people come to call."[18]

Mary's worries about work were prompted by Ellmann's letters. On August 3, from his father's office in Detroit, he reports that he has been typing up his Michaux translations, reading Feidelson's thesis, proofing the index to *Yeats: The Man and the Masks,* and having "long talks with my father." A topic likely to have figured in these talks is suggested in an undated letter his father wrote to him after his return to Harvard, probably in late August. His father understands and accepts that while in Highland Park, Ellmann had to devote "much consecutive time to the Michaux job." But work is not everything. "I feel that you must give attention now—in the next year—to the central job of finding a suitable mate who will not make your future course more difficult. I tried to warn you in the past by the force of an unsuitable example." The example the father has in mind is that of Erwin and Steffani, from whom he feels alienated. In addition, he thinks Erwin's marrying a non-Jew has hindered his career. He is now, his father thinks, neither a Jew nor a Christian: "If he were a Jew he would make many of the contacts which he would normally inherit [from me, that is]. If he were a Christian he would move in that direction more normally. But being neither it is tough and will be getting tougher for the three of us—Erv, Steff and me. And soon the baby will be confused even more than the rest of us." Whether or how Ellmann responded to this letter is unknown, nor is there any indication that the father knew of Mary, or of the growing seriousness of his son's feelings for her.

That Mary herself was unclear about these feelings is suggested in several letters written to her by her best friend at Minnesota. This friend, Esta Klein, also an instructor in English at Minnesota, was two years younger than Mary and at work on a PhD in American Studies (her dissertation was titled "The Changing Image of the American Woman in a Mass Circulation Periodical, *The Ladies Home Journal,* 1890–1919"). As well as sharing an interest in women's issues, the two young instructors had been alike in having complicated love lives. Both were involved with married men or soon-to-be-married men. "You and I will never be completely free of Bob or John," Esta writes to Mary in a letter of September 10, 1948, given "the dangerous excitement" of secret or adulterous affairs. If Mary finds relations with Dick "a little flat and unromantic" (as with the men Agnes and Lily marry in "The Sisters"), that is only to be expected. "All I can say is to concentrate on getting him to marry you, without knowing what advice to give you as to how to accomplish the fact. Just give it time, I guess, and try not to get too depressed in the meantime." "Bob" in Esta's letter is Hivnor, who, like Mary, had come to Minnesota from Yale, where Ellmann had known him (Mary only met him in Minnesota). Whether he was married to Mary Otis, the elevator heiress, at the time of his affair with Mary Donahue, or only engaged to her, or only going out with her, is uncertain.

At the end of the month, in a letter of September 29, 1948, Esta returns to the subject of Mary's love life: "Oh, Mary, what is it that holds your Dick back from marriage? He seems 70 per cent ready and willing—what stupid thing comes to his mind to stop him? I wish now you had been pregnant. It would have made him do what I'm almost certain he really wants to do and yet for some reason is afraid to do. I could shake him until his head rattled." The "stupid thing" holding Ellmann back was the likely reaction of his parents. To avoid facing their displeasure in person, or to avoid having them boycott their wedding, the lovers decided to marry in Paris. "All goes well," Mary writes to Ellmann sometime in the spring of 1949, in an undated letter. "Monday I give the Cunard place $80—the rest not until June." Mary has obtained a passport at the State House in Boston, "the work of five men, all chewing gum and all it seemed to me Irish—it is comforting to see them all with sinecures." Ellmann's father, meanwhile, in a letter of April 28, 1949, writes to him to ask "what your plans are for the summer—how long away and when are you going, and where." In a subsequent letter of May 2, he again raises the question of marriage. "Every day someone stops me to congratulate me on your book or the reports about it. You cannot live on that forever, of course." Proud of his son's accomplishments, and sure more are to come, he is nonetheless "anxious to see you get off the literary reservation and into the matrimonial one, but then again you are too busy methinks."

Sometime in the summer of 1949 Ellmann drove to Newburyport to meet Mary's family. "My family will be glad, if shy, to meet you," Mary wrote on June 14, "and I hope you will like them—I think you will." Mary's mother was all for the marriage (once she was reassured that Mary was not getting married because she was pregnant). Neither she nor Mary's father made any trouble about Ellmann's being Jewish. In the June 14 letter, Mary writes about having bought a black dress and of Katty approving it. "It troubles me even to pack it. I've got the American Express checks, tomorrow I go to Boston for $5—I feel sort of light-headed and birds-in-stomach about now" (in "The Sisters," Lily is married in a black suit).[19] On June 21, Mary writes to Ellmann from the Biltmore Hotel in New York. "TODAY IS THE DAY. Until today I felt reasonably calm but now there's nothing to do about it." The day before, she and Esta had wandered around New York, ending up at the Algonquin Hotel, where they drank martinis. "When I lost her support I called up Bob Hivnor and went out to see him baby-sitting and met his wife Mary and saw their baby (microscopic) get fed. . . . But for all these gallant efforts I must admit I've never felt so terribly lonely in my life. . . . When I get to London I will write to you in Paris."

Writing or work commitments may have prevented Ellmann from traveling with Mary. It is also possible, Maud and Lucy think, that their mother was concerned about the propriety of traveling with a man to whom she was not married. On June 13, a week before Mary set sail, Ellmann flew to Detroit, ostensibly to tell his parents about their plans to marry. When Mary boarded the *Queen Mary* on June 21, a telegram was waiting for her. It consisted of a poem Ellmann later described as written in telegraphic and abbreviated form. The unabbreviated version she received when she arrived in London. It begins: "Darling though the seas are wide/My Doppelganger's at your side;/You need not fear another land,/My alter ego's there at hand." It ends: "Why say you're lonely then when you/Pay for but one but sail as two?/For thus to you who cross the sea/I send not love, my love, but me." The unabbreviated poem was sent from Kirkland House in a letter of June 23.

In the June 23 letter, Ellmann urges Mary to contact Geoffrey Tillotson, professor of English at Birkbeck College, London, recently returned from a visiting professorship at Harvard. Mary was shy about making such contacts—in this respect, Ellmann's "opposite." When she did contact Tillotson, he was warm and welcoming, she reported in a letter of July 2, and the benefit of having done so was immediately apparent: "I was going to busy myself soon about Sir Charles Tennyson [the poet's son]—really I was—but Mrs. T [Kathleen Tillotson, herself a distinguished Victorian scholar] knows him so G.T. says he will get me introduced." In addition to encouraging Mary to make contacts, Ellmann seems to have schooled her about nurturing them: "I brought him [Tillotson] a package of Chesterfields," she reports, "so evidently feeling this must be outdone properly he gave me a first edition of *Maud* which he'd just found somewhere for threepence. Against my secret will he thought I should get on a moving bus, so I saw the last of him as I swung round and round a pole on the back platform—in the utmost fear." At a subsequent meeting over coffee, Tillotson "congratulated me on Our Plans at which point I was modestly embarrassed and stared into my coffee (better there than most places)."

Also in his letter of June 23, Ellmann informed Mary that he had arranged to leave Cambridge for Quebec on June 26 and sail from Quebec for France on June 28. After making preliminary inquiries about getting married in Paris, he did some touring of his own: to Geneva, where he stayed with friends, to Florence for two days, and to Rome, where he was entertained by the master of Kirkland House, Mason Hammond, director that summer of the School of Classical Studies at the American Academy. In an undated letter of early August, having finally sorted out arrangements in Paris, Ellmann wrote again: "Come at once! I am assured that we can be married very quickly and I don't want to wait any longer." The wedding took place at the city hall of the fourteenth arrondissement on August 12, 1949, in a ceremony that seems to have been conducted in French by an official of the American Embassy. What little of this ceremony Mary understood (her French was not good), she resented, on feminist grounds. Henri Michaux was there and as a wedding present gave the newlyweds a drawing, now hanging in Maud Ellmann's house, described by Lucy as "hilariously gloomy."[20] Who else attended the ceremony and where the subsequent wedding celebration was held, the daughters do not recall hearing or having been told. In "The Sisters," the weddings are also civil ceremonies, with only a very few guests. The wedding feasts involve much drinking and eating, in Lily's case at a Chinese restaurant, in Agnes's at Locke-Ober in Boston, an improbably grand location for the union of a garage mechanic and his bride. Both are described as happy occasions. According to Lucy, her parents "never seemed the least bit regretful about eloping. And my siblings and I were always impressed with them for doing so."[21]

* * *

Ellmann found it hard to disappoint his parents, let alone to defy them. Despite having flown to Detroit only two weeks before sailing to France, it was not until June 25, on the eve of his departure from Cambridge, that he finally told them about Mary, without disclosing their plans for the summer:

> Dears,
>
> For a long time now I have been in love with a girl named Mary Joan Donahue, who teaches at Wellesley. For the first time in my life I have had a feeling of complete intellectual and emotional companionship. She is a bright girl, graduated first in her class from college, held a better fellowship at the Yale graduate school than I did, and got a doctorate there. She gave me a great deal of help on my Yeats and Michaux books, as I indicated in the preface to the former; and any distinction in style in either book is largely owing to her good taste. She has a good sense of humor, and is attractive looking. But besides all these things, and above and beyond them, she is a very sweet, loveable person, such a girl as you were, mother. While she has no religion herself, she understands the importance to me of retaining mine. I feel sure you will like her very much. I wish I had been lucky enough to find a girl who would meet all your requirements and ambitions for me, and I have tried very hard to do so. But no one else has seemed anywhere near so well suited to me, and I no longer want to look any further. I wanted to tell you about this while I was home, but found it impossible. I love you all very much and hope you will try to understand my position.
>
> Love,
>
> *Dick*

As anticipated, the parents did not react well. In a letter of August 2, written from Rome, Ellmann described himself as "greatly distressed at not hearing from you in Paris. I very much hope that you will take a more indulgent view of what I am sure is a wise decision. It was very difficult for me to write to you about it, and even harder not to hear from you." In an effort to please or reassure, he adds a passage about recent encounters: with a *New York Post* reporter on the bus to Rome, who was just back from Palestine and "claimed there was still sniping in the street"; with "a Cockney Englishman, non-Jewish, who said Jerusalem [above the line he writes "and Palestine in general"] is one of the few places he keeps going back to. . . . I hope it will soon become less expensive to get there."

This letter typifies Ellmann's manner when faced with parental disapproval: pained, patient, propitiating. When the parents finally responded, they did so in a telegram sent to Dublin, where the newlyweds stayed after their wedding. It read "We forgive you."[22] "We were delighted and grateful for your telegram," Ellmann replied in a brief undated note, an odd feature of which is that it refers to Mary as "Joan," her middle name. According to Lucy and Maud, "Mary" was simply too Christian a name for their grandparents. Equally odd was the fact that Mary not only went along with being called Joan but always used the name (which Maud says she "hated") when signing letters and thank-you notes to her parents-in-law.[23] Her first communication with them was a short note appended to a letter from Ellmann. The letter is undated but was written in London, on the journey home: "Dear Mother and Dad—I share Dick's feeling that it will be very good to be home again—it seems to me that the tourist's life is the most arduous of all and we've been especially flurried. I hope we may all see each other not long after Dick and I get back. Affectionately—Joan."

Mary's name change seems to have been agreed to or accepted in a letter written sometime between Ellmann's June 25 letter and his note thanking his parents for the "We forgive you" telegram. As he discovered in Dublin, his father had written two letters to him after the June 25 letter, one on August 17, which he only sent with a second letter, written on August 24. The first letter was addressed to "My Dear Dick," the second to "My Dear Dick and Joan." The earlier unsent letter the father includes because it "said the things that would always be on my mind and might have remained unexpressed. You are entitled to know how I felt and why," also because, in a letter now lost, "Joan" had written to say that "my whole wish is to share the tradition to which Dick is always 'loyal,'" a statement the father says can mean "much or little."[24] The effect of Ellmann's letter of June 25, he writes in the August 17 letter, was to leave him "stunned and unhappy," not only because his son was pledging his future to a non-Jewish girl, but because "you decided to say nothing about it, and you left us completely in the dark." He writes "in a spirit of despondency" rather than in "artificial exaltation, which Lord knows, I have tried to stimulate in myself." Toward the end of the letter, he declares, "We shall bow to the inevitable," but "not unmurmuringly, without letting you in on our bitter disappointment. We have always tried to be honest with you."[25]

When James Ellmann wrote these words, "Dick and Joan" were married and honeymooning in Dublin. Their time in the city had been exhaustingly social. In the letter to his parents of August 20, Ellmann reports that they were received "very cordially. Mrs. Yeats took us to dinner and so have a lot of other people. . . . Dr. Hayes of the Library was very grateful for all the cigars—we're going out there tomorrow. . . . Tonight we're going to O'Faolain's and on Monday to Jack Yeats's. . . . I expect to see Maud Gonne next week."

What Mary thought of Dublin is not recorded; the letters she wrote while there have not been saved. Although she and her sister Katty corresponded "continuously" (Lucy Ellmann's word), sometime in the 1980s Katty, described by Lucy as "very houseproud," decided, as Lucy put it, "to throw out *all of my mother's letters*—purely for tidying purposes. . . . My father was beside himself when he heard this, claiming that the whole history of our family was in those letters." As for letters home to Newburyport, or to Esta Klein or to Mary's Wellesley colleague, Sylvia Berkman, none survive.[26] What has survived are Mary's letters about England, sent to Ellmann while he was still at Harvard and later in Paris or on his travels to Geneva, Florence, and Rome. These letters are funny and affectionate and show Mary to have been an intrepid tourist, well-suited to what would become a life filled with extended research trips and relocations. She visited cultural sites in London, Oxford, Cambridge, Canterbury, Bath, Stratford, and the Cotswolds. Stratford looked to her like "every Tudor front in the town was built last March."[27] In London, buying theater tickets, she spotted John Gielgud, "so I stared at him and—gratification to report—he stared at me. I consider it a milestone in my Grand Tour."[28] The Wren Library at Trinity College, Cambridge, was "heartbreaking—so much there and not a bit of it can be copied or published. . . . I haven't felt the true scholarly zeal so keenly in years."[29] At Ellmann's recommendation, Mary visited the English Speaking Union, which she found full of "fat bleary old Tories. . . . I try to like it there but it irks my proletarian soul—and I suppose intimidates it too which irks it more."[30] Interspersed with tourist observations are complaints about missing Ellmann. On July 7 she confesses, "I rush around and do enjoy seeing places and try to believe I am perfectly blissful but I think of you too much to be convincing."

* * *

The newlyweds sailed home from Rotterdam on August 31, arriving in New York on September 11, a trip Ellmann characterized as "very dull, eleven days long, with just as many lectures, discussion groups, and square dances as I had endured on the way over."[31] When they arrived in Cambridge, Ellmann found a letter from his father written on September 9. As Ellmann knew, his mother had been unwell for some months. Now her doctors "urged the immediate use of radium followed within four to six weeks by an operation." Ellmann and Mary called right away, which pleased both parents, and then flew out to Detroit. The visit was a success, as was a subsequent letter from "Joan." "We were very pleased with your letter," Ellmann's father wrote, "it is evident you will be growing in our esteem and affection." Two days later, on October 13, the parents sent "a formal token from mother and myself to celebrate your wedding." Money, presumably.

It took Mary and Ellmann a while to find a place to live in Cambridge. They eventually settled on a half-furnished apartment in a Victorian house at 42 Mount Vernon Street, about fifteen minutes from Harvard. On October 8 Ellmann wrote to Ellsworth Mason, now teaching at Williams College in Massachusetts, describing the apartment as "expensive, badly furnished, but very nice, and we're gradually stocking it with desks, lamps and Jameson's [Irish whiskey], which I hope you'll share with us before long. At present we've only a couch to sleep on." Mason sent them a frying pan as a wedding present, which in a thank-you note Mary described as "very useful and unlike the rest of our kitchen (very clinical), very decorative—so we keep it out where it shows all day." Although her housekeeping and cooking were "wholly unpredictable," "I hope you'll take these domestic risks and come just the same." Less welcome, also unpredictable, was another friend's wedding present, which had to be given away: a Siamese kitten that kept leaping onto people's shoulders from behind and getting stuck between window and screen.

Mary was returning to teach at Wellesley for "at least this year," and Wellesley was about ten miles from the Mount Vernon apartment, so she began taking driving lessons.[32] She had been hired at Wellesley in the expectation of teaching Romantic poetry as well as Victorian literature. Her field of specialization, she wrote in a faculty questionnaire, was "Tennyson—Poetry." In 1947–1948, her first year in the job, she taught two sections of freshman composition (Wellesley's equivalent of English A) and a course on the Romantic period. In her second year, 1948–1949, she again taught the Romantic period course. That autumn, however, the Romantic period course recruited fewer students and was taught by only one faculty member, and all of Mary's teaching was on introductory or lower-level courses.[33]

There were at least two courses on Victorian literature in the English Department at Wellesley, but Mary was never assigned to teach them. These courses were taught by Walter Edwards Houghton, an associate professor who had come to Wellesley in 1942 from Harvard. Houghton had been educated at Yale, where he was a member of Skull and Bones. He and Mary had each taught a section of the Romantic period course in Mary's first two years. In this third year, however, Houghton taught the course by himself. He believed that Mary was responsible for the fall in student numbers, and in the spring of 1950 she learned that she would not be promoted from instructor to assistant professor, a promotion awarded to several fellow instructors and one she had expected.

On learning of the decision not to promote Mary, Ellmann protested to Houghton in a letter now lost. Houghton's reply of April 2, 1950, began: "Dear Dick, I can well understand why you and Mary feel unhappy." Mary, however, had received "an absolutely fair 'trial.'" It was not true, as Ellmann seems to have suggested, that the decision was made "on insufficient evidence, nor because her anti-romanticism shocked the traditional academics." A number of factors were considered in decisions about promotion: "class visiting, publications, personal impressions in conversation and in department meetings, and student opinion." In Mary's case, student opinion "told heavily," as evidenced by the drop in student enrollment for the Romantic period course. "One can be critical of the romantics while at the same time *primarily* emphasizing their positive achievement for their time, judged by their own standards, and to some extent still, for us today. If one's teaching of a whole group of writers is largely critical in the derogatory sense, the students rightly wonder what's the use of studying these men at all. The word goes round. The course falls off seriously." For Houghton, the decision not to promote had worrying consequences: "My notion is that Mary should not teach the Romantics or the Victorians. When we offered her a job here, we naturally supposed that she would fit in, but that was a mistake for which she has suffered." The letter ends with praise for Mary's "fine mind, her alert perceptions, and her wit," qualities that he "very much" hopes will earn her a promotion at some point (where is not specified). It is signed: "With cordial regards, Walter."

Traces of Mary's purported "anti-romanticism" are visible in *Thinking about Women,* as when she contrasts "the eighteenth-century imagination of sociability, poise and wit" with "the nineteenth-century celebration of feminine inexperience, seclusion, innocence and timidity." In Wordsworth's "Lucy" poems, "Lucy is 'the difference' to Wordsworth [in "She Dwelt among the Untrodden Ways"] because she is nothing to everyone else."[34] Later in the book, Mary disparages "the intimidating *laws of Nature,* the sweeping *sole voice* [a male voice] of moral guidance. Wordsworth comes to mind, and all our loose, benevolent and deadly dull associations with Nature" (p. 156). Mary's students at Wellesley may well have been put off by views like these. They may also have been put off by Mary's manner, at times acerbic, unsentimental, blunt ("Mustn't get mushy"). "She was charming, witty, a pleasure to be with," recalls a friend, "but her intellect was unmistakeable . . . she was direct and could be challenging." In this respect, the friend adds, Mary was "unlike Dick who would allow your opinions, however half-formed, taking in what he might find useful—he was a collector, after all."[35]

By the time of Houghton's letter of April 2, 1950, the Ellmanns had moved to a second apartment in Cambridge, at 79 Martin Street, also about a fifteen-minute walk from Harvard Yard. In addition, they had acquired a dog, Pierre, a black standard poodle (to be succeeded in the 1961 by Pepito, a brown standard poodle). This was a time of great excitement for the Ellmanns, despite Mary's setback at Wellesley. To begin with, she was pregnant. At roughly the same time, Ellmann was asked if he would consider applying for a position in the English Department at Northwestern University, in Evanston, Illinois. In the course of negotiations, he mentioned that he had been offered a full professorship the year before by Iowa, which "perceptibly raised the tone of conversation."[36] He was offered a full professorship. He then asked if he could delay taking up the professorship for a year. The reason for the delay he explained in a letter of July 3, 1950, to Simeon Leland, dean of Northwestern's College of Liberal Arts. "My Guggenheim fellowship began in February 1950, and extends until February 1951. . . . I am also collaborating, during the spring term, in a General Education course, where at this late date it will be difficult to replace me; and since I've just had a sabbatical term from Harvard, I'm reluctant to cause any embarrassment there." The dean was accommodating. "It is far more important that you decide to join us than that we should importune you to neglect the obligations you had previously assumed. I am sure that you will enjoy your work and your career here. . . . If there is any way in which we can make it more pleasurable or profitable to you, do not hesitate to write."[37] A year later, the head of the English Department, Frederic E. Faverty, sent the dean a report on the year's activities. Under "New Appointments" it describes Ellmann as "one of the most promising men in the country in [his] field."[38] At thirty-one, Ellmann would become the youngest full professor of English in a major university in the United States.[39]

Mary resigned her post at Wellesley in December 1950. If she had worries about returning to the Midwest, Ellmann's salary may have helped to allay them, being generous enough to enable them to buy a house in Evanston, the first house of Mary's life. Sometime in the spring she visited the campus with Ellmann, met faculty and wives (there were no women faculty in the English Department in 1951), and had a preliminary look at houses and apartments. By May, a month before the baby was due, the Ellmanns had completed the purchase of the house at 2733 Thayer Street, a corner property in a leafy neighborhood in north Evanston. The house had a tenant, however, who would not leave until the place she was moving to was ready. "The whole business is nerve-wracking," Ellmann wrote to Mary, who sympathized, especially over his having to negotiate through a realtor she remembers as "flaccid and vague with halitosis and an atrocious suit."[40] As the birth date approached, Mary's mother moved in with her in Cambridge, "though she'd prefer to be at home, poor duck."

On June 20, 1951, Stephen Jonathan Ellmann was born. He was late and the birth was difficult. Meanwhile, the tenant at Thayer Street refused to move. Lawyers were engaged. On August 13, Ellmann wrote from Cambridge to start eviction proceedings. "Any date after September 15 will seriously inconvenience us, because it will involve maintaining a Cambridge residence for my family as well as my living somewhere in Evanston." Sometime in mid-September, Ellmann drove ahead to Evanston, taking Pierre and stopping in Highland Park to see his parents. Mary and Stephen were scheduled to fly to Chicago on September 22. In the period between vacating the Cambridge apartment and the Chicago flight, they moved in with Katty and her family in Salem, Massachusetts (as Agnes and her new baby move in with Lily and her family in "The Sisters"). The tenant finally vacated the Thayer Street house on September 19, the day the Ellmann furniture arrived from Cambridge.

In the midst of upheavals and uncertainties, Ellmann faced a drama in Highland Park. Relations between his parents and Erwin and Steffani had deteriorated. "Very sorry to hear of all the trouble," Mary wrote to him on September 15. "Nothing is more exhausting and nerve-wracking for everyone than these not-speaking situations." When he arrived in Evanston, a long letter awaited Ellmann from his father. Why had he left Highland Park earlier than planned? He knew there were "many things" they needed to talk about. When his mother had complained to him about feeling alienated from Erwin and his family, Ellmann told her to try to live her own life, a comment that offended both parents: "Your counsel to us: 'You'll have to try to live your own lives,' is not quite as easy as it seems to you." He raises the matter of Stephen's birth. "You have a child. Practically not a word from Joan in a month regarding the difficulties she was enduring during that time. We had lived with some hope, because you and Joan made some pledges to us. Do these have meaning?" In the paragraphs that follow, the father makes it more than clear how upset he is:

> From the many things you have not said, and Joan has not written, I am spelling out some meanings. And I am bitterly disappointed. You are slowly doing away with all of the last vestiges of things that have bound us together.
>
> In this emotional turmoil, I feel completely lost—more and more—I am trying to fortify myself and fortify mother to carry this new emotional burden. But how are we to withstand this strain? How much can one human being take? When I start slipping who will hold me up? The complete breakdown may come sooner than is good for anyone's comfort.

The parents now feared that both daughters-in-law "will separate us from the grandchildren." Meaningful relations, wrote the father, need more than "an occasional weekly or monthly visit or letter." "Why did neither of you find it in your heart to take your mother or Dad into your confidence about our grandchild [there were concerns about Stephen's health as well as Mary's in his first weeks]. It was easier to tell Steff or Erwin about it." The father's oft-repeated worry that by marrying out his sons would lose or discard their identity as Jews resurfaces. "What will you tell your students and associates, when they are curious or fresh enough to ask you about your faith? Will you tell them that you are of the Jewish faith?" Relations with Erwin and his family did not bode well: "In the past few weeks, we have had some sample or two of what it means to watch your children breaking away entirely from the fold, becoming annoyed with you more and more, and even beginning to hate you. . . . I am in real trouble, my son, and I do not know to whom to go for counsel."[41]

When Mary received news of the father's letter, she wrote immediately to Ellmann, "Sorry that with all you've been doing, you should have been plunged into it upon arrival."

> I hope you tried to explain that I haven't had time to write even thank-you notes—it's probably some total mismanagement but certainly not intention—my not writing your parents. I will of course write them at once and of course they should come to Evanston very soon. . . . I fully intended a visit soon for them to see their new grandchild. Try not to be dejected—perhaps our house will cheer you up and I'm delighted to hear we will have it—and I will be with you next Saturday—or should I change the reservation and come sooner in the week? My love, Mary.[42]

After receiving his father's letter on the morning of September 19, Ellmann spent the rest of the day moving furniture into and cleaning the Thayer Street house. He had hired two college students to help him. It took eleven hours of washing ceilings and walls, shelves and floors, to make the place "fairly decent."[43] That night Ellmann sat down to answer his father's letter, beginning with the admission that he had been thinking of "nothing else" but the situation in Highland Park since he had left it and that he felt "miserable." He was "shocked to hear you still torment yourself over whether or not Joan and I and Stevie are Jewish. It's hard to know what more to say on this matter." That "Joan" had not written for a month

> is indicative of nothing except the difficulties she's been having with the child—she knew I was keeping you generally posted and we've been on the verge of leaving on the 27th, the 1st, and finally the 15th, though with constant uncertainty. . . . Every spare moment—and by this I mean while she was nursing the baby—she's been trying to finish reading my manuscript [the volume of Michaux translations, with its lengthy introduction], since I rely heavily on her criticism. Nevertheless, if she had had any idea that you were so misinterpreting her silence, she would have written you constantly.

It distressed Ellmann that his parents had "failed to understand her character," to see that "she is a very gentle, loyal, and affectionate person, and there is no animus in her nature." Although these traits may not always have been evident to her Wellesley students (let alone to readers of *Thinking about Women*), they are everywhere evident in the letters she wrote to her parents-in-law. The letters support Ellmann's assertion that in respect to them, "her only desire is to be a good daughter to you. She fully understands the necessity of Stephen being brought up as a Jew, and herself always speaks of us as Jewish."[44] Of course, they will be warmly welcomed in Evanston: "I thought we had warmly welcomed you in Cambridge, we certainly meant to; I have nothing but affection for you and mother. . . . Joan feels the same way, and I can't repeat too often that she is of a loving nature, and that to suppose anything else of her is to do her a great injustice."

In this letter Ellmann explains the reasons he and Mary decided to elope—chief being "because I did not think I could ever win you and mother to appreciating her fineness, because you would always have had the Jewish issue predominant."

> I wrote you a letter about her first to see whether you would consider her, and you never answered it. I foresaw that you would give me excellent reasons for not doing what I believe is the best thing I have ever done—and I loved and respected you too much to feel I could be proof against such reasons. Then too, I knew the embarrassment of seeing her in her poor but honest home surroundings would be extremely painful for you, and I wanted to spare you this. I don't say I was right—I feel I was probably wrong; but I had hoped you would both come to see at last how well I had chosen. . . . I'm sorry I didn't stay longer at home, though I find it harder to say things than to write them. I want to say that I know that whatever I have done stems from what I learned at home—I mean that all my interests were shaped by the best of fathers and mothers—and that I only want to do you honor.

Shortly after reading these words, Ellmann's father wrote to thank him for his "reassuring letter."[45] On October 6, mother and father visited Ellmann and Mary in Evanston and as subsequent correspondence suggests were further reassured. What Mary really felt about her parents-in-law, as opposed to what she told them she felt, is open to question, as is the accuracy of Ellmann's description of her feelings. In later years her memories of them were mostly critical. Maud remembers Mary telling her that when Lucy was born, "our paternal grandmother took care of me and Steve, but she drove our mother crazy—she was bossy, opinionated, and interfering. She was also full of prejudices: she told our [Irish American] mother that she'd had to teach her Irish 'maids' how to wash their hands. But my mother thought her father-in-law was even worse: she said he turned her into a feminist."[46]

That James and Jean Ellmann were "the best of mothers and fathers," others besides Mary and her daughters may disagree, but it seems clear that Ellmann sincerely wished to do them honor, and that his interests were shaped by them, even when they differed, as over questions of affiliation or assimilation, the sorts of questions that figure as well in the life and work of James Joyce. In Ellmann's account of Joyce's relations with his parents, the prominence he gives to Joyce's father may owe something to his own experience, which is not to say it is therefore inaccurate. The same could be said of his treatment of the different attitudes Joyce and his brother Stanislaus took toward their father, in particular toward Joyce's attachment to him.

Other aspects of Ellmann's personal life and background influenced the biography. Joyce's politics, as Ellmann depicts them in *James Joyce,* have been described by a recent Irish critic, Emer Nolan, as "mild liberalism," a label applicable to Ellmann's politics, certainly in the period when he was writing *James Joyce.* According to Nolan, this depiction was once "entirely unacceptable" to Joyceans but was becoming "belatedly embraced" as truer than more extreme views, both those from independent Ireland in the period of the Troubles in Northern Ireland and from today's postcolonialists or critical theorists.[47] Another example of biographical influence—the influence of the biographer's life on the biography—is the treatment of Joyce's relation to established religion. For example, what Ellmann says in *James Joyce* about the "divinity" of Leopold Bloom echoes William Blake, about whom Ellmann knew a great deal, having taught as well as written about Blake's poetry, mostly in connection with Yeats. "There is god in him," Ellmann says of Bloom in *James Joyce,* though "by God Joyce does not intend Christianity. . . . Nor is he concerned with the conception of a personal god. The divine part of Bloom is simply his humanity—his assumption of a bond between himself and other created beings" (p. 372). This assertion recalls Blake's "The Divine Image," in which "Mercy, Pity, Peace and Love" dwell in the human form: "And all must love the human form,/In heathen, turk or jew,/Where Mercy, Love, and Pity dwell,/There God is dwelling too." That Joyce, like Yeats, thought much of and about Blake, Ellmann's biography amply demonstrates.[48]

In depicting the marriages of Nora and Joyce and Molly and Bloom, Ellmann may also have been drawing on personal experience. Mary Ellmann was very different from Nora Joyce or Molly Bloom. Unlike Nora, who never read a word of her husband's books, Mary was intimately involved in Ellmann's writing, as he openly acknowledged; unlike Molly, there is no evidence that Mary was ever unfaithful, and Maud has described her as "rather prudish."[49] Like them, however, she was caustic, opinionated, straight-talking, and teasing or mocking in her relationship with Ellmann, who not only accepted her teasing but enjoyed it, was attracted to it, perhaps needed it. Nora, as Ellmann puts it in *James Joyce,* "had no understanding of literature and no power or interest in introspection. But she had considerable wit and spirit, a capacity for terse utterance as good in its kind as Stephen Dedalus . . . and if her allegiance would always be a little mocking, it would be nevertheless thoroughgoing" (p. 163). As for how Joyce reacted to this treatment, "he was content to find her stronger and in her way more self-assured than he was" (p. 195). In drawing Molly's character, Ellmann writes, Joyce "had a model at home for [her] mind. Nora Joyce had a similar gift for concentrated expression, and Joyce delighted in it as much as Bloom did. Like Molly she was attached to her husband without being awestruck" (p. 376). With everyone else Joyce was prickly about the way he was treated, but "Nora handled [him] as if he were still half a child" (p. 447). "He was pleased that she 'saw through him,' as he said, and detected the boy in the man" (p. 305). Ellmann was the mildest and most emollient of men, quite unlike Joyce, but as Michael Anania recalls, when Mary "wanted to draw him up short, she would call him Dickie Boy, not so much a rebuke as a reminder of something crucial between them."[50] Hence, in part, the inwardness, sympathy, and humor Ellmann brings to his accounts of Nora and Molly and their marriages.

* * *

For the next seventeen years, from September 1951, the Ellmanns lived in Evanston, Illinois, the suburban township where *James Joyce* was conceived and written. Evanston is ten miles north of downtown Chicago. Affluent, staid, and in the 1950s overwhelmingly Republican and dry, it was founded in 1857 by the same Methodist business leaders who six years earlier had founded Northwestern University.[51] The town's main street, Sheridan Road, winds through the university's lakeside campus, past spacious Victorian and turn-of-the century mansions with wide manicured lawns. The Ellmanns lived on Thayer Street from 1951 to 1955, and in a slightly larger house at 2523 Harrison Street from 1955 to 1968. Both houses were in North Evanston, a ten-minute drive from campus. In the years of *James Joyce*'s making, Stephen was joined by Maud in 1954 and Lucy in 1956.[52] All three children were born by caesarean section, and though Mary wanted a fourth child, the doctors advised against a fourth caesarean. In these years Mary lived the life of a suburban mother and homemaker. In 1959, the year *James Joyce* was published, Lucy was only three and Maud five. The daughters remember babysitters when their parents went out in the evenings but no regular childcare. Mary returned to teaching in the 1960s, first at Kendall College in Evanston, then at Roosevelt University in downtown Chicago.[53] Only then, moreover, did she begin publishing the reviews that would lead to *Thinking about Women*.

Northwestern in the 1950s was an ambitious research university, though Ellmann felt it "just fell short of being first rate."[54] Yet he stayed for seventeen years, despite being continually pursued by other offers. That he did so was a product both of how well he was treated and how much he liked the place, in particular the community of colleagues who would become his and Mary's lifelong friends. When he arrived, he was by far the youngest of the English Department's eight full professors, which partly explains why most of his and Mary's friends were drawn from the ranks of assistant and associate professors (all of whom went on to become full professors). The Ellmanns were social beings and quickly found themselves invited to parties, picnics, outings, weekly lunches. They were also party-givers, though anxious ones, often cross and flustered in preparation ("enough to make Maudie and me decide NEVER to have parties when we grew up," Lucy reports). Lucy remembers their mother's signature buffet dishes, classic 1950s party cuisine: chicken cacciatore, eggplant parmigiana. Often the dinners were given for visiting speakers. Among the visitors Ellmann brought to Northwestern in the 1950s were John Crowe Ransom, W. H. Auden, Dwight MacDonald, Frank O'Connor, and Allen Tate.

Although Evanston was dry, the parties were not. The Ellmanns, however, were moderate drinkers, as were their closest faculty friends. Every night after five, depending upon when he came home, Ellmann and Mary had a drink together, usually just one, a whisky and soda, with snacks. This routine Mary fictionalized in "The Sisters." "Since they rushed all day

[Agnes, newly married] had decided, one of those beautiful first resolutions, that before dinner every night they must sit and have a drink and do nothing at all" (p. 206). Of the many ways Ellmann was different from Joyce, his moderate drinking is mentioned first by his daughters. "He had almost no experience of the level of drinking Joyce spent most of his life reaching," Lucy writes. "He would have gotten bored drinking in a pub for more than an hour, however good the company."[55] After the drink and dinner, Ellmann would return to his study to work. "He worked all day," Maud recalled, "he was completely absorbed in his work."[56]

The affection Ellmann felt for his circle of friends at Northwestern is memorably recalled in an address he delivered on June 14, 1980, on the occasion of the university awarding him an honorary degree. He was at the time Goldsmiths' Professor of English Literature at Oxford, and to amuse his American audience he described several oddities of Oxford life, among them the nude bathing sites, Parson's Pleasure and Dame's Delight. These sites he contrasted with faculty beach gatherings on Lake Michigan, emblematic of what he describes as "the best seventeen years" of his life. "Whatever the advantages of nudity in that damp and chilly climate, I find myself longing for the gregarious domesticity of the warm Northwestern University beach, where in the old days we used to see Walter and Elizabeth Scott, Harry and Jo Hayford, Lyn and Barbara Shanley, Jean and Ruth Hagstrum, Bob and Pauline Mayo, Carl and Isabel Condit, Jules and Ruth Marcus, George and Connie Cohen, sometimes even Erich Heller. It was worth wearing bathing suits to be in such company."

Walter and Elizabeth Scott are the first names mentioned in this list because Walter Scott was in some ways the key figure in Ellmann's circle of faculty friends. Ellmann was taken with him from the start, describing him to Mary in a letter of May 1951 as "very sharp and pleasant," the most "remarkable" person at a dinner given for him by Lyn and Barbara Shanley.[57] Scott stood out in several ways. He was older than others in the circle, born in 1906, and was a member of the School of Speech rather than the English Department (his title in 1951 was associate professor of dramatic literature). He also stood out because he published almost nothing in his thirty-seven years at the university, from 1939 to 1968. Instead he busied himself with what Gerald Graff, a colleague and close friend, described as a one-man "office industry" of mimeographed satire: "an unendingly delightful, not infrequently outrageous, stream of letters, parodies, travesties, faked

The beach at Northwestern University.

official notices, faked photographs, and other items falling under no known classification. Many of these creations were wildly (at times obscenely) illustrated with cut-outs from newspapers or magazines or drawings from Walter's own hand. . . . The products of the Scott workshop went out almost daily to Northwestern colleagues, administrators, and students lucky enough to be on Walter's mailing list."[58]

A small coterie not on Scott's mailing list learned of him through the few things he did publish, almost always, in Ellmann's words "buried in other men's anthologies and in magazines and in privately printed commentary." When several of his parodies appeared in 1950 in *Furioso,* Edmund Wilson enclosed them in a letter to Vladimir Nabokov, who agreed that they were up to standard, "very funny and successful." Nabokov even approved Scott's French (in a parody titled "Gaetan Fignole: Pages de Journal"), which Wilson had queried.[59] When Scott eventually turned his hand to Nabokov himself, in a Pnin-esque "Letter to a Festschrift" (for a collection of tributes to Nabokov edited by colleagues), Nabokov described it in the *New York*

Times as "a masterpiece. It was so full of plums, that I read it three times. It's absolutely splendid." Over the years, both Katharine White of the *New Yorker* and Barbara Epstein of the *New York Review of Books* sought without success to persuade Scott to contribute what White called "anything."[60] Why Scott declined such overtures he himself did not understand. In a letter to Ellmann, he lamented his "lifelong incapacity for collaboration, meeting deadlines, etc.," calling it "nothing to be proud of."[61]

To Northwestern's credit, at a time when it was keen to raise what today would be called its research profile (as in the recruiting of Ellmann), it not only retained Scott but in 1963 made him a full professor. It seems to have mattered that to those who knew him, or knew of him, he was, in Ellmann's words, "one of the wittiest men in America."[62] As a teacher, he was demanding, popular, but no cult figure, clear-eyed about his own abilities as well as those of his students. "At my best moments," he admitted, "I am a pretty good teacher, as many students have told me. I am neither a showman nor a charlatan. I do not think the business of education is to entertain students, or to make them feel good . . . if inadvertently in the course of being instructed they *should* feel good, so much the better."[63] Scott's view of his students is suggested at the end of a letter of November 1, 1970, to the painter George Cohen, a close friend of the Ellmanns. "Now I must return reluctantly to thinking about tomorrow's classes—what can I find to talk about that the little bastards don't already know—a whole universe opens up before me! It's the most exciting college generation I've ever encountered—they are full of life and zip and energy and they don't know a god-damned thing!"

This could hardly be said of Scott himself, who was learned as well as witty. He knew six languages besides English—Greek, Latin, Italian, French, German and Spanish—plus some Danish and Old Norse. When Ellmann founded a *Finnegans Wake* reading group at Northwestern, Scott was a valued resource. The group met in the Ellmann living room to go over passages distributed earlier, "reading for all possible puns, allusions and neologisms." Academics from a range of disciplines were invited, each with a distinct expertise. Whiskey circulated during meetings and eventually, according to Michael Anania ("My specialty was picking metrical stanzas out of the text"), jokes took over from scholarship, "entirely appropriate for a Wake."[64] The delight Scott took in these meetings and in linguistic arcana more generally, is suggested in a letter he wrote to the Ellmanns when he learned they were going to Spain. He had two words for them, which he had also offered to "a small group of friends who DIG this sort of thing." "*Cagarrache,* m. one who washes the olive pits in an oil mill" and "*Caniculario,* m. beadle who drags dogs out of Church." These words, he told the Ellmanns, were to be found "in Appleton's New English-Spanish and Spanish-English Dictionary; I bought my copy in Evanston in 1950."[65]

Three times a week during term, some combination of the friends Ellmann lists in his honorary degree address would meet for lunch at Michelini's, an Italian restaurant on Foster Street, a short walk west of campus. Newcomers who were invited could find the wit of the regulars "at once compelling and a bit hazardous." Gerald Graff, who would go on to coedit a collection of Scott's parodies, felt he had to prepare before attending. When literature came up, according to Anania, it involved "puzzles, puns or little nuggets of learning in Walter's incessant researches into other people's questions." Ellmann was an irregular attendee, often away on research leave, but upon his return "he would join in as though he had never been away."[66] Scott kept him up to date, as he did all friends, in letters and circulated diary entries, often highly imaginative. One such diary entry, undated, concerns the Americanist and textual scholar Harry Hayford, general

Walter B. Scott.

editor of *The Writings of Herman Melville.* "Lunch at Michelini's today. Harry not there, being busy at home 'creating' a few original Melville documents against his trip to Paris next week, where he is to appear as one of the stars of a Melville conference. . . . Harry told me over the phone that he has got Melville's handwriting and signature down to a 'T' after all these years of 'f—ing around' (his words) with them and hopes to spring a number of crucial notes and letters on the conference." The same entry also describes Gerald Graff's physical appearance at the lunch: "He had a 'mouse' on his cheekbone, a split lip, and some sort of band-aid on his right ear. When I asked him about them he said he had once again absent-mindedly tried to get out of his car without opening the door first."[67]

On Saturdays there was a Michelini lunch for families, at one of which, Scott reports, an infant by the name of Ferguson Parker, grandson to the Hayfords, was included. "After a while," Scott writes, "everyone gets to feel that Ferguson is the only possible name for him." Ferguson becomes a Saturday regular, "much admired and much loved by all hands . . . a great addition to these festive gatherings." When two other babies were brought to Michelini's, the result was "a remarkable, in all senses, lunch hour," with "much passing of the three babies from hand to hand. I am always afraid that I may drop a tiny child [the Scotts had no children], or that he'll break, so I pass them fast."[68]

Several figures in Ellmann's circle—Robert Mayo, Jean Hagstrum, Lyn Shanley—went on to administrative positions, both in the department and beyond, promotions that proved useful for both Ellmann and Scott, with their very different academic records.[69] Ellmann himself steered clear of such positions, focusing on research and teaching. While in Italy on holiday, well after the success of *James Joyce,* he received a letter from Jean Hagstrum, whose term as English Department chair was ending. There were deep divisions in the department, Hagstrum reported, and it was not clear if either of the candidates for the chair would have sufficient support from the faculty to be nominated. He wrote to alert Ellmann "to the very real possibility that you could be nominated and accepted by the Dean. Most of us respect your wishes to escape the burdens now; but I have to say, bluntly, that I feel that anyone we can agree on should feel morally obligated to serve. . . . I thought you should know how things stand."[70] Ellmann replied on March 24, 1964: "You ask whether I would be willing to serve as chairman in the event it became necessary. I would." He had a condition, however. "I would hope you will make clear to Ernest [Samuels, who had just won a Pulitzer Prize for the third volume of his biography of Henry Adams] that I did not initiate my own candidacy and in fact fully intend to support him." When Samuels was eventually nominated and approved, Ellmann wrote to Hagstrum in a letter of May 21: "In an aberrant moment, I may have conceived of myself in that position, but I am very happy not to occupy it. I voted for Ernest and I hope he will do a good job and be happy in it." This reaction did not surprise Hagstrum. Before he (Hagstrum) became department chair at Northwestern, he was offered a similar role at Indiana University. When called upon for advice, Ellmann replied, "It is of course a position of eminence and authority, and I hope Northwestern will compensate you in salary if as I assume and hope you don't take it. . . . In short, drain the treasury but don't leave us. Let's both live it up in Evanston."[71] Using an offer to bargain for better pay and conditions is a common tactic in academic life and one Ellmann several times adopted. He remained at Northwestern, in Mason's words, "because it steadfastly topped every other salary he was offered and allowed him princely teaching loads."[72] Throughout his life Ellmann took a keen interest in what other professors of English were earning, mostly as a measure of rank or standing, equivalent to his wartime interest in gaining a commission. According to Mason, toward the end of his time at Northwestern, in addition to having one of the highest salaries of any English professor in the nation, his teaching load consisted of "one course the first semester and two courses the second semester with every third year off with full pay." The result of this generosity, Mason adds, "was twenty-one distinguished books, three of which (including the Wilde) will remain monuments in their fields."[73]

Although Ellmann had little interest in running things, he wished them to run well. He kept up with department affairs, also department gossip, and was conscientious when consulted, keen to forward both the department's and the university's reputation. When asked to comment on the scholarly claims of colleagues and potential hires, he was firm and frank. "I'm afraid I can't endorse for promotion any of the people you name," he informed Hagstrum in a letter of October 5, 1960. Of the five candidates, "two have published a little but their work does not seem to me exciting," two he scarcely knew, and the last "seems to be pleasant but unambitious." With colleagues whose work he admired, he made efforts to showcase their scholarship, also to give advice and encouragement.[74] In discussing requirements for students majoring in English, his standards were high. Hagstrum credits him with the idea "of what through the years has been considered one of the best features of the English program at Northwestern—the two-year required course in English and American literature, taught in small sections." When asked the chief aim of this expensive as well as intensive program, Ellmann replied, "Exhilaration," an answer Hagstrum describes as being "much to the dismay of the more doctrinaire among us."[75]

Although Ellmann knew and liked his Northwestern administrators—in particular Simeon Leland, a "shrewd and humane man," the dean who hired him and made sure he stayed—he mostly steered clear of university as opposed to departmental affairs.[76] He served on two major university committees. The first oversaw the creation of the new library, an effort he was proud to have played a part in. "No committee has ever worked harder," he claimed in his honorary degree address. The second committee reviewed preliminary designs for future university buildings, "to see whether they harmonize with the rest of the campus." Ellmann's friend Carl Condit, who moved from English to the Department of Art History (his specialties were architectural history and urban planning), chaired this second committee and persuaded his friend to join it.[77] In doing so, he rekindled an interest sparked in Ellmann in Charleston, South Carolina, during the war, when he and Frank Trager toured the historic buildings of Savannah and Charleston.

Recollections of Ellmann as teacher come mostly from the 1960s and beyond, after *James Joyce* had made him a star, but they largely conform to descriptions from earlier periods. Like many successful teachers, Ellmann treated his students as if they were equals, asking of them "not much less than he demanded of himself ('take a look at Heidegger' or 'you should read Ibsen in Norwegian')" (this last, hard to credit).[78] His students describe him as exceptionally polite, unthreatening in manner, not at all "the big, corpulent professor, strutting around the MLA" (though at Northwestern he did put on weight).[79] He had something of the formality of the academics who taught him, belonging to what Joseph Epstein, a longtime lecturer at Northwestern and editor of the magazine *The American Scholar,* described as "the last generation of professors as adults—suits and ties, didn't use the F-word in class, didn't call students 'Frosty' or 'Muffin.'" (Epstein also described Ellmann as "looking nothing like his prose style.")[80] But Ellmann seemed genuinely to enjoy hearing from the students in his courses, and was curious about them. The courses he taught at Northwestern were C-level (advanced undergraduate courses), held in the largest of the university's lecture halls. He was not a dynamic lecturer, though as a friend recalled, he invariably began with "a challenging and witty first sentence accompanied by a little turn of the head, a signal to his listeners that he was glad to be addressing them."[81] He lectured from notes rather than a fixed script and for the most part steered clear of what one of his teaching assistants described as overarching theory.[82]

In small classes or E-level graduate seminars, Ellmann was patient and encouraging, keen for his students to share his enjoyment in the works assigned ("Let us take the poet's part"). The amount of reading required in his courses, however, struck many students, including quite able students, as unrealistic. Laurence Senelick, later a professor of drama, took Ellmann's course on the European novel. He remembers a reading list that included *The Red and the Black, War and Peace, The Brothers Karamazov, Ulysses, Man's Fate, The Castle,* and *Confessions of Zeno.* Ellmann "assumed that we would do the reading," Senelick recalls, which meant that "every free moment you're reading a novel." To make sure they kept up, he set weekly short-answer quizzes, with questions like "What is the name of the town in which the Karamazovs live?" (The answer is "Skotoprigonyevsk," a name derived, appropriately given what goes on there, from the Russian word for stockyard or pigsty.)[83] As a PhD supervisor, he was tough on drafts, sometimes irritating students "with his obsessive editing, even though he intended it to be beneficial."[84] John Sutherland, a professor at University College London, tells of a PhD oral examination in which Ellmann was the external examiner. The candidate's original supervisor had done a bad job—had, in effect, abandoned him—and Sutherland was his second supervisor. In Sutherland's words: "Ellmann breezed in. . . . He filled the room. In the pre-viva session he said, 'I really like [the candidate]—a very nice man. . . .' Pause. 'But I can't pass this.' The oral was amiable, began with a laugh. Ellmann disemboweled [the candidate's] work, in the most friendly way. Afterward, with great difficulty, he was prevailed upon to award a severe referral. I believe he helped [the candidate] get it passable. I found him scrupulous, winningly pleasant, and unbending."[85]

Ellmann published two books in addition to *James Joyce* in the period 1951–1959. In his first year at Northwestern, before he began work on the Joyce biography, the Michaux book was published by New Directions. In the *Saturday Review of Literature,* Justin O'Brien, a professor of French at Columbia, called his translations "scrupulous and intuitive."[86] Two years later Ellmann's second book on Yeats, *The Identity of Yeats,* was published in London by Macmillan and in New York by Oxford University Press.[87] This book he dedicated to Mary. It differs from *Yeats: The Man and the Masks* in focusing on the poems as poem instead of as evidence of Yeats's sources or influences or working methods. In the preface to a 1963 second edition of *The Identity of Yeats,* Ellmann admits, in reference to *Yeats: The Man and the Masks,* to "an uneasy feeling that I have not been blameless"

Mary Ellmann, early 1960s.

in helping to turn "all that marvellously innovative poetry into a résumé of what other people have written."[88] His purpose in the second book, he declares in the1963 preface, was "to display the patterns of Yeats's poetry" rather than "to understand his life." Beneath this admission lies the success of *James Joyce,* which seems to have allayed anxieties about the biographical nature, or partial biographical nature, of the earlier Yeats book. The differences between biography and criticism are now clear to Ellmann. Biography "must necessarily emphasize beginnings, efforts, forays, while a critical work can dwell upon accomplishments" (p. xxiii). As for the book's title, it serves "a dual purpose": to "search for Yeats's essential mode of transforming experience," and to "insist also upon the integrity of his work, no matter in what period of his life it was composed" (p. xxiii).

* * *

Here, then, is something of the life Ellmann led in the years 1952–1959, from the age of thirty-two to forty—minus the work that most preoccupied him. This is where he lived, what his wife and family were like, who his friends and colleagues were, the social life he led, what and how he taught, what else he wrote. The sort of a person he was, and how he came to be such a person, have been the concerns not just of this chapter but of the whole of the first half of this book. In the chapters that follow, the focus will be on how Ellmann came to the decision to write a biography of Joyce, the factors involved in its making, and the nature of the resulting work. *James Joyce* is an extraordinary achievement, all the more so given the fullness of the life Ellmann led over the years of its creation.

PART II

The Biography

Yet as the nobility of his heroes gradually overcomes their ingloriousness, so the tenacious craftsman, holding to his idea, gradually surmounts that roving, debt-ridden scene through which Joyce kept his elegant way. Implicit in his work there is a new notion of greatness, greatness not as an effulgence but as a burrowing that occasionally reaches the surface of speech or action. This kind of greatness can be perceived in life, too, though camouflaged by frailties.

—RICHARD ELLMANN, *JAMES JOYCE* (1959)

CHAPTER SIX

Choosing Joyce

"I BEGAN THIS BIOGRAPHY of Joyce in perhaps the happiest way, without knowing I was beginning it." This reflection, from an unpublished, untitled, and undated document in the Ellmann Papers, refers to the moment in Dublin in 1945 when Yeats's widow proved (to Ellmann, at least) that Joyce did say to Yeats at their first meeting: "You are too old for me to help you." The arrogance of the remark "delighted" Ellmann. It also led him to look further into the several meetings between the two men and in 1950 to write an essay about them ("Joyce and Yeats," *Kenyon Review,* Autumn 1950). As we have seen, in the preface to the 1982 edition of *James Joyce,* Ellmann says of his 1945 meeting with Mrs. Yeats: "My book had its origin at that time." The book's dedication is: "To George Yeats."

Seven years after his meeting with Mrs. Yeats, after much weighing of practical and professional considerations, Ellmann made a decision to begin research on the book. In coming to this decision he was helped by his friend Ellsworth Mason, whose interest in Joyce predated his own and who played a key role in the making of *James Joyce.* Mason had studied economics as an undergraduate at Yale, then went on as a graduate student to earn an MA and a PhD in English. His PhD on Joyce and Vico ("James Joyce's *Ulysses* and Vico's Cycle") was awarded in 1948, a year after Ellmann's PhD on Yeats.[1] It was only the second Yale dissertation on a twentieth-century writer. During the early years of the war Mason worked at the Board of Economic Warfare in Washington while Ellmann worked at the Office for the Coordinator of Information. Like Ellmann, he was then drafted into the Seabees, though he was stationed in the Pacific rather than the States. There he helped to build and maintain airstrips and related military facilities, keeping in touch with Ellmann through correspondence, for the most part about literary and academic matters.

Mason's interest in writing a dissertation on Joyce and Vico ("*if* nothing serious has been done on the subject already") was communicated to Ellmann as early as September 6, 1943. By February 23, 1945, Mason was deep into matters Joycean, reporting to Ellmann from the Marshall Islands of "the New Directions edition of Joyce's *Stephen Hero* . . . from which was distilled his *Portrait.* The manuscript has been at Harvard for some time (Levin mentioned it in his 1942 *Joyce*). . . . I've wondered what was in it ever since I learned of its existence. Both the Portrait and Stephen are on their way out here, so I should have some fun in the near future. Levin also mentioned a bibliography on Joyce in progress in '42. I hope it comes to light before I get back to civilian life."

In late 1946 Mason was back at Yale, while Ellmann was in Dublin on a Rockefeller Post-War Fellowship. Ellmann wrote that he had completed two-thirds of his Yeats dissertation. He also reported meeting A. Norman Jeffares. "You remember Jeffares," he writes to Mason on October 27, "the guy who had the article on Byzantium that you showed me." Ellmann was not impressed: "Very pleasant and not very intelligent. . . . I'm anxious to try to publish before he ruins the material by misinterpreting it." When writing to Mason from Dublin, Ellmann is uncharacteristically bullish, partly because he knew he had Mrs. Yeats's support, partly under the influence of what Stephen Dedalus in *A Portrait* describes as the "gibes and violence of speech" of literary Dublin, and partly out of worry about rivals.[2] At the end of a letter of November 11 he reports, "My big problem here is people stealing my stuff; and since a lot of other people have the same problem we all live haunted lives, or rather ghost-like ones in which we conceal 9/10 of what we are thinking and meet the world, as in the Japanese fairy tale, with a face without features in it." Hence the autocratic or perhaps mock autocratic tone of the advice he gives Mason at the beginning of the letter. After warning him not to write on Auden—"Auden is a living man; I am thoroughly convinced that it is impossible to handle with any degree of finality any subject which has to do with anyone animate"—he moves on to Joyce:

> Do not write on Joyce. The problem here is admittedly more complicated: the man is unquestionably in his grave. But listen to me attentively: it is

> impossible to do Joyce outside of Dublin, Paris, and possibly Zurich. I know Levin did, but Levin wrote a very small book and confined himself to special problems. . . . To understand Joyce you have to come here; you have to get hold of letters; you have to talk to people who knew him; all this stuff about Vico and so on is, so far as I am concerned, all balderdash so far as a creative writer who is not a philosopher is concerned.
>
> I have said you can't do Joyce out of Ireland; you also can't do Joyce without a very careful study of Catholic doctrine and literature. If you try to, you will go off. I can only prove this by telling you my own experience with Yeats; when I was making notes before going to Washington, the coherent picture was getting further away; when I worked on the GD [Golden Dawn] and Theosophy, I overestimated their importance; when I first arrived here I got overly involved in the father-son split. You will think that these are the displacements which always occur, but I assure you that outside this milieu I should have been constantly askew. It is the same way with almost every *Southern Review* [that is, American] article on Yeats; even when they are on the right track, they quote somebody like George Moore as an authority and are instantly derailed. You can't work on a man so recently dead without being the constant prey of his friends' misconceptions.
>
> If you could come over here I think Joyce is still doubtful, although you could undoubtedly find enough for a thesis which would be authoritative so far as it went. But exegesis with Joyce is in an earlier stage even than in Yeats, and your problems would therefore be greater than mine which are, God knows, great enough.

Ellmann then suggests alternative subjects. Why not write on Disraeli's novels or "some obscure work of Melville, say, or somebody from New England which you know well." This last suggestion prompts a return to Joyce: "Are you prepared to do the biographical work which is the prerequisite to any new study of Joyce? Every creative artist has a life so bound up with his work that the questions of value—here I speak largely of Yeats and Carlyle, whom I know best—are constantly impinging upon facts of his life. I am positive that this is so with Joyce, and if you start attributing something or other to Vico you'll find in the end that it is really due to Clongowes, Aquinas, or the revolving door of a Dublin brothel." There were also professional or career difficulties to be considered: "I am not writing to be clever and I hope you will consider what you are doing very seriously.

You will gain nothing in traditional English depts.—which category includes most—by working either on Joyce or Auden; and you will gain little in the modern ones when it is discovered that you have only a graduate school contribution to make, however good of its kind. I was lucky enough and got to Dublin—otherwise my book would have been silly" (this last sentence is an afterthought, added in pen).

Ellmann's letter annoyed Mason, who was neither a delicate flower nor himself averse to giving advice. After hearing nothing from Mason for some weeks, Ellmann wrote again, admitting, "Since I wrote to you last I have seen some dissertation subjects at other American universities, and gather that the act of writing on the living is not so rare." But he continued to argue that Mason should not write on Joyce, suggesting that he contact John Kelleher for a second opinion. He again offered alternatives. Why not write on Rossetti? Pound? Vachel Lindsay? Edwin Arlington Robinson? "But you have probably already decided."[3]

Here is how Mason begins his reply to Ellmann's initial letter of November 11, in a letter written over a month later:

> Dear Dick,
> I have held off answering your unfortunate last letter since my instinct all along has been to kick your teeth out one by one. In a softer mood, I merely say, for Christ's sake stop playing Sir Oracle and get back here before you're beyond redemption. There has been some apprehension in these parts as to what was happening to you in the light of your letter published in the LonTimes Lit Sup [about being "on leave" from the Harvard faculty] and of a certain tone that was creeping into certain of your correspondences. This last business makes it perfectly clear that you've completely lost your self-perspective. What is worse, you seem to be losing perspective on your general field, and we can only hold out in hopes that you have kept your perspective on Yeats. The tone of your letter made you sound so foolish, and its substance seemed to be so wrong that I immediately took it to Feidelson, as you had suggested, and he corroborated both my impressions. If you don't hurry back to where you are evaluated by your accomplishments rather than by your social charm you will really be insufferable. I have been urged to burn your letter lest it should one day fall into strange hands, but I'm damned if I will. You wrote it and you must stand by the consequence.

At this point Mason draws a line under the subject of Ellmann's advice, moving on to Yale gossip and ending with a request that "the next time you're in the National Library will you please see if they have Joyce's broadsides: *The Holy Office* and *Gas from a Burner,* which are reprinted in Gorman's biography. Also whether they have the original version of his *Day of the Rabblement,* which appeared together with an article by F. J. C. Skeffington in *Two Essays,* Dublin, 1901."[4]

Within two years Mason had finished a draft of his dissertation and was considering sending it to Levin or Kelleher. During these years the two friends commented in detail on each other's work, Ellmann having dropped his objections to Mason writing on Joyce.[5] They also kept each other informed about their scholarly activities. In a letter of January 27, 1948, for example, Mason reported having attended a meeting of the James Joyce Society in New York:

> Of course, there were many people there who were more interested in throwing light on themselves than on Joyce. Robert Kastor showed some home movies of Joyce and his family, fine shots of Nora, Giorgio and Lucia. [Padraic] Colum read from the Cyclops episode with a fine Dublin accent, but not too much understanding of the scope. A Prof from National Univ. named MacHugh was there, said that he had met you in Dublin. . . . He has a movie of Dublin as represented in *Ulysses* from the Martello Tower to Nora's bum, he says. . . . [Eugene] Jolas was there and I asked him about his wife's collection of letters—he claims that there are very few Joyce letters around, says the project is coming along very slowly. The latest on letters, according to Slocum and Kastor, is that Stuart Gilbert is collecting them to edit. Nora to pass on what is to be included. Your buddies [Kelleher and Levin, presumably] will be interested to know, if they haven't heard, that Slocum has just received 18 packages representing all the newspaper clippings on Joyce that Harriet Weaver has collected since 1922.[6]

Mason later recalls that he was equally generous in sharing what he called his "discoveries": "about the interconnections between *Portrait* and *Ulysses,* about Stephen's aesthetic theory, about Levin's book and an article that James T. Farrell published in the *New York Times.* To all this Ellmann replied rather casually, little realising his future as a Joycean."[7] While at work on Yeats, Ellmann occasionally came across Joyce material, or had a thought about Joyce, which he passed along to Mason. In a letter of October 14, 1947, for example, he describes Freud's *Traumdeutung* as "anticipating Joyce by two years"; he also alerts Mason to "2 recent French books on Joyce—Louis Gillet, *Le Stele de James Joyce* and another short one. Have you seen them? Why not write Sylvia Beach? I'll get her address if you want it. I think Joyce did more journalism than anybody knows. Glad to hear that diss. is going well."

As Ellmann's career flourished, Mason's faltered. While at Williams College, he made a drastic mistake. Confident of being awarded a Fulbright Fellowship, he allowed the chair of the English Department to fill his job for the coming year. When the Fulbright fell through, the chair had nothing left to offer him. Ellmann was "horrified at your generosity with your dept.; your self-abnegation is beautiful but hardly prudent."[8] Ellmann also attempted to find a post for Mason. "Deeply grateful for your persistent efforts in my behalf," Mason wrote to him in an undated letter of autumn 1950, "and although I never expect you to be in my present situation, I hope to be able to repay your kindness sometime. Maybe I can babysit for you?" When Mason applied for a Rockefeller Post-War Fellowship, Ellmann offered detailed suggestions. The Rockefeller also fell through, as did a 1952 application for a fellowship from the American Council of Learned Societies.[9] During these years Mason found work teaching at Marlboro College, a small liberal arts college in Vermont.

In a letter to Ellmann of July 5, 1952, Mason summed up his career prospects. Failing to win a fellowship "quite effectively brings to an end any ambitions I may have had along scholarly lines. They can go blow it out their academic asses for all of me. I will write me a few articles sometime, and teach well, and if this isn't enough for whothehell, then I'll get out of the profession." This is pretty much what happened. As a graduate student, Mason had worked in the reference department of the Yale University Library (alerting Ellmann to all Yeats items in the catalogs). An avid book collector, he was from the start interested in archives, manuscripts, library holdings, and bibliography (in the tradition of Tinker, Potter, and other English professors at Yale). He had a wife and a baby daughter to support, and a few months after the July 5, 1952, letter about getting out of the profession, he decided to accept a job as a librarian at the University of Wyoming. This job, he wrote to Ellmann in a letter of November 27, he was enjoying. The staff were "excellent," except for the librarian, "but since he is in England on a Fulbright (see what thrives), it is a happy group. I am working *40* hours a week, and it is wonderfully refreshing after teaching. I am not at all convinced I am going back to teaching. Time alone will tell. Meanwhile, I'm catching up on reading I had been out of touch with at Marlboro."

Going to Wyoming was a wise move for Mason and the beginning of a distinguished career. From there he went on to work on the library staffs of Montana State University, Colorado College, Hofstra University, and the University of Colorado at Boulder, for the last three as chief librarian. In 1976 he was nominated to run for the presidency of the American Library Association. He served as a consultant in the planning of many library buildings, was awarded several honorary degrees, and found time to produce ten books, including two on Joyce—*The Early Joyce: The Book Reviews, 1902–1903* (1955), coedited with Stanislaus Joyce, and *The Critical Writings of James Joyce*, coedited with Ellmann and published the same year as *James Joyce*. Mason also wrote more than a hundred scholarly and professional articles.

* * *

With Mason working forty hours a week as a librarian and his scholarly career "effectively [brought] to an end," and Ellmann having delivered *The Identity of Yeats* to his publishers, the question of a new project for Ellmann loomed large. Mason's opinion, which he urged "very actively," was that Ellmann should consider writing a biographical work on Joyce.[10] "I'll give you all the help I can," he promised in the July 5 letter. "You can do it, not many other people could. Right now, I don't know what kind of a book you could complete, because there are yawning gaps in the available information which cannot be closed quickly." Mason then offered Ellmann names and addresses of the most important Joyce collectors and archives, together with detailed instructions about how they were to be approached. "When you definitely decide when you are going [to Ireland, then Europe, on paid research leave] and what you are going to do, write me, and I'll go through everything I have and send you anything pertinent."

* * *

Mason may have been unsure about the "kind of a book" Ellmann could produce, by which he meant the kind of biography, but he knew something of Ellmann's views on Joyce, both as a writer and as a man. This knowledge he acquired not only from correspondence and visits to Evanston but from Ellmann's 1950 *Kenyon Review* article "Joyce and Yeats," his first published writing on Joyce. The article begins by contrasting the larger outlook of the two writers. "Even when it uses local and national themes," Ellmann writes of Yeats's poetry, what it "longs for" is "'a place of stone'" (a phrase from the Yeats poem "To a Friend Whose Work Has Come to Nothing"), by which is meant a place beyond the local and the national.[11] Joyce, in contrast, "exiles and isolates himself, only to make his subject Dublin and a congress of men. Joyce rooted his work in natural acts as intently as Yeats in esoteric experience."[12]

This view of Joyce's "place" as "Dublin and a congress of men" was complicated by Joyce's views on theater policy and the Irish language. Joyce had reservations about the Irishness of Irish theater, wanting it, writes Ellmann, "to be part of Europe, while Yeats feared special qualities might thereby be lost. The insularity which repelled Joyce was to Yeats, if properly maintained, a source of intensity." The attitudes of the two men to the revival of the Irish language were also at odds, "Joyce opposing and Yeats sponsoring it" (p. 33). In identifying Joyce as a modernist, Ellmann quotes Yeats, from the first edition of *A Vision* (1926), "brilliantly" relating *Ulysses* "to the seemingly dissimilar writings of Pound, Eliot and Pirandello, as fragmenting an earlier unit of consciousness" (p. 50).[13] To Ellmann, as to Yeats, it is the European context that matters most for Joyce.

In discussing the two writers' shared interest in system or myth (Mason's territory), Ellmann begins with a crucial difference: "Yeats's impulse toward order makes the myths which appear in his work, such as the annunciation of a new era, ritualized, heraldic, supernatural." For Joyce, "similar myths appear unrehearsed, casual, part of the order of things. Yeats felt the need for sharp outlines, for a protrusive, exigent form; Joyce preferred to flesh out a more Gothic form with a multitude of particulars. He revels in the clutter by which Yeats, conceiving of art as purgation, was repelled. His manuscripts, at least the later ones, are revised by accretion, Yeats's by reduction" (p. 55). There is a similar difference between Joyce's attitude to cyclic myths and T. S. Eliot's: "For Joyce, whatever differences may exist between ages are not to be put in valuative terms. As he said of Stephen, all ages were as one to him, resulting from the same laws of behavior, and equally remote from perfection" (p. 56).

Ellmann's point about the "Gothic form" of myth in Joyce connects to his account of Joyce's language or style. "Yeats has no barrier about subjects," Ellmann writes toward the end of the article, "but in responding to unexalted occasions he guards a verbal formality. Even at his wildest, he maintains the poise, the authority of language. It is just this poise and authority which Joyce seems always to be disturbing, as if he were mounting a revolution against that worst of tyrannies, the lexical kind. Yeats is always looking to further and to celebrate an aristocracy of culture, while Joyce, who depends more than Yeats upon such an aristocracy to read him, declines to endorse it, and in his work is concerned only with people who, he said, make less than a thousand pounds a year" (p. 55).

Two points are worth noting about this passage, both characteristic of *James Joyce*. The first is the poise and authority of Ellmann's own writing, Yeatsian rather than Joycean (one recalls Joseph Epstein's crack about Ellmann looking "nothing like his prose"); the second is the knowing irony of the remark about Joyce's culturally aristocratic readers. "Like other people," Ellmann writes elsewhere, in a similar spirit, "Yeats devoted more time to thinking about *Ulysses* than to reading it" (p. 50). When Joyce denounced Synge's play *Riders to the Sea,* Ellmann tells us, "Synge paid absolutely no attention, the one attitude toward criticism by which Joyce could be impressed" (p. 41). In Yeats, the beloved is "a Dantean symbol binding heaven and earth"; in Joyce, she is "a more cajolable entity"—the effect of which, Ellmann suggests, is to turn love into "a romantic convention so exhausted as to be slightly undermined" (p. 35). After a paragraph detailing Joyce's arrogance at his first meeting with Yeats ("I really don't care whether you like what I am doing or not"), Ellmann begins the next paragraph: "In terror of excessive charm, Joyce took up his objections to Yeats's recent work" (p. 38). What these instances suggest is that Ellmann's prose, like his attitude to Joyce more generally, can be viewed as combining Joycean as well as Yeatsian elements or impulses. "For Yeats the method of literature was to raise the ordinary to the heroic, for Joyce a movement down was as required as a movement up, and he mingled ordinary, heroic, and mock-heroic without wishing to compound them" (p. 54).

Mason singled out the final paragraph of "Joyce and Yeats" for special praise. "Just got in the offprint," he writes to Ellmann in an undated letter: "I think that the ending is now just the right thing to top off a good job on the whole." (He then goes on to point out that Ellmann gets the date of the publication of *Ulysses* wrong.) The paragraph ends by distinguishing between the *voyeur* and the *voyant,* Joyce belonging to the first category, Yeats to the second. "The sharpness of Joyce's perceptions comes from a conviction that all things are worth observing," concludes Ellmann, "while the vigor of Yeats's aspirations comes from an unwilling and yet acute acknowledgment of experience and of its shortcomings. In this middle ground their troubled friendship was possible" (p. 56).

* * *

In his several accounts of how he came to write Joyce's biography, Ellmann singles out the moment in 1952 when "a lawyer called me and said, 'Come and see my Joyce collection.'" This lawyer, James F. Spoerri, lived in Evanston and his Joyce collection consisted of over 900 items. The strength of the collection was in printed materials, both books and periodicals, including all first editions of Joyce's books (excepting "five minor items printed for copyright purposes which exist in only one, two or three copies").[14] Spoerri had collected over 200 books and pamphlets devoted wholly to Joyce and his works and another 200 or so books containing critical and biographical material. Although initially Spoerri claimed not to have manuscript material (which was not true, Mason told Ellmann in a letter of November 29, 1952), he was otherwise forthcoming and friendly and Ellmann was characteristically quick to reciprocate. In addition to arranging an exhibition of items from Spoerri's collection to be displayed in the lobby of the Deering Library at Northwestern, he invited Spoerri to talk about Joyce to his class on contemporary English, Irish, and American literature.

Once he had seen the Spoerri collection, Ellmann claimed, "it occurred to me that one might be able to do another biography. The only one at that time was by Gorman, Herbert Gorman. That was written while Joyce was alive and under great restrictions. He didn't know about half of Joyce's life and there were big gaps which he filled in by telling us what was going on in the rest of the world. And so I thought, well, I could do better than this, even if I only use the secondary material that has accumulated."[15] Gorman's *James Joyce: A Definitive Biography* was published in 1939, nine years after he began work on it. It was his second book on Joyce, the first being a laudatory critical study, *James Joyce: His First Forty Years* (1924). Gorman was a New Yorker whose Greenwich Village circle included Theodore Dreiser, Sinclair Lewis, and Eleanor Wylie. He wrote novels and verse as well as other biographies (of Hawthorne, Longfellow, Dumas *père,* Mary Queen of Scots). He was also a frequent reviewer for the *New York Times.* Ellmann was not alone in his low opinion of Gorman's Joyce biography: Hugh Kenner recalled "struggling to extract even rudimentary chronology from Gorman"; Brenda Maddox, the biographer of Nora Joyce, described the book as "uninformative, obsequious, and lifeless."[16]

For Ellmann, Gorman provided a perfect object lesson in the dangers of writing about a living author. These dangers he spells out in his discussion of Gorman in *James Joyce,* beginning with Joyce's being sometimes cooperative, at other times "oddly reticent," evasive, uninterested (p. 632). Originally Joyce wanted Stuart Gilbert, an Englishman, to be his biographer, following on from his *James Joyce's Ulysses: A Study* (1930). But when offered the job in the late 1920s, Gilbert wisely declined, on the grounds that he was still at work on the *Ulysses* book.[17] As Gorman was living in Paris at the time, and the Joyces had become friendly with him, he was offered the job and accepted. "Without saying so directly to Gorman," Ellmann writes, Joyce "made clear that he was to be treated as a saint with an unusually protracted martyrdom" (p. 631). (Tom Stoppard, an admirer of Ellmann, described Joyce in similar terms, as "an essentially private man who wished his total indifference to public notice to be universally realised.")[18] Toward the end of his life, in a "bilious" mood, Gilbert imagined how a better or freer biographer than Gorman might have depicted his subject: "A whole chapter would have been given to the description and illustration of the method by which he got people to put their time—and sometimes money—completely at his disposal; to follow him wherever he wanted them to accompany him: boring plays and operas, dull expensive restaurants; to [cancel] their agreements if he wanted their assistance in some trivial, easily postponed task; to run errands for him, undertake delicate and distasteful missions which exposed them to snubs, rebuffs, and ridicule at his bidding."[19] "I will never write another biography of a living man," Gorman complained to his publisher after Joyce had delayed the book's publication: "It is too difficult and thankless a task."[20]

* * *

In his letter of July 5, 1952, after "very actively" urging Ellmann to do the Joyce biography, Mason warned him that "there are Joyce letters scattered . . . throughout large libraries all over the country."[21] To locate these letters as well as other Joyce materials, he would need the help of two men: Herbert Cahoon (1918–2001), a Joyce collector who for the past dozen years had worked as assistant director of the Rare Book Room at the New York Public Library (in 1954 he became head of the Morgan Library, where he stayed for thirty-five years), and John J. Slocum (1914–1997), the most important collector of Joyce materials in the immediate postwar period. Like Cahoon, Slocum had been educated at Harvard and Columbia, but he also had a career away from books and collecting, as a diplomat working for the Inspection Corps of the United States Information Agency. Slocum was rich, and in 1951 he gave his Joyce collection—letters, manuscripts, clippings, photographs, printed books, and pamphlets—to the Beinecke Library at Yale.[22]

"You cannot do without his help," Mason said of Slocum in his letter to Ellmann of July 5. "He is intensely interested in having work done on Joyce, especially if it involves use of his material at Yale, and he would help any serious effort." That Norman Pearson, now back at Yale, was in charge of the Joyce papers in the Beinecke was an added incentive. In 1952 Slocum was stationed in Germany, and the only address Mason had for him was with the Office of the US High Commissioner in Germany, care of its Office of Public Affairs in New York. Mason therefore suggested that Ellmann write to Cahoon, with whom Slocum had been collaborating on their soon-to-be-published *Bibliography of James Joyce: 1882–1941* (1953), the fullest and most reliable source of data about Joyce's writings for decades to come. On scouting trips to Europe, the two Joyceans sought out items to document and describe, also for Slocum to buy, while plotting ways to house as many of them as possible under the same roof.

The roof under which Slocum originally intended his Joyce's papers to be housed was at Harvard, not Yale. A letter Slocum wrote to Stanislaus Joyce on May 25, 1949, sheds light not only on his *modus operandi* but on his concern for the needs of scholars. It also suggests something of the "reglar Desparrados" (Sylvia Beach's term) with whom he was dealing:

> Considering the possible sale of any manuscripts or other book material that you might be willing to dispose of, you have probably heard from a "Dr." Jacob Schwartz, an engaging rascal if there ever was one, but a rascal as I learned some ten years ago to my sorrow. Providing you don't

> mention my name to him or the conditions, I will top any effort he makes you for any material by twenty-five percent. Recently he has been getting hold of Joyceana all over France and England and scattering it all over the world, while I am trying to get it together in one place, catalogue it and then deposit it in the Harvard College Library where it will be available to students for all time. If you ever wanted to part with an appreciable amount of material by and about your brother, books or manuscripts, I would be happy to have them go into the library as a group identified and known as the "Stanislaus Joyce Collection."[23]

That Harvard declined to have Slocum's collection, for what were described as administrative reasons, partly accounts for Mason's warning to Ellmann in the July 5 letter: Slocum "was not happy with your refusal to let him have a copy of the Joyce-Yeats stuff [presumably related to the first meeting of the two writers in London] and he has you classified with 'that Harvard group.' His reaction to them is summed up in his placing the collection in Yale. . . . When you approach him . . . I suggest some jocose reference to your disconnection from Harvard." As it turned out, it took a while for Slocum to respond to Ellmann's inquiries.

Ellmann's way with Slocum was smoothed by Mason's endorsement, also by his suggestion that he approach Cahoon for Slocum's address in Germany. In mid-August Ellmann wrote to Slocum to ask if they could meet sometime in the spring, when Ellmann planned to be in Europe.[24] By mid-December Slocum had not replied. Nor was Ellmann able to arrange to meet with him in New York, when Slocum returned for two weeks in February. Undeterred, Ellmann wrote to Cahoon on February 14 with questions for Slocum, principally "whether he has any leads in Ireland. . . . I'd also like to know whether he'd have any time to talk with me if I could get over to Germany to see him." In the same letter, he asked Cahoon for the addresses of Joyce's son Giorgio, Stuart Gilbert, Harriet Weaver, and J. F. Byrne, Joyce 's closest friend at University College Dublin and the model for the character "Cranly" in Joyce's novels.

Throughout December, Ellmann pursued Mason with queries about Joyce and Joyceans. He was particularly concerned to find out "whether Stanislaus would be accessible in Trieste, and whether he ever comes to Italy, and exactly what he's up to in his Autobiography. He seems the key figure in any biographical work, and I'm afraid to write to him for fear of starting off

Stanislaus and Nelly Joyce, 1926.

on the wrong foot."[25] In reply, in a letter of December 11, Mason warned Ellmann to be careful in approaching Stanislaus, who, "as he wrote me is writing a book about Joyce based on his personal knowledge of him and unpublished material which he has on hand. . . . He says 'My aim in writing is to present my brother's character and outlook as I knew and understood them in about thirty years of life together.' I had thought of mentioning your project to him, but did not for the same reason. If he thinks you're trying to beat him to his book, he will not tell you a thing."

In later correspondence, Mason pushed Ellmann about his research plans. "From my original talk with you, and the fact that you're sailing past the American materials and going to Dublin, I gather that you're going to do a book on Joyce in Ireland. But from your present questions, you seem to have in mind a full biography."[26] Ellmann himself was uncertain. All he was sure of was that he would be free to conduct research on Joyce in the spring quarter at Northwestern and in the following summer, from March to September 1953; that he would begin in Dublin; that he would go on to Paris; and that, if time permitted, he would make preliminary visits to other locations in Europe where Joyce had lived (Trieste, Pola, Rome, Zurich). He would be accompanied by Mary and two-and-a-half-year-old Stephen in Dublin and Paris, if not on further trips. "Your question about my precise plans is hard for me to answer," he wrote to Mason in an undated letter in February:

> I think I'd like to do a complete biography, but I begin to fear that insuperable difficulties may get in the way. I am still hopeful, however, that things may become easier once I get to Europe. If I can't do a complete job, I'd like to do the Irish years. If I can't do either, I hope to do an article or two. I've fallen into a habit of saying I'm doing a biography of Joyce, but am trying to keep my head above water for a few more months till I understand the situation better. The trouble with doing the Irish period alone is that I learned in my work on Yeats that the later life made many things clearer about the early, and at getting at so difficult a temperament as Joyce's you perhaps have to know everything there is to be known.

Other difficulties with a full-scale biography concerned the nature of Joyce's life. Unlike Yeats, Joyce lived a life away from the public sphere, largely without incident. "Everyone warned me that Joyce's life was as dull in private gestures as it was wanting in public ones." Nor did Joyce have much to say publicly or in print about the nature of his art. Ellmann, however, found it hard to believe "that a writer could have so much extravagance inside him and express it only in his art? Was it possible that a man so sensitive to language had never said anything memorable?"[27] He also cited the example of Joyce's own interest in the private lives of the undistinguished, as well as his ability to make their lives memorable. "Many of the things that interest me will probably appear trivial to you," he wrote to Jacques Mercanton on April 6, 1954, "but I am endeavoring to treat Joyce's life with some of the same fullness that he treats Bloom's life." As he wrote to Joyce's sister May Monaghan on November 22, 1953, his task was to make "as accurate a picture as possible of the relatively uneventful outward life . . . allowing the occasional flash of what a French poet I know [Michaux] calls 'the space within' to give the ordinary events new meaning. This is I suppose close to your brother's own method in *Ulysses,* and seems to me to be enormously difficult." Ellmann, in other words, was taking Joyce's part ("Let us take the poet's part") in several senses, becoming like him in order to understand him.

In the letter of November 29, Mason encourages Ellmann, but he also makes clear the many difficulties he would face (in something of the spirit of Ellmann's 1946 letter warning Mason against writing a dissertation on Joyce). "You could do a hell of a good biography," Mason writes, "but you can't do so in your present rush[ed] state of mind."

> You could probably do it in about ten years on a full job. You could probably do it in five but not sooner. I was the first serious person into Slocum's collection and the doors stood yawning open, but from the very first I resisted it, because it is an enormous job. In dealing with Joyce's character you are dealing with a man about as different from Stephen [Dedalus], from what he seems to be in his works, from what he seemed to be to people, as you can imagine. You weave your way through rumor and confusion and darkness. There are parts of his life that are fully documented and parts that are completely blank. What information there is is scattered all over. Just yanking together the presently known material is a two year job, and even then there would be great yawning gaps, serious enough to impair any picture you might form of the man. There have been perhaps three thousand articles on him, many on the continent. Most of them are useless, some of them contain priceless information. Some of Joyce's friends are still living. . . .
>
> By all this I do not mean to discourage you. If you set your mind on it, you can do the job that can be done better than anyone. But knowing the eagerness of your beaverosity, I'd hate to have you find yourself two or three years along and developing an impetuosity that would hurl into print something that would sound good for a while, but would not be basically sound.

Ellmann was not just telling friends and colleagues that he was embarking on a biography of Joyce, he was telling publishers as well. Random

House had turned him down but his editors at Oxford University Press were interested and would eventually offer him a contract; his editors at Macmillan also offered him a contract, contingent on his securing the cooperation of the Joyce family. When Ellmann declined this offer on the grounds that "the point of my seeking a contract in advance . . . was to help me in my dealings with Joyce's family and friends," Macmillan waived the contingency. Ellmann's negotiations with OUP and Macmillan began on the eve of his departure for Europe, grew more complicated after his arrival there, and will be treated more fully later in this chapter. They were conducted at a time when he was telling friends that he was uncertain whether he could do any sort of biography, let alone the full-scale life he was promising. They also involved his agreeing to delivery dates he knew would be impossible to meet.

* * *

On March 25, 1953, the Ellmanns departed New York for England on the SS *America.* After a brief stopover in London to consult with Macmillan not only about the Joyce biography but about proofs for the English edition of *The Identity of Yeats,* they set off for Ireland, arriving in Dublin on April 3. There they were greeted by Richard J. Hayes ("Jim" to his friends), director of the National Library of Ireland, whom Ellmann had met on his first trip to Dublin in September 1945.[28] Hayes knew and approved of Ellmann's plans: "We all *reJoyce* to hear you are coming back to your spiritual home," he wrote as early as August 12, 1952. "I am very pleased that Northwestern are giving you a quarter to do a biography of James Joyce. I intend to add another quarter to this to make up the even half dollar which I feel your work will well earn."[29] At the Dublin station, Hayes met the Ellmanns and guided them to the train to Killiney, where Sean O'Faolain had found a place for them to rent for the spring and summer. Killiney, where the O'Faolains lived, had once been a village but was now a rich Dublin suburb and popular summer resort ten miles south of the center of the city. In a letter to his parents on April 5, Ellmann calls it "one of the beauty spots of Ireland. . . . a sort of Evanston to Dublin—full of big estates and large homes. Ours is a five-room house, all on one floor, with a lovely garden. The railroad station is two blocks away, the town is about half a mile up the hill, so we order things by telephone."

When the Ellmanns arrived at the house, the O'Faolains welcomed them, having turned on the gas and electricity, lit fires, arranged vases of flowers and filled hot water bottles. Two days later Mary wrote to Ellmann's parents with a mixed report: "I think neither Dick nor I has ever lived in a more beautiful or more uncomfortable place!" "Tigin," the name of the house, was "a charmingly designed cottage" with views of Killiney Bay and the mountains in Bray (a nearby seaside resort) "from almost every window." The Irish Sea "is simply *there* at the foot of our little lane." But the cottage was cold, poorly heated by "tiny fireplaces and rather crude and ineffectual electric heaters," dangerous for two-year-old Stephen. Hayes had warned Ellmann about the weather: "Mary and your firstborn will, I am sure, be happy here during our gorgeous Summer. He will be able to make mudpies on the dryer days and swim in the backyard in the wetter."[30]

Although trains from Killiney to Dublin ran every twenty minutes, Ellmann rented a car to "take little drives into the country as well as to Dublin."[31] "I go in every morning," he wrote to Cahoon, on April 16, "and search for old friends or old documents of Joyce." At Killiney, he explained to his parents, they had "a retinue of servants, a nice girl who works three hours a day Monday, Wed., and Thurs., and stays on into the evening to babysit if we want her; an older woman who comes for two days a week; and a gardener whose expense is borne partly by us and partly by the owner." What made the servants affordable was the fact that "a maid costs $1.40 a day here, and a gardener about the same."[32] As a consequence, the Ellmanns' Dublin social life was almost as busy as it had been on their honeymoon in 1949. In a letter of May 10, Mary writes to Ellmann's parents that they have been to a new play with Mrs. Yeats (who fell asleep in the third act), have seen the Montgomerys and the Sheridans, "both very pleasant couples," and that "Niall [Mary has written "Neil"] Sheridan, as Dick perhaps wrote you, has lent Dick a great deal of Joyce material."[33] At another party, Mary writes in the same letter, "we met Owen Sheehy-Skeffington [interviewed by Ellmann three days earlier] whose father was a friend of Joyce's [and the model for "McCann" in *A Portrait*]—the whole family is outstanding in Dublin affairs."[34]

At first Ellmann's daytime forays into Dublin were not productive. "So far I've not turned up anything sensational," he writes to Cahoon, in a letter dated April 16, "but I've at least seen the records of occupancy of the Martello Tower and that sort of thing, and begin to feel familiar with the material.

But it is slow work, and always when I am hottest on the scent I am told the information will be ready the *next* time I come in, or that the office is closed for the 'half day,' or for the interminable lunch period, or not open until after 10." When he went to interview Richard I. Best (1872–1959), Hayes's predecessor as director of the National Library, his spirits were hardly lifted. Best had been an acquaintance of Joyce's as a young man. He was eighty-two at the time of his interview with Ellmann and was much exercised about Joyce's portrayal of him in the ninth, or Scylla and Charybdis, episode of *Ulysses,* set in the National Library. The Richard Best of the episode (Joyce used his real name in the novel) is given a catchphrase, "Don't you know," which the real-life Best denied was his. Best then informed Ellmann (maliciously?) that Joyce had once sent him "a great many articles and notes from Trieste and elsewhere," but that he had thrown them out, along with all the other Joyce material he had kept stored in a drawer. In the same interview he lamented how many of his and Joyce's acquaintances were no longer alive. "There were a 100 people who used to come to my house," he told Ellmann, "and all of them are dead now; all dead. It's a terrible thing," a lament that left Ellmann complaining to Cahoon: "I should have done this ten years ago."[35]

The interview with Best, though depressing at the time, was not without its uses. In the *James Joyce* chapter "The Backgrounds of *Ulysses,*" Ellmann sees Best's "Don't you know" denial as "a useful warning. Even in a *roman à clef,* which *Ulysses* largely is, no key quite fits. Art lavishes on one man another man's hair, or voice, or bearing, with shocking disrespect for individual identity. . . . 'Are you in it?' or 'Am I in it?' The answer was hard to give" (p. 374). What is noteworthy about Ellmann's earliest interviews and inquiries, as in this instance, is how often he asks about episodes or aspects of *Ulysses.* For Ellmann, *Ulysses* is at the center of his understanding of Joyce, both as man and as artist, the place where his character is most fully revealed, the point of connection or conjunction between the Joyce of *Dubliners* and *A Portrait of the Artist as a Young Man* and the Joyce of *Finnegans Wake.*

* * *

Three days before the interview with Best, Ellmann reported receiving what he called his first "good lead." Its source was the Yeats biographer Joseph Hone, whom he had invited to lunch. He wrote to his parents, "One thing

I have been wanting to get into was the relation of fact to fiction in Ulysses, which opens in the Martello Tower a few miles north of us." Hone was able to identify the real-life model for "Haines," an Englishman staying in the Tower with Buck Mulligan and Stephen Dedalus, fictional versions of Oliver St. John Gogarty and Joyce himself. Ellmann already knew that "Haines" "was a real person and that his name was Trench, but Hone told me that he was an Irishman—so I feel I'm beginning to get a notion of what Joyce did to the facts for his artistic purposes."[36] (In fact, Samuel Chenevix Trench came from an old Anglo-Irish family, so he was neither wholly Irish nor wholly English.) Ellmann describes him in *James Joyce* as "insufferable," having "embraced the Irish revival so passionately, and to Joyce so offensively, that he called himself Diarmuid Trench" (pp. 178–79).

A second lead was provided by Niall Sheridan, who had himself once planned to write a biography of Joyce. The papers Mary Ellmann reported "Neil" as having given to Ellmann were those Sheridan was collecting for the biography. Ellmann described these papers as "very helpful," though not as helpful as he had hoped they would be. Also helpful was Arthur Power (1891–1984), an art critic for the *Irish Times,* who had known the Joyces in Paris in the early 1920s when he wrote on art for the Paris edition of the *New York Herald.* For a period in the early 1920s, Power was Joyce's closest friend in Paris, approved of by Nora in part because of his moderate drinking habits. Power appears as a character in *James Joyce* and is frequently cited in the notes as a source of quotations, anecdotes, and observations, not only from Ellmann's 1953 interview with him but from his memoir, *From an Old Waterford House* (1940).

These leads, reported in Ellmann's April 21 letter to his parents, were balanced by "a serious setback" concerning Constantine Curran (1883–1972), one of Joyce's college friends. According to Curran's daughter Elizabeth, "her father wouldn't give me any help because he is himself doing a life of Joyce in Ireland—I mean the Irish period." Curran's refusal to help mattered because "he is the only person surviving who knew him well in youth as well as maturity."[37] Undaunted, Ellmann wrote the same day to Stuart Gilbert, who lived in Paris and was now editing Joyce's letters (a safer prospect than writing his biography). After Ellmann explained that he was considering a biography, he asked Gilbert if he could meet with him in Paris. He also reassured Gilbert that he understood the magnitude of the task he was considering taking on, describing his current trip to Europe as "of necessity only a preliminary one." When he learned that Gilbert would be away from Paris on the dates the family planned to be there, he arranged to come to meet him by himself in mid-May.

Ellmann then set about arranging other interviews for the trip. On April 23 he wrote to Harriet Weaver, to introduce himself, to tell her his plans for a biography, and to arrange a meeting in Oxford, where she lived. Weaver replied on April 29, expressing guarded enthusiasm for these plans and a willingness to meet, but declining to be interviewed or to offer anything in the way of formal support or approval. On May 2 Ellmann wrote to thank her, also to inform her that he had "taken the liberty of sending you two of my books." As Amanda Sigler comments: "Sending books to his fellow Joyce scholars and Joyce sources was a technique that Ellmann frequently employed with varying results, and in this case his generosity proved effective. When *Yeats: The Man and the Masks* arrived on her doorstep on May 5, Weaver wrote to Ellmann that she looked forward to reading the biography, and when Ellmann's translation of Henri Michaux's *The Space Within* arrived on May 7, she exclaimed, 'I shan't know which of the two books to read first."[38]

In London, Ellmann arranged to meet with Frank Budgen (1882–1971), the English painter and writer, a close companion of Joyce's in Zurich during the war years. Ellmann was a great admirer of Budgen's memoir, *James Joyce and the Making of Ulysses* (1934), describing it to his father, who was now reading everything he could by and about Joyce, as "the most useful book to help in reading Joyce."[39] To Budgen himself, Ellmann declared that it "would be a great privilege for me to meet you" and that in addition to the memoir, "which has been of tremendous help to me," he had read "all the excellent articles you have written about Joyce."[40]

Other interviews Ellmann arranged in London were with George Roberts, the Irish actor and publisher, and W. R. ("Bertie") Rodgers, a poet and essayist. Rodgers gave Ellmann "quite a few leads." Roberts was trickier. In his capacity as managing director of the Dublin publishing house Maunsel and Company, Roberts had angered and disappointed Joyce by backing out of publishing *Dubliners,* after years of successive demands for alterations. This was in 1912, described by Ellmann as "the most disheartening year" of Joyce's life (p. 329). Roberts's mistreatment, a product of fears of prosecution for libel or obscenity, was seen by Joyce as the last of a series of indignities visited on him in Ireland. The place itself seemed hostile to him, as if it intended "to weary me out and if possible strangle me."[41] He would never return. On the train back to Trieste a furious Joyce composed the scatological broadside "Gas from a Burner" (the work Mason was eager for Ellmann to find for him in 1946), unmistakably spoken by and mocking Roberts. In *James Joyce,* Ellmann describes the broadside as a work of "wholly personal invective" (p. 346). Perhaps unsurprisingly, when Ellmann came to interview Roberts in London in May 1953, he found him less than forthcoming, though he "let drop a few useful things." Roberts was eighty at the time of the interview and claimed to be writing his own memoir. He died six months later with the memoir unfinished, though excerpts were published in the *Irish Times* in July–August 1955, mostly about his early years as an actor in Dublin. Roberts's papers were deposited in the National Library of Ireland, where Ellmann was able to consult them.[42]

There was one other destination on the trip, aside from London, Paris, and Oxford. Ellmann reported to his parents early in May, "I finally called Slocum . . . in Germany, and he sounded very cheery and invited me to stay with him when I go to see him." Slocum was living in Bad Godesberg, just outside Bonn, in a lavish apartment on the west bank of the Rhine. In addition to offering to put Ellmann up, he promised "access to his whole collection," precisely the help Mason thought Ellmann required. He would see Slocum first, then Gilbert in Paris, then Budgen, Roberts, and Rodgers in London, then Harriet Weaver in Oxford, all in less than ten days, from May 14 to May 23. A "whirlwind tour" Mary called it.[43]

* * *

The tour proved to be a great success. Slocum was as good as his word, showing Ellmann a list of all his holdings, including materials not at Yale (Ellmann knew of these, but pretended not to know), and keeping him up on the activities of other Joyce scholars, one of whom, Richard Kain, had also been considering a biography. Slocum suggested that Ellmann write to Kain "to the effect that if he were not himself doing a biography, I'd be grateful for his suggestions about mine. Slocum thought, I believe, that Kain would be put off the book if he knew I were doing one."[44] This is not quite what happened, as we shall see. In Paris, Gilbert was somewhat evasive when pressed about a publication date for the letters, but he was otherwise "affable" and supplied Ellmann with addresses for several other Joyce contacts. Especially welcome was the news that Constantine Curran's letters were in Gilbert's possession. Also encouraging was the fact that Gilbert had obtained access to the letters of Valery Larbaud, thanks to the American literary critic Patricia Hutchins Greacen, wife of the Irish poet Robert Greacen. In *James Joyce,* Ellmann describes Larbaud as "the most respected critic of foreign literature, especially of English and Italian, in Paris" (p. 514). Sylvia Beach and Adrienne Monnier had introduced Larbaud to Joyce in the 1920s, and when Larbaud read *Ulysses* he described it as "great and comprehensive," like Rabelais's *Gargantua and Pantagruel.* Larbaud had translated Coleridge, Whitman, and Samuel Butler, and was crucial not only in helping to present Joyce to the French literary world but in overseeing Auguste Morel's translation of *Ulysses.*

Harriet Weaver, who was at least as important to Ellmann's project as Slocum and Gilbert, also proved accommodating. She was "gracious," Ellmann wrote to Slocum, and showed him "several books and manuscripts," including an unpublished five-page fragment of *Stephen Hero* "which seemed to me to establish that Joyce originally carried the Portrait much further along in his life, presumably up to 1904, if not later."[45] Like almost all of Ellmann's interviewees, she offered additional leads, which he assiduously followed, afterward making sure, quickly and fully, to thank and compliment everyone involved. "Tell Mrs. Budgen how much I appreciated her inviting me to supper," he writes to Frank Budgen on May 31, from Killiney. "It was very pleasant meeting you both and your charming daughter, and it is nice to know that Joyce had such good company in Zurich." This remark suggests the role sympathy as well as objectivity played in Ellmann's approach to his subject.

* * *

On his return to Killiney, in a letter of May 23, Ellmann wrote to Fred Faverty, chair of the English Department at Northwestern, to report what he called "reasonably good success." Working on Joyce was different from working on Yeats. With the Joyce family, he noted, "I have to contend with shabby gentility, with the friends I contend with memoir-writing of their own, and (on a higher plain) simple loyalty promoting concealment. I have nevertheless found out quite a lot and feel that the book can be written." A week or so later the Ellmanns were invited to dinner by Arthur Power. "Eva Joyce, the sister, was there," he reported in a June 3 letter to his parents:

> She is awfully hard to get to, but turned out to be very nice. And we had lunch on Monday. She has her reserves, but told me a great deal of stuff that I could not have got elsewhere. As a result for the first time I felt moved to begin organizing stuff, and got a few pages of material together on the family. She looks like Joyce and she lived in his house in Trieste for two years. Though not particularly educated, she has a certain sharp perceptiveness. And of course she could tell me a lot about the family history.

The impression Ellmann made on Eva Joyce seems to have opened the way to the other sisters. Before setting off with his family on July 8 for the Paris leg of their trip, Ellmann had seen "all the available Joyce sisters (three of them) a good many times, usually separately, and they told me a great deal of stuff which I think no other investigator has obtained from them—at least, so two of them informed me."[46] By June 9 he was writing to C. G. Bowen of OUP "to correct a misleading impression I gave you that the family wouldn't cooperate. As a matter of fact they have been very helpful. I arranged my approach to them carefully, and they turned out to be very kind-hearted. One sister, Mrs. Eileen Schaurek, will talk about anything, with what seems complete frankness. The other two, Eva Joyce and Mrs. Monaghan, have their reserves, but they're helping too." In addition to helping Ellmann identify characters in *Dubliners,* May Monaghan later wrote him a five-page letter in which she argued for her mother's importance in Joyce's early life.[47]

One source of the sisters' "reserves" was the hostility some Catholics felt toward Joyce. "Being a relative of Joyce is very difficult in this country," wrote Ellmann to James Spoerri on May 5, 1953. "At least one of the sisters feels persecuted, claims she has been discharged from jobs because of her late brother and his works." In the week before the Power dinner, Ellmann had experienced Catholic hostility to Joyce firsthand. On May 25 he had written to Father D. P. Kennedy of Belvedere College SJ, where Joyce went to school after the family moved from Bray to the Dublin suburb of Blackrock. Ellmann was keen to see Joyce's "grades, to know the exact dates of his attendance, the date when he became the head of the Sodality [year or class in this context], and to see any programmes of plays in which he acted." Kennedy replied on June 3 that he feared he could be of little help. In addition to having no records of payment, he could not explain how

Joyce was allowed to attend the school after his family could no longer afford fees. All he could offer was the speculation that Jesuit schools like Belvedere were reluctant to lose promising students.[48] Ellmann also wrote to Father Roche, rector of Joyce's previous school, Clongowes, in Clane, County Kildare, a boarding school about thirty miles from Dublin. The rector agreed to a meeting but he, too, did not think he had much information for Ellmann. When Ellmann arrived at the school the next day, May 29, the rector was unavailable, and Ellmann was given a tour by his secretary and the Father Minister, "his second-in-command, a short tough-looking priest."[49] Ellmann reported to Frank Budgen two days later that the Father Minister "went into a brief fury, demanding whether I would want my children to read Joyce's books." When Ellmann tried to calm him, he barked "Yes or no!" When Ellmann replied "Yes!" the Father Minister was briefly silent, then retorted "No, surely not all that muck." Then he softened (worried, Ellmann guessed, that "the absent rector might feel that his zeal was excessive"). Apologetically, he introduced Ellmann to a small pupil who "told me how thick Clongowes pandybats are. (Very thick, it appears.)" Although the rector's secretary then showed Ellmann "that Joyce's father had failed to pay the last tuition fees," Clongowes was able to produce little more in terms of records than had Belvedere. Nevertheless, Ellmann wrote to Budgen, "I pick up a few details wherever I go."[50]

* * *

Ellmann characterized his last few weeks in Dublin in a letter of July 13 to Bowen, written from Paris. The material he collected was "of several kinds." In addition to Joyce's sisters, he interviewed Nora's sister in Galway, who "also told me a great deal and claimed that no one else had got it from her." He found people "who had been neighbors of the Joyces during the 'nineties, several of his classmates at school and at the university, and a lot of casual acquaintances." Then there was the material Sheridan had collected and the material collected by a hired assistant, "interesting documentary evidence (deeds of sale and mortgage, addresses etc.) of the decline of the Joyce family fortune of the nineties." Altogether, "it is quite a pile of anecdotal and biographical detail." Ellmann found this detail "exciting," but added, "I suppose I was myself most exhilarated by my success in finding out the background of *Ulysses* and identifying the characters in Joyce's books. People have been talking for years about identification, but nobody has done it, and one reason is that aside from a few obvious identifications there are fairly considerable difficulties. One of Joyce's sisters helped me with many of the stories in *Dubliners,* his school friends were useful with the *Portrait,* but *Ulysses* was harder because the milieu he deals with there is largely that of the pub-crawlers whom the educated university boys wouldn't have known." In two typed pages, single-spaced, Ellmann then recounted to Bowen all he had learned about possible real-life models for a range of characters.

Joyce himself admitted that he wrote close to life, which partly explains Ellmann's interest in real-life models. To Ezra Pound, Joyce claimed that he had "little or no inspiration or imagination." As far as he was concerned, he told Budgen, "imagination is memory." Rather than having to make things up, he confessed to the Swiss writer Jacques Mercanton, "chance furnishes me with what I need. I'm like a man who stumbles: my foot strikes something, I look down, and there is exactly what I am in need of."[51] In *James Joyce* it is not always clear how or why the real-life models Ellmann identifies, for minor characters in particular, were "exactly what I am in need of" (or worth readers knowing about, perhaps), but searching them out brought ancillary benefits. The chief of these benefits Ellmann explained by an example from the Dublin leg of his trip, an example he recounted on numerous occasions, including in the letter of July 13 to Bowen. It concerned his attempts to find a real-life model for Molly Bloom's lover Blazes Boylan. Here is a version of the story from a speech Ellmann gave in London when accepting the 1982 Duff Cooper Prize, awarded for the second edition of *James Joyce.*

> One day somebody referred me to Thomas Pugh, a blind man. Before he went blind he had read *Ulysses* several times over, and as a young man he had knocked about the various parts of Dublin much as Joyce had in the same period and with the same retentive memory. Mr. Pugh could remember many of the minor characters in the novel, some of whom retain their own names, some have closely similar ones. . . .
>
> But neither Mr. Pugh nor anyone else seemed able to suggest who might have been the model for Blazes Boylan, the swaggering, strawhatted Lothario about whom we are told little except that he managed a prize fighter and was the son of a horse trader. Just before I was to leave Dublin, someone proposed that I consult a man named Ted Keogh, who ran the

> Old Curiosity Shop on the quays, because he was knowledgeable about old times. I went to the shop and after some preliminaries said to Keogh, "Did you know anyone who wore a straw hat, managed a prize fighter, and had a father who was a horse trader?" Keogh thought for a moment, rustled through innumerable papers in a drawer of an old chest, and came up with a photograph of a man in a straw hat. Would that be him? I didn't know. Then he pointed out on the wall behind me a photograph of the same man with a prize fighter. That seemed warmer. So I said, was his father a horse trader? He was. Who was it? I asked Keogh, and Keogh replied, "That's me." So it may have been Keogh who supplied at least some details for the character of Boylan. You may wonder what was the point of hunting down problematic live models for the characters. Well, one reason was that Joyce did work with living people, sometimes assigning them their own names. . . . . But the other reason was that by asking questions about people who lived at the time, I often got some sense of the quality or texture of life then, and that was what I was really after.

"Keogh's character," Ellmann admits in *James Joyce*, "was not . . . what Joyce needed for Boylan's" (p. 389), but his appearance and background immediately presented themselves, as Joyce put it, as "exactly what I was in need of." On June 15, some three weeks before setting off on the Paris leg of their trip, Mary wrote to her parents-in-law about Ellmann's research:

> Dick is zooming along these days, as he's told you, one lead seems to tumble after another and he's rushed to follow them all up. . . . [A]t this point even Dick feels he has more than anyone else except perhaps Stanislaus Joyce himself. He is giving a talk on Thursday to a group of Trinity College students—suggested by his old friend Professor H. O. White—it will be on Joyce but it's *not* to give away any of the new stuff. He's with old Mr. Pugh today who's not a literary person but knows a tremendous amount about the Joyce background. . . . So all's fine, you see, with the research.

A week later, on June 23, Mary wrote again, this time with the address of the house they would be staying at in Paris: 18 Avenue des Peupliers in the Villa Montmorency, in the sixteenth arrondissement. In the earlier June letter she had announced that she was pregnant. Now she wrote with disturbing news. There had been a scare about a possible miscarriage and she had spent the week confined to bed. "We feel grateful that it seems to have been avoided. But it has been worrisome and depressing. But as I say, I believe the risk is past." (She was right that the risk had passed: Maud Ellmann would be born in Evanston on January 16, 1954.) On July 8 the family left Killiney for Cobh, the Cork seaport town. From there they sailed to Le Havre and traveled on to Paris, arriving on July 10.

The house in the Villa Montmorency belonged to Edme and Daniela Jeanson. Ellmann had known Daniela for some years, at least since autumn 1944, when she was Daniela de Prevaux.[52] In a letter to Ellmann of October 1, 1951, she sends her love to Mary as well, so they must have met in Paris in August 1949, at the time of the Ellmanns' marriage. By this date Daniela was married to Edme Jeanson (1924–2015), a wealthy entrepreneur and philanthropist and president of a celebrated classical music festival in the town of Lessay (where his father had been mayor).[53] When Ellmann wrote to Daniela in November 1952 to ask if she could help him to find a place to live in Paris for the summer, she suggested that they take over the third floor of her house, an offer Mary described to her parents-in-law as "a much better thing than it looks at first glance." Mary explained: "We would have three small rooms and bathroom of our own on the third floor but also have daytime use of the living-room, dining room and kitchen on the first [ground] floor. Moreover, the house is in a very pleasant quiet part of the city and has a large and pretty garden where, I remember, it was possible to eat outdoors during the early evening." Daniela and the children (four of them, very small) would be away at their house in the country, the family cook would be away, only Edme would be in occasional residence. The cost to the Ellmanns (surprisingly, there was one) would be $100 a week, a small price to pay to live in what Mary calls "fine Parisian style." Leafy and beautiful, the Villa Montmorency, a nineteenth-century gated community with mansions scattered around a large park, was (still is) home to celebrated actors, politicians, industrialists, and writers. Gide had a house there; Victor Hugo, Henri Bergson, Apollinaire, and Sarah Bernhardt had lived there.[54]

"Now begins the siege of my second city," Ellmann declared on July 15 to Bertie Rodgers. By mid-July he had written to Sylvia Beach; Dr. Bertrand-Fontaine, Joyce's Paris doctor; Cornelius ("Con") Cremin, Irish ambassador to France; Samuel Beckett ("a nice guy . . . said to know everything about

Joyce");[55] the Italian writer Nino Frank; Maria Jolas, editor of *transition;* Valery Larbaud; Joyce's son Giorgio, who lived in Zurich; Lucie Leon, a fashion journalist and wife of Paul Leon, a scholar and lawyer, who were friends of the Joyces in the 1930s; Philippe Soupault, a writer and a prominent Surrealist; and John Sullivan, a singer whose career Joyce had been keen to forward. Amanda Sigler neatly summarizes the standard formula Ellmann used in introducing himself in such letters:

> First stating who, if anyone, had suggested that they make contact; second, identifying himself as a scholar working on a biography of Joyce; and third, requesting information from his correspondent. Ellmann would then conclude with a paragraph that further established his credibility, such as the following paragraph in a letter to the Irish ambassador:
>
> > I ought perhaps to identify myself as the author of a life of Yeats, published by Macmillan [and] of a critical book on Yeats's poetry, to be published later this year by the same firm, and of a translation of the prose poems of Henri Michaux, published last year by Routledge [New Directions in the States]. I am a professor of English literature at Northwestern University in the United States.

Sigler, herself an academic, notes that "in this final paragraph, Ellmann established himself as a biographer, secondly as a literary critic, thirdly as a translator, and finally as a professor," an ordering that "reflects well his academic priorities, especially his tendency to elevate his research and publication over his teaching and university responsibilities."[56] Without disputing this ordering of priorities, it is worth pointing out that none of the people to whom Ellmann was writing were academics or likely to be impressed by the title "professor," especially at an American university little known in Europe.

Remarkably, Ellmann managed to interview almost all the people he wrote to in Paris, "even during the month of July when it is supposed to be entirely deserted."[57] He also saw people on short trips out of the city—to Vichy, where he interviewed Valery Larbaud ("who is ¾ paralyzed and can only speak a rare word or two, but managed by signs and stammers to give me some rather interesting points"); to the village of Saint-Gérand-le-Puy, where Joyce lived for almost a year during the war; and to the Savoy region, where Sylvia Beach and Adrienne Monnier had a small chalet. Beach could be difficult, especially with what she called "Joycean rag-pickers."

Although she eventually approved of Ellmann, there had been tensions between them over access to Michaux, as well as over Ellmann's translations of Michaux (published two years after Beach's translation of Michaux's *A Barbarian in Asia,* about his early travels in the Far East). When Ellmann arrived at the chalet in the summer of 1953, he was poorly received. Beach recalled in a letter to Harriet Weaver: "He suddenly appeared at night at the door of our little chalet in Savoie summer before last, and told us he was doing a biography of Joyce. I fear I wasn't helpful at all—shooed him away as soon as possible from our mountain retreat."[58]

That Ellmann arrived at the chalet unannounced is hard to credit, given his habitual care and formality with sources. That Beach treated him poorly is less surprising. As the critic Bernard McGinley puts it, Beach "regarded these fellow-Americans' pursuit of Joyce's life and works as something worse than stamp-collecting." She also had material reasons for resenting them: "Their scavenging of materials was likely (she believed) to lower the value of her own collection—which was essentially her pension, her only asset after decades of poverty in the service of James Joyce. (Her world was not one of professorial tenure and Marshall Aid.)"[59] When in 1931 Joyce sought to secure an American publisher for *Ulysses,* Beach, who held the rights, named a price so high ($25,000) that the chief publisher involved in the bidding withdrew his offer. Sales of the Shakespeare and Co. edition of the novel, mostly to American tourists, had been earning her about £1,000 a year; once there was an American edition, she wrote to Harriet Weaver on October 1, 1931, she would be forced to "give up my shop and sell chickens."[60]

* * *

In August, Ellmann ventured further afield—to Geneva to consult again with Stuart Gilbert; to Zurich to meet Joyce's son Giorgio and to interview Carl Jung (who had examined both Joyce and his daughter Lucia); and to Trieste where, aided by Mason, he had secured an interview with Stanislaus Joyce. Had there been time he would have gone on to Pola (now Pula, in Croatia), which he was to visit the following summer (Joyce and Nora had lived in Pola in 1904 for six months). The meetings with Gilbert and Stanislaus Joyce will be discussed in Chapter 7. The meeting with Giorgio, which Ellmann approached with "trepidation," proved surprisingly pleasant. Giorgio, he wrote to Bowen in the August 30 letter, was "supposed to be an ogre—but he proved very mild, said he had never given an interview before but seemed glad to give one now; we spent three evenings at two very fine Zurich restaurants."

In the course of the trip, Ellmann obtained a researcher in Zurich and was in the process of obtaining another in Pola. Researching Joyce's life, he reported to Bowen, was "like some gigantic financial operation conducted over about eight countries." One of the things the operation revealed was the importance of family to Joyce. For example, in an interview of August 8, Carl Jung recounted to Ellmann a disagreement he had had with Joyce over his daughter Lucia's poems, which he described as betraying "schizoid elements." To Joyce, as Ellmann puts it in *James Joyce,* drawing on notes from the interview, these elements "were anticipations of a new literature." Lucia, Joyce argued, was "an innovator not yet understood." In reply, Jung granted "that some of her portmanteau words and neologisms were remarkable, but said they were random; she and her father, he commented later, were like two people going to the bottom of a river, one falling and the other diving."[61] Leaving aside the question of who was right about Lucia's neologisms, Ellmann took Joyce's defense of his troubled daughter as evidence of paternal feeling.

This view, crucial to Ellmann's conception of Joyce, had been supported the day before in an interview with Giorgio, who stressed not only his father's love for his children but his involvement in family life more generally. Earlier, on July 28, Samuel Beckett had also emphasized Joyce's closeness to his family, in addition to suggesting that the "young thin pale soft shy slim slip of a thing" referred to in a passage from *Finnegans Wake* (202:27) was based on Lucia.[62] On July 22 Maria Jolas had told him of Joyce's admiration for "the family attachment of Jews" and his sense of Ulysses as "a kind of family man." Lucie Leon's view of the importance of family to Joyce was more mixed. In her 1950 memoir, *James Joyce and Paul L. Leon: The Story of a Friendship,* she describes Joyce as "very much a family man, a devoted husband, a good father, and a loyal son."[63] On September 2, however, she told Ellmann that she felt Joyce "had but one object in mind, the work he was engaged in." She also had a warning for Ellmann: to steer clear of any suggestion of impropriety in the relation between father and daughter. "PLEASE PLEASE be careful what you write about Lucia. Her sickness is not of syphilitic origin, neither was Joyces [*sic*] love *ever* incestuous." To Maria Jolas, Lucie worried that Ellmann was digging "a bit too deep for discretion."[64] Presumably Lucie and Maria's worries had been fed by gossip. It is possible that they were also fed by *Finnegans Wake,* which Jolas and her husband had serialized in *transition* under the title *Work in Progress.* In the first installment of the serialization, published in 1927, there is an episode intimating father-daughter incest (the episode begins "This is the way to the museyroom [museum/nursery room]." It is found on pages 8–10 of the published work. No mention of this passage or of the scurrilous gossip that may have worried Joyce's defenders appears in either edition of *James Joyce.*[65]

* * *

Ellmann began negotiating with publishers about a Joyce biography well before he felt confident enough to sign a contract. On March 25, 1953, the morning of his departure for Dublin and Europe, he wrote to his parents about his meeting the previous day with Oxford University Press, which was publishing the American edition of *The Identity of Yeats.* "It became clear that they regard the Joyce book as something of a find—and they offered up to $1500 advance on royalties—I told them I wasn't sure I wanted that much but would let them know." As mentioned earlier, Ellmann had also received an offer on the biography from the New York office of Macmillan, which was willing to waive its precondition that Ellmann secure the cooperation of Joyce's family. In London, with his options open, Ellmann visited Macmillan, where Thomas Mark, Yeats's editor and a director of the firm, informed him that it was company policy not to publish books on Joyce.[66]

C. G. Bowen ("Curley" to his friends), the editor Ellmann dealt with in the New York office of OUP, was in the trade division of the firm. In steering *The Identity of Yeats* into print, he helped to shape its character, as he would later shape the character of *James Joyce.* "Keeping in mind the wide, and in many instances, quite amateur, reading public interested in Yeats," he wrote to Ellmann on February 26, 1952, a revision of the "almost discouraging heaviness" of chapters 2 and 3 was worth considering. "The book is too good to be one merely for the specialist."[67] To this request, Ellmann acceded: "I want to be read by amateurs as well as professionals, as you suggest I should."[68] A month later Bowen wrote with bad news. Despite the book's purported wide appeal, OUP (that is, the trade division of OUP) had now decided, because of "market conditions," that they could only publish the book if Ellmann could find an English publisher to split the costs, or from whom it could purchase "books or printed sheets in considerable quantity."[69] Ellmann immediately approached the London office of Macmillan, which had published *Yeats: The Man and the Masks,* and after eight months of dithering it agreed to publish the English edition.

On April 28, 1953, Bowen wrote to tell Ellmann that he was sending contracts to him for the Joyce biography. The contracts stipulated a submission date two and a half years from signature, a date Ellmann knew full well he could not meet. On June 3 he reported to his parents that he had signed the contracts. Five days later he reported to Jean and Ruth Hagstrum that "the floodgates have opened and I've got a mass of stuff, several times as much (I think) as Gorman had. . . . It is astonishing how much material there is around here. Some of it is hard to pry up, but generally if people are reluctant to tell a biographer they have confided something or other to their friends, who have less compunction." On July 15, in a letter to Charles Feidelson, Ellmann admitted that "the ambition to do a complete biography is so inordinate that almost nobody has tried it." The letter was written from Paris, five days after having arrived from Ireland, with the daunting prospect of still having to research Joyce's thirty-seven years in Europe. In *James Joyce,* the number of pages devoted to this period are four times the number for Joyce's Dublin years.

In addition to the daunting size of the task Ellmann faced, he was worried about competitors—not just Richard Kain of Kansas but Joseph Prescott of Wayne State University, and Patricia Hutchins, whose *James Joyce's Dublin* was published in 1950 and who was now "trying to do for Joyce in France and England what she did for him in Ireland."[70] Against these worries, there was the thrill of the hunt and the glamour of the terrain, especially to an eager and resourceful traveler like Ellmann. As he later put it, "My scholarly needs *obliged* me to go to the most interesting places in Europe, to Paris, to Zurich, to Trieste."[71] To Herbert Cahoon, on July 16, he describes himself as "on the whole increasingly exhilarated, sometimes very excited, not so much by scandalous revelations as by illuminating details which seemed to come together into a fairly coherent image."

But worries persisted. At the end of the July 13 letter to Bowen, with its detailed account of Dublin discoveries, Ellmann makes a radical suggestion.

Sylvia Beach and Harriet Weaver, at the *Paris in the Twenties* exhibition, in 1960.

One way to create a "coherent image" of Joyce without being swamped by detail or scooped by rivals, would be to produce a different kind of book, a biographical study rather than a full-length biography.

> My notion is that I could do in something over a year a short book of perhaps 150 pages which could be not only of biographical interest but would also illuminate [Joyce's] method of composing his novels out of family reminiscences and personal recollections. It would deal with the backgrounds of all his books through *Ulysses,* and to some extent with *Finnegans Wake.* I have a fairly coherent image of him and of his writings, which I think would do much to counteract the view of him which Harry Levin and others have propagated as the impersonal artist, cold and aloof.

Bowen was quick to reject this suggestion, understandably, given the likely readership of a full-length biography as opposed to the sort of book Ellmann was proposing. Ellmann received Bowen's reaction in Paris shortly before he set off on his two-week trip to Geneva, Zurich, and Trieste. He did not answer until August 30, after returning from Trieste. "I think you are probably right," he admitted, "though on the other hand I shall feel very upset if somebody anticipates my results. But I agree that the complete life will be much better done together, and I'll try to make even that impossible time table we agreed upon." For the next six years, as materials accumulated and worries about rivals intensified, Ellmann's image of Joyce began to cohere. Central to the image was a quality Ellmann himself needed and came increasingly to value: "tenacity of purpose."[72]

CHAPTER SEVEN

People and Papers

THANKS TO GENEROUS FUNDING from the Rockefeller Foundation and Northwestern University, Ellmann was able to make two more research trips to Europe, both taken alone, each lasting roughly two months.[1] In 1954, from mid-June to mid-August, he traveled to Dublin, London, Paris, Pola, Zurich, Lugano, and Florence. In April and May 1956, he traveled to Dublin, London, Copenhagen (which Joyce had visited in 1936), Paris, Zurich, and Trieste. On both trips, in addition to conducting interviews, Ellmann collected the names and addresses of people he was unable to contact or had learned about in his travels. To all these people he wrote with queries. He also hired research assistants to follow up leads and conduct interviews. How he set about finding and interviewing people who knew Joyce or had information about him or about his papers is the main subject of this chapter.

Perhaps the best example of the sorts of questions Ellmann asked of interviewees comes from a letter he wrote shortly after the publication of *James Joyce*. Tom Staley was a lifelong Joycean, first at the University of Tulsa, where he founded the *James Joyce Quarterly* and *Joyce Studies Annual* (he later convinced Ellmann to deposit his papers at Tulsa), then in Austin, Texas, where for twenty-five years he served as director of the Harry Ransom Humanities Research Center. In December 1959, as a twenty-four-year-old graduate student, Staley took part in a discussion about Joyce on the radio. Several days later he received a letter from the nephew of a woman who had once been a maid in the Joyce household in Trieste. This woman, who now lived near Pittsburgh, also possessed a letter from Joyce. Staley arranged to interview her, but unsure what questions to ask, wrote to Ellmann, whom he had never met, asking for advice. Ellmann replied in a letter full of suggestions:

> It would perhaps be well to begin by getting all the names straight, the exact or approximate dates, the location of the farm. You could perhaps try to ask the aunt directly about the children's going to church—how often, with their father or mother, with the aunt? Did she remember Eileen Joyce or Eva Joyce or was she the housekeeper before their time, that is, before the late summer of 1909? (I assume from your letter she did some sort of maid service.) What was Nora like? Household management? Did Joyce write? What was his day like? When did he get up? What did he do with his time? Was he teaching English? What were Giorgio and Lucia like? If at all possible, try to get any remarks by any member of the family. Children or parents, and of course anything Joyce said above all. The point is to treat no detail as too trivial, for the more dense the recollections, the more likely to be accurate, and of course people don't themselves know the value of their own information. I think it would be worth asking them about Francini Bruni, Prezioso, Svevo, etc. It would be useful to know what they charged for boarding the children, what the children did around the farm, what sort of household was maintained in Trieste, and so on. Nora's degree of proficiency in speaking Italian or Triestino, Joyce's; how they dressed, what they ate and drank; whether Joyce was often drunk; whether he had trouble with his eyes, whether they remember Nora's miscarriage, births, whether she nursed the children, what his language pupils were like. Did they know Dr. Sinigaglia, who delivered Giorgio? Or Moise Canarutto, at whose house the Joyces stayed rather early in their Trieste period?[2]

While still a graduate student, Staley wrote up the interview with the woman and published it under the title "Joyce in Trieste" in the *Georgia Review* (Winter 1962). The article was accompanied by a first printing of the letter Joyce had written to her when she took Giorgio and Lucia to stay with her parents in the country for a few days.

* * *

The way Ellmann himself approached interviews has been described by his friend John Kelleher. In 1946 Ellmann was at work on Yeats, and on their cycling trip to Sligo, Kelleher sat in on interviews Ellmann conducted with some of the poet's relatives, "none of whom seemed particularly interested in cousin Willie." Staley had felt "bombarded" by Ellmann's suggestions; the people interviewed in person by Ellmann were immediately put at their ease. "His way was to come armed with more, and generally more detailed and reliable, knowledge than he could expect the person interviewed to have, yet never to bring this forward, never to contradict, scarcely ever to interrupt. He let them talk; he showed himself grateful for what they told him; now and then with a quiet question he would elicit some particular point of information, and in leaving would express his thanks again. He left them smiling and thinking, what a nice young man!"[3]

In a letter of October 6, 1953, to Herbert Cahoon, Ellmann claimed that on his first research trip he had seen between fifty and a hundred people in Ireland. On the whole trip he had seen "nearly everybody that one could think of readily as associated with Joyce, except for a few who were inaccessible in South America, Tangier, Spain and one or two other places. It meant writing hundreds of letters." In the preface, notes, and acknowledgment pages of *James Joyce,* Ellmann names over 330 people from over thirteen countries who "made it possible for me to assemble this record of Joyce's life" (pp. 819–21). Even Joyceans who were critical of aspects of *James Joyce* praise Ellmann's prodigious research. Phillip Herring, who has doubted the "verifiable accuracy" of a number of the book's assertions, describes its critics, presumably including himself, as "like a few small mice nibbling around a royal wedding cake." Bernard McGinley, another doubter, admits "our debt and our gratitude to Ellmann." Hugh Kenner, the most persistent and severe of Ellmann's critics, called *James Joyce* "the best Joyce biography we are likely to see," adding that its author has "earned our gratitude for all he has preserved."[4]

What *James Joyce* preserves derives not only from Ellmann's industry and persistence, but also from luck. In letters, interviews, and talks about the book, he often cites an example from his 1954 trip to Pola, now Pula, part of Croatia. Joyce taught English in Pola's newly opened Berlitz School for six months in 1904–1905, just after he and Nora had in effect eloped from Dublin. Ellmann had wanted to visit Pola on his 1953 trip but had been unable to do so owing to a border dispute between Italy and Yugoslavia. On the 1954 trip he hired a driver in Trieste at considerable expense and, after a ten-hour drive, arrived in the city at 9:00 A.M. In "Writing

Joyce's Biography," the undated and unfinished draft of a talk, he describes what happened next: "I had the address where Joyce had lived, and I thought that with that, at least we would see where he had lived, and perhaps there might be some way of finding out where the Berlitz School had been in 1904 and 5. We drove to the street where Joyce was supposed to have lived, and the driver made enquiries of the neighbors, who said they didn't know anything about Joyce, and that since 1904–5 the street numbers had been changed twice." The neighbors suggested that Ellmann drive to the National Library in Pola, which he did, arriving at 11:35. There he was told that the library shut at twelve and would not open again until five.

> It seemed impossible for me to stay the night, since I could scarcely afford to be there myself, let alone pay for the chauffeur. So I explained to the librarian as well as I could what I was looking for, and this time in German [his Italian was only rudimentary in 1954], and he said that he knew there had been a Dichter named Joyce in Pola, but that he had no idea where he lived or where the Berlitz School had been. And so I was thinking, that I had come for nothing or almost nothing, when suddenly a man approached. You know how in Greek tragedy the god is suddenly let down by pulleys, and it seemed to me as if this man, although he came in a conventional manner towards me, was in effect a Deus ex machina. He said to me in quite good English "I am Professor so and so [his name was Mijo Mirnovic], I am an economist [at the University of Zagreb] and what's more I am a poet. I have been on trade missions for the Yugoslav government to Washington. I have recently written a book on Pola and I can show exactly where Joyce lived, and also where the Berlitz School is.

The professor then revealed that his son, a journalist in Zagreb, had recently interviewed a woman who had taught alongside Joyce in 1904–1905 at the Berlitz School. Her name was Amalija Globocnik, she came from Ljubljana, and she taught Croatian and offered private lessons in Italian. She was also assistant to the school's director. Ellmann was able to find her address in Zagreb through "a society of Yugoslav authors" and arranged to have her interviewed by Stanislav Simic, who had translated *A Portrait of the Artist as a Young Man* into Serbo-Croatian.[5]

In *James Joyce,* Fraulein Globocnik (as Joyce habitually addressed her) is said to have "liked the Joyces and [to have] visited them often in their little room, where Joyce would usually be sitting on the bed writing when she came in." The vivifying particulars in Ellmann's account of Joyce and Nora's months in Pola mostly come from her, as in the sentences that follow:

> The poverty of the young couple distressed her: Joyce never changed his suit, and Nora never changed her dress, and once they even had to borrow paraffin from her for their lamp. The room had no stove and by December it became chilly and then cold. Nora was nonetheless hospitable, and if there was money she would make, at Joyce's request, English puddings which their friends would be invited to share. Fraulein Globocnik found Joyce affable but impenetrable; he showed emotion chiefly in the scorn with which he would speak of priests or dismiss Ireland as "L'Isola di santi e savi" [The isle of saints and sages]. (p. 194)

Yet of all the things Ellmann learned from the Fraulein, he mentions only one in "Writing Joyce's Biography." On a visit she paid to the Joyces in Trieste, after they had left Pola, "Mrs. Joyce told her that there was a man who said to her that the sun rises for you. This seemed to me of considerable interest, because I remembered that Leopold Bloom is represented as having told Molly during their courtship, the sun shines for you, and this is the fondest of their fond memories of that period in their love. It seemed extraordinary to dig this up from someone in Zagreb."[6]

* * *

Although much will be said in this book about Ellmann's fear of academic competitors, he was greatly assisted by academics throughout Europe and North America. In another talk, "Adventures and Misadventures of a Biographer," he tells of coming across a letter in Paris in a collection of "some Joyce family papers" (which collection he does not say) from a woman who lived in Saskatoon, Saskatchewan. The letter was written to Joyce on February 7, 1935: "I was in the public library in Saskatoon today, and I saw a book by a man named James Joyce. I took it off the shelf and I found my own name." The name was Eileen Vance. "And I realized that she was the Eileen Vance in *A Portrait of the Artist,*" writes Ellmann, "living a few doors from the Dedalus family in Bray." When Ellmann wrote to her, his letter was returned: "Unknown at this address." "Then I thought—shd I go to Saskatoon? Paris was one thing, Saskatoon another. I bethought myself that there is or should be a freemasonry of professors of English around the world, so I wrote to the chairman of the English dept of the University of Saskatchewan, and asked if he had a graduate student willing to help trace Eileen Vance." As it turned out, the chairman, Professor Carlyle King, "got interested in the matter himself." "He searched the death lists since 1935 and didn't find her name, so he advertised in the newspapers, and several people replied that she was teaching at an Indian reservation 100 miles north of Saskatoon. I asked him to interview her for me, and furnished him with questions, which he did. She made it possible for me to feel that I had got back to the years immediately after Joyce's birth." The interview with Professor King took place on December 28, 1953. By the time *James Joyce* was published, Eileen Vance had become Mrs. Eileen Harris. One of the details she provided about Joyce's early years was a story Ellmann included in the biography. On visits home from Clongowes, where Joyce attended school between the ages of six and nine, he and Eileen, who was four months his junior, were "inseparable." The Vances were Protestants but the two families got on well. Eileen was "a pretty girl . . . and the two fathers often spoke half-seriously of uniting their first-born" (p. 25). One Valentine's Day, however, Eileen's father "sent Joyce a Valentine purporting to come from her, on which he had written, paraphrasing a rhyme of Samuel Lover,

> O Jimmie Joyce you are my darling
> You are my looking glass from night till morning
> I'd rather have you without one farthing
> Than Harry Newall and his ass and garden.

Drawing both on Eileen's interview with Professor King and her 1935 letter to Joyce, Ellmann explains: "Harry Newall was an old and disquieting cripple who drove his cart around Bray, so the compliment was not so extravagant as it first appeared. Mrs. Joyce may have intercepted the Valentine, as Stanislaus Joyce says, but James found out about it. Eileen, hearing of the trick that had been played on her, became shy with her playmate and for years blushed at the sound of his name. He in turn faithfully kept the verse in mind and put it into *Ulysses*" (p. 31). On the same page, in a footnote, Ellmann tells us where: in the "Nestor" episode in which "Bloom remembers having sent the Valentine to his daughter Milly." In an earlier footnote, Ellmann mentions that Eileen Vance was now living in Saskatoon (p. 25). Twenty-five years later, in the second edition of the biography, he retained the footnote, and as he explains in "Adventures and Misadventures of a Biographer," "one reviewer complained that she could not possibly be still alive. So I wrote to the man who helped me [Professor King], and he said I've lost touch with her but I'll try to find out when she died. A few days later he wrote again. She had not died. She was still very much alive in Saskatoon, at the age of 101. And since then she has celebrated her 102nd birthday."[7]

Almost as generous as Professor King was Heinrich Straumann, professor of English at the University of Zurich, who had done Joyce himself a great favor in September 1940 when he (Joyce), fleeing France, applied for permission to stay in Zurich for the duration of the war. The Swiss authorities refused his application on the grounds that he was a Jew—"'*C'est le bouquet, vraiment,*' Joyce exclaimed on being informed of this" (p. 749)—but they changed their minds after representations from the mayor of Zurich, among other notables. Included among these notables was Professor Straumann, who "certified that the works of Joyce were without question the best published writings of the English-speaking world" (p. 750). One of Straumann's favors to Ellmann shed light not only on Joyce's life but on his art, in particular on the art of *Ulysses* and on the moment in *A Portrait,* at the end of chapter 4, in which Stephen Dedalus, in Ellmann's paraphrase, "walks along the north strand, towards the end of his school days, and suddenly sees a handsome girl, skirts drawn up, wading in the water. Her beauty affects him like an illumination of truth, and vindicates his choice of life and art, even if life means also disorder and art suffering." Straumann's favor was to provide what to Ellmann seemed proof that "the incident actually occurred to Joyce about this time" (p. 56), that is, toward the end of Joyce's own school days.

The proof came from a woman named Marthe Fleischmann, who, after Joyce's death, sold Professor Straumann four letters Joyce had written to her. Marthe first appears in *James Joyce* at the beginning of chapter 27:

> Early in December, 1918, Joyce was going home to his flat at 29 Universitätstrasse [in Zurich] when he observed a young woman walking ahead of him. She moved with a slight limp, her head held high. As she turned to enter a house he saw her face, and his own was lit up—as she discreetly noted—"*mit grosstem Erstaunen.*" For it seemed to Joyce that he was seeing again the girl he had seen in 1898 by the strand, wading in the Irish Sea with her skirts tucked up. That girl had appeared to him like a

> vision of secular beauty. . . . The sight of this woman who looked so much like her—for she was not of course the same—struck Joyce as of equal talismanic significance. His passion for coincidence impelled him towards a passion for her. (p. 462)[8]

After this first sight of Marthe, Joyce wrote to her asking if they could meet. He described himself as a writer "at a pivotal point in his life: his age . . . the same as Dante's when he began the *Divine Comedy,* and as Shakespeare when he fell in love with the Dark Lady of the Sonnets." He praised her beauty and hoped that she would not mind "if he suggests that perhaps she was Jewish" (pp. 462–63), which she was not. In a second letter, he "begged her to see him, and eventually, with suitable archness, she did." Further letters and meetings ensued, until relations were broken off at the end of March 1918. "He saw Marthe as often as he could," Ellmann writes. "Like Bloom peeping on the Strand [in the "Nausicaa" episode, begun in the autumn of 1919], he eyed her from the street as she moved about her sitting room" (p. 464). Joyce himself alluded to the resemblance in a lost postcard to Marthe. According to Straumann, who learned of the postcard from Marthe's sister, its contents "consisted of greetings sent to 'Nausikaa' by 'Odysseus,'" written, the sister recalled, "by the same hand as the letters."[9]

In *James Joyce,* Ellmann has little to say about Marthe that is complimentary. She "did not work; she spent her days smoking, reading romantic novels, and primping. She was vain and wished to be snobbish. When she realized that Joyce was in some way distinguished, she wrote to him, and they began a correspondence that was kept both from Nora's eyes and Hiltpold's [Rudolf Hiltpold, a Swiss engineer with whom Marthe was living as his mistress]" (p. 463). Whether Joyce's infatuation with Marthe was ever consummated is unclear. In the biography Ellmann suggests that "Marthe liked to be looked at, not embraced, so that Hiltpold kept other mistresses at the same time that he maintained her in his flat, and in later life she always sugared over her intrigue with Joyce as '*eine Platonische Liebe* [a platonic love]'" (p. 464).

When Joyce's son Giorgio was shown the letters Professor Straumann had purchased from Marthe, he gave Straumann what in "Writing Joyce's Biography" Ellmann calls "a good deal of trouble." Giorgio had never heard of Marthe Fleischmann and neither, he claimed, had his mother. He not only doubted that his father and Marthe had had an affair, he doubted

Marthe Fleischmann and her "guardian" Rudolf Hiltpold in Zurich, about 1918.

the authenticity of the letters, claiming that they were not in his father's hand. As evidence, he cited the fact that the letter "e" was written in the Greek style (as an epsilon, ε], a style that he claimed his father never used. By refuting this claim, Ellmann returned a favor to Straumann. "I was able to solve this problem because of remembering that in the text of *Ulysses* there is a place where Leopold Bloom is writing a letter to a pen-pal, whose name is also Martha though it is Martha Clifford, and he decides to disguise his handwriting by writing with Greek *e*'s. I was able to confirm in this way the authenticity of these letters, which do provide a very interesting window to Joyce's life."[10]

In *James Joyce,* Ellmann devotes several pages to Joyce's involvement with Marthe Fleischmann, which occurred while Joyce was at work on *Ulysses.* As for his motive for using Greek epsilons in his letters to her, "It seems unlikely that he could have supposed that this slight graphic change would be of any use in a court test of handwriting." It was more likely, to Ellmann at least, that the graphic change "could have meant to him little more than a sign that he was reserving part of himself in the correspondence, amusing himself with his own folly. . . . Joyce evidently felt himself a little absurd in yielding to his rhapsodical inclination; but he yielded to it nonetheless" (p. 463). The attraction to Marthe "was a final burgeoning of his desire for dark, unknown, passionate, preferably Semitic women who would envelop him in their arms" (p. 464).[11]

The melodramatic style of the letters to Marthe Fleischmann also suggests to Ellmann that Joyce was "amusing himself with his own folly." "I imagine a misty evening to myself," Joyce writes in the first letter. "I am waiting—and I see you coming towards me, dressed in black, young, strange and gentle. I look into your eyes, and my eyes tell you that I am a poor seeker in this world, that I understand nothing of my destiny, nor of the destinies of others, that I have lived and sinned and created, and that one day I shall leave, having understood nothing in the darkness which gave birth to both of us."[12] A similar sense of drama marks the meeting Joyce staged with Marthe on February 2, 1919, his birthday. The meeting took place in the Zurich studio of his friend Frank Budgen, the artist, and in preparation for it Joyce borrowed a Menorah from a Jewish friend, Ottocaro Weiss. In *James Joyce,* Ellmann describes the Menorah as "a ceremonial candlestick, lighted during the Jewish festival of Hannukah, and so appropriate to [Joyce's] first impression of Marthe." February 2 was also the date of the Christian festival of Candlemas, the Feast of the Presentation of the Virgin Mary, celebrated by the lighting of candles, so doubly appropriate. "On the pretext that the light there [in Budgen's studio] was poor," writes Ellmann, "he lit the candlestick so that she might be seen at once more clearly and more ceremoniously." When asked later by Weiss why he had borrowed the Menorah, "Joyce replied a little shamefacedly, '*Per una serata nera*' (For a Black Mass)" (p. 465).

James Joyce omits several revealing details about Joyce's involvement with Marthe, including about the Black Mass. These details first appeared in print in Frank Budgen's memoir *Myselves when Young* (1970), but it is possible Ellmann knew of them before the publication of his biography.[13] For example, before the meeting on February 2, to heighten the Bohemian atmosphere of the studio, at Joyce's request Budgen drew a large charcoal sketch of a female nude "in a recumbent position and a rear aspect, to which I accorded as much bulk as I reasonably could." ("As an old shipmate would have described her," Budgen writes of Marthe, "she was high up in the fo'c'sle and fairly broad in the beam.") When Marthe saw the drawing, "Joyce received the reproachful smirk he fished for."[14] Both, it seems, were amusing themselves with their own folly.

Budgen claims to have been a reluctant participant in Joyce's "Black Mass." He had no desire to deceive Nora, and agreed to play a part only because Joyce begged him to and because he sensed that Joyce's motives had more to do with art than with seduction. "Sometimes I thought that Joyce's memory did fail him," Budgen writes, "not so much in the recollection of an event as in the subjective joys or agonies associated with it. This could necessitate the reconstruction of the event in order to relive the moment again in all its immediacy." Budgen likens the night's staging "to performances I have seen when some painter, his inner vision failing him, reconstitutes the whole scene in his studio, placing his models in the exact light and relationships of his original design." He recalls a tearful Nora telling him "'that Jim wanted me to go with other men so that he would have something to write about.'" "To my mind there were in Joyce's affair with Marthe Fleischmann similar literary intentions."[15]

Other details missing from the first edition of *James Joyce* concern Joyce's initial glimpse of Marthe, as well as his visits to her rooms. In the first edition, as quoted above, the initial sighting is in the street. To Budgen, Joyce claimed that it occurred when he looked out his back window and saw her rise from the lavatory seat and pull the chain. According to Brenda Maddox, in her biography of Nora, "If Joyce did glimpse Marthe in her bathroom, he must have strained his eyes very hard. The two buildings are not positioned directly opposite one another; besides, by 1919 Joyce's sight was so reduced that he used to carry papers over to the window and bring them close to his eyes in order to read."[16] When Joyce visited Marthe in her rooms, he told Budgen, she was in her nightgown and they discussed women's lingerie. "Every reader of Joyce," Budgen wrote, "will be well-aware of the kind of mid- to late-Victorian lingerie he admired."[17]

The absence of these details in the first edition of *James Joyce* was remedied in the 1982 second edition (*JJII*), in which chapter 27 now begins: "Early in December 1918, Joyce looked out of a side window of his flat at 29 Universitätstrasse and saw a woman in the next building pulling a toilet chain." In a footnote, Ellmann adds that "Earwicker's crime in the Phoenix Park [in *Finnegans Wake*] is often indicated to be that of peeping on micturating girls" (p. 448). The second edition holds nothing back. After quoting Joyce's claim to Budgen that on one visit to Marthe's rooms, he "explored the coldest and the hottest parts of a woman's body,"[18] Ellmann includes Budgen's estimate, recorded elsewhere, that Joyce had not had intercourse with Marthe: "as Bloom says of Gerty MacDowell, she had been 'fingered only'" (*JJII,* p. 451).[19] Had Ellmann known of these details while at work on the first edition of *James Joyce,* he would not have included them. By 1982 times had changed, the details were already in print, and there was no threat of permissions being withheld.

A similar intermingling of artistic and real-life motives, including erotic motives, is described by Ellmann in Joyce's attraction to a second young woman, also drawn to Ellmann's attention by an academic. In this case Ellmann learned of the woman only after the first edition was in print, but like the Marthe Fleischmann episode, it illustrates a key theme of the biography. Sometime in 1962 James Atherton, a Joyce scholar and the author of an influential study of *Finnegans Wake,* gave a lecture in Manchester after which a woman came up to him and said she had a friend in Germany who had known Joyce in Locarno, where he and his family had gone in the autumn of 1917 for health reasons. In a passage in "Adventures and Misadventures of a Biographer," Ellmann writes, "The woman's name was sent to me eventually, and I wrote to her." Her name was Gertrude Kaempffer, she lived in Bat Tolz in Bavaria, and while studying for her medical degree during the war she contracted tuberculosis. "Her father took her to one part of Switzerland after another, in the hope that the climate would cure her. Eventually, she ended up in Orsolina above Locarno." In the second edition of *James Joyce,* Ellmann describes Dr. Kaempffer as "twenty-six, tall (almost five feet eight inches), and attractive, with delicate features and somewhat subdued manner" (p. 418). As it happened, she had friends staying in the same pension as the Joyces, and they introduced her to "the famous intellectual of the pension," to quote again from the talk. Joyce, interested in the young doctor, "soon approached her as a man [an oddly antique locution for Ellmann] and told her he would leave the matter of intimacy to her." When she declined his approach, being not only ill but sensing "that he was more interested in his own mind than in hers," Joyce urged her to write to him at the Poste Restante in Zurich. This urging she also declined.

Undeterred, Joyce wrote two letters to Dr. Kaempffer, which, as she told Ellmann with apologies, she had torn up. Ellmann recalled, "There was something about her manner of disclosing this which made me feel that she might have remembered these letters, and when I coaxed her she replied that she had torn them up because she thought they were indecent." In one of the letters, Joyce recounted his first sexual experience. It was with a family retainer on a canal bank, a nanny. "She had told him to turn his head, but when he heard her piss he had jiggled like anything. She [Dr. Kaempffer] did not know the word jiggle, and her friends told her it was a wild Scottish dance. But she recognised the tone of the letters." A year after receiving this letter, Dr. Kaempffer came across Joyce again, when she was visiting friends in Zurich. Once more he proposed that they meet up. As Ellmann puts it in the second edition of *James Joyce:* "Foreseeing embarrassment, she refused again. Joyce looked pained, shook hands, and said goodbye. All that he had left was a recognition of having been aroused by a woman named Gertrude. It was enough to bolster him in naming *Gerty* the pallid young woman that Bloom excites himself over in the *Nausicaa* episode. As he had said in *Giacomo Joyce,* 'Write it, damn you, write it! What else are you good for?'"[20]

What Joyce once described to Budgen as his "cloacal obsession"—a term first applied to him in an early and influential review of *A Portrait* by H. G. Wells ("How right Wells was," Joyce admitted to Budgen)—figures in both the Marthe Fleischmann and the Gertrude Kaempffer episodes.[21] In the latter, it is traced to Joyce's first sexual experience, the intensity of which he seems to have sought to recapture in the Marthe episode. Ellmann does not say this. What he does say, in the opening paragraph of the introduction to both editions of *James Joyce,* is this:

> The life of an artist, but particularly that of Joyce, differs from the lives of other persons in that its events are becoming artistic sources even as

> they command his present attention. Instead of allowing each day, pushed back by the next, to lapse into imprecise memory, he shapes again the experiences which have shaped him. He is at once the captive and the liberator. In turn the process of reshaping experience becomes a part of his life, another of its recurrent events like rising or sleeping. The biographer must measure in each moment this participation of the artist in two simultaneous processes.

* * *

Kaempffer, Budgen, and Straumann spoke good English, but other people Ellmann sought to interview or correspond with did not. Even when language posed no problems, there were time constraints, the need to return to teaching and family in Evanston. Not all leads could be followed up personally, and at times Ellmann relied on research assistants.[22] Ellmann contacted one such research assistant, Dr. Alfred Dutli, in the summer of 1953, shortly after his first trip to Zurich. Dutli had been a pupil of Professor Straumann, who had recommended him. Ellmann asked him "to undertake a small research job for me in Zurich," which Dutli offered to do for free, though Ellmann insisted on paying him.[23] The "small research job" lasted several years and was important in documenting Joyce's years in Zurich. "You are too modest about what you've done," Ellmann wrote to Dutli on October 10, 1953. "It would have taken me a great deal of time to cover the same ground, and you have opened up a lot of possibilities." In the same letter Ellmann mentions "a new lead: there is a woman called Evelyn Cotton who is in the Zurich phone book—she acted in the English Players [the amateur theater company for which Joyce acted as business manager in 1919–1920] and she might have the program notes which Joyce wrote. . . . She might also have information about Joyce and the players."[24] On October 23 Dutli reported on his efforts to contact Joyce's eye doctors. As in his dealings with Tom Staley in 1959, Ellmann offered Dutli careful instructions. Before approaching Joyce's doctors, he wrote on November 5, Dutli should obtain a copy of a report by an earlier doctor. "The idea would be to point out that you already have a good deal of information. I have been in touch with the following French doctors, whose names you might wish to mention to him." These doctors Ellmann then lists.

Special care was needed when Ellmann asked Dutli to contact Joyce's son Giorgio. "If I write directly to Giorgio he won't answer," Ellmann told

Dutli in the November 5 letter, but by writing to him, Ellmann would make it "possible for you to write to him and then call (he's insistent on punctilio)." On November 14, Ellmann wrote again to Dutli, enclosing a letter for Giorgio "which I think you might like to send along with one of your own, in which you hope he will not mind your telephoning him to arrange to see him. When you phone him you might suggest dropping in on him at the Kronenhalle [a restaurant near the Opera] late in the evening." Dutli is to pay all restaurant bills and Ellmann will reimburse him. On March 9, 1954, Ellmann writes to congratulate Dutli on another matter: his success at the Bezirksgericht (district court) in Zurich. In 1918 Joyce had brought suit in the court against one of the actors in the English Players. The actor (who countersued) worked at the British consulate in Zurich and Joyce claimed not only that he had libeled him but that he (the actor) owed the English Players money for tickets.[25] "Your description of the second case [for libel] as a wonderful joke, a real Bleak House affair, is wonderfully apt," wrote Ellmann. "You are right about the absurd figure Joyce cuts. I see no great harm in sending George [Giorgio] an account of the trial, especially since he has put us under obligation; but if you have time, it might be better to do it in person rather than give him a written account. . . . However, do whatever seems proper to you; the main thing is to keep George on our side." Later in the letter Ellmann suggests that Joyce may be "parodying his own ludicrous behavior in Zurich in a libel suit that Mr. [Denis] Breen is conducting in *Ulysses* [in the "Lestrygonians" episode] and your report made me see this for the first time."[26]

In addition to paying Dutli for his efforts and thanking him in the preface to *James Joyce,* Ellmann sought to forward his career as a scholar. Dutli had written a book on Bernard Shaw, and Ellmann volunteered to draw it to the attention of "some of the libraries and scholars here [in Evanston and Chicago]; one of my colleagues is Arthur Nethercot, who has just written a book on Shaw to be published by the Harvard University Press; do you have a copy you could lend me or would you give me the name of the distributing agent, the price, and so forth."[27] In this case, Ellmann's favor was a kindness pure and simple. The two men became friends and their correspondence often contained news about family and personal matters as well as about Joyce.

With other favors, kindness and calculation combined.[28] One of the trickiest of Ellmann's interviewees was J. F. Byrne, Joyce's closest friend at

University College Dublin and a model in part for the character of Cranly in *A Portrait* and *Ulysses*.[29] Like Joyce, Byrne studied medicine briefly. He then went on to a career as a journalist, emigrating to New York in 1910. In 1953 he published *Silent Years: An Autobiography with Memoirs of James Joyce and Our Ireland.* In interviewing Byrne, Ellmann sought to learn more not only about his and Joyce's student days at University College but about two later moments in their friendship. The first occurred in 1903, when Joyce was in Paris and wrote to another friend from University College, Vincent Cosgrave, a model for the abrasive Lynch in *A Portrait.* Byrne thought Cosgrave coarse and careless and had warned Joyce explicitly against confiding in him. When Cosgrave showed Byrne a postcard he had received from Joyce recounting his experiences in the Paris brothels (it was written in dog-Latin), Byrne was doubly shocked, both by the details themselves and by the fact that Joyce had ignored his warning against confiding in Cosgrave. As a result, when Joyce returned to Dublin, Byrne snubbed him, a reaction Joyce claimed to have found baffling. For five years Byrne persisted in keeping his distance from Joyce, while Joyce took to referring to him as "His Intensity" and "the Sea-Green Incorruptible" (p. 120).[30]

What brought the two former friends together again was a second moment Ellmann was keen to hear about from Byrne. In August 1909, on a visit to Dublin from Trieste, Joyce met Cosgrave for a drink and Cosgrave led him to believe that in the summer of 1904, while Joyce and Nora were courting, he was also seeing her. According to Byrne, in an interview of March 1954 with Ellmann, what Cosgrave told Joyce was "that he had slept with Nora before Joyce did." In *James Joyce,* Ellmann says nothing about Cosgrave's having slept with Nora, either before or after she began seeing Joyce. What he says is that on evenings when Nora was off from work at Finn's Hotel (as a chambermaid and at the hotel bar), she and Cosgrave had "gone for walks in the darkness along the river bank."[31] Whether Cosgrave said he had slept with Nora or only implied it, Joyce came away from their meeting tormented by what Ellmann calls "the horrible possibility that she had betrayed him" (p. 288). Two days later Joyce went to Byrne's house in great distress and told him what Cosgrave had said. "I had always known that Joyce was highly emotional," Byrne writes in *Silent Years,* "but I had never before this afternoon seen anything to approach the frightening condition that convulsed him. He wept and groaned and gesticulated in futile impotence as he sobbed out to me the thing that had occurred." The sympathy Byrne felt for Joyce at this moment ended their estrangement. As Byrne puts it, it "was enough to obliterate forever some unpleasant memories."[32]

Byrne insisted to Joyce that what Cosgrave had told him was "a blasted lie," part of a malicious plot hatched by Cosgrave and Oliver St. John Gogarty to wreck Joyce's relationship with Nora.[33] Some days later, Joyce's brother Stanislaus also helped to calm Joyce, claiming that in 1904 Cosgrave had confessed to him that he had tried and failed to seduce Nora at the time she was seeing Joyce. This news, in Ellmann's words, "helped Joyce to reassert his self-esteem" (p. 290). The episode led to the fevered letters Joyce wrote to Nora in August and early September of 1909—letters of anguish, recrimination, self-pity, and, after the reassurances of Byrne and Stanislaus, relief, contrition, renewed declarations of love, and explicit sexual detail. Nora's responses have not survived, but Joyce's letters suggest that to the explicit detail she replied in kind. Brenda Maddox describes Joyce's letters of 1909 as "central" not only to "the relationship between Joyce and Nora" but also to "the origins of *Ulysses*."[34] To Ellmann, they "present Joyce with more intensity than any others," they are "psychologically the most important that he wrote." As for the episode as a whole, it was, he wrote to Byrne, "as you pointed out to me in Chicago—of crucial importance in Joyce's life, and in any effort to fathom his character."[35]

Ellmann's efforts to interview Byrne took tact and patience. It also took a favor. On November 30, 1953, he wrote to Byrne to introduce himself as a biographer of Joyce and to compliment the "unforgettable picture of Dublin" in *Silent Years*. Would Byrne consent to an interview, thus helping him to "avoid the faults of Gorman and Gilbert"? Byrne wrote back on December 7, 1953, saying that he was unwell (he was seventy-four) and had personal reasons for saying no. "You can understand my attitude to this matter when I remind you that I knew James Joyce intimately, and that there are some things that one simply cannot talk about." Ellmann reassured him on December 25 that his questions would "not involve any breach of confidence."

Byrne's wariness was habitual, but in late 1953 it also owed something to a review of *Silent Years* in the *Herald Tribune*. The review was written by the Joyce scholar William York Tindall of Columbia, whom Ellmann thought of as a rival.[36] Tindall had already interviewed Gogarty and Byrne, neither of whom Ellmann had interviewed. However, in interviewing Byrne he had caused offense by asking personal questions about Joyce and Nora. When his review of the *Silent Years* appeared, it was hostile, which Byrne explained as a product of his deliberate failure to answer two letters Tindall had sent him after their interview. As a result, Byrne explained to Ellmann in a letter of February 3, 1954, "Tindall did his best in his review to hit back at me in a personal way." Ellmann valued *Silent Years* and quickly offered to give it a positive review. On March 13, 1954, the review appeared in the *Saturday Review of Literature* under the title "Cranly's Memoirs." Nine days later, on March 22, Byrne granted Ellmann an interview. On his way to California, Byrne stopped in Chicago and met Ellmann at the Brevoort Hotel in the Loop. There he gave Ellmann much of the information he sought. Ellmann suggested that they meet again on Byrne's return from California, but Byrne declined. As for "your kindly expressed 'hope' of having me address your class in Northwestern University, that is an experience with which I feel quite sure your class could very readily dispense."[37] In a letter to Maria Jolas of May 11, Ellmann complained that "J. F. Byrne, after his short burst of confiding in me en route to California, has sunk into his previous evasive reticence."

Byrne was also prickly. On August 21, in reply to a letter Ellmann had sent him addressed to "Dear Jeff," Byrne wondered, "Where did you get the name 'Jeff.' My intimates of yesteryear—I might better say yestercentury—called me by that name, but those who still address me by it are very few." In the same letter Byrne writes of having given a "cursory" reading to an article by Ellmann about *Ulysses* ("The Backgrounds of *Ulysses*," *Kenyon Review*, summer 1954) which, he wrote, "gave me the impression of its having been done hastily. It is not your intention, I presume, to incorporate this article 'as is' in your forthcoming book." Ellmann's reply, on August 27, was again addressed to "Dear Jeff":

> It was good to hear from you, even if the Jewish Hospital sojurn has dispirited you; perhaps the tests and the xrays will yet turn out to be, if not helpful in themselves, helpful in the treatment to which they lead.
>
> I hope you were not offended by my use of the name "Jeff," but in fact you were quite gracious about it. When we met in Chicago you told me your name was often elided to that ["J. F." becoming "Jeff"], and I took this as an authorization for me to do it.

> I am sure that my article has many flaws, and I wish I could claim it had been done hurriedly, though in fact it was not. I know of certain factual errors; and I should be grateful if you would point out those which you recognize, as well as errors of interpretation. But I don't mean to overtask either your patience or your strength. It will be two or three years I suppose before my book will be published, though most of the preliminary work has been done as far as I know how to do it.

The letter then offers news about recent interviews (T. S. Eliot, Wyndham Lewis) and reflections on the difficulty of dating Joyce's activities. It ends:

J. F. Byrne.

"This is a rather disconnected letter, but I wanted you to know that I was thinking of you and wishing you well."

A year later, a second Ellmann essay about Joyce, "The Limits of Joyce's Naturalism" (*Sewanee Review,* Autumn 1955), elicited further criticism from Byrne.[38] In discussing Joyce's distress in August 1909 over Cosgrave and Nora, Ellmann describes Cosgrave as having attempted to "cuckold" Joyce. Byrne took issue not only with the term "cuckold" ("To my knowledge, Joyce neither could nor should, have thought of himself as a 'cuckold.'") but also with Stanislaus's suggestion that there had been no sexual contact between Cosgrave and Nora, either before or after she began going out with Joyce. According to Byrne, in the letter of January 29, 1954, Cosgrave *had* slept with Nora, but before she had met Joyce.[39] Ellmann's defense of Stanislaus's view came in a letter to Byrne of February 2: "Stanislaus was emphatic and very circumstantial that the charge related to her behavior while Joyce was courting her. He mentioned Joyce's letters to her, the theme of which was betrayal and infidelity, not pre-Joycean sexual indulgence. This seems more in keeping with the anguish you describe so well in your book. . . . I suppose Stan's story not unfounded." As Amanda Sigler puts it, "Having secured the information from Byrne he so desperately wanted, he ultimately rejected it."[40] Some three years later, Ellmann sent Byrne a copy of Stuart Gilbert's edited volume *Letters of James Joyce* (1957). In a thank-you note of October 9, 1957, Byrne wrote: "I think it was a very kindly thing for you to do, and it prompts me to say that I believe you are from the tips of your toes to the top of your head a gentleman."

* * *

Ellmann's relations with Stuart Gilbert were also smoothed by favors. The two men had got on well in Paris on Ellmann's first research trip in the summer of 1953, and within a year, in a letter of February 27, 1954, Gilbert wrote to Ellmann to ask if he would produce a "skeleton biography" or chronology to accompany the *Letters* volume. Ellmann readily agreed, not only because it would be good for his reputation among Joyceans to be associated with the edition, but because he wished to do all he could to hurry it along. Although Harriet Weaver had granted him permission to see the letters, Gilbert's publishers, Viking in the United States and Faber and Faber in Britain, would not let him quote from them until they were in print. It was in Ellmann's interest to have the edition out as soon as possible. On

May 10, Harriet Weaver likened Ellmann's biography and Gilbert's letters to horses in a race ("Perhaps it will be neck and neck!"). Ellmann replied on May 27 that his biography would "undoubtedly appear after Mr. Gilbert's edition. . . . Perhaps I shall be able to spur him on this summer!" By the end of May, Ellmann had produced a preliminary version of the chronology. On June 13 he wrote to Gilbert asking if, in addition to the letters he was about to publish, he could also have access to "whatever letters you do not plan to use in your selection." Weaver had already agreed to let him see these letters, having been reassured that his main motive was "to avoid going astray in my interpretation." If something turned up that he needed to quote, he told her, "I should ask specific permission for that."

Gilbert had almost as much trouble editing Joyce's letters as Gorman had had writing his biography. He was formally appointed editor on August 28, 1948, after Miss Weaver had done a fair bit of preliminary work selecting, deciphering, and transcribing the letters, and censoring those containing what Gilbert described as "passages relating to personal and private matters, of no general interest" (Gilbert, "Note on Editing," in *Letters of James Joyce,* vol. 1, p. 39). Once Gilbert was appointed, his main tasks were "sorting, labelling and eventually annotating."[41] From the start, gaps in Joyce's correspondence were a concern not just to Weaver and Gilbert but to the book's publishers, so much so that in February 1950 Benjamin W. Huebsch of Viking (who soon would figure prominently in Ellmann's life) suggested that instead of printing a volume of letters alone, Gilbert should write a biographical narrative of Joyce's life "illustrated" by letters, under the title "Letters of James Joyce, Presented by Stuart Gilbert." (By omitting the definite article, Huebsch thought, readers would be alerted to the incomplete character of the collection.) This suggestion Gilbert rejected, claiming that he had "no first hand knowledge of the subject previous to about 1927."[42] "I am accumulating such a load of guilt regarding the Letters," Gilbert wrote to Huebsch on July 11, 1950, "that I soon shall need the services of a psychoanalyst. The truth is, of course, that those Letters weigh on my mind as no job I have ever undertaken has weighed." By this date Gilbert had hired an assistant, Patricia Hutchins Greacen, author of *Dublin's Joyce* (1949). She had been hired in April 1949, principally to scout out and annotate the Irish letters. The scale of the work that remained, however, so alarmed Gilbert that on November 4, 1950, he wrote to John Slocum asking if he would consider collaborating with him on the edition, an offer Slocum declined.

In May 1955 Gilbert submitted the finished manuscript of *Letters* to Weaver, including his introduction, his note on editing, and Ellmann's "skeleton biography." He had been at work on the volume for over seven years, as long as it took Joyce to write *Ulysses*. Galleys were examined in April 1956 and the book was published a year later, on May 24, 1957. According to Weaver, the main reason it took so long for Gilbert to edit the *Letters* was that it was only "a sideline" for him. What took precedence was a commitment to the Swiss publisher Albert Skira, whose art books Gilbert was contracted to translate. Ira B. Nadel thought the delay owed to Gilbert's "overall inertia [hence the "guilt"] when confronted by the 690 letters sent to him from London that required sorting, annotating, and emending."[43] When yet more letters surfaced, making clear the need for a second volume, Gilbert was asked if he wanted to be its editor.[44] He declined—and Harriet Weaver turned to Ellmann. "There is no-one with a greater right than yourself to undertake the task," she told him, "or who would do it better." This was Gilbert's view as well.[45]

The death of Stanislaus Joyce on June 16, 1955 ("Bloomsday"), played a part in the choice of Ellmann as editor. A year after Stanislaus's death, Ellmann visited Nelly Joyce, who gave him access to her husband's papers, including over 150 letters Joyce had written to him, plus other family correspondence. Hence, in part, Weaver's talk of no-one having a "greater right" to the role than Ellmann. Although still at work on the biography, Ellmann accepted the appointment, in part because as editor he could restrict access to the new letters until after publication of the biography.[46] Weaver enthusiastically greeted Ellmann's acceptance in a letter of December 5, 1956, though she worried about when he would be able to begin work on the new volume. In August 1958, when Ellmann sent her the completed manuscript of *James Joyce*, he reassured her that he would now be able to start on the letters in the fall. Ellmann also sent a copy of the manuscript to Gilbert, who after reading it sent him all the letters not included in the 1957 edition. Writing to Huebsch of Viking on September 23, 1959, Gilbert praised Ellmann as much better qualified for the job than he was, "much more modern in outlook, and objective. I am . . . sadly old-fashioned in my view on these matters and have always felt a—very likely—misguided 'loyalty' to J. J., whom I liked as much as I admired."

* * *

Ellsworth Mason's support had been fundamental to Ellmann's gaining the trust of Stanislaus Joyce and his wife Nelly, and thus access to Stanislaus's papers, including diaries and letters. Mason and Stanislaus had been brought together by John Slocum and collaborated on an edition of Joyce's early book reviews.[47] In addition, as Joseph Kelly puts it, "Mason provided Stanislaus with a tireless advocate before the American scholarly community, increasing his circulation and his credibility." He not only recommended Ellmann to Stanislaus but cautioned him against talking to any other biographer or would-be biographer.[48]

On Ellmann's first visit to Trieste in 1953, Stanislaus had been courteous, helpful, but "obviously taken up by his own book," the memoir that would eventually be published posthumously as *My Brother's Keeper* (1957). He was also, Ellmann continued in a letter to Mason, "crotchety but intelligent. He is about through with the 4th of nine chapters. I'm sure it's hard for him to write, and he has an enormous amount of material, I should guess. He said he would try to finish soon, but will he? His book will be enormously interesting, and I'd be much happier about my own if I could see his first."[49] Ellmann encouraged Stanislaus to finish the book as soon as he could, and Stanislaus seemed "glad to be urged."[50] He also offered to help Stanislaus publish an article titled "An Open Letter to Oliver Gogarty," described by Ellmann as "an eloquent attack on Gogarty's attack" on Joyce.[51] The publisher Ellmann had in mind was his friend John Train, the first managing editor of the *Paris Review*.[52] In addition, Ellmann wrote to his publishers at Oxford University Press on Stanislaus's behalf to see if they might be interested in publishing the memoir.[53]

On his second trip to Europe, in the summer of 1954, Ellmann met Stanislaus in London for a stroll in Hyde Park. Stanislaus told Ellmann that in the memoir he had reached the year 1904, the moment when Joyce and Nora left Ireland for Europe. He also informed Ellmann that T. S. Eliot was reading the memoir for Faber and Faber.[54] To Harriet Weaver, Ellmann described Stanislaus on this occasion as "very affable, and as you predicted, . . . glad to have someone to talk to. His writing is sometimes truculent, but his manner face to face, while it is often very positive, is rather impressive and always winning."[55] In a later letter to Weaver, written a year after Stanislaus's death, Ellmann recalled being "impressed by his strength and youthfulness" when they met in Hyde Park, especially given that "as he probably told you, he had had a heart attack on his way to London, but preferred to believe that it was only a temporary strain and shopped among doctors until he found one who agreed with him. I understand that he did not tell his wife about it, and did not recognize the disease even up to the end." As for the memoir, Ellmann was certain that, "even if incomplete, [it] should be invaluable; it is a pity he was deprived of the fame that it would have given him during his lifetime if he had lived."[56] When Mason learned from Ellmann of Stanislaus's death, he felt it as a blow to Joyce scholarship as well as a personal blow. "An important part of the information on Joyce's life," he wrote to Ellmann on June 26, 1955, "will never be told. This will make your biography easier, but it will certainly cut back the total picture considerably."

After Stanislaus's death, Ellmann wrote a letter of condolence to Nelly Joyce, whom he had talked with over the telephone but had never met. In the letter he offered "any help I could on getting his manuscript ready for the printer."[57] He also brought forward a planned third trip to Europe. He wrote to Maria Jolas on October 14, 1955, "The death of Stanislaus on June 16 has made me think it would be better to try to go abroad this coming summer (1956) than wait until 1957." In fact he returned to Europe at the end of March. In London, early in April, he met with Peter du Sautoy of Faber and Faber, who asked him to edit Stanislaus's book, which would be published concurrently in the United States by Viking (publishers also of Joyce's letters, both those edited by Gilbert and those to be edited by Ellmann). By May 17, 1956, Ellmann and du Sautoy had even "chosen some passages from [Stanislaus's] later journal to go with the original text—which ends in August 1903."[58]

By far the most important interview Ellmann conducted on this third trip to Europe was with Nelly Joyce, whom he described to Harriet Weaver as "a very nice woman . . . who is not very strong and has had a difficult two years, losing a brother as well as a husband."[59] According to Mason, Stanislaus had instructed Nelly that, if he died, she should "trust only Mason to advise her on James's and Stanislaus's papers."[60] In a moment equivalent to the moment when Yeats's widow took Ellmann into her husband's study in Rathmines, Stanislaus Joyce's widow took Ellmann into the

The cellar where Nelly Joyce showed Ellmann Stanislaus's papers.

cellar of their home in Trieste, where he found "a great mass of papers . . . miscellaneous stuff which [Nelly] couldn't identify." Ellmann offered "to put it all in order for her," a task that took him three weeks.[61] "The most important part of the collection," he later reported to Weaver, "was a group of about a hundred and thirty letters and letter-cards written by James to Stanislaus, mostly between 1902 and 1914, but continuing until a few days before James's death. These describe his activities in great and fascinating detail. . . . From the point of view of a biographer, I had tumbled into King Tut's tomb."[62]

Ellmann returned to the United States in May 1956. In September he received from du Sautoy both the original typescript of Stanislaus's memoir and a second typed copy along with editing instructions. Chief among these instructions was that he focus squarely on Stanislaus's observations about

Joyce and that he cut back on his criticisms of religion. Ellmann reported his first reactions to the manuscript in a letter of October 1, 1956, to Weaver. "I rushed to it hoping that all veils would be removed. . . . Although occasionally he achieves felicities of style, in general the book lacks a strong purposive structure, probably because of the ambivalence of the fraternal relationship. A good deal of it is about Stanislaus, who is not altogether likeable though one feels sorry for him. Unfortunately it ends in 1903, before James's life really is under way." To du Sautoy, on the same date, he wrote that the manuscript "presented more problems than I had anticipated."

In his Introduction to *My Brother's Keeper,* Ellmann is more admiring. Also admiring is T. S. Eliot, whom Ellmann persuaded to write a preface to accompany the introduction. "I have read the book twice," Eliot writes,

> and find myself fascinated and repelled by the personality of this positive, courageous, bitter man who was prey to such mixed emotions of affection, admiration and antagonism—a struggle in the course of which, as Mr. Ellmann in his Introduction points out, he saw his famous brother, at certain moments, with a startling lucidity of vision. . . . Possessed as he was by the subject of his memoir, Stanislaus Joyce, under the exasperation of this thorn under his flesh, became himself a writer, and the author of this one book which is worthy to occupy a permanent place on the bookshelf beside the works of his brother.[63]

Eliot's preface also contains surprising remarks about biography, the sort likely to have encouraged Ellmann: "In the case of James Joyce we have a series of books, two of which at least are so autobiographical in appearance that further study of the man and his background seems not only suggested by our own inquisitiveness, but almost expected of us by the author himself. We want to know who are the originals of his characters, and what were the origins of his episodes, so that we may unravel the web of memory and invention and discover how far and in what ways the crude material has been transformed" (pp. 11–12).

What Eliot calls the "startling lucidity" of Stanislaus's depiction of his brother, Ellmann extends to his depiction of himself. For Ellmann, the title of the memoir, *My Brother's Keeper,* is Stanislaus's way of disarming "the criticism he expected of his candor." "Mainly he wished to present his case before an imagined tribunal, and sardonically presented himself as

Cain because the evidence would show he was not. Yet he may also have felt his own role as helper to be a little ambiguous, confused, even, by a muted struggle for mastery over the creature who so mastered him. Like all his family, including his many sisters, [Stanislaus] was capable of such great and sudden insights. It is not difficult to understand how genius cropped up in his household" (p. 15). Stanislaus was for Ellmann a trustworthy witness not only because of his closeness to Joyce, but because of his intelligence, evident throughout the book, and his honesty, manifest in the mixed character of the portraits he paints both of Joyce and of his relation to Joyce. In his introduction, Ellmann calls the memoir "remarkably frank and searching, but what gives his record its special force is that complex mixture of frustration, affection, resentment, and regret Stanislaus had for the days when he was closest to his brother" (p. 24). A similar mixture marks Ellmann's depiction of Joyce in the biography, in which flaws and failings mix with heroic abilities and virtues.

That Stanislaus was funny, with a sardonic sense of humor like Ellmann's own, also appealed. "Though for the second half of his long life my father belonged to the class of the deserving poor," writes Stanislaus, "that is to say of the class of people who richly deserve to be poor, he was born into a middle-class family." The father's father was a model in this respect: "After the second bankruptcy he lived with his wife and young son at Sunday's Well, a fashionable suburb of Cork, on an allowance from his father . . . and perhaps on some desultory occupation. His wife had an annuity settled on her by her father. My grandfather died young, in his forties, and his death seems to have been sincerely mourned even by his wife" (p. 43). Stanislaus's hostile remarks about religion are similarly sardonic. At Belvedere, early on in his time there, "I was startled and awestruck to see our Jesuit teacher turn a boy of about nine across his knees and whack him with a leather pandy-bat for writing the 'Our Father' at dictation in pencil instead of ink. But after all, priests have so few pastimes" (p. 70). For all his hostility to religion, though, Stanislaus openly acknowledges its influence on his brother's writing and thought, as in an exchange between the brothers about transubstantiation. "'Don't you believe,' said Joyce to Stanislaus, choosing his words without haste, '[that] there is a certain resemblance between the mystery of the Mass and what I am trying to do? I mean that I am trying in my poems to give people some kind of intellectual pleasure or spiritual enjoyment by converting the bread of everyday life into something that has a permanent artistic life of its own . . . for their mental, moral and spiritual uplift'" (p. 116).

Stanislaus's influence upon Ellmann has been detected in several aspects of *James Joyce*. In addition to the mixed nature of the portraits of Joyce and of Stanislaus's relation to Joyce in both memoir and biography, there is the prominence both works give to the father (of whom Stanislaus has almost nothing good to say) rather than the mother. Stanislaus's favoring of Joyce's earlier, more realistic or "realist" fiction, as opposed to his later writing, is another possible influence. For Stanislaus, Joyce was "an uncompromising realist," in the tradition of Zola and Balzac; what little Stanislaus has to say about *Finnegans Wake* in the memoir (inevitably, given its 1904 end date) is hostile. For readers of *James Joyce*—even non-Joycean readers such as Ellmann's father—too little is said not only about *Finnegans Wake* and the nonrealist elements in *Ulysses*, but about the role of language as a subject for Joyce, including his skepticism about fiction's claims to faithful representation. Similarly, Ellmann's treatment of Joyce's politics in the biography resembles Stanislaus's approach in his memoir. For Stanislaus, Joyce's "political leanings" (p. 174) take a distant second to literary concerns. "My brother considered even a European, or even a world, war to be just literally a bloody nuisance interfering with his work" (p. 186). "To his last days, when he was fleeing before the invading hordes in France, he regarded the European upheaval as one might observe a blizzard or a tornado, and only wondered whether it was still possible to get a book he needed from Paris" (p. 124). In a review of *James Joyce* in the *New Statesman*, William Empson takes Ellmann to task for just this attitude to Joyce's politics, in particular for his failing to take Joyce's socialism seriously.[64]

* * *

Mary Ellmann's role in the making of *James Joyce*—with respect to research as opposed to as a reader—is worth considering at this point. The 1956 trip could not have been made without Mary, and was made at considerable sacrifice for her, as is clear from correspondence. On April 3 Ellmann was dining at the Dolphin Restaurant in Dublin at the same time that Mary was in Evanston longing "to eat out with [an] adult." Stephen was four, Maud was two, and Mary was pregnant with Lucy, who would be born on October 18. Mary was a loving mother, but by 6:30 each night, she told Ellmann, she "could not bear the sight of either child." The weather in

Evanston did not help. The spring was "ridiculously and disgustingly hot" and her days consisted of "much outdoor stuff, increased fatigue, schizoid between housework and yard—all neighbors raking and poking indefatigably, feel honor of the house at stake." Ellmann's enormous correspondence, including letters forwarded to her by the department secretary, had to be sorted. "It is my sincere wish," she writes on April 6, "that the flood may abate as you are longer away. I particularly value my evenings." The letter ends: "I cannot write about myself. . . . I *should* have gone to Newburyport, as I once had thought of doing. I will never again live in this house by myself. I will go back to my own family. I cannot bear it. I feel myself being destroyed. I will mail this walking Pierre [the poodle] who has brightened my day by vomiting all over the rugs. The home front. Love, Mary."

Ten days later, after Ellmann offers to cut short his trip, Mary replies: "I am glad to hear that matters went so well in London. I acknowledge the importance of this trip to your project and the importance of the project to you and I do not want you to shorten it on my account. Nor do I honestly mean to seem 'unfriendly' when I write. What you must try to understand is that I live in a constant horrified contemplation of my own life. I am half sick, alone and burdened with stupid monotonous work." A visit from Ellmann's parents was to follow. "I have set a kind of goal with them," Mary writes. "I feel that once I have got through their visit I will also have got through April and that therefore somehow I will be bound to feel better." Later in the letter, she writes: "Please do not call by telephone—I can't bear that kind of call and what good could it do? Steve's pestering me intolerably so I will go and make his orange juice."

Before Ellmann left for Europe, a student was recruited as a lodger, to help Mary with babysitting. She was of little help. On April 23, presumably in response to a worried letter from Ellmann, Mary writes reassuringly:

> I do not want you to shorten your trip *at all.* I have become emotionally reconciled to its length (I was *always* intellectually)—in fact I now feel a kind of *commitment* to its original length and I will be very disconcerted if you alter it on my account. In terms of our lifetimes, it is very brief and I don't want to feel for *that* length of time that I rather squashed it. And sent you through Europe, like Byron, in an aura of gloom. We are getting along OK, we are through a month already, and I really want you to do it as thoroughly as you planned.

Pierre the poodle.

The letter ends: "Must to bed without you. My love, Mary." Five days later, after mentioning the erotic frustrations of Pierre, the poodle, and Bev, the student lodger, Mary's letter ends: "All my love—in my own way in as bad a way as Bev and Pierre."

At some point early in May, in his excitement at gaining access to Stanislaus's papers in Trieste, Ellmann raised the possibility of extending his stay in Europe. Mary's response of May 7 begins without salutation: "You should not have been so vocal about returning soon when the possibility of this about-face in Trieste must always have been in your mind. You will want to know how we are. Steve has an ear infection, Maudie has a cold and I have a wretched incessant cough. Meanwhile your father writes me that *you* must have a good rest when you get back here. After six weeks I still rack my brains to think of some means of escape. But there is none. I am bound by this student and by this insane pregnancy. Mary."[65] Three days later, in a letter of May 10, Mary is more composed, though still obviously fed up:

> Dear Dick,
> What is this business about your hospitalization in Paris? What happened to you? Too many snails? So very cryptic, lesser-man-than-I stuff—I daresay intended to embarrass. Long since resigned to your winning these pathological contests.
>
> I am glad that you had such good luck in Trieste. Regret last angry letter.

There follows news of a scare. Steve had been wrongly diagnosed with mumps, a possible threat to the pregnancy. Then she recounts more mundane calamities:

> Maudie flooded bathroom again, great flood down through light fixture but this time *not* put on blink. Pierre had back leg trouble yesterday, better today without vet. Couldn't get to vet, car on blink, so money saved. Obviously we have entered a new phase of catastrophes confronted and stared down. Rather exhilarating.
>
> *My love to you—Mary*

On May 29 Ellmann wrote to Maria Jolas: "You probably decided that I was at the bottom of the Adriatic by now, but what happened was that I decided to cut short my trip and console Mary in her lonely pregnancy so I did not stop in Paris but came straight on home."

CHAPTER EIGHT

Rivals and Restrictions

IN MID-JUNE 1956, shortly after his return to Evanston from Europe, Ellmann traveled with Mary and the children to Bloomington, Indiana, for six weeks. He was to teach a summer course at the School of Letters, part of the University of Indiana. The School of Letters was created in 1948 at Kenyon College in Gambier, Ohio, where it was known as the School of English. It was funded by the Rockefeller Foundation and founded by John Crowe Ransom, Lionel Trilling, and F. O. Matthiessen. It moved to Indiana in 1951, when the Rockefeller Foundation shifted its literature funding to individual writers rather than institutions. The school was New Critical, emphasizing interpretation or close reading rather than literary history, philology, or biography. Ellmann's course on Joyce and Yeats met on Mondays, Wednesdays, and Fridays, and had six students, all studying for the MA or PhD.

The course was more demanding than Ellmann had expected. "The small size did not translate into ease of instruction," he reported to H. K. Croessmann.[1] To Harriet Weaver he complained about the school's "tradition of energetic questioning which is quite out of keeping with the hot humid climate" (Bloomington, he pointed out, is 250 miles south of Evanston).[2] Students as well as teachers proved alarmingly sophisticated. "I committed myself to giving a public lecture on Wallace Stevens," he wrote in the letter to Weaver, "thinking that the subject was recondite enough so that nobody would be knowledgeable about it, but it has turned out that several people at the school are getting up articles and lectures on him and I have been obliged to prepare more energetically than I had intended." The lecture was published as "Wallace Stevens' Ice-Cream," *Kenyon Review* (Winter 1957).

Ellmann's complaints show the pressure he was under in the summer of 1956. As well as writing Joyce's biography, he had Stanislaus Joyce's memoir to edit and its introduction to write (to meet a publication date of 1958, a year before the biography). The page proofs of Gilbert's edition of Joyce's letters had to be read ("They still contain a number of errors," he reported to his parents).[3] Meanwhile, he and Ellsworth Mason were to edit *The Critical Writings of James Joyce,* which was due to be published the same year as the biography. Ellmann took on these projects partly because they afforded him exclusive access to materials sought by rival scholars, and partly to establish his reputation. Pressed as he was, almost as soon as he arrived at the school he became embroiled in an increasingly acrimonious negotiation over the sale of Stanislaus Joyce's papers, something that threatened his friendship with Mason and their coediting of *The Critical Writings.* Here, too, anxieties about access and rivals were involved.

Ellmann was one of four fellows at the School of Letters in 1956. The others were the critics and literary theorists Northrop Frye and Richard Chase, and the poet Karl Shapiro. The senior fellows that year were Ransom, Trilling, Philip Rahv (editor of *Partisan Review*), Allen Tate, and Austin Warren. Ransom was Ellmann's chief supporter, an admirer since the summer of 1941 when both were at the Bread Loaf School in Vermont. Ellmann was a budding poet at that time, as well as a budding academic, and he excelled in Ransom's course on criticism and philosophy; he was also chosen to read his poems in the company of William Carlos Williams, Theodore Roethke, and Robert Frost. Although in 1956 he was at work on a biography, his most recent book, *The Identity of Yeats* (1954), was a study of the poet's verse, and his most recent essays appeared in the *Kenyon Review* and *Sewanee Review,* journals associated with the New Criticism. This association, given academic fashion, was in Ellmann's interest, as it would be also in the reception of the biography.

Ellmann published six essays on Joyce during the years he was writing the biography. All the essays are interpretative, but three of them, two in the *Kenyon Review,* one in the *Sewanee Review,* contain biographical material that he wanted to be the first to publish. "Here is the article I've been threatening you with," Ellmann writes to his brother Erwin on April 7, 1954, speaking of "The Backgrounds of *Ulysses,*" *Kenyon Review* (Summer 1954). "I'm more or less obliged to publish it because my rivals are breathing down my neck; chiefly Tindall, whose edition of Chamber Music (just out) is lousy, but indicates that he's looking for exactly the stuff I am, and he's just gone to Dublin for four months. I imagine he won't find much of what I have, but he will find some, and will talk to many of the same people."[4]

In "The Backgrounds of *Ulysses,*" Ellmann maintains that "Joyce built his art upon a rock, and the rock was reality, which he understood with deliberate naïveté as a collocation of what Blake called 'minute particulars.'"[5] These particulars Joyce subjected to "a continual transposition and re-composition" (p. 339). How the characters in *Ulysses* differ from their real-life models is the essay's ostensible subject, but what is most striking is Ellmann's detailed knowledge of those models. For example, in discussing "Aeolus"—the seventh episode in *Ulysses,* set in the Dublin offices of the *Freeman's Journal* and *Evening Telegraph*—Ellmann identifies the prototypes or partial prototypes for all the fictional journalists Bloom encounters, and offers particulars for the real-life journalists who appear in the episode under their own names. Here is his account of the named real-life journalists:

> His uncle John Murray worked on the advertising staff of the *Freeman's Journal* and is mentioned here in that capacity; he was called "Red" Murray to distinguish him from Chris Murray, also on the advertising staff, who was known as "Black" Murray. Braydon, whose imposing entrance is observed by Red Murray and Bloom at the beginning of the episode, was at the time the editor of the *Evening Telegraph.* The description of him as bearded and with hunched shoulders is true to life. Paddy Hooper and Jack Hall were two reporters; Hooper, the son of an alderman mentioned elsewhere in *Ulysses,* was to be the *Evening Telegraph*'s last editor. About 1909 he was usually assigned to London; hence he is depicted here as having come over to Ireland only the night before. Hall was a famous reporter with old-world manners and tastes, who in 1901 highly praised Joyce's acting in his review of a play called *Cupid's Confidante.* Nannetti was foreman printer of the *Freeman's Journal* in 1904; Joyce probably saw his son, who was foreman printer of the *Evening Telegraph* in 1909. Chris Callinan, whom Lenehan mockingly calls Ignatius Gallaher's brother-in-law, was a reporter who had the Dublin coast as his province and was famous for his Irish bulls. These personages were not of much importance in the book, but they peopled Joyce's newspaper world and gave it lights and shadows. (p. 365)

The detail paraded in this passage is intended to impress, as it does in the essay as a whole and in the biography into which the essay was incorporated.[6]

Its "importance," Ellmann would argue, is that it gives "lights and shadows" to Joyce's working methods. "To trace the materials of *Ulysses,*" Ellmann writes at the end of the essay, "is to discover a fuller admiration for the hand that changed them or, with equal mastery, let them alone" (p. 386). That Ellmann was determined to be the first Joyce scholar to reveal this mastery was the reason he had proposed, in 1953, publishing a short book before a full-length life. "We must protect the book's novelty" is how he put it to his editor at OUP, after listing potential rivals (Richard Kain, Joseph Prescott, Patricia Hutchins).[7] OUP vetoed this proposal, but journal articles, unlike a short book, posed little danger to the wide general market sought for in a full-length biography.

The "novelty" Ellmann sought to protect was literary critical as well as biographical, particularly in respect to the characterization of Leopold Bloom. In his discussion of the "Circe" episode in *Ulysses,* William Blake and Leopold von Sacher-Masoch are identified as presiding spirits. Once again, divergence from sources is shown to be as important as resemblance. Bloom's masochistic fantasies in "Circe" are likened to those of Sacher-Masoch, but in "vaudeville" style. They also "occur in his unconscious mind," unlike Severin von Kusiemski's experiences in *Venus in Furs* (1879) (p. 373). Ellmann shows that Blake is alluded to several times in the episode, most importantly at the end, when Stephen is confronted by the soldiers who attack him after hearing him declare, tapping his brow: "But in here it is I must kill the priest and the king" (4437). As Ellmann puts it,

> Joyce has in mind here an episode that occurred during Blake's stay at Felpham, when he put two soldiers out of his garden in spite of their protests that as soldiers of the king they should not be handled so. He replied, or was alleged to have replied, "Damn the king," was therefore haled up for treason, and barely got off. (In *Finnegans Wake* the two soldiers become three, and have an equally unpleasant role to play.) Stephen does not put the soldiers to flight; rather they knock *him* down, but not before he has stated his contention that the authorities, religious and secular, must be defeated in spiritual rather than corporeal warfare.

In this case, difference or divergence reveals a deeper resemblance, because "this is Blake's central conception of the conquest of tyranny by imagination" (pp. 373–74).

In the rest of the essay, in addition to surveying possible real-life models for Bloom, Ellmann considers the significance of the character's Jewishness, his passivity, his feeling for family, and his ultimate heroism, in ways that were at odds with influential predecessors, notably Harry Levin, T. S. Eliot, and Pound.

> The kindness of Bloom on June 16, 1904, begins with animals and ends with human beings. So he feeds the cat in the morning, then some seagulls, and in the *Circe* episode feeds two dogs. He remembers his dead son and dead father, he is also concerned about his living daughter, and he never forgets his wife for a moment. He contributes very generously—beyond his means—to the fund for children of his friend Dignam who has just died; and, when he begins to see Stephen as a sort of son, he follows him, tries to stop his drinking, prevents his being robbed, risks arrest to defend him from the police, and feeds him and takes him home. . . . So we have Stephen and Bloom, the mental men, ranged against Mulligan and Boylan, the burly men, and Joyce's partisanship is clear.
>
> The scheme of value of *Ulysses* comes closer to explicit expression in the *Circe* episode than it does anywhere else.[8] (pp. 375–76)

Ellsworth Mason was startled by several aspects of the *Kenyon* essay, beginning with where it appeared. "I must congratulate you on the tour de force of getting Ransom to accept an article this long that is largely non-critical," he writes in a letter of October 13, 1954. He then takes issue with several of the article's assertions. He reminds Ellmann, "I argued at length in my dissertation that Circe is not the climax of Ulysses and that the Father-son theme is not the central theme of the book." For Mason the episode ends not with "some sort of communion or call it what you will" but with "complete or utter frustration, although Bloom does not yet realize it." Mason also questions Ellmann's account of Joyce's working methods, which present him as "more deliberate than he actually was. Much of the welding of persons that you described undoubtedly was unconscious, conscious though your tracing of it may be."

More generally, Mason objected to the prominence Ellmann gives to "fact." "You make Joyce out as far less inventive than he actually was. Say what you want, up through the portrait, in *Ulysses* invention is the dominant thing. Throw the directory and biography and landscape at me, and you have not begun to get to the heart of Ulysses." Early in the essay, Ellmann recounts a story Beckett tells about taking dictation from Joyce for *Finnegans Wake:* "There was a knock on the door and Joyce said 'Come in.' Beckett, who hadn't heard the knock, by mistake wrote down 'Come in' as part of the dictated text. Afterwards he read it back and Joyce said, 'What's that "Come in"?' 'That's what you dictated,' Beckett replied. Joyce thought for a moment, realizing that Beckett hadn't heard the knock; then he said, 'Let it stand.' The very fact that misunderstanding had occurred in actuality gave it prestige for Joyce" (pp. 359–60). To Mason, however, "If Joyce said 'Let it stand' it was not because the words had occurred in reality, but because they were artistically appropriate to the passage being written. . . . Fact does not liberate Joyce's genius, his genius scoops up facts and absorbs them in a larger unit that is only partially factual."

In Ellmann's defense, he does not claim that Joyce said "Let it stand" *because* it "occurred in actuality," only that its occurring in actuality gave it "prestige."[9] Easier to credit are Mason's reservations, leavened with praise, about the implicit connection between Ellmann's and Joyce's working methods:

> While you do up the mélange in a very pleasing package, I couldn't help feeling that you had blurred both by trying to write both biography and criticism. I do not think that the biographical details you have gathered, most of which were new to me, have clarified anything in my own mind about Joyce. They rather show that you have been having a fine time in Ireland. I hope that you will find it in your heart to give up this idea of playing a duet with Joyce in his biography, because really, old thing, although Joyce was in many ways less interesting than you, and obviously not nearly as pleasant, he *was* more important. And I don't think you really are the one to write Ellmann's biography, largely because you underestimate him a good deal of the time.

A year later, in a much shorter essay titled "The Limits of Joyce's Naturalism" (*Sewanee Review,* Autumn 1955), Ellmann again begins with "fact," both in Joyce's life as a person and in the lives of the characters in *Ulysses*. Its opening sentence is: "Joyce used to boast that if Dublin were destroyed, it could be reconstructed from his books." Here, too, there is some parading of real-life origins—of characters, settings, incidents. In "Penelope," for example, Molly, in stream of consciousness mode, thinks first about the beauty of flowers, then about atheists, who are wrong to ask "who was the first person in the universe before there was anybody who made it all." A recollection follows: "how she herself lay beside Bloom in the natural paradise of rhododendrons on Howth and gave him a bit of seedcake out of her mouth" (that Nora Joyce did the same with Joyce, also at Howth, a matter of dispute, is not mentioned in the essay).[10] At this point Ellmann invokes a biblical rather than Homeric source: "Are not Bloom and Molly reenacting the scene which took place in another garden. When the woman gave the man a bit out of the apple, the 'seed-fruit,' as *Finnegans Wake* calls it? As so often in Joyce's work, an ordinary situation [in this case in Molly's 'real life'] swells to mythical proportions, but only fleetingly. Only for a moment do Howth fade into the Garden of Eden, Bloom and Molly into Adam and Eve, the seedcake into an apple from which Joyce has withdrawn the bitterness. Quickly we are back with Bloom and Molly again" (p. 571). Although this reading is omitted from *James Joyce,* it finds its way into Ellmann's *Ulysses on the Liffey* (1972), an "interpretation" of the novel, accompanied by references to St. Augustine and Dante.[11]

Of the essays Ellmann published prior to *James Joyce,* the finest, in part because its real-life origins are so striking, is "The Backgrounds of 'The Dead'" (*Kenyon Review,* Autumn 1958), which appears, so-titled, as a chapter in the finished biography. Only when discussing the annual Christmas party that opens the story do real-life parallels seem extraneous. Mason's objection to Ellmann's earlier *Kenyon* essay—that Joyce's literary or artistic aims are depicted as secondary to documentary ones—is acknowledged tacitly in Ellmann's description of the selection of details in "The Dead" as "choices which, while masterly, suggest the preoccupations which mastered him" (p. 254). There is only one place in the essay in which real-life models are identified *as* fictional characters, as opposed to a source of fictional characters, a rare slip. It occurs at the beginning of the second paragraph: "Although the story dealt mainly with three generations of his family in Dublin, it drew also upon an incident in Galway in 1903" (p. 252). The phrase "dealt mainly with," unlike "drew upon," used in relation to the Galway incident, wrongly suggests that the story is *about* Joyce's family,

The "incident in Galway" occurred in 1903 and involved Nora and a youthful suitor, Michael ("Sonny") Bodkin, who, when confined to bed with tuberculosis, stole out one night in cold and rainy weather to sing goodbye to her on the eve of her departure for Dublin. "Nora soon learned that Bodkin was dead, and when she met Joyce she was first attracted to him, she told a sister, because he resembled Sonny Bodkin" (p. 252). This is the obvious source for Gretta Conway's revelation to her husband at the end of the story, that as a girl in Galway she was courted by a young man named Michael Furey, who died young. "What did he die of so young, Gretta?" asks Gabriel. Gretta's answer, writes Ellmann, "terrifies and silences him." She answers: "I think he died for me'" (p. 258). Like Nora's Michael Bodkin, Gretta's Michael Furey, confined to bed with tuberculosis, left his sickbed on a cold and rainy night to sing to the girl he loved, and died as a result. It is easy to imagine why Ellmann was keen to be the first to reveal this key bit of biographical background.

Ellmann makes much of Joyce's changing the name Michael Bodkin to Michael Furey. The change implies, "like the contrast of the militant Michael and the amiable Gabriel, that violent passion is in her [Gretta's] Galway past, not in her Dublin present." At this point in the essay, biography takes over, in what Ellmann calls "one of Joyce's several tributes to his wife's artless integrity":

> Nora Barnacle, in spite of her defects in education, was independent, unself-conscious, instinctively right. Gabriel acknowledges the same coherence in his own wife, and he recognizes in the west of Ireland, in Michael Furey, a passion he has himself always lacked. "Better pass boldly into that other world, in the full glory of some passion, than fade and wither dismally in age," Joyce makes Gabriel think. Then comes that strange sentence in the final paragraph: "The time had come for him to set out on his journey westward." . . . What the sentence affirms, at last, on the level of feeling, is the west, the primitive, untutored, impulsive country from which Gabriel had felt himself alienated before: in the story, the west is paradoxically linked also with the past and the dead. (p. 258)

It is also linked with the folk, and thus with the Irish revival for which Gabriel, as we shall see, has little time.

Ellmann begins the essay by writing about Rome, where Joyce lived for six unhappy months in 1906–1907, and where "The Dead" was conceived. Joyce did not begin writing the story, however, until he had left the city. In Rome, "the obtrusiveness of the dead" was unavoidable, writes Ellmann, everywhere apparent in a profusion of relics, ruins, statuary.[12] So, too, in Dublin, "the equally Catholic city he had abandoned, a city as prehensile of ruins, visible and invisible. His head was filled with a sense of the too successful encroachment of the dead upon the living city; there was a disrupting parallel in the way that Dublin, buried behind him, was haunting his thoughts" (p. 253).

Dubliners was submitted to the London publisher Grant Richards before the Joyces arrived in Rome. Once there, Joyce found himself impelled to write two more stories for the volume. After leaving Rome, Joyce told Stanislaus, in a letter of September 25, 1906, that he still had more to say about the city, singling out its "ingenuous insularity and its hospitality." The party that opens "The Dead" lovingly details Dublin hospitality, drawing many particulars from the festive gatherings of Joyce's childhood. As for the city's "ingenuous insularity," it figures in several ways. At the party, Miss Ivors, a nationalist, presses Gabriel to visit the Irish-speaking Aran Islands in the west. These islands, Ellmann tells us, are where Synge went, on the advice of Yeats, "to find his inspiration in the Irish folk" (p. 254). When Joyce received similar advice from Yeats, he rejected it, as Gabriel rejects the advice of Miss Ivors, who "twits him for his lack of patriotic feeling" (p. 254).

Gabriel is internationalist in outlook and associates the west of Ireland with "a dark and rather painful primitivism, an aspect of his country which he has steadily abjured by going off to the continent" (p. 257). Ellmann's own objection to insularity, which perhaps was most evident in his accounts of the Jewish community in Charleston, South Carolina, was lifelong. It is implicit everywhere in the decisions he made about how and where to live. Miss Ivor's accusation that Gabriel lacks patriotic feeling is connected at the end of the story to what he comes to think of as his lack of feeling in general, at least in comparison to the passion of his wife and Michael Furey. As Ellmann presents him, Joyce seems in the story to be interrogating aspects of his own life and character. This is something that also could be said of Ellmann in the essay. He, too, thought of himself, and was thought of, as internationalist, mild or dispassionate, and wary of political engagement.

The most striking of the literary sources Ellmann suggests for "The Dead" are those Joyce drew on for the story's ending. Gretta's revelation about Michael Furey "terrifies and silences" Gabriel at the very moment he is overcome with desire and love for her, after the party, alone in their room in the Gresham Hotel. Ellmann introduces the source, the name of which he initially withholds, by likening Joyce's method of composition to

T. S. Eliot's, which he calls "the imaginative absorption of stray material," "the only way he could work" (p. 259).

> He borrowed the ending for "The Dead" from another book. In that book a bridal couple receive, on their wedding night, a message that a young woman whom the husband jilted has just committed suicide. The news holds them apart, she asks him not to kiss her, and both are tormented by remorse. The wife, her marriage unconsummated, falls off at last to sleep, and her husband goes to the window and looks out at "the melancholy greyness of the dawn." For the first time he recognizes, with the force of a revelation, that his life is a failure, and that his wife lacks the passion of the girl who has killed herself. He resolves that, since he is not worthy of any more momentous career, he will try at least to make her happy. Here surely is the situation that Joyce so adroitly recomposed. The dead lover who comes between the lovers, the sense of the husband's failure, the acceptance of mediocrity, the resolve to be at all events sympathetic, all come from the other book. But Joyce transforms them. For example, he allows Gretta to kiss her husband, but without desire, and rarefies the situation by having it arise from a memory of young love. The book Joyce was borrowing from was one that nobody reads anymore, George Moore's *Vain Fortune,* but Joyce read it, and in his youthful essay, "The Day of the Rabblement," overpraised it as "fine, original work." (pp. 259–60)

Those who might quibble that "The Day of the Rabblement" was written six years before Joyce wrote "The Dead" are provided with a footnote: "He [Joyce] evidently refreshed his memory of it when writing 'The Dead,' for his copy of *Vain Fortune,* now at Yale, bears the date 'March 1907.'"

The end of the essay moves beyond biographical specifics to a larger and more dramatic sense of Joyce's life and literary evolution, a fitting expansion given the famous ending of the story, which moves from "a few light taps" of snow upon the hotel window to a vision of snow falling everywhere in Ireland, including "on the churchyard on the hill where Michael Furey lay buried." As Gabriel's soul slowly swoons, he hears the snow "falling faintly through the universe and faintly falling, like the descent of their last end, upon all the living and the dead." Ellmann's essay seeks a comparably sonorous close: "Joyce had a special reason for writing the story of 'The Dead' in 1906 and 1907. In his own mind he had thoroughly justified his flight from

Ireland, but he had not decided the question of where he would fly *to*. In Trieste and Rome he had learned what he had unlearned in Dublin, to be a Dubliner. As he had written to his brother from Rome with some astonishment, he felt humiliated when anyone attacked his 'Impoverished country.' 'The Dead' is his first song of exile."[13]

The anxieties about competitors that led to Ellmann's publishing these essays before their appearance in *James Joyce* were sparked by interviewees as well as rival scholars. In his dealings with Maria Jolas, whom he first interviewed in Paris in 1953, they were compounded by worries about Joyce's forty-three-year-old son Giorgio and twenty-one-year-old grandson Stephen. In September 1939, after Germany invaded Poland, Joyce and Nora began reading over their correspondence to see what needed saving and what could or should be destroyed. At this time Joyce was frantically revising *Finnegans Wake,* preoccupied with moving Lucia to a clinic outside Paris, and in search of a safe place for the rest of his family to live. In the correspondence he and Nora sorted through were a number of personal letters, many to Lucia in the hospital. When, in the summer of 1939, they finally left Paris, some of the remaining papers, including, presumably, those they had not reread, were left behind in a large trunk, which they instructed Jolas "to dispose of."[14] Jolas hid the trunk in a closet in her apartment in Paris, where it still remained in 1953 when Ellmann called upon her on his first research trip. As we have seen, after swearing him to silence, Jolas showed him the papers in her possession.

Jolas knew the importance of the materials in her closet and chose only Ellmann to view them. The way he earned her trust and kept it can be seen in his correspondence as well as in accounts of his manner in person. William Brockman, coeditor of a forthcoming edition of Joyce's uncollected correspondence, offers a template for the sort of letter Ellmann sent not just to Jolas but to all of those from whom he sought information: "He customarily opened his letters with cordial greetings, proceeded in engagingly persuasive but deferential tones to discuss the matter at hand, and closed his letters with snippets of informal news. One can follow through these letters the renovation of the study on the third floor of the Ellmann house, the birth of a child, the health of his wife, and other such family matters."[15] The element of calculation in these passages is muted by touches of sardonic humor. Here is Ellmann to Stuart Gilbert, on January 2, 1959: "We got through the Christmas festivities without too many wounds and scars from our (may I say it?) omnipresent children."

Richard Ellmann and his children (*left to right:* Maud, Stephen, and Lucy) around the barbecue, early 1960s.

When animals figure, there is nothing cloying. "I got home last night to discover that Stevie's turtle had just laid 7 eggs," Ellmann writes to Harriet Weaver on July 23, 1960. "It then laid six more, and one more since. The pet shop where 'he' was bought had never experienced any such phenomenon and had no advice as to how the eggs might be hatched. However, the children were vastly impressed, and the turtle itself looked rather dazed."

Ellmann shared Jolas's fear that if Joyce's son Giorgio or his grandson Stephen learned of the existence of the papers she held, and if they learned that she had let Ellmann see them, they would not only claim them but lock them away. Jolas put it to Ellmann in a letter of September 10, 1953, "It is to my mind very much to your advantage to 'let sleeping dogs lie.'" On January 20, 1954, she reiterated the need for secrecy, adding of the letters that "many would love to see them," and that "eventually they will be asked for by their logical owner [Giorgio] even though his mother gave them to me." (Nora had died in 1951.) Ellmann was therefore obliged not to disclose the nature of the letters or the identity of their possessor either to his editor at OUP or to John Slocum, whose help had been crucial to the biography. When he met Giorgio in Zurich in July and August 1954, he said nothing of the trunk or its contents.

Jolas herself, or perhaps her friend Lucie Leon, wife of Paul L. Leon, Joyce's de facto secretary in Paris, seems to have been less discreet. On February 11, 1955, Jolas wrote to Ellmann with the news that several other scholars had learned of the existence of the trunk. Stuart Gilbert knew of it. Patricia Hutchins, at work on the book that would become *James Joyce's World* (1957), did, too, asking Jolas directly if she knew where Joyce's letters to Harriet Weaver were (a number were in the trunk). In response, as Carol Shloss, Lucia's biographer, puts it, Jolas "equivocated."[16] When Giorgio learned of the trunk, the pressure on Jolas increased. "The trunkful of documents rather burns my closet," she confessed to Ellmann in a letter of February 11, 1955. "I am getting rather weary of the whole affair and the fact is that if Georgio [*sic*] were to die before it is settled (Stevie told me he almost did die last summer) it would be an awful mess." In an earlier letter, Ellmann had advised Jolas to have the contents of the trunk microfilmed at the Bibliothèque nationale. "This process is quite cheap," he assured her in a letter of December 16, 1954, and "I rather think I could get money from Northwestern to pay for it." He reiterated his advice in a letter of February 16, certain that once Giorgio got his hands on the letters, he was "sure to lose or destroy some of [them]."

The prospect of Stephen Joyce possessing the letters or having a say in access to them was especially unnerving. In the letter of December 16, 1954, Ellmann called it "frightful." Jolas had raised this prospect in a letter of December 11, announcing, "Stevie is very curious about the material features of his grandfather's fame, and is anxious to get his hands on the famous trunk, not to mention, eventually, the management of the literary executorship. I was a little taken aback when I realized this and could only be grateful that not only Miss Weaver but Giorgio himself are still there to stand between any such arrangement." In his December 16 reply, Ellmann revealed that he had suspected that Stephen, not Giorgio, had "got up" the aesthetic objection Giorgio had made to the Marthe Fleischmann letters, "a more convenient pretext than the moral objection or the objection in the name of family pride." As for Stephen's interest in the "material features" of Joyce's fame, Ellmann imagined that he might claim to his father that he could "get big prices for the papers; but I very much doubt that he knows enough about the market to do this." If Stephen got control of the papers, Ellmann thought, he was likely to sell them piecemeal ("he could probably get more money for [them] that way now"), in the process "destroying any possibility of [scholars] using the collection together."

Ellmann voiced another worry in the December 16 letter, this one concerning Giorgio. Would it be right for him to "have those pathetic, over-sexed letters from his mother to his father," possibly the letters Nora wrote in response to Joyce's "dirty letters" of 1909? These letters and others are likely to have been in the unchecked correspondence Nora had given to Jolas in 1939, in what Jolas called "a gesture of fatigue and helplessness."[17]

Jolas's fears about what would happen to the letters when Giorgio got his hands on them were fully justified. Once she delivered the trunk in 1955, the letters became unavailable to anyone outside the Joyce family. Ellmann may therefore have been the only Joyce scholar to have seen Nora's side of the "dirty letters." If so, it is odd that they are not mentioned in the extensive notes he took on the correspondence he was shown by Jolas in 1953, in some cases copying whole letters. Nor are they mentioned elsewhere in his papers or published work, including in the editorial apparatus of *Selected Letters* (1975), which publishes Joyce's side of the erotic correspondence in full. His reasons for not doing so can only be guessed at. Although in later life, especially after the *Selected Letters,* he was vilified for allowing literary or biographical interests to override family sensibilities, in this case the sensibilities may well have been his own. The first (1959) edition of *James Joyce* gives little sense of the number and nature of the erotic letters—necessarily, given the prejudices of the day and the influence of Joyce's executors—and the result, to some, risks distorting our view of what Ellmann called Joyce's "conjugal life."[18] His decision to remain silent about Nora's letters, after printing Joyce's in full, is distorting in a different way. To Brenda Maddox, the omission diminishes Nora, which presumably was the exact opposite of Ellmann's intention. Nora "certainly would not have wanted her letters published," writes Maddox, but her admirers "have special cause for regret." Maddox, an admirer, makes it abundantly clear in her biography how bold and obscene Nora's letters were, as recalled by Joyce in his side of the correspondence. For Maddox: "Nora's initiative in writing what Joyce dared not be the first to do showed great courage, erotic imagination and loyalty for which she has been deprived of recognition [!]

by everyone except Joyce. When he wrote 'Your letter is worse than mine,' it was praise indeed."[19]

Maria Jolas's generosity to Ellmann earned his deep gratitude. "If it hadn't been for the famous trunk," he wrote to her on June 22, 1981, "and your decision that I should see its contents with or without authorization I should hardly have had the courage to press on with my biography." But Jolas herself had, at moments, sought to restrict or censor. Early in 1959 Ellmann sent her the proofs of *James Joyce.* She had a number of suggestions and corrections, objecting especially to Ellmann's inclusion of a letter that suggested that Joyce had had an adulterous affair in the 1920s in Paris. In this letter, to an unnamed woman addressed as "My darling, my love, my Queen," Joyce professes himself to be in despair at having been abandoned. He also writes of experiencing a fainting fit in Sylvia Beach's bookshop after the woman left him. The letter shocked Jolas, as it did Sylvia Beach. When Ellmann first brought it to her attention in 1957, Jolas told him that she and Beach were "dumbfounded, had never expected anything, never heard a name even whispered."[20] She urged Ellmann not to publish the letter while Giorgio was alive. By 1959, however, Ellmann had established that the woman in question was not, in fact, a mistress, but Nora, as was made clear in the proofs. So he felt free to include it. The letter was written in April 1922 and the despair it records was the result of a quarrel Joyce and Nora had on the eve of her departure for Ireland to visit her family. The quarrel led Nora to issue what Ellmann calls "a final threat not to return" (p. 548). Jolas, however, continued to object, worried about Giorgio's reaction and the impression the letter would give readers of Joyce's marriage. Again, she urged Ellmann not to publish, threatening to draw the letter to Giorgio's attention.

As soon as he received Jolas's letter, Ellmann cabled her asking her not to contact Giorgio until she had heard from him. That same day, February 25, 1959, he wrote to explain:

> The fact is that in the total context of what has been written about Joyce, by others as well as by me, this letter to Nora is only confirmation of what is known, that he and Nora sometimes quarrelled, that he loved her (and she him), that she disapproved of *Ulysses,* and that he felt both submissive and passionate towards her. Joyce himself made this quite clear in *Exiles, Ulysses,* and *Finnegans Wake,* and Budgen's book and

> others have added details. I need the letter because it points these matters up. It is not at all disgraceful; if anything, it makes both Joyce and his wife more human and attractive.

Ellmann then adds that Harriet Weaver and the Society of Authors, Joyce's co-executors, had raised no objections. Nor had Stuart Gilbert (Jolas had asked about his reaction). Ellmann assured Jolas that he did not dismiss her views. On the contrary, "I made the changes you suggested . . . including the removal of passages that were too blunt, and in general tried to heighten what was always my intention, to bring the reader into sympathy with Joyce, his life and his work, while not sacrificing honesty and objectivity." If she tells Giorgio about the letter, he will be "bound" to be censorious: "His inclination is to disapprove, and as you know, it is very hard to persuade him to change his mind." Ellmann's letter ends: "I must beg you very earnestly not to write to George about this. My book is written in ultimate praise both of his father and of his mother, and of their marriage. I'm sorry to trouble you further with my work, and hope you'll forgive me."

* * *

Sometimes the restrictions involved in the making of *James Joyce* were those Ellmann imposed on his rivals, as opposed to those imposed on him. On July 8, 1953, the Joyce collector H. K. (Harley) Croessmann wrote to Ellmann from his home in Du Quoin, Illinois. "Dear Mr. Ellmann, I have just come across your letter in the June 19 IRISH INDEPENDENT. Very glad indeed you are working on a Biography. The Lord knows one is needed. I wish you the best of luck!" Croessmann, an optometrist, lived all his life in Du Quoin, a small town south of Chicago. He was born in 1894 and became interested in Joyce in 1923 while studying optometry. In Chicago he came across a first edition of *Ulysses* in the Covici-McGee bookshop and was fascinated. Too poor to purchase the volume, he stood for hours reading it. By the time he wrote to Ellmann in 1953, he had become a serious collector of Joyceana, and he and Ellmann soon became close friends through correspondence. Croessmann was twenty-four years older than Ellmann and took a fatherly interest in him, also in his family, about whom Ellmann wrote amusingly. The friendship had benefits for both men. William Brockman explains: "For Croessmann, isolated in a small town, Ellmann was an insider through whom he could vicariously enjoy an international world of scholarship and book collecting. For Ellmann, Croessmann was an accommodating collaborator who had at his disposal unique primary materials."[21]

For several years Ellmann had sought access to the papers of Joyce's first biographer, Herbert Gorman, because, as he put it, "to some extent both Gorman's books [*James Joyce: His First 40 Years* (1924) and *James Joyce: A Definitive Biography* (1939)] were command performances." Ellmann's hope was to find letters among Gorman's papers in which Joyce demanded changes or made suggestions.[22] When Croessmann purchased the papers in 1956, two years after Gorman's death, Ellmann asked if he could be granted exclusive access to them. "For you to state that 'it is essential for my biography' is enough for me," Croessmann replied. "You may be certain that no part of the Gorman material will be used by any other writer until the appearance of your biography."[23]

Ellmann felt some scruples about what he was asking of Croessmann, writing on September 19, 1956, "I hope you will not mind reserving the papers for me for another year or two. By which time I ought to have finished my book. . . . I should not wish you to think that I wanted to tie your hands." A day earlier Croessmann had written to Ellmann to say that he had recently turned down a request from Marvin Magalaner to see the papers, about which Magalaner intended to write an article. "My promise to you precludes my furnishing him with anything like he would like to have." Magalaner was a serious scholar, the coauthor with Richard M. Kain of *Joyce: The Man, the Work, the Reputation* (1956), and Croessmann asked Ellmann if it would be all right to send him a copy of Herbert Cahoon's catalog of the Gorman collection, which had been in circulation for some time. "Of course, I don't mind." Ellmann replied. A month or so later, Croessmann refused Magalaner permission to see correspondence in the collection concerning Joyce's "schema" for *Ulysses*. "I promised you to reserve the Gorman material until the publication of your book and I meant it."[24]

At the same time as Croessmann and Ellmann were restricting access to the Gorman papers, Ellmann was doing his best to fend off a rival to his and Mason's edition of *The Critical Writings*. On December 7, 1957, Herbert Cahoon wrote to Ellmann that a lecturer at University College Dublin, Eileen MacCarvill, had been compiling an edition of previously unpublished Joyce essays, under the title "James Joyce: A Documentary." MacCarvill had written to Cahoon for help in finding an American publisher. To Cahoon, as much a friend and supporter of Ellmann as Croessmann, it sounded as if MacCarvill's book would "very seriously conflict" with the one Ellmann and Mason were editing.[25] Four days after receiving Cahoon's warning, Ellmann wrote to Marshall A. Best of Viking, saying that MacCarvill's book was "nearly identical" to his and Mason's, adding, "I am naturally concerned. She claims she has 'full permission from the Joyce Estate and has paid her fees.' Is there anything that can be done to prevent our being anticipated by this book?" Ellmann urged Best to contact Cahoon to see if together they could head off MacCarvill.[26] He also wrote to Harriet Weaver, on February 19, 1958, in the hope that she could somehow dissuade MacCarvill from publishing, despite having granted her permission to do so.

By this date, as William Brockman puts it, MacCarvill had written to Cahoon "and offered in a conciliatory way to change the book's title and to eliminate over a dozen items to avoid competition with Ellmann's and Mason's book."[27] Hearing of these concessions calmed Ellmann, as they had calmed Benjamin Huebsch of Viking, his and Mason's publisher. On February 19, 1958, Ellmann wrote again to Harriet Weaver, informing her that Huebsch had assured him that MacCarvill's book "will not preclude the publication of the book Ellsworth Mason and I have compiled, since the latter contains a great deal of new material."[28] In the end, MacCarvill's book was never published, either in America, Ireland, or Britain. Pressure from Ellmann and his powerful allies had played its part in seeing it off.[29]

As early as 1953, Ellmann's father had expressed concern about his son's fear of rivals. "The more I think of it," he writes in a letter of September 15, 1953, "the more I realize that you will have . . . not to worry too much about some letters or efforts of others. You can get sick about it if you want to or get down to work and set forth all of your own conceptions plus what you have already gathered. Plenty of material there, I am sure to fill more than one volume. Prescott [Joseph Prescott, of Wayne State University in Detroit] is an able fellow I am told and he too will move forward into the field as you are doing. A little competition may be good. But in any event the less you worry about him or others the better." In a later, undated letter, his father seeks to remind Ellmann, "Joyce will be written about for many years to come. So no matter how authoritative your work may be it can't be the final word. . . . Your publisher is right and has a better perspective on the subject than you can have. In any event, you will have much material for every sort of occasion it would seem—philosophical, literary, dramatic, and most human too."

* * *

The anxieties Ellmann's father sought to allay figure prominently in negotiations to find a suitable home for Stanislaus Joyce's papers. Ellmann's aims as advisor to Nelly Joyce, Stanislaus's widow, were threefold: to provide her with money; to keep the collection together, at least in large measure; and to restrict access to all other scholars until *James Joyce* was in print. In November 1956, shortly after his daughter Lucy's birth, Ellmann learned that Arthur Mizener, a professor of English at Cornell University, had inquired about Cornell obtaining the Stanislaus papers. Mizener wrote on modern authors (Fitzgerald, Ford Madox Ford) and this news raised the unsettling prospect, wrote Ellmann, of other scholars "anticipating my results," a prospect that receded a little on December 4, 1956, when Harriet Weaver offered Ellmann the job of editing a second volume of Joyce's *Letters*. This volume would not appear until after the biography, so Ellmann would retain exclusive access to what was for him the crucial part of the Stanislaus collection: the letters.

Before Weaver offered Ellmann the job as editor, he had considered another way of heading off competitors: to publish his biography in two volumes. In a letter of November 27, 1956, to OUP, he noted that the first such volume would cover the years 1882 to 1915, "the exciting, formative period of his life." As Amanda Sigler points out, these years happened to be "the most pertinent to the Stanislaus Joyce collection."[30] OUP was as quick to scotch this idea as it had been to scotch Ellmann's earlier idea of producing a short book before a full-length life. "The appearance of the book in several volumes at different times," wrote Lee Grove of OUP, "would be fatal to its success." If Ellmann was frightened of rivals, Bowen suggested, his best course was to focus his energies on finishing the biography "in the near future."[31]

Ellmann immediately relayed Bowen's advice to Frederic Faverty, the chair of the English Department at Northwestern, adding, "I do not see how I can possibly complete the book in less than a full year of work," by which he meant a full year free of teaching. To get such a year, he would need a renewal of his Guggenheim fellowship, which he had planned to apply for in 1958, to take up in 1959. He had written 500 pages of the biography and estimated that he would need another 300 pages to get to the end. Given "the fierce competition among Joyce scholars, and the imminent availability to others of some of my best material," would Faverty be willing to support his applying immediately for the Guggenheim renewal, to be taken up next year? Doing so would head off the possibility "that the results of my four years of work will be anticipated." Faverty was sympathetic, as was Simeon Leland, dean of the College of Liberal Arts, and in April the Guggenheim granted Ellmann's application for the renewal of his fellowship. He would have no teaching for a year. When the Guggenheim money turned out to be less than half of what Ellmann expected ($4,000, not $10,000), the dean agreed to make up the difference.[32]

* * *

At this point, in May 1957, negotiations for the Stanislaus papers were heating up. Since the previous autumn, at Ellmann's urging, the sale of the collection had been put in the hands of Ottocaro Weiss, a Triestine friend of Stanislaus. (It was Weiss who had loaned Joyce his Menorah for the Marthe Fleischmann "Black Mass.") Weiss had met Joyce in 1915 in Zurich, where he had gone to study political science. Oscar Schwartz, a young pupil of Joyce's, introduced the two men, who soon became friends. At the end of 1915, though, a year into World War I, Weiss was called up to serve with the Austrian army on the Russian front. Returning to Zurich after the war, in January 1919, he resumed his friendship with Joyce, though not for long. In both editions of *James Joyce*, as in Gorman's biography, Joyce is said to have dropped Weiss in October because he wrongly suspected him of alienating an important patron. Ellmann sees Joyce's behavior in this instance as characteristic. Expecting treachery everywhere, Joyce was "accustomed to look for it among his close friends" (p. 481).

Brenda Maddox and Carol Shloss, Lucia's biographer, believed instead that Joyce's shunning of Weiss may have been the product of suspicions of treachery of a quite different nature. Maddox cites Claude Sykes, whose wife Daisy was for a period Nora's close friend. Writing in confidence to Herbert Gorman, Sykes claimed that Weiss had been in love with Nora and that Nora had repelled his advances. Maddox also cites Lucia, who, although only twelve at the time, had noticed Weiss's fondness for Nora and recalled that her father had "quarrelled with Weiss about her mother."[33] Maddox then connects Joyce's break with Weiss both to "his voyeuristic love affair with Marthe [Fleischmann]" and to the first performance of *Exiles* in August 1919, suggesting that the play's love triangle may have caused Joyce to see a similar triangle in his life, in relations between Nora, himself, and Weiss. Unsurprisingly, in view of Joyce's surveillance of his work, Gorman makes no mention of these matters. That they are "hidden" (Maddox's word) by later biographers, unmentioned in either edition of *James Joyce,* she attributes to a combination of sexism and Weiss's later wealth and influence:

> The suppression of any mention of the Weiss attachment is an example of the distortion of fame. Because of Joyce's celebrity and the continual quest for the background of *Ulysses,* the Fleischmann escapade was chronicled and written into the record of Joyce's life and the history of *Ulysses.* Because Nora was considered unimportant, because a woman's reputation was so much more easily tarnished by rumour than a man's and also because Weiss himself, by the 1930s, when Gorman was collecting biographical information on Joyce's past, was an important figure in international banking and insurance, his youthful fondness for a married woman (and her husband's resentment of it) remained buried in unpublished notes in libraries hundreds of miles apart.
>
> Yet in the real lives of Nora and James Joyce, the flirtations with infidelity were simultaneous and related. Weiss, in fact, seems to have been the man toward whom Nora complained that Joyce was pushing her.[34]

There are several problems here. Maddox's suggestions about the Weiss episode—more than suggestions as the paragraphs proceed—make it sound as relevant to "the continual quest for the background of *Ulysses*" as the Fleischmann episode. Nor can it be right to describe Nora as "unimportant" to Joyce's biographers. That she rejected Weiss's attentions, moreover, would seem to burnish rather than tarnish her reputation. A more likely explanation for the absence of the episode, certainly in the case of Ellmann's biography, concerns Weiss's influence—not in banking or insurance, but as a direct source of information about a crucial period in Joyce's life. If anyone was "tarnished" in the episode, it was Weiss, to whom, as we shall see, Ellmann was indebted.

Where suppression does come into effect, in Ellmann's case, is in a letter he wrote to Gilbert on May 4, 1956, by which time Weiss had offered to negotiate the sale of the Stanislaus collection, with Ellmann as advisor. At the time Ellmann was reading the galleys of Gilbert's edition of Joyce's *Letters:*

> The Mr. Weiss mentioned on Galley 46 is very much alive. He is a man of wide culture, a friend of the conductor Toscanini as he was of Svevo [the novelist Italo Svevo, whose real name was Ettore Schmitz]. . . . I know him very well and I know how hurt he would be if these references to him were published, even with your saving note that Joyce's suspicions were wrongful. In pleading his case before the court, I should like to call to your honor's attention that Weiss and Joyce were intimate friends for two years, and that the extent of their friendship is not clear from correspondence. When Joyce makes a derogatory remark about Sylvia Beach or someone like that, it can be discounted in the light of their known friendship over many years. But the case is different with Weiss. . . . All these remarks were written while Joyce was still convinced of Weiss's treachery, and can hardly be thought of as his considered judgment. . . . I should personally favor omission, but I'm embarrassed to find myself on the side of the censor. But it has always seemed to me that the feelings of the living are more important than those of the dead.[35]

* * *

At the time of negotiations over the Stanislaus collection, Weiss was living in New York, having fled Trieste in 1938 to escape Italian antisemitism. By the 1950s he was chairman of the board of two large insurance companies: the Assicurazioni Generali di Trieste e Venezia, Italy's largest and oldest insurance company, which operated in the United States as well as Europe, and the Buffalo Insurance Company, which the Assicurazioni Generali had purchased in 1950. Ellmann introduced Weiss to Mason in a letter of June 8, 1956, as "a mutual friend of Stan, Mrs. J's, and mine" who "was offering to help her dispose of some of her papers. . . . (He is a rich man and wd do it for nothing; if he does do it, he will work closely with us in making arrangements.)" Later in the letter, Ellmann thanks Mason for having written to Nelly Joyce on his behalf, adding that his "very noble letter of introduction . . . was extremely helpful; that and Mr. Weiss's were determining factors." To Harriet Weaver, in a letter of January 12, 1957, he described Weiss and Stanislaus as "good friends, he regularly visited Mrs. Joyce

[Nelly] after her husband's death. When he heard of the difficulties she anticipated in disposing of Stanislaus's papers, he offered to help her, of course without fee. . . . She was glad to accept his services and sent the papers to him in New York."

Negotiating the sale of the Stanislaus collection was not Weiss's first involvement in the market for Joyce papers. In 1949 Weiss had alerted the University of Buffalo to the existence of the papers Joyce and Nora left behind when they fled their Paris apartment—papers that, when sold to Buffalo, became the most important collection of Joyce materials in the United States (it comprised more than 10,000 pages of working papers, notebooks, manuscripts, photographs, portraits, publishing records, memorabilia, Joyce's private library, and correspondence).[36] According to Brenda Maddox, it was Weiss "more than anybody who was responsible for tugging two of the world's most important collections of Joyce papers into the hinterland of New York State."[37]

Ellmann's loyalty to Weiss derived not only from his having recommended Ellmann to Nelly Joyce, but also from the help he gave him in depicting Joyce's daily life and milieu in Zurich in 1915 and 1919. In addition, Weiss provided Ellmann with insights into Joyce's opinions on literature, politics, music, women, and Jews, through telling details and anecdotes. That he was a shrewd and successful businessman, and with some experience of the market for Joyce papers, also influenced the choice of him as agent in the sale. When, therefore, Bob Vosper, the librarian at the University of Kansas, called Ellmann to inquire about possibly purchasing the collection, Ellmann immediately contacted Weiss, advising him to take the bid seriously. "I should be very glad if you could come to suitable terms with Kansas," he wrote on November 2, 1956, adding that "if the agreement with Kansas works out, I should be most grateful if you could stipulate that the material not be available to anyone but me for a year." As for price, "I'm utterly convinced that $10,000 is not excessive as a guarantee. After all, when the previous collection was sold to Buffalo, there was only one serious collector in the world—John Slocum. Now there are at least five libraries and at least five collectors strongly interested in it, and I have no doubt there could be others."[38]

Ellmann's collector friend from Evanston, Jim Spoerri, had been hired by Kansas to act on the university's behalf and flew to New York to begin

Ottocaro Weiss.

negotiations with Weiss. What happened next Ellmann recounted in a letter of December 8 to Mason:

> You have no doubt heard from Vosper about the proceedings over the Mrs. S. Joyce collection. Jim Spoerri was in New York and acted for Kansas: he bid five, then ten, then twenty thousand dollars, all within one week; at that point Mr. Weiss cabled Mrs. Joyce to find out what she thought, and she wondered whether more couldn't be obtained. Vosper called me and asked me to intervene on Kansas's behalf, and I did so, urging Mr. Weiss to consider them as a repository for some if not all the collection. Then I heard no more until this evening, when Mr. Weiss called to say that Cornell is considering the purchase.

* * *

The story of the Cornell bid for Stanislaus Joyce's papers shows how fraught and competitive the business of acquiring modern literary manuscripts had become during the period of postwar university expansion in the United States. It also shows how fraught Ellmann himself became in the years running up to the publication of *James Joyce*. The Cornell bid was Weiss's idea; he had sent a list of the contents of the collection to his friend Mario Einaudi, a professor of politics at Cornell. Einaudi came from a well-to-do family of Italian intellectuals. After World War II his father had been elected the first president of the Italian Republic. Like Weiss, Einaudi left Italy in the 1930s, in his case on a Rockefeller Fellowship to Harvard, where he went on to teach political theory. He then taught at Fordham before moving to Cornell. Einaudi took Weiss's list of contents, and its accompanying letter, to the Cornell literature scholar M. H. Abrams, who, mightily impressed, took them to Cornell's librarian, Stephen McCarthy, and, presumably, to Arthur Mizener. McCarthy presented the university president, Deane Malott, with the idea of purchasing the collection, and Malott's immediate response was, "Buy it," he would find the money. This he did, thanks to an initial donation from a wealthy alumnus, William Mennen, chairman of the Mennen aftershave company.[39] Cornell's motive in obtaining the collection was described by Ellmann in a letter of January 12, 1957, to Harriet Weaver: it would "add luster to their new library, which will be finished in a couple of years. They hope, in fact, to keep the purchase unknown, at least to the public, until the library is finished." Cornell, he reassured Miss Weaver, had one of the most beautiful university campuses in the country. "It lies somewhere between Yale and Buffalo, and perhaps this dispersion westward of Joyce materials is a good thing, an aid in breaking the cultural hegemony of the eastern seaboard." When the dean of the College of Arts and Sciences at Cornell learned of the collection, he described it as being "to the English Department what a cyclotron is to the Physics Department."[40]

From the start, for reasons unclear, Mason questioned Weiss's suitability to conduct the negotiation. When he asked to be put in touch with Weiss, in a letter of June 9, 1956, Ellmann hesitated. When Ellmann did send him Weiss's address, on July 31, he warned Mason to treat Weiss "with great respect." Weiss could be touchy, and Mason could be forceful in argument. ("I rushed off my comments on your article ["The Backgrounds of *Ulysses*"]," Mason wrote to Ellmann on October 26, 1954. "In the process, I find, I don't seem to have made clear that, on the whole, I liked it.") Ellmann admitted to Mason in the letter of July 31, "[I was] a little afraid of your offending him by being too forward with advice he would otherwise be glad to take." He then warned Weiss about Mason. "You will remember my friend Ellsworth Mason," he wrote on August 6: "I think he would like to make you some suggestions about possible sale of some of the material, and if you have no objections I will tell him to go ahead and write you. . . . But don't feel you will offend me in the slightest if you ignore all his suggestions." Mason's suggestions were not specified by Ellmann. Most likely they concerned possible divisions of the collection.

What sparked the feud between Mason and Ellmann was Mason's reaction to Ellmann's letter of December 8, in which he recounted the increasing bids of Jim Spoerri on behalf of the University of Kansas, and the news that Cornell had entered the picture. "You probably have good ideas about this," Ellmann wrote to Mason. "I must confess that it is getting too damned complicated for me—and I wish you'd send them to him [Spoerri] either directly or through me." Two days later Ellmann wrote again to Mason, upset at having discovered not only that Mason had written to Nelly Joyce disparaging Weiss, but that Mrs. Joyce had then sent his letter to Weiss. That morning Weiss called Ellmann to read him parts of Mason's letter. "He is a man of sixty years old and this criticism of him is almost overwhelming," Ellmann wrote to Mason. "Frankly I cannot understand why you did not write first to me or to Mr. Weiss to get the whole picture. Here is a distinguished man who has been working indefatigably in Mrs. Joyce's behalf only to be faced suddenly with a most serious charge."

Mason's charge was that Weiss had advised Nelly first to accept and then to reject each of Spoerri's bids—in effect, that he had acted dishonorably. Ellmann disagreed:

> Both his [Weiss's] and Jim Spoerri's conduct of the matter is quite explicable if you consider it calmly. They are men of opposite temperaments, Jim as forceful as Mr. Weiss is tentative. Mr. Weiss was exploring possibilities and Jim was consolidating them. Their interpretations of what happened are necessarily different. Purchasers who do not get what they want are not often pleased; but I fail to see how you can object to Mr. Weiss's obvious effort to get as much money for Mrs. Joyce as possible. . . . Mr. Weiss told Jim that he thought the papers were worth between $25,000 and $50,000, and within four or five days Jim's offer went

> from \$5,000 to \$20,000. In this situation any seller would become cautious, and Mr. Weiss understandably felt that he must cable Mrs. Joyce for authority, Mrs. Joyce hoped the price might be higher, and the proceedings temporarily fell through. The buyers are unhappy. This is the history of most unsuccessful negotiations.

Ellmann added that Spoerri was "almost as upset as Mr. Weiss by your criticism of Mr. Weiss to Mrs. Joyce" (principally because the Kansas offer was still open). He advised Mason to write to Mrs. Joyce to reassure her about Weiss.

Two days later Mason wrote back to Ellmann. Weiss had made agreements with Spoerri and he had "broken" them. "This is dishonorable dealing." Because Mason had "directed people to deal with a man who deals dishonorably," he believes his "personal integrity . . . has been compromised." He will not apologize. "I see no reason for retracting what I have said to Mrs. Joyce, and most certainly will not write Weiss." The person he wrote to was Stephen McCarthy of Cornell, who immediately wrote to Ellmann "asking the extent to which we are associated." The letter to McCarthy Ellmann describes as "much more serious" than the earlier letter to Mrs. Joyce:

> It is opposed to her interests, and although you said in your letter to me that the most important thing at stake was your own integrity, that was not in question at Cornell where they didn't know about you. . . . At the end of your letter you refer to our association and ask for access to the papers [for materials to be included in *The Critical Writings*]. I should not want you to take so important a step in any case without consulting me, but especially not in connection with an attack on Mr. Weiss. Your letter seems contrary to the spirit of our collaboration. I mentioned to you before, when the tone of your letter to our publisher [Huebsch of Viking] seemed unfortunate, that I insisted upon being informed in advance of any serious steps in our affairs. Instead you have gone ahead on your own.

Mason's letters, Ellmann declares, "are destroying everybody's peace of mind" and must stop. "We can't risk anything like this happening again." Later that day, December 24, 1956, Ellmann wrote again, to make clear what he thought Mason needed to do. "If a retraction was advisable before, it seems to me to be indispensable now. Nobody likes to retract, but I see no other way out." Three days later, in a cable, Mason agreed to desist. "No need to phone will keep quiet. Writing."[41] But Mason offered no retraction.[42]

What happened next is that Weiss threatened Mason with a libel suit unless he retracted, and Mason hired a lawyer, whose advice was that he must refuse to retract. As Mason told Ellmann in a letter written on New Year's Eve, his lawyer had told him that retracting would "in no way alter my legal responsibility and will merely increase the strength of Weiss's position in the event that he should bring suit." Mason claimed in his letter that before he was threatened with libel he had drafted a letter to Weiss that he intended to send first to Ellmann to vet. "The matter is now a legal matter and I am completely unable to give Weiss the kind of retraction that I would want to give." He then defends his views on Weiss, reminding Ellmann that "it is a common fact that men of business can apply two different sets of standards to their personal and to their business lives." Ellmann has made much of possible confusions between Spoerri and Weiss, but "you never state that it is absolutely impossible that Weiss might have committed himself to sell the collection, and you give no reason in seeming to favor Weiss' position over Spoerri's."[43] The letter ends with Mason telling Ellmann not to be "concerned with my position. He has a very weak libel case, and will have to prove damages. I am in no danger here at the college. . . . The end product, depending upon what my lawyer comes up with tomorrow, will probably be a generalized retraction which will say nothing. I am grateful to you for your concern over me, at any rate. Best regards to the family."[44]

In his letter Mason also offered general observations about the differences in character between himself and Ellmann, especially marked in this time of anxiety for his friend. "My approach to the world," he writes, "is far less apprehensive than yours. . . . You did, indeed, object to the tone of one of my letters to Huebsch, and subsequent events have shown that your objections were quite unjustified. If people are not as rugged as I sometimes think, neither are they as brittle as you sometimes think." When Huebsch sent Ellmann the contract for Joyce's *Critical Writings,* Ellmann hesitated before signing it, at the same time confessing to his parents that "he would be very sorry to give up this project and will try to hold on to it no matter what."[45] In the months that followed, the dispute between Mason and Weiss was handled by lawyers. Ellmann signed the contract and the two friends resumed work on *The Critical Writings*. In a subsequent letter to his parents, written on April 13, 1957, Ellmann wrote that their work was "getting on well." In the end, Cornell purchased the Stanislaus Joyce collection for $37,000 and the fears that plagued Ellmann throughout the years in which he wrote *James Joyce*—of having his results "anticipated"—were not realized.

Ellsworth Mason.

CHAPTER NINE

Writing

ELLMANN WROTE *James Joyce* while he was still doing the research, so he was also frequently redrafting. Before he began writing, he had to reorder his notes, a complicated process that began in June 1953. "For the first time," Ellmann announced to his parents in a letter of June 3, he felt "moved to begin organizing stuff." "My own work is coming along," he wrote to Ellsworth Mason six months later, on December 7, 1953. "I've put my multifarious notes in chronological order, and am struggling to find adequate form and image." To Herbert Cahoon, the same day, he confessed that having "at last begun to put my notes in order . . . I begin to see more clearly what you meant about the amount of time the job would take." Two years later, Ellmann was still organizing his material. He wrote to Frank Budgen on November 12, 1955, "I hope to have a rough draft done by next summer," although "my own days are spent entirely on trying to bring together my notes and what-not into some sort of order." It was a task for which he was well suited. As a child he had delighted in playing with the papers his father brought home from work. "He was in his glory when he was up to his chin in important papers," his mother recalled in her memoir. "He would fondle them and arrange them." At the Office of the Coordinator of Information (COI), precursor to the OSS, his wartime job had been to index and classify secret documents from a range of sources. His work on Yeats drew on notes from interviews, manuscripts, correspondence, criticism, diaries, and notebooks.

The structure Ellmann chose for the biography was largely chronological. All but five of its thirty-seven chapters are titled by date, the exceptions being chapters 1 ("Introduction"), 2 ("The Family before Joyce"), 15 ("The Backgrounds of 'The Dead'"), 18 ("The Growth of Imagination"), and 22 ("The Backgrounds of *Ulysses*"). The chapters are grouped into five parts, named after locations: "Dublin" (1882–1904, eight chapters), "Pola, Rome, Trieste" (1904–1915, thirteen chapters), "Zurich" (1915–1920, five chapters), "Paris" (1920–1939, eight chapters), and "Return to Zurich" (1939–1941, one chapter). The printed book has 756 pages of text and 842 pages in total, including notes, further acknowledgments, and index.[1]

Although chronology is central to the biography, it figured only intermittently in its composition. The first chapter to be written was the *Kenyon Review* essay "The Backgrounds of *Ulysses*," published in the summer of 1954 but written in 1953.[2] It became chapter 22, appearing between "1913–1914" and "1914–1915." The earliest of Ellmann's progress reports on the writing of the book occurs in a letter of October 15, 1955, to Mason. Writing was "proceeding slowly. I have done a draft of the Zurich years, and am going back to 1903–4." Three days later, to H. K. Croessmann, Ellmann reports that he is "now working on the banner year of 1904, and expect to jump from here to 1920 and 1921, so that eventually my muddy footprints will be everywhere." On January 5, 1957, in answer to a query from J. F. Byrne, he provides an update. "I have written 500 pages and have about 300 more to go. I don't write quickly and feel the necessity of trying to verify everything as well as I can, so I suppose it will be another year or two before the book is done. I began it in 1953 so that if I finish it in 1957 or 1958 I shall have written it much more quickly than Gorman, who took nine years."

A month and a half later, on March 19, 1957, Ellmann writes to Croessmann that he is now "working up" the years 1893–1902, by which he seems to have meant revising or redrafting them. "I hope to finish up Belvedere days [1893–1898] before I have to start teaching again." A week later, again to Croessmann, having reached the year 1898, he has only four more years to go "in order to get up to where I had previously started. Then I am going to start a wholesale revision. I've now completely done the last years of Joyce's life, but I think I will leave them till I get the first forty-five or fifty years done over."

On April 13 he writes to his parents that he has won a second Guggenheim fellowship, which will enable him "to put a high polish on the book." By July 19, 1957, he has at last reached 1902 "in this draft" (the second draft, according to a letter of August 7 to J. F. Byrne). In a letter of November 8, 1957, to Croessmann, Ellmann confesses to a Joycean ambition: "to finish this draft before March 15"—that is, before his fortieth birthday (*Ulysses*

CHAPTER III
1882 - 1894

~~Tell me all. Tell me now. You'll die~~ when you hear.
Finnegans Wake

James Joyce was born on February 2, 1882. In later life, fond of coincidences, he was pleased to discover that his friend James Stephens was born in Dublin on the same day, and improved upon the fact by asserting that their births had also occurred at the same hour. That February 2 was Candlemas helped to confirm its importance, and he made the day even more his own by contriving, with great difficulty, to see the first copies of both Ulysses and Finnegans Wake on that day.

CHAPTER VII
TRIESTE: 1905

Joyce now had an opportunity to appraise "the jewel of the Adriatic," as Leopardi's rhetoric characterized Trieste. The city had the only merchant port of the Austro-Hungarian empire, and therefore received handsome treatment from its emperors. Maria Teresa built up the Citta Vecchia, the old city with its almost medieval narrownesses, and her son Joseph II developed the more spacious, modern part of the city. The harbor was crowded with ships, some at port, others waiting impatiently to put in. Away from the city, in the high hills known as the Carso, grew the vines which have since the twelfth century produced a wine of a special type. It was in these hills and the mountains beyond that a great deal of desperate fighting took place during the first World War. Its embattled terrain is brilliantly described in A Farewell to Arms.

Trieste's cultural history long antedates the coming of Ernest Hemingway and Joyce. Though today the city's

Ellmann early manuscript drafts.

was published on February 2, 1922, Joyce's fortieth birthday). Although Ellmann succeeded in his ambition, finishing the draft on March 5, he still faced, as he admitted to Croessmann, "revision, checking etc., which will last into the summer. Without the year off I should certainly have been unable to do this much at all. Have over 500 pages written now."

The draft Ellmann completed on March 5, 1958, was 917 pages long. He told his parents, "It will no doubt swell a bit more before it's done." He would embark on a third rewrite "by the end of the month." His emotions on the day were complicated: "I felt a sudden pang at finishing and a strange excitement—it seems inconceivable it should be done, even in this form. New material still keeps coming in—somebody sent me some journal entries about Joyce in 1904 and Miss Weaver has sent me some letters to her from Paul Leon between 1933 and 1939—very useful, I think, since he reports on Joyce's activities in each at some length. I have a lot of books and articles to read or reread, and am a little afraid that two more drafts will be necessary." A month later, in a letter of April 5, 1958, to Erwin and Steffani, he reported that the manuscript was 935 pages long "and still growing, to the evident annoyance of my publishers." In the months to follow, in addition to accommodating new material, he had the responses of friends and family to consider. "I think all these suggestions are excellent," he wrote to his parents on October 28, 1958, "and will certainly quiet hostile reviewers." "But I wince at all criticism, beginning with Mary's which she has given me steadily over the last years, and including the comments of Spoerri, Kelleher, etc. I had a phone call from Weiss today, and he obviously objects to some things too. . . . The arrows are coming in from all sides, you see. So I didn't mean to seem ungrateful; it is just that I am smarting from the general barrage." Before the book was published, in October 1959, Ellmann took care to date the preface "March 15, 1959," his fortieth birthday. He also ensured that it was published in the blue binding Joyce used for *Ulysses*.

* * *

The question of the book's length had been a continuing source of worry for both author and publisher. Having rejected the idea of two volumes in 1956 (an idea born out of Ellmann's anxieties about competitors), OUP had to consider it again. In a letter of December 18, 1956, OUP had warned Ellmann that "if the book is too long, we will price ourselves out of the market." But the book continued to grow. When the idea of two volumes was raised again, this time by the publisher, Ellmann resisted. "My friends here," he wrote to OUP on October 10, 1958, "including Jim Spoerri, who's a well-known book collector, have been urging upon me that two volumes, no matter how handsome, deter readers whom one would attract, that the index is hard to use with two volumes, that two volumes are much harder to hold than even a fairly standard single volume." OUP then raised the idea of publishing the book as a two-volume boxed set, the format it favored up to early January 1959, to Ellmann's dismay.[3] In mid-January, however, OUP reverted to the idea of publishing the volumes at different times, an idea Ellmann disapproved of even more strongly. In such a scheme, he believed, "the second part would be an awful anticlimax."[4] What Ellmann now argued was that it ought to be possible to publish the book as a single volume of 750 "fairly large" pages. After considering this idea for several weeks, OUP agreed. The book would be published as Ellmann wished, as a single volume.

* * *

James Joyce is long for several reasons. Ellmann came to think of *Yeats: The Man and the Masks* as driven by a single theme or thesis, that of duality in the poet's life and work. To the extent that it is a biography, it bears the mark of his teacher, F. W. Pottle, for whom, as we have seen, the biographer must begin "with a trial impression of the personality he is attempting to reconstruct"; collect his facts "with this tentative reconstruction always in mind"; and modify his reconstruction if the facts he collects "won't fit." The biographer builds on an "imaginative core; he does not simply collect facts and wait for something to quicken the chaos." In the case of *James Joyce,* Ellmann took a more open approach, as he explains in a letter of March 1, 1959, to Stuart Gilbert, one of several readers of the finished draft.

> I am particularly pleased that you liked the fairly straightforward presentation without superfluous comments; as I get older I find that I am dissatisfied by heavily analytical biography and want instead as many facts as possible, organized of course, and selected, but not transformed to illustrate a thesis. I have also become more partial to a method which proceeds chronologically (pretty much), sacrificing hereby some fine effects but giving a much more total sense of the subject's life at any given time. It was particularly hard to do this in Joyce's later years, where there is so much material; but insofar as I have a biographical theory I suppose this is it and I must sink or swim with it. You will remember that my first book on Yeats was much more a pursuit of "essence" and besides that I didn't want to do this one in the same way. I think Joyce's life would resist such treatment.

Many of the facts Ellmann collected for *James Joyce* are mundane or commonplace, the sort most biographers omit. "Don't you think the way a genius ties his tie is important?" he once asked the Irish filmmaker Sean O'Mordha. "I feel it would be shirking my duty as a biographer not to give [Joyce] the same attention that he gives to Bloom," Ellmann told Georg Goyert, who had translated *Ulysses* into German.[5] In minutely documenting Joyce's everyday activities and routines, Ellmann was consciously following in his subject's footsteps in several senses. At the beginning of the book he declares: "The initial and determining act of judgment in [Joyce's] work is the justification of the commonplace. Other writers had labored tediously to portray it, but no one knew what the commonplace really was until Joyce had written. There is nothing like Joyce's commonplace in Tolstoy, where the characters, however humble, live dramatically and instill wisdom or tragedy in each other. Joyce was the first to endow an urban man of no importance with heroic consequence" (p. 3). In *Finnegans Wake,* Joyce mocks this sort of commonplace: "business, reading newspaper, smoking cigar, arranging tumblers on table, eating meals, pleasure, etcetera etcetera, pleasure, eating meals, arranging tumblers on table, smoking cigar, reading newspaper, business; minerals, wash and brush up, local views, jojo coffee, comic and birthday cards; those were the days and he was their hero" (127:20–25). In *James Joyce,* routine is given its due. Here is one of several descriptions of a typical day for Joyce, in this case shortly after his return to Trieste from Dublin early in 1910:

> Since leaving the Scuola Berlitz Joyce had grown accustomed to a gentlemanly morning, an industrious afternoon (when, he said to Budgen, "the mind is at its best"), and a chaotic evening. He woke about 10 o'clock, an hour or more after Stanislaus had breakfasted and left the house. Nora gave him coffee and rolls in bed, and he lay there, as Eileen [Joyce's sister] described him, "smothered in his own thoughts" until about 11 o'clock. Sometimes his Polish tailor called, and would sit discoursing on the edge of the bed, while Joyce listened and nodded. About eleven he rose, shaved, and sat down at the piano (which he was buying slowly and perilously on the instalment plan). As often as not his singing and playing were interrupted by the arrival of a bill collector. Joyce was notified and asked what was to be done. "Let them all come in," he would say resignedly, as if an army were at the door. The collector would come in, dun him

> with small success, then be skillfully steered off into a discussion of music or politics. That visit over, Joyce returned to the piano, until Nora interrupted, "Do you know there's a lesson?" or "You've put on a filthy shirt again," to which he'd reply calmly, "I'll not take it off." There was lunch at 1 o'clock, cooked by Nora with some skill now.[6] (pp. 318–19)

The description goes on until bedtime, for two more paragraphs of equal length focusing primarily on material matters. "When I was working on Joyce," Ellmann told an interviewer in 1982, "I realized I really must try and deal, as he did, with external things . . . because he attaches so much importance to external things,"[7] even small or imperfect external things. As Ellmann puts it elsewhere: "Stephen Dedalus is perhaps the first hero in an English novel who has lice, and Bloom the first to use a cup that has a broken handle, or to carry a humpy tray, or to notice the button under the cat's tail." Ellmann parts company with Joyce in this respect only in relation to what one critic calls "the body's everyday workings and needs: urinating, defecating, menstruating, farting," though in later years he was bolder.[8]

A second feature of *James Joyce* that accounts for its length was Ellmann's determination to show what it was like not only to meet Joyce but to be him, to "know or almost know what the subject was thinking at any given moment."[9] The modern biographer, he declares in "Freud and Literary Biography," a lecture he delivered at All Souls College, Oxford, in 1984, "conceives of himself not as outside but as inside the subject's mind, not as observing but as ferreting" ("burrowing," in another talk). Elsewhere, in "Literary Biography" (1971), Ellmann's inaugural lecture as Goldsmiths' Professor of English Literature at Oxford: "Biographies will continue to be archival, but the best ones will offer speculations, conjectures, hypotheses."[10]

As a literary psychologist, Ellmann was shrewd, jargon-free, and Freudian ("We are all still under his long shadow").[11] Here he is hypothesizing about Joyce's relations with his mother and his wife:

> His attitude towards his mother is clarified by his attitude to Nora Barnacle. In the letters he sent to Nora in that discomposed summer of 1909, there are many testimonies that Joyce longed to reconstitute, in his relations with her, the filial bond which his mother's death had broken. Explicitly he longs to make their relationship that of child and mother, as if the relationship of lovers was too remote. He covets an even

> more intimate dependence: "Oh that I could nestle in your womb like a child born of your flesh and blood, be fed by your blood, sleep in the warm secret gloom of your body. . . ." He was attracted, particularly, by the image of himself as a weak child cherished by a strong woman, which seems closely connected with the images of himself as victim, whether as a deer pursued by hunters, as a passive man surrounded by burly extroverts, as a Parnell or a Jesus among traitors. His favorite characters are those who in one way or another retreat before masculinity, yet are loved regardless by motherly women.[12] (p. 303)

These speculations about Joyce and his mother, or his idea of the mother, Ellmann then applies to Joyce's relations with the Church: "It was not a mother church but a father church, harsh, repressive, masculine. To give it up was both consciously and unconsciously to offer his mother's love its supreme test, for his mother was deeply religious. She was disconcerted but did not abandon him. Yet her death not long after one of his open defiances of her beliefs seemed a punishment; he felt as if he had killed her by trying her too far. This thought he confided to Nora" (p. 304). Ellmann then extends his theory about Joyce and his mother to *Dubliners,* which he describes as

> written on the assumption that Ireland is an inadequate mother, "an old sow who eats her farrow," and he [Joyce] associates himself with the masticated children. As he wrote to Georg Goyert, the book did not describe the way "they" are in Dublin, but the way "we" are. We are foolish, comic, motionless, corrupted; yet we are worthy of sympathy too, a sympathy which, if Ireland denies us, the international reader may give. But the reader must be tested like a loving mother by an errant child, must be forced to see the ugly, undecorated reality before he is allowed to extend his pity, a pity compounded of outraged affection, amusement, and understanding. (p. 305)

Support for conjectures like these about Joyce's inner life comes from correspondence and interviews, particularly with members of his family, but also, at times, from his fiction. It is not enough, for example, for a biographer to discover the dates of Joyce's attendance at Clongowes Wood College, or what he was taught there, or who his teachers were, or the identity of his fellow students and what they thought of him; the biographer must also convey something of what Joyce thought of the place, of his fellow students, of his teachers, and of what they taught him. In the absence of direct evidence, Ellmann turns to the fiction—in the case of Joyce's early schooling, to *Stephen Hero* and *A Portrait*—seeking out congruencies or discrepancies between the actual life and the life as portrayed in the novels.

Ellsworth Mason objected strongly to this aspect of Ellmann's approach. "You are weaving both the works and the non-works [the life] into a single, supposedly factual, fabric," he wrote in a letter of November 9, 1958, after Ellmann had sent him a copy of the completed manuscript. "We simply must have a biography that will tell us what can and what cannot be determined as actually having existed outside Joyce's works." Earlier, in a letter of October 26, 1954, Mason had chided Ellmann for depending "only on a thin line of evidence." "The most difficult thing for a man bent on finding something out, is to admit that he can't, but such an admission is centrally important in the soundness of results." What made Ellmann's tendency to identify "the plausible with the actual" especially dangerous, according to Mason (and many subsequent Joyce scholars) was that he wrote so well. "The trouble with your performances," he warns in a letter of March 20, 1955, "is that they have a kind of self-contained beauty of their own, and even in deepest error you have an intelligence of expression that is rare in Joyce criticism. I hereby predict that your errors about Joyce will be the last to depart from this earth."

Ellmann was unperturbed. He seems never to have considered confining himself to "the actual" or banishing speculation. Responding to Mason's strictures, in a letter of November 20, 1958, he is casual, as if confident that readers will trust his judgment and honesty. He also stands firm on the biography's length.

> Dear Ellsworth,
> Thanks for your preliminary comments. I have been making up the footnotes for the book, and these will at least indicate whether there's any source for a given fact. Beyond JJ's books. I'm not sure that this will meet your objections. In some cases the Gorman papers—which include some of J's answers to questions—confirm what the books say; also Joyce went over Gorman's proofs, though I admit his accepting something in Gorman does not prove it is true. It is however some

> evidence, even if shaky. I may be able to indicate in the text places where the evidence of the books is unsupported, but I don't know how often such statements should be inserted. Well, I value your objection.
>
> I hope to finish revising the book by early January. Oxford is still waiting for third reader's report, but says first two are very complimentary, and they will not, I think, ask me to reduce it in size—something I feel rather keenly about.

"I may be able to indicate . . . I don't know how often such statements should be inserted." The concern here is with narrative, the danger of distracting from or slowing down the narrative, or of leaving gaps. The fiction is invoked in cases where evidence from the life is unavailable or needs bolstering, or where Ellmann sees interesting connections between life and work, including connections that contradict rather than corroborate. It is unfair of Mason to describe the narrative Ellmann weaves, the book's "fabric," as "supposedly factual." On the whole, Ellmann is careful to distinguish the factual from the speculative, the actual from the plausible.[13]

The Irish critic Denis Donoghue shared Mason's worries about the mixing of biographical and fictional evidence, not so much in *James Joyce* itself as in the works of subsequent biographers. "Ellmann gave his authority to this bad habit," he writes. "He made it respectable for lesser biographers to assume . . . [that] if something is in the novels, it must have happened." When Ellmann describes *Stephen Hero* and *A Portrait* as "both autobiographical and fictional," adding that "while some details of Joyce's life are stylized or otherwise changed, many are kept intact," Donoghue objects that "those 'some' and 'many' could be distinguished only if there were independent evidence for them." Like Mason, however, he largely trusts Ellmann.

The example Donoghue provides of the danger of mixing fact and fiction concerns Joyce's first date with Nora in 1904, in which they walk out to Ringsend, a southern suburb of Dublin. He begins by quoting the "complete propriety" of Ellmann's treatment of the episode in *James Joyce:* "On June 16, as he would afterwards realize, he entered into relation with the world around him and left behind him the loneliness he had felt since his mother's death. He would tell her later, 'You made me a man'" (p. 163). The words Ellmann quotes here come from Joyce's letter to Nora of August 7, 1909: "O, Nora! Nora! Nora! I am speaking now to the girl I loved, who had red-brown hair and sauntered over to me and took me so easily into her arms and made me a man." "Scholars have usually taken the sentence to mean that at Ringsend on June 16 Nora Barnacle masturbated Joyce," writes Donoghue, adding that Ellmann, in his critical study, *The Consciousness of Joyce* (1977), "merely says that they 'touched each other's bodies,' a mild conjecture."

Donoghue then quotes Brenda Maddox on the episode, from *Nora: A Biography:* "To Joyce's grateful astonishment, she unbuttoned his trousers, slipped in her hand, pushed his shirt aside, and, acting with some skill (according to his later letter) made him a man." Maddox quotes a passage from the "Proteus" episode of *Ulysses,* in which Stephen, on Sandymount Strand, recalls giving a "keen glance" to a woman in the window of Hodges Figgis, a bookshop. Stephen thinks to himself, "Touch me. Soft eyes. Soft soft soft hand. I am lonely here. O, touch me soon, now. What is that word known to all men? I am quiet here alone. Sad too. Touch, touch me." Donoghue comments: "All this to eke out the sole fragment of evidence, five words, 'You made me a man.'" He then quotes Peter Costello, author of *James Joyce: The Years of Growth 1882–1915* (1992):

> Nora made the first approach and he was left in little doubt about her feelings for him. There was not intercourse—that would have been unthinkable—but Nora was knowledgeable enough to manipulate her partner to a climax.
>
> Like so many of Joyce's experiences, this event also made its way into *Ulysses* transferred to the memory of Molly Bloom: . . . how did we finish it off yes O yes I pulled him off into my handkerchief pretending not to be excited but I opened my legs and I wouldn't let him touch me inside my petticoat I had a skirt opening up the side I tortured the life out of him first tickling him . . . he was shy all the same I liked him like that morning he I made him blush a little when I got over him that way when I unbuttoned him and took out his and drew back the skin . . .

Donoghue comments: "So Nora is supposed to have performed at Ringsend the service here quoted, inaccurately too, from Molly Bloom's account of an episode with Lt. Harry Mulvey in Gibraltar." Donoghue also points out that Joyce had been with prostitutes before Nora, "so her making him a man may refer to a loftier achievement than masturbation." Ellmann's treatment of the episode (unaltered in the second edition, when sex could be treated more freely) resists the temptation to cite the fiction, which Donoghue describes as the product of an "occasional" scruple.[14]

What is odd about Donoghue's scorn here, is that there *is* clear evidence that Nora masturbated Joyce at Ringsend, and in a manner quite like that described by Maddox and Costello. In a letter of December 3, 1909 (the "later letter" Maddox mentions), Joyce wrote to Nora: "It was not I who first touched you long ago down at Ringsend. It was you who slid your hand down inside my trousers and pulled my shirt softly aside and touched my prick with your long tickling fingers and gradually took it all, fat and stiff as it was, into your hand and frigged me slowly until I came off through your fingers, all the time bending over me and gazing at me out of your quiet saintlike eyes." When challenged about the omission of this passage, Donoghue replied: "I have never doubted that on the evening of June 16, 1904, Nora Barnacle masturbated . . . James Joyce at Ringsend. Nothing in my review carries any other implication. What I disapproved of is the biographical procedure by which passages from Joyce's fiction have been quoted as glosses on the event at Ringsend."[15] Given Joyce's letter, it is hard to see what is wrong with conjecturing that the passages from *Ulysses* quoted by Maddox and Costello draw on reminiscences of what happened at Ringsend on the night of June 16, 1904.

* * *

The willingness of readers, including readers as caustic as Donoghue, to trust Ellmann's judgment may derive from the evenhandedness of his overall assessment of Joyce and his works. Seeing both sides, like attending to the commonplace material aspects of Joyce's life or connecting the life to the writing, also plays a part in the book's length. Here is how Ellmann's larger view is set out in the book's introduction:

> Joyce will not make it easy for us either to condemn or adore. If we go to him thinking he may be the apostle of brotherhood, he shows us brothers in violent quarrel. If we go to him to find a defender of the family, he presents his central hero—a cuckold. If we ask him to be the celebrant of the isolated individual, Joyce shows isolation making him morose and defenseless. If we look for the spokesman of life, he introduces us to the dead. The reconciling factor is the imagination, which, working through

> wit, brings opposite ends of the mind together, and makes our seeming unlikenesses suddenly gregarious.
>
> Joyce is the porcupine of authors. His heroes are grudged heroes—the impossible young man, the passive adult, the whisky-drinking greybeard. It is hard to like them, harder to admire them. Joyce prefers it so. Unequivocal sympathy would be romancing. He denudes man of what we are accustomed to respect, then summons us to sympathize. . . . We can move closer to him by climbing over the obstacles of our pretensions, but as we do so he tasks our prowess again by his difficult language. He requires that we adapt ourselves in form as well as in content to his new point of view. His heroes are not easy liking, his books are not easy reading. He does not wish to conquer us, but have us conquer him. There are, in other words, no invitations, but the door is ajar. (p. 4)

Passages like these led Ellmann's friend Seamus Heaney to describe his prose, in the inaugural Richard Ellmann Lecture at Emory University, delivered a year after Ellmann's death, as "Johnsonian," by which he means possessed of a capacity "to judge what the text was worth to the fuller enjoyment or better enduring of our unspecialized lives" (the full quote is "He could maintain subtle receptive vigilance over a text and explicate it within the idiom of his profession; but he could also produce a kind of Johnsonian meditation that considered what the text was worth to the fuller enjoyment or better enduring of our unspecialized lives").[16] An example of Ellmann's "Johnsonian" manner is his account of the complications of Joyce's earliest attitudes to sex. At fourteen, Joyce "precociously began his sexual life" (a maid at the Joyce home assisted). At the same time, he was a prefect in the school's "Sodality of the Blessed Virgin."

> The position suited him very well; he had an adolescent thrill in adoring the Virgin Mary while his lips still savored "of a lewd kiss." His mind longed to adore and to desecrate. Yet virginity still engrossed him, and he was readier than he knew for the retreat which began on November 30, 1896. In charge of the retreat was Father James A. Cullen, and his sermons, delivered, as was customary, according to the prescription of St. Ignatius Loyola's *Spiritual Exercises,* elicited a more than customary number of twinges from hell-fire. All Joyce's mounting scruples against his own conduct found a fierce justification. He saw himself as a beast,

> eating like a beast, lusting like a beast, dying like a beast, and dreamed of a pure love with a virgin heart. (p. 49)

Ellmann's style here is "Johnsonian" in its psychological shrewdness, balance, and air of authority. Elsewhere it is Johnsonian in its wit, often a product of ironic oppositions. Here is Ellmann on Joyce's drinking: "Joyce was abstemious during the day, and drank only at night. He drank with a nice combination of purpose and relaxation: during his convivial evenings he filled his mind with the way people talked and behaved, storing up what he needed for his writing; he also confided to intimate friends the latest anxieties of his life; and as the hour grew later he sang and cavorted to forget his troubles and circumvent his reticences. He engaged in excess with considerable prudence" (p. 693).

Insofar as wit of this kind undermines certainties and expectations, it could be said to be Joycean as well as Johnsonian. Ellmann quotes Joyce on his father, John Stanislaus, whose death affected Joyce deeply: "I got from him his portraits, a waistcoat, a good tenor voice, and an extravagant licentious disposition (out of which, however, the greater part of whatever talent I may have springs)." Ellmann then comments: "The 'extravagant licentious disposition' was something James always cherished, and much of his seemingly irrational spending and drinking justified itself to him as a way of holding the source of his talent inviolate" (p. 657).[17]

Wit can be a way of seeing the world. Johnson describes it as an "unexpected copulation of ideas, the discovery of some occult relation between images in appearance remote from each other." As Ellmann himself puts it at the beginning of *James Joyce:*

> Joyce had to see joined what others had held separate: the point of view that life is unspeakable and to be exposed, and the point of view that it is ineffable and to be distilled. Nature may be a horrible document, or a secret revelation; all may be resolved into brute body, or into mind and mental components. Joyce lived between the antipodes and above them; his brutes show a marvellous capacity for brooding, his pure minds find bodies remorselessly stuck to them. To read Joyce is to see reality rendered without the simplifications of conventional divisions. (pp. 3–4)

Prominent among these divisions, the critic Patrick Hayes writes, are "the unilluminating and devitalizing moral oppositions that religious and political traditions have bequeathed us." Ellmann is to be commended, writes Hayes, for documenting Joyce's resistance to them in "both writing and living."[18]

Ellmann combines every form of what one of Johnson's biographers, W. J. Bate, calls "balance and antithesis," as does Joyce.[19] For example: "He depended on Nora to hold his life together by her loyalty and by her contempt for his weakness" (p. 620).[20] Or consider the titles Ellmann initially suggested for the biography: "The Golden Codger, The Wistful Tyrant, Languid Fury."[21] The cumulative effect of a propensity to "live between antipodes" is to create the impression that nothing is single or simple. Here, for example, is Ellmann's description of the fame that came to Joyce in 1920:

> In a few days he had met dozens of people, in a few weeks he had received visitors, reverent or merely curious, from New York, London, and Dublin, made new friends and enemies, and played the starveling and then the seigneur, both rather convincingly. Money came in and he spent it. Fame appeared, in Rilke's sense of the quintessence of all the misunderstandings that collect around a new name; and he was sometimes diverted by it. More to the point, Joyce, the artist, now thirty-eight, completed *Circe* and then the final three episodes of *Ulysses*. (p. 500)

The paired oppositions in this passage ("reverent/merely curious," friends/enemies," "starveling/seigneur," "Money came in/and he spent it") are characteristic. Another example is his account of the relations between Stanislaus and Joyce, an example that also helps to counter notions that Ellmann was unduly influenced by Stanislaus:

> It is easy to see that James was a difficult older brother, yet Stanislaus was a difficult younger one. If James was casual and capricious, Stanislaus was punctilious and overbearing. James knew his laxity of behavior to be an appearance he could, in sudden tautness, brush aside; Stanislaus knew his own self-discipline to be largely a revolt against his brother's faults. The artist and the reformer made poor house-mates. Stanislaus remembered with many instances that he had been abused in Trieste. Yet he had also been lifted away from ignominy in Dublin and given a career and an intellectual life. The debts were due and had been paid on both sides. (p. 496)

The question of the book's title is worth returning to, in regard to claims of Ellmann's bias or partiality. After discarding "Languid Fury," Ellmann settled for a time on "The Hawk-Like Man," a title he gave to several drafts. It was disapproved of not only by his mother ("not euphonious") but also by Jim Spoerri and Harry Levin. On October 8, 1958, only months before the book went into production, Spoerri wrote: "I dislike the title. . . . I think the definitiveness of the book should be asserted by entitling it simply with the name. Second, most of the implications of hawk are unsympathetic and unflattering." Harry Levin, one of the readers OUP chose to assess the finished manuscript, also disapproved: "The epithet strikes me as illuminating only one side of Joyce, and only doing that for those who knew him already to some extent. It would be perfectly all right for just another book on Joyce; this demands something more comprehensive, because it is going to be *the* book on Joyce."[22] Ellmann explained his problem in a letter of January 9, 1958, to Erwin and Steffani: "The hard thing is to get over that he was witty, romantic, profligate, silly, scheming, passionate, dedicated, suffering, masochistic, all in two or three words." In the end, he took the advice of Spoerri and Levin: the book would be titled *James Joyce.*

* * *

As has been suggested, not all critics have accepted Ellmann's trustworthiness or objectivity, particularly when he draws on the fiction to illuminate the life. An example cited by several critics comes early in *James Joyce.* Ellmann claims that six-year-old Joyce was unhappy at Clongowes, despite Stanislaus's saying that his brother was "happy and well" there, a view corroborated in correspondence by a former fellow student, Lieutenant Colonel P. R. Butler. Ellmann bases his account of Joyce's early days at Clongowes on *A Portrait,* in which six-year-old Stephen Dedalus enters a school clearly modeled on it. Here is how Ellmann describes Joyce on arrival at the school:

> His immediate response to Clongowes is less clear than one would expect; his brother Stanislaus, who had already begun to worship him, remembers him as happy and well there, while *A Portrait* represents him as unhappy and unwell. That a boy of this age, suddenly removed from his family, could have been untroubled is hardly conceivable. The authorities are said to have considerately allowed him to live in the infirmary, instead of a dormitory, so that a nurse, "Nanny Galvin," might look after

> him. Apparently she could not prevent his feeling homesick and tormented by the other boys' ragging for at least the first few months at Clongowes. The snobbery of small boys was new to him; he counters it, *A Portrait* asserts, by making his father a gentleman, one of his uncles a judge, and another a general in the army. The worst event of the early months was the incident described in *A Portrait* and confirmed by Joyce to Herbert Gorman, when another boy broke 'Stephen's' glasses. (p. 27)

That Joyce himself confirmed Gorman's account of the incident with the glasses, as well as the subsequent "pandying" (being hit with a wooden bat) Stephen receives at the hands of "Father Dolan" (in real life Father James Daly), is reason enough for Ellmann to accept as autobiographical the novel's account of Stephen's initial unhappiness. Stanislaus's memory, Ellmann suggests, was colored by his hero worship; that he was four at the time is also worth recalling. In this case, a side other than Stanislaus's is taken, although Stanislaus's contrary view is also registered.

What, though, of Lieutenant Colonel Butler's views, which are not mentioned here? Amanda Sigler finds it "surprising that Ellmann would not only refute Stanislaus's description of Joyce at Clongowes, but that he would ignore Butler's memories altogether."[23] The implication is that in this case taking a side involves suppression. But when Butler questions the autobiographical origins of episodes in the early school scenes in *A Portrait,* it is mostly because he has no memory of them, which is hardly proof that they did not happen or that they are inaccurately depicted. The scenes he does recall and takes issue with concern six-year-old Joyce's feelings. Joyce's account of Father Daly in the novel, Butler told Ellmann in a letter of February 6, 1954, is "extremely exaggerated": "We were afraid of him, it is true, but to nothing like the extent described." How, though, would Butler know the "extent" of six-year-old Joyce's fear, even if we are meant to include him in the "we" who were less frightened than Stephen?

Where Ellmann is culpable in the extended passage quoted above, allowing the plausible or probable to be taken for the actual, is in describing *A Portrait* as representing "him [Joyce] as unhappy and unwell." What Ellmann should have written is that it represents "Stephen" as unhappy and unwell. So, too, with Ellmann's description of Joyce's response to the snobbery he encountered at Clongowes. He says that *A Portrait* "asserts" that Joyce, like Stephen, responded "by making his father a gentleman, one of his uncles a judge, and another a general." Given the absence of evidence from Stanislaus or Butler or Joyce himself, as in the confirmation Joyce provided for Gorman about the broken glasses episode, the word Ellmann should have used here was "suggests," or he should simply have written "in *A Portrait* Stephen counters it by making his father. . . ." Later in the paragraph, talking about what happened to Joyce after he was wrongly punished over the glasses, Ellmann is careful and qualified: "On this occasion he bravely protested to the rector, Father Conmee, and was sustained by him. Probably at this time the other boys began to respect him; such a development is suggested, a little obscurely, in *A Portrait,* and is borne out by accounts of Joyce's life at the school by contemporaries. Even if, as seems likely, he really was pushed into the square dish or cesspool by a fellow-pupil and laid up with fever as a result, probably in the spring of 1891, he was generally in good health." In this instance, the difference between the actual and the plausible is clearly signaled: "Probably"; "suggested"; "as seems likely"; "probably," "generally."

On other occasions when Ellmann's judgment or objectivity is said to falter, artistic or writerly concerns, specifically about narrative, override archival ones. The Irish critic Declan Kiberd, a friend and pupil of Ellmann's, provides an explanation. For Kiberd, "though ostensibly a critic, Ellmann seemed intent on creating works of art." As a result, "although he was honest enough to include much that was unflattering about Joyce's selfishness, his neglect of his children and his exploitation of his brother while writing *Ulysses,* he overrode those elements with a narrative of his own about the essential decency of a great artist. It was as if Ellmann were in agreement with Dr. Johnson who believed that a good artist cannot be a bad man."[24]

In support of this view, Kiberd and others cite the "resounding declaration" that ends the book:

> The surface of the life Joyce lived seemed always erratic and provisional. But its central meaning was directed as consciously as his work. The ingenuity with which he wrote his books was the same with which he forced the world to read them; the smiling affection he extended to Bloom and his other principal characters was the same that he gave to the members of his family; his disregard for bourgeois thrift and convention was the splendid extravagance which enabled him in literature to make an intractable wilderness into a new state. In whatever he did, his two profound

> interests—his family and his writings—kept their place. These passions never dwindled. The intensity of the first gave his work its sympathy and humanity; the intensity of the second raised his life to dignity and high dedication. (p. 756)

"Splendid extravagance" is an indulgent way of describing Joyce's relations with money—not just his squandering, but his consequent cadging, scrounging, and failure to repay loans, all documented by Ellmann in the course of the narrative. "Smiling affection" is too mild a term to describe Joyce's relations with Stanislaus or Nora, nor is it all that accurate a description of Joyce's feelings for his children. His relations with Lucia, as the biography makes clear, involve emotions more intense and complicated than smiling affection. As for Giorgio, so little is said in *James Joyce* about Joyce's relations with him, that in effect the biography supports Kiberd's claim of neglect. A more accurate, carefully qualified summary of Joyce's relations with his children is provided three chapters earlier: "As a father, Joyce wished to interfere as little as possible with his children's lives, a principle which was better suited to his own insuperable personality than to theirs. Because he rarely ordered or forbade them anything, and always treated them kindly and generously, he assumed they had their freedom. But by delicate requests, by sighs, by suggestions, he bound them into his affairs. They were slow to make their own careers" (p. 624).[25]

If the final paragraph of *James Joyce* tips the scales in Joyce's favor, the rest of the biography is more evenly balanced. Ellmann was no "biografiend," but he was clear about Joyce's failings. It is hard to see him, as Kiberd imagines, agreeing with Johnson that a good artist cannot be a bad man. How, then, does one explain the softening in the final paragraph, its eulogistic ring? Kiberd's suggestion that Ellmann "was intent on creating works of art" suggests a possible answer. In writing the last paragraph of his book, Ellmann had his eye on the needs and expectations of his audience, in his case a general audience, though he hoped also to gain the approval of specialists. For such an audience, the last paragraph of a traditional cradle-to-grave narrative, especially of an admired subject, is like a speech at a funeral: no place to stress flaws. Joyce, of course, challenged the needs and expectations of his audience, but his provocations, like Ellmann's propitiations, depended on a comparable understanding of what his audience expected.

Ellmann's efforts to meet the expectations of a general audience are most obvious at the ends of chapters, sites of drama and suspense. Here are some examples:

> When they arrived in the city [London], Joyce left Nora for two hours in a park while he went to see Arthur Symons. She thought he would not return. But he did, and he was to surprise his friends, and perhaps himself too, by his future constancy. As for Nora, she was steadfast for the rest of her life. (p. 185)

> The new business manager [of the English Players] mismanaged; the reconciliation with the consulate never took place; and the financial difficulties of the Players increased. It was perhaps as well that just at this moment Joyce's interests shifted in a remarkable way. (p. 461)

> Switzerland, where they arrived a few hours later, was more than a refuge; it was a symbol of artistic detachment, *au-dessus de la mêlée,* and it was fitting that Joyce should not only write the bulk of his greatest book there, but also return there in the end to die.[26] (p. 397)

Another sign of artistic or writerly calculation is the way Ellmann shapes his narrative, moving back and forth from topic to topic, from life to work, inner world to outer world, analysis to narrative. The smoothness of the transitions in *James Joyce* is equivalent to the smooth transitions in multistranded novels—from Anna to Levin, say, or Dorothea to Lydgate. This feature of narrative is rarely commented upon by academic theorists or critics, perhaps because their own readers are meant to tolerate any amount of elaboration or documentation. When, therefore, Joyceans—that is, academic Joyceans—discuss Ellmann's shaping and patterning in *James Joyce,* it is mostly with suspicion. For Finn Fordham, biographies like Ellmann's "compress" the inevitable blank periods in a life; such periods "leave scant traces," being "infertile, boring, ordinary, barren." *James Joyce,* Fordham believes, is "noisier" than Joyce's actual life, projecting "a noisy life onto the work."[27] Earlier in the same essay, Fordham describes the biography as "stylish and gorgeous in detail but also, upon close inspection, with parts tacked on over gaps, creating illusory effects of completion and tidiness."[28] Hugh Kenner complains of "what we're having to trust all through *James Joyce,* [Ellmann's] sense of what will fit his narrative." For Ellmann, Kenner continues, "biography is finally fiction, and . . . it works the way imperfect fiction does, filling sag with cellulite generalities when the data continuity requires are lacking. If, unlike the novelist, the biographer can't invent fact, he can invent ways to cover its absence."[29] John McCourt, not as severe as Kenner, makes similar points: "Part of Ellmann's genius was to cover cracks, conceal ellipses in the narrative by the brilliance of his storytelling, by his patterning and arranging of events." Sometimes, McCourt claims, Ellmann even "misplaced events to make them fit better, and . . . aimed at tying up loose ends, giving a sense of causality and completeness where there was none."[30]

McCourt gives no examples. It is not clear if he is claiming that Ellmann makes things up or misdates the material he "misplaces," falsifying chronology. What he, Kenner, Fordham, and other academic Joyceans distrust about biographies is what most readers want from them: a narrative or story. Stories, after all, are how most people, including most academics, know and present not only the lives of others but their own lives. As Montaigne puts it, "each of us constructs and lives a 'narrative' . . . this narrative *is* us, our identities." That Joyce and his fellow modernists challenged such a view contributes to the anti-narrative suspicions of Ellmann's critics. Here is Virginia Woolf in "Modern Novels" (1925), an influential attack on her immediate realist predecessors (Wells, Bennett, and Galsworthy):

> If a writer were a free man and not a slave, if he could write what he chose, not what he must, if he could base his work upon his own feeling and not upon convention, there would be no plot, no comedy, no tragedy, no love interest or catastrophe in the accepted style, and perhaps not a single button sewn on as the Bond Street tailors would have it. Life is not a series of gig lamps symmetrically arranged; life is a luminous halo, a semi-transparent envelope surrounding us from the beginning of consciousness to the end.

In the most read of Woolf's novels, however, this "luminous halo" or "semi-transparent envelope" emerges over the course of a plot or plots, sometimes comic, sometimes tragic, with love interests, catastrophes, and carefully timed transitions from one narrative strand to another. As for the shaping of narrative in biography—far from distrusting it, Woolf saw it as inevitable. The biographer, she writes, "chooses; he synthesizes; in short, he has ceased to be the chronicler, he has become an artist."[31] Joyce's best-known novels also have plots: *A Portrait* proceeds from infancy to childhood to youth; *Ulysses* from morning to afternoon to evening. (*Finnegans Wake,* not one of Joyce's best-known novels, is another matter.)[32] Nor is Joyce's view of biography any different from Woolf's. He may not have thought of Herbert Gorman as an artist, but he expected him to choose, to synthesize, to be more than a chronicler, to tip the scales.

* * *

Even those Joyceans who are wary of Ellmann's shaping and tidying, admire his prose. Fordham, quoted above, calls it "stylish and gorgeous." Kiberd writes of "the wonderful clarity of his style."[33] McCourt begins his account of *James Joyce* by describing it as "a triumph of style, clarity, eloquence and readability, in a style which puts that of most rival biographies to shame."[34] In addition to the stylistic features already mentioned—Johnsonian weight, balance, wit—Ellmann has a talent for figurative language. Here he is on Ettore Schmitz (Italo Svevo), a possible model for Bloom:

> Schmitz was in many ways quite different from Bloom, but he had married a Gentile, he had changed his name (though only for literary purposes), he knew something of Jewish customs, and he shared Bloom's amiably ironic view of life. Joyce could not abide the inner organs of animals and fowl, while Schmitz, like Bloom, loved them. Some of these are small similarities, but Joyce had a spider's eye. (p. 385)

Here is Ellmann on the extremity of Joyce's despair over Lucia:

> Joyce had not wept in a letter since he suspected Nora of infidelity in 1909. Though not so blind as Homer, nor so exiled as Dante, he had reached his life's nadir. "People talk of my influence on my daughter," he said to Mrs. Jolas, "but what of her influence on me?" His exasperation and despair exfoliated like a black flower. (p. 697)

Here he is on J. F. Byrne:

> His power over Joyce came from his habit of refraining from comment: Joyce's admissions about his feelings towards family, friends and church, about his overweening ambition, struck like waves against Byrne's cryptic taciturnity. (p. 66)

Finally, on religion:

> He was no longer a Christian himself; but he converted the temple to new uses instead of trying to knock it down, regarding it as a superior kind of human folly and one which, interpreted by a secular artist, contained obscured bits of truth.[35] (p. 68)

* * *

Joseph Epstein's quip about Ellmann not looking like his prose style can be extended: his prose style does not read the way he spoke (nor does it read like his letters). The prose of *James Joyce* is literary, at times antique in diction and phraseology. Consider the construction "his capacity for alcohol was small." "Small" is not the word one would use here in speech. Nor would one say, again about Joyce and alcohol, that "his soul, fed on pride, and declining attachments, longed to give way, to swoon, to be mutilated, and he brought this happy consummation about with the help of porter" (p. 137). "Happy consummation" is historical as well as literary, used by Andrew Jackson to describe the odious "Indian Removal Act." Were Ellmann to speak the above sentence, "happy consummation" would require tonal quote-marks. Or consider the words "dear" and "discomfited" in the following passage, about Joyce and Nora: "She refused to believe he was evil; she cut through his posturings so ruthlessly that sometimes, when they happened not to be posturings or were especially dear posturings, he was discomfited" (p. 177). The speech of literary academics can be mannered (I once heard an English professor use the word "perforce" in conversation), but there is no evidence that this was true of Ellmann's speech. The prose of *James Joyce* combines the virtues of writing and speech, being literary *and* colloquial. Joyce's writing was literary, while making fun of itself, as in a story he told, skillfully recounted by Ellmann, about consulting two London ophthalmologists: "Doctors Henry and James, whose names, he noted with fine indifference to a fellow-author, were also the name of a clothing store in Dublin" (p. 551).

* * *

Ellmann loved anecdotes and good stories, and *James Joyce* is full of them. Here he is on Joyce's dealings with the publisher George Roberts, whose delays drove his author half mad. In 1912 Roberts wrote to Joyce to say that he would publish *Dubliners* only if he received two sureties from him of £500 each, to cover expected libel costs.

> Joyce received the letter at Roberts's office, where it had been left for him. "I read it," he wrote Nora, "and walked down the street feeling the whole future of my life slipping out of my grasp." He had no money, hope, or youth left. He sat for an hour on a sofa in Lidwell's office [George Lidwell, a solicitor friend of Joyce's father], and considered buying a revolver to "put some daylight into my publisher." Lidwell, appealed to once more, was now on Roberts's side. John Joyce, who told Charles [Joyce's brother] privately that *Dubliners* was a "blackguard production," urged James to buck up and find another publisher. But after pawning his watch and chain so he could stay a little longer, Joyce went back to Roberts for a last try. At his most dogged, ironic, and practical, he took up one by one the points made by Roberts's solicitor. (pp. 342–43)

Joyce's responses to these points Ellmann then reproduces. There are nine of them, numbered, the last being overarching in nature: "that his lawyer encouraged correspondence and litigation for his own profit."

Sometimes, if stories were too amusing to leave out, Ellmann included uncorroborated or conflicting ones, including some from questionable sources. Here he is on Joyce and Proust meeting in May 1921, on the eve of the publication of *Ulysses*, a happening that "quickly became legend."

> Sydney Schiff ("Stephen Hudson"), the English novelist whom Joyce had met a few times, invited him to a supper party for Stravinsky and Diaghilev following the first performance of one of their ballets. Joyce appeared late and apologized for not having dressed; at this time he had no formal clothes. He was drinking heavily to cover his embarrassment when the door opened and Marcel Proust in a fur coat appeared, as Joyce said later, "like the hero of *The Sorrows of Satan*." Schiff had mentioned the party to Proust but had not ventured to invite him because of Proust's known unwillingness to emerge from his flat. Joyce followed Schiff and Mrs. Schiff to the door, was introduced to Proust, and remained seated beside him. The conversation has been variously reported. According to one account, which William Carlos Williams heard and set down, Joyce said, "I've headaches every day. My eyes are terrible." Proust replied, "My poor stomach. What am I going to do? It's killing me. In fact, I must

> leave at once." "I'm in the same situation," replied Joyce, "if I can find someone to take me by the arm. Goodbye." "*Charmé,*" said Proust, "oh my stomach." Margaret Anderson writes that Proust said, "I regret that I don't know Mr. Joyce's work," and Joyce countered, "I have never read Mr. Proust," the conversation ending there. Joyce told Arthur Power that Proust asked him if he liked truffles, and Joyce answered, "Yes, I do." He commented, "Here are the two greatest literary figures of our time meeting and they ask each other if they like truffles." To Budgen he gave a slightly more extended version: "Our talk consisted solely of the word 'No.' Proust asked me if I knew the duc de so-and-so. I said, 'No.' Our hostess asked Proust if he had read such and such a piece of *Ulysses.* Proust said, 'No.' And so on. Of course the situation was impossible. Proust's day was just beginning. Mine was at an end." (pp. 523–24)

Not all the stories in *James Joyce* are humorous or ironic, some are somber, appalled. Here is Ellmann on the last days of Joyce's mother, who had been bedbound for months:

> His father became increasingly difficult to handle as his drinking caught up with the pace of May Joyce's decay. One hopeless night he reeled home and in his wife's room blurted out, "I'm finished. I can't do any more. If you can't get well, die. Die and be damned to you!" Stanislaus screamed at him, "You swine!" and went for him murderously, but stopped when he saw his mother struggling frantically to get out of bed to intercept him. James let his father out and managed to lock him in another room. Shortly after, tragedy yielding to absurdity, John Joyce was seen disappearing around a corner, having contrived to escape out a second-floor window.
>
> May Joyce died on August 13, 1903, at the early age of forty-four. In her last hours she lay in coma, and the family knelt about her bed, praying and lamenting. Her brother John Murray, observing that neither Stanislaus nor James was kneeling, peremptorily ordered them to do so. Neither obeyed. (p. 141)

* * *

Another noteworthy feature of *James Joyce* is its use of quotations, not only from interviewees, or sources such as Stanislaus's memoir, or from the fiction, but from correspondence. For Ellmann, as for all biographers, letters were a crucial source of evidence, though not always in a straightforward way. Writer and recipient play what Ellmann called "a game of concealment and revealment" (as Ellmann's own letters do). "What we have to read in correspondence," he writes in "Adventures and Misadventures of a Biographer," "is what is not written there, as at a party we notice who has not been invited. For earlier biographers, letters were like saints' relics; for biographers since Freud, they are likely to be duplicitous or at least incomplete." Ellmann cites Lacan, in what Donaghue would call an "occasional" lucidity: 'What the unconscious forces us to examine is the law according to which no utterance can ever be reduced simply to its own statement.'" Joyce's letters, Ellmann believes, whether open or disguised, "were already set in the three modes that he held to throughout his life: the assertive, the plaintive, and the self-exculpatory" (p. 207). The aim of quoting so frequently from them, often at length (chapter 11 includes an entire three-page letter to Stanislaus about Pola, and chapter 33 includes a four-page letter to Harriet Weaver), is only partly to convey the information they contain. They also provide a crucial counter-voice for the reader. As Ellmann explained in an interview:

> I don't like it when the biographer claims omniscience. I think it's better for him to claim a certain distance between himself and the subject. I mean he offers his views, but I always feel he has some duty to present material so that a reader can judge it independently. I always put in a fair number of letters of Joyce. I felt that even if my construction of his situation at a given time might be valid, it was just as well to see how he was writing himself about it. Not that one would necessarily agree with everything he said either, but at any rate one could have some sort of check upon the biographer's interpretation.[36]

* * *

One final feature of the finished biography is worth noting, in part because it raises again the issue of audience, a key to many of the choices Ellmann made in writing *James Joyce*. This is the fact that each chapter begins with an epigraph from *Finnegans Wake*. With most of these epigraphs it is possible for the general reader to make out a connection with the chapter that follows, though only a very general one. Here is the epigraph to the first or introductory chapter:

> As often as I think of that unbloody housewarmer. Shen Skrivenitch. Always cutting my brhose to please his phrase, bogorror, I declare I get the jawache! Be me punting his reflection he'd begin his beogrefright in muddyass ribalds.

The epigraph to the chapter that follows, a chapter titled "The Family before Joyce," is

> Wharnow are alle her childer, say? In kingdome gone or power to come or gloria be to them farther? Alllivial, allalivial. Some here, more no more, more again lost all stranger.

Most readers of the first epigraph should be able to see that it is about biography and its distortions, and some of the portmanteau joke-spellings are funny ("beogrefright," "in muddyass ribalds"). In the second epigraph, the connection with past generations is even easier to make out. With later epigraphs, however, particularly those titled by date, the connections with the chapters they introduce are less clear. Is the reader meant to go back to them after having read the chapter? For specialist readers, the tricks, puzzles, puns, and joke-spellings will be familiar. Readers who only know of *Finnegans Wake* but have not read it, or who have tried to read it and given up, life being too short, are likely, eventually, to skip the epigraphs, or only glance at them. The interpretive effort they call for is not explained or defended until the end of the book, when the making of *Finnegans Wake* is recounted.[37]

Ellmann's decision to draw the epigraphs from *Finnegans Wake* is perhaps a sign of authorial anxiety. They are there to reassure or impress specialist readers. One such reader, Patrick Hayes, calls them "an understated but deft" response to a major anomaly in *James Joyce:* "Joyce, after all, had 'turned literature and life on end,' as Ellmann put it, creating a 'Joysprick' that could start to think outside its own norms. What does it mean to navigate Joyce's experiment in living through a biographical prose that can readily recount the story of such a life?"[38] This anomaly Ellmann chose not to discuss, though the epigraphs bring it to mind. When the *Wake* itself is discussed, nothing is said of the larger implications of its strange language, what later Joyceans see as the challenges it poses to representation, the autonomy of the subject, narrative reliability. Instead Ellmann focuses on traditional novelistic features, or what can be made of them, in the novel, features such as plot, setting, characterization, theme, symbol.

It was Ellmann's father who first raised questions about the biography's treatment of *Finnegans Wake*. On October 21, 1958, after reading a completed draft, he wrote: "I was expecting that you would stop somewhere along the way and give a more complete explanation of what makes Finnegan's [*sic*] Wake a great book, and why it has made the imprint which [it] did or should." Ellmann's father also wanted to know, "Why did Joyce stick to it in spite of the many objectors to it? What has he actually achieved by it? What will the future literary historians do about it?" These questions Ellmann seems to have been reluctant to answer, not wanting to alienate readers, either specialist or nonspecialist, but it is possible to intuit answers. For Ellmann, *Ulysses* is the pinnacle of Joyce's achievement. What followed, though Ellmann is careful not to say so, is decline. At the time of the publication of the biography, this was the view not only of nonspecialist or general readers (as it remains today), but of most specialist readers. Today, though, many academic Joyceans see the earlier works, including *Ulysses,* as steps or "staging posts" on the route to *Finnegans Wake,* which alone offers what one critic summarizes as a "full realization" of Joyce's views not only on language, but on the instability of the subject and the unreliability of narrative. These views, they argue, are detectable not only in the later and most difficult episodes of *Ulysses,* "The Oxen of the Sun" and "Circe" and "Eumaeus" episodes, but in all of Joyce's fiction, from *Dubliners* onward.[39]

It was not that Ellmann had no idea about this way of viewing Joyce. He was first exposed to it, or a version of it, at the very start of his work on the biography, when it was a minority view. In a letter of May 16, 1948, his friend Ellsworth Mason writes of the later episodes of *Ulysses:*

> It has always amused me that this chapter ["The Oxen of the Sun"] is the favorite scapegoat of anyone demonstrating his "objective" approach to *Ulysses* (i.e. anyone trying to show that he is not a hero-worshipper, that he can tell when Joyce is off the beam). Levin kicked it all over the lot in his book [*James Joyce: A Critical Introduction,* 1941] and if he'd stand by a single statement in this section of this book, I'd really be surprised. Kain also hauled out this chapter to knock around [in *Fabulous Voyager: A Study of James Joyce's "Ulysses,"* 1947]; others have done so in shorter commentaries. From the first I have maintained that not only was it one of the most skillful of Joyce's chapters, but one of the most

important in the book. The style is one of Joyce's major statements in the book that words, communication, have broken down in modern society (and he shows this in several ways in different parts of the book); and he does this by showing the tradition of the language in the past, and its gradual breaking down into the confusion of present jargon, the offspring of the past. The implications of the style carry over into the matter of the chapter, since the baby being born is also the inheritor of a social tradition that has broken down. The way Joyce uses the different styles makes for some of the best humor in the book, and begins to prepare us for the fantasy and breakdown of language in the next chapter, *Circe.* But the experts go on stating that this is merely Joyce parading his virtuosity.

This defense of the style of late Joyce differs in an important respect from that of many current Joyceans, in that it connects the late style to a specific moment in history, that of postwar disillusion. Mason takes Levin to task for kicking the late style all over the lot, but he shares with him an Eliotic or "Waste Land" view of the style's origins, seeing it as a product or reflection of cultural degeneration. In such a view, as Levin puts it, Bloom is "this apologetic little man," "thoroughly uninteresting."[40] Ellmann set his face against the "Waste Land" view. The closest *James Joyce* comes to offering a defense of the language of *Finnegans Wake* is courtesy of Joyce himself:

> That *Finnegans Wake* should be a night book as *Ulysses* was a day book was also already decided. The night required and justified a special language. "*Je suis au bout de l'anglais,*" Joyce said to August Suter, and he remarked to another friend, "I have put the language to sleep." As he explained to Max Eastman . . . "In writing of the night, I really could not, I felt I could not, use words in their ordinary connections. Used that way they do not express how things are in the night, in the different stages—conscious, then semi-conscious, then unconscious. . . ." To the objection of triviality, he replied, "Yes. Some of the means I use are trivial—and some are quadrivial." . . . He said to Edmond Jaloux that his novel would be written "to suit the aesthetic of the dream, where the forms prolong and multiply themselves, where the visions pass from the trivial to the apocalyptic, where the brain uses the roots of vocables to make others from them which will be capable of naming its phantasms, its allegories, its allusions." (p. 559)

Ellmann at the typewriter.

That this language puts great demands on readers—exorbitant demands, some would say—is a point Ellmann addresses only briefly, less than thirty pages from the end of the book:

> In retrospect it seems clear that the "monster," as Joyce several times called *Finnegans Wake* in these days, had to be written, and that he had to write it. Readers may still sigh because he did not approach them more directly, but it does not appear that the alternative was open to him. . . .
>
> In his earlier books Joyce forced modern literature to accept new styles, new subject matter, new kinds of plot and characterization. In his last book he forced it to accept a new area of being and a new language. What

> is ultimately most impressive is the sureness with which, in the midst of such technical accomplishments, he achieved his special mixture of attachment and detachment, of gaiety and lugubriousness. He was no saturnine artificer contriving devices, but one of life's celebrants, in bad circumstances cracking new jokes, foisting upon enemies and miseries his comic vision. (pp. 729–30)

Readers must decide if this defense answers the questions Ellmann's father posed in his letter of May 15, 1958. In an earlier letter, written on April 11, 1953, shortly after Ellmann embarked on his first research trip for the biography, his father had written: "It seems to me that before you write you must make up your mind what kind of mind you wish to attract. Is it an audience going to read Finnegan's [*sic*] Wake or rather one that wants to know just what he tried to do, why and how he accomplished his objectives." Ellmann's answer was both, with the attendant danger, as here, of satisfying only one or the other or neither.

CHAPTER TEN

Reception / Afterlife

ELLMANN "COMPLETED" the text of *James Joyce* on March 5, 1958, but he continued to work on it, as he predicted he would, revising and adding materials for another four months. It was delivered to the typist on July 1, but not sent to OUP until late September (Ellmann wrote to Harriet Weaver, once the draft was typed, "I had it reproduced by a special process so that it would be easier than a carbon copy to read").[1] Harry Levin and John Kelleher were the book's readers for OUP, and on November 15, 1958, Ellmann reported to his parents that Sheldon Meyer, his OUP editor, had told him that their reports were "very complimentary, and suggested only minor changes."[2] Also complimentary were the unofficial responses from James Spoerri and Harriet Weaver. "With your encouragement and theirs," Ellmann wrote to Miss Weaver on October 20, 1958, "I will begin to like it a little myself."

In a later letter to his parents, Ellmann had more to report about the book's readers. Sean O'Faolain "had heard from Kelleher that the book was very good, though K. didn't like Joyce." As O'Faolain explained, 'John is the nicest fellow in the world and wants everyone else to be as nice.'" Advance word of Levin's report came from a student at Northwestern, who "told me she had heard from a Harvard student that Levin considers the book 'absolutely tremendous.'"[3] As it turned out, Levin's report was tough. Like Mason and others, he urged Ellmann to untangle "the historic James Joyce from the fictitious Stephen Dedalus." "He should be at special pains to keep from blurring one from the other." Levin also complained that Joyce's mother was "not painted at all." As for length, "I do not think it should be cut very much, since breadth of treatment is one of the ways in which it out-classes its rivals. On the other hand, certain chapters tend to

Harry Levin.

deal with the specific background of particular works; these tend to get in the way of the more chronological treatment and could be eliminated or redistributed." The chapter he thinks most in need of eliminating or cutting is "The Backgrounds of 'The Dead.'" "The space devoted to it is out of proportion to the rest of the work." Moreover, "as literary criticism it is rather mediocre."[4] (The space Levin himself devotes to "The Dead" in *James Joyce: A Critical Introduction*, is less than two pages, only two sentences of which are devoted to literary criticism as opposed to plot summary.)[5] Surprisingly, given his strictness about untangling author and character, Levin describes Gabriel Conroy as presiding over "the Christmas party of his musical maiden aunts—incidentally Joyce's."[6] In the same letter to his parents, Ellmann confesses that Levin's report "kept me in a frazzle all last month . . . about five pages of almost unrelieved attack. I can't say I didn't profit from a few details of it."

The book's line editor at OUP, Elizabeth Cameron, was assistant to Sheldon Meyer. Cameron and Ellmann got on well and her suggested changes, nowhere near as radical as Levin's, were mostly approved. He also got on with the book's copyeditor, Helen Marlas, only once objecting to her imposition of house style, asking Cameron to intervene over the possessive plurals "Joyces's" and "Flynns's."

> I am sorry to be stubborn, but the "house rule" as applied in these instances seems to me ridiculous. Where do your house rules come from? I should like to write to their originator, who I suspect would agree with me. A friend of mine suggested to me that the clinging of Oxford to its house rules is symptomatic (perhaps causative) of the ruin of the British Empire. In any case, dear Elizabeth, I will not yield on this point. Please let me know to whom I should write, even to the sacred precincts of the Clarendon Press itself.[7]

Mostly Cameron's suggested changes served what she saw as the tastes and needs of the general reader. "The new first page is an improvement," she writes on February 18, 1959, "but perhaps we can all think about that first sentence some more. I hate the thesis sound of 'this book attempts . . .' I would like something more direct like 'James Joyce is . . .'" Earlier, on February 10, in a discussion of footnotes and endnotes, she worries that "in a book of this length it is difficult to avoid the textbook appearance, especially with the extracts, verse, and notes adding to the 'heavy' character." At the same time, Cameron acknowledges, the general reader of a biography of Joyce is expected to be educated. Hence her attitude to quotations from other languages: "I'm all for keeping as much of the foreign language material as possible because I liked the flavor of it and because I thought anyone reading this book should be able to read the French at least" (also, presumably, the book's several phrases and brief passages in Latin, German, and Italian). Only on rare occasions does Ellmann resist a suggested alteration on the grounds that it misses meaning or nuance. On February 11, responding to earlier suggestions, he thanks Cameron "for your re-writing of the first paragraph of THE DEAD chapter—I thought it an improvement except that I want to keep the word 'so,' as I indicated in sending the page with the last batch of MS." The word "so" occurs in the opening sentence of the chapter: "The stay in Rome seemed purposeless, but during it Joyce became aware of the change in his attitude toward Ireland and so toward the world." Ellmann wants the word "so" retained to suggest that Joyce's changed attitude to the world *comes from* a changed attitude to Ireland, as if to emphasize the more-than-local influence or character of the story's Dublin setting.

In the weeks leading up to publication, Ellmann was peppered with requests from Fon Boardman, OUP's manager for advertising and publicity. *Time, Newsweek,* the *New York Times,* the *New York Herald Tribune,* and the *Saturday Review* all wanted to take Ellmann to lunch and to interview him. He was sent a list of advertisements OUP had placed in over fifty US publications, either for *James Joyce* singly or with other OUP books. Boardman asked him to name other publications to add to the list. He also sent Ellmann requests for radio and television appearances. Meanwhile, Frances Steloff, of the Gotham Book Mart, offered to host a launch party for *James Joyce,* to be held from 6:30 to 8:30 on October 22, 1959, publication day. Steloff also arranged for the James Joyce Society to hold a meeting directly after the party, at which Ellmann would be asked questions about the book. Sheldon Meyer urged Ellmann to skip the meeting; he would be exhausted by the day's activities, and more were to come. Ellmann, though, was determined, as with the book itself, to please both general and academic audiences.

Mary accompanied Ellmann to the launch, staying with him three nights at the Biltmore Hotel. The children stayed in Evanston, looked after by "a nice woman named Mrs. Bolton. . . . I want them to get used to her in case we want to take a day off again some time."[8] In a letter to Harriet Weaver, Ellmann described Steloff as "wildly excited" about the party.[9] "I think it is going to be quite a mob scene," Fon Boardman wrote to him on October 8, "but I suppose the more the merrier." Attendees included Sylvia Beach (who was in the States to promote her own recently published book, *Shakespeare and Company*), Lucie Leon (widow of Paul Leon), Ottocaro Weiss, Helen Joyce (Giorgio's ex-wife), Ben Huebsch of Viking (publisher of Joyce but also of Ellmann and Mason's edition of *The Critical Writings of James Joyce,* which had come out earlier in the year, and of Stanislaus Joyce's *My Brother's Keeper* (1958), edited and introduced by Ellmann).[10] In a letter of November 1, 1959, Ellmann described the days immediately following the launch. "There have been several radio and TV programs, book-and-author luncheons and the like. I've been asked to write articles, give lectures, take new jobs, and in general this temporary emergence from obscurity has been hysterical enough, though I will not pretend that it is disagreeable."

When the US reviews appeared, they were every bit as good as OUP had predicted they would be. Three weeks before publication, on October 1, Sheldon Meyer had reported to Ellmann that the biography had received

Mary Ellmann, Richard Ellmann, John R. B. Brett-Smith, president of Oxford University Press in New York, and Frances Steloff, at the launch party at Gotham Book Mart.

"the most ecstatic advance reaction I have seen on any book I have known anything about" (a quote used in this book's Introduction). Two days earlier, Elizabeth Cameron had written to Ellmann that it was "the only Oxford book I remember being read by 90% of the staff." On September 26 Ellmann reported to his parents that Mark Schorer, a critic and professor of English at Berkeley, wrote to say that he had read the book twice, "the second time probably for a review though he doesn't say so. He writes 'An *incredible* achievement . . . I am at once exalted and laid low (for us lesser ones) by the dimensions and the detail of the utterly fascinating book.' I rather hope he may be doing it for the NY Times. Also had another letter, which you *mustn't* mention, but it implies that the New Yorker will have a long and favorable piece." Schorer's review appeared in the *San Francisco Chronicle* (November 1, 1959) rather than the *New York Times*. Its first sentence reads: "This is not only the most important book that we have had on James Joyce until now (and the only reliable biography), it is also, almost certainly, one of the great literary biographies of this century, a book that will last for years, probably for generations."[11]

The book was published simultaneously in the United States and the United Kingdom. In a lengthy front-page review in the Sunday *New York Times,* Stephen Spender described it as an "immensely detailed, massive, completely detached and objective, yet loving biography." Later, in discussing *Finnegans Wake,* Spender says Ellmann "seems to accept the view of all good Joyceans that 'Finnegans Wake' is Joyce's masterpiece and not an immense aberration." The word "seems" rightly hints at something unclear or evasive about Ellmann's view ("all good Joyceans" is perhaps patronizing). Later in the review, Spender declares that "Mr. Ellmann is to be respected, for, although a Joycean, his love of his subject never comes between Joyce and the reader. Indeed, he writes with a cool and masterful detachment, which allows the reader to approach Joyce with a completely open mind, sometimes liking the warm humanity, sometimes detesting the cold arrogance of the man, always having the sense that he who was often a fool in his life was always wise in his work."[12]

Just as important as the *New York Times* for attracting general readers was *Time* magazine. To its anonymous reviewer, the "great and fascinating merit" of the book was "that it demystifies Joyce without debunking him. It will be read as long as James Joyce is read." The book's style was praised in terms likely to appeal widely: "Out of minute factual detail, Ellmann fashions a Ulyssean portrait that has the lived-with, lived-through intensity of a major novel." This was the view also of Horace Reynolds, in the *Christian Science Monitor:* "It absorbs the reader like a great novel."[13] For the *Time* reviewer, the book's "only drawback" is its treatment of *Finnegans Wake,* or rather Ellmann's valuation of it. Whereas Spender is not quite sure of Ellmann's opinion, the *Time* reviewer complains that Ellmann "attempts no critical revaluation."[14] Reynolds says nothing about the *Wake,* nor does William York Tindall in his review in the *New York Herald Tribune.* Ellmann distrusted Tindall, saw him as a rival, but the review opens by calling *James Joyce* "definitive—or all but. It has abundant news for Joyceans, however adept, and for plain readers, human interest."[15]

When the *New Yorker* review finally appeared, in the December 12 issue, it was, as predicted, very long and wholly favorable. Dwight Macdonald, its author, begins by calling the book "definitive . . . a model for future scholarly biographies," distinguishing its fact-filled bulk from that of most academic biographies, "great lumbering dinosaurs with brains the size of a teacup. We have endured their wooden writing, their congenital lack of ideas, their magpie heaping-up of Facts . . . Facts presented with so little sensibility (or simple common sense) that the subject never emerges from their scholarly welter." Macdonald establishes his generalist credentials by making clear what he thinks of *Finnegans Wake.* After praising "the fine peroration" of chapter 23, in which the *Wake* figures prominently, he quotes Ellmann's description of Joyce's genius as "a trap from which he did not desire to extricate himself." Macdonald, in contrast, wishes "he *had* extricated himself," describing the novel as "a crossword puzzle of genius, here and there funny or moving but in general almost as dead an end as Gertrude Stein's prior experiments." Macdonald had spent time at Northwestern, at Ellmann's invitation. In the review, he describes having "once attended a session of a Finnegan Club . . . in which a dozen savants from various departments, including Mr. Ellmann, spent two hours on three on four pages; I was struck by the ingenuity of their hypotheses and also by the number of words they had to give up on."

In addition to reviews in places most likely to attract potential general readers, *James Joyce* was reviewed in a wide range of regional newspapers and periodicals. At the time of the National Book Awards, the *Saturday Review* published an article titled "SR Polls the Nation's Press for 1959's Best." "Curious to know how the daily and weekly newspaper book critics would vote were they on the [National Book Award] panel," the magazine asked some forty respondents to name one title in each category, poetry, fiction, and nonfiction. With poetry, "there were so many abstentions that no title could be said to have won." Fiction, one respondent wrote, voicing "the opinion of many," "was pretty undistinguished last year. . . . My selection represents not so much enthusiasm as the necessity for singling out something." Nonfiction, in contrast, "presented no real problem." "Critics have agreed that Ellmann has written a definitive biography." The *Saturday Review*'s own review, written by Stuart Gilbert, called *James Joyce* "a biography that we are justified on every count in regarding as definitive." Gilbert never mentions *Finnegans Wake,* despite identifying Joyce as "above all a great creator in the sphere of language."[16]

Reviews in England were mixed. In the *Spectator,* Frank Kermode began by describing the biography as "superlatively good."

> It assembles with a mastery Joyce himself would have admired, a great mass of published and unpublished testimony; it proceeds without the least fuss or affectation; and it is informed by critical comment of high quality, all the more effective for being sparingly inserted. Joyce himself once tried to explain how difficult everything must be "when your life

> and work make one," and couldn't even finish his sentence. Here, in 800 pages of remarkable authority, Mr. Ellmann finishes it for him, and fixes Joyce's image for a generation.

After voicing reservations about the appeal of *Ulysses,* Kermode turns to the "Joyce industry," whose denizens "know so much about *Ulysses* that they call 'the older studies' merely the work of cultivated amateurs. The articles in such a miscellany [the *James Joyce Quarterly,* mentioned earlier in the review], some dry, some brilliant, are not in need of defence. At worst they contain useful hints, or they are part of a very intelligent game like that played by the Austenite *élite* who send each other incredibly difficult questionnaires about the *oeuvre.* The underlying assumption is that the books involved are *fully* meaningful, that the reality of each is confirmed by occult relations and laws that often wait long for discovery."[17]

At the time of Kermode's review, both academic and general readers in Britain shared a common skepticism about Joyce, shaped in part by the influence of F. R. Leavis and *Scrutiny,* the literary journal he founded in 1932. Leavis had granted Joyce "genius" but thought him fundamentally unserious. *Ulysses,* despite moments of power, was disfigured by "inorganic elaborations and pedantries," *Finnegans Wake* "in any bulk [was] not worth the labour in reading." Critics who compare Joyce's mastery of language with Shakespeare's fail to appreciate a crucial difference between the two writers: Shakespeare's "medium was for him strictly a medium"; for Joyce, "the interest in words and their possibilities comes first."[18] Writing in 2004, Joseph Brooker reformulated this view: for Joyce "words are savored for their own sake, material signifiers sundered from the meanings with which they ought rightly to be coupled. The Joycean word, allowed to revolt against referentiality, is confronted only with its equally autonomous fellows; language grows sick on its own narcissism."[19]

William Empson's review in the *New Statesman* is largely free of the Leavis viewpoint. Like Kermode, he begins with praise: "It is a grand biography, and must be the last of its kind about Joyce, because Mr. Ellmann, as well as summarising all previous reports, has interviewed a number of witnesses who are now dead." Then comes what Empson elsewhere calls "argufying," principally over the nature of the evidence Ellmann draws on and the attitude he takes toward Joyce's politics. Empson accuses Ellmann of "often reporting gossip," credulously believing that "Dubliners usually make the remarks which are attributed to them" (a quote found on p. 105 of the biography). The prime example Empson cites concerns Joyce's treatment of Nora when in 1904 they eloped to Paris. Stopping in London, as we have seen, Joyce left Nora in a park "for two hours while he went to see Arthur Symons. She thought he would not return." This anecdote (retold on p. 185 of the biography) came from Joyce's sister Eva, whom Empson suggests had ample reason to bring it "to quite a high polish when it was reported forty years later. This is not really a scientific way to write biography. . . . It is a libel on Nora to believe so easily that she ran away with a man whom she was expecting to abandon her; and other sources report her as merely cross at the time." What especially bothers Empson in this instance is that the source of the anecdote is identified in an endnote rather than in the main text and that "if you follow the index under Eva Joyce" you eventually learn that on the way to Trieste with Joyce in 1909, in Empson's paraphrase, she was "greatly upset by being left with his young son in a park in Paris while he succeeded in recovering a ring given him by Nora."

Empson's objection to Ellmann's treatment of Joyce's politics is that when Joyce says he is a socialist "he gets jeered at heartily" by Ellmann, who jokes that "he needed a redistribution of wealth if he was to be a spendthrift." As Empson points out, "Joyce went on saying he was a socialist, and showed understanding of the theory in talking about it." He also made clear his distance from the right-wing views of fellow modernists, declaring, "The more I hear of the political, philosophical, ethical zeal and labours of the brilliant members of Pound's big brass band the more I wonder why I was ever let into it." Empson claims to have been baffled at first by Ellmann's ridiculing of Joyce's politics: "then I realised that, to an American, a socialist is a Commy, and it would hardly be more shocking if Joyce had said he was a cannibal, so the only thing for Ellmann to do is to laugh it tenderly off." Ellmann "has every right" to find Joyce's ideas "harmful and ridiculous, but he is somehow committed to a duty of insinuating that Joyce hadn't really got any revolutionary ideals at all."[20]

Ellmann fared better in the English broadsheets. In the *Sunday Times* Cyril Connolly marveled at his "scholarship, patience, industry, and devotion." So detailed is *James Joyce,* he writes, that "I must be about the only person who knew Joyce [who was] not to be mentioned in it." Ellmann is also praised for moments in which "he steps in for a judgment or a brief estimate of one of Joyce's works." In such moments, "he is both penetrating and sympathetic." For Connolly, "it is this gift of criticism held in reserve which makes this book a truly masterly biography, wise in its completeness. If Joyce is a great writer, then this is a great book." But *is* Joyce a great writer? Connolly is not sure. To begin with, "he asks too much of his ideal reader." This view he describes as "an English heresy and may account for the way we lag behind America in our appreciation of Joyce (or is it our lack of subsidised theses?)." "Am I the only person," Connolly wonders, who finds "the plans and keys and clues and commentaries on Joyce's books more exhilarating than the originals?" The review ends with Connolly's admission that he has "marked some sixty interesting points (and only one mistake) in this most admirable book, and not left space to deal with them. Anything further to be said I must leave to Mr. Ellmann's fortunate readers."[21]

There were two other reviews in influential broadsheets. In the *Daily Telegraph,* Anthony Powell described the biography as "definitive . . . excellently done . . . presenting in a palatable form an enormous amount of material and research." Powell distinguishes between early Joyce and the Joyce "dedicated to making a revolution in writing, the infinitely accomplished parodist, the etymologist obsessed with words. Finally, in 'Finnegans Wake,' the etymologist won, driving out the artist." Ellmann's biography "shows how all this happened." The review ends: "He [Ellmann] is admiring but not abject; he does not moralise, but at the same time he does not evade all moral issues. He has, in short, written a fascinating book about an extraordinary man and a great writer—even if Joyce were not quite so great as he himself liked to think."[22] The last of the broadsheet reviews, in the *Guardian,* was written by Matthew Hodgart. It, too, begins with praise for Ellmann's research, "a triumph of mid-twentieth-century technique, based on the tape-recorder and the card-index." Hodgart especially admires Ellmann's "judgment and tact," his "sense of comedy," his "elegant prose," and his literary criticism ("here Mr. Ellmann is at his best"). His only complaint is that the prose "never quite catches fire."[23]

A complaint similar to Hodgart's was voiced in the lead review of the November 20 issue of the *Times Literary Supplement,* which was important to Ellmann and OUP because of its wide academic as well as general readership. The anonymous author of the review, Anthony Cronin, an Irish poet and critic, begins by praising the wealth of new information provided by the book. He then accuses Ellmann of missing the wood for the trees, objecting also to Ellmann's even-handedness, the fact that Joyce is sometimes presented as heroic and sometimes as weak and foolish. Ellmann's depiction is "confusing," "undiscriminating," especially given the "endlessness" of the research. It is "rather difficult, as in life itself, to see the central figure steadily, and to see him whole." That Joyce *was* difficult to see steadily or whole, of course, is why the biography depicts him as such. Hodgart's complaint that Ellmann's prose "never quite catches fire" may owe something to this objection, which admirers praise as detachment or balance.

Like other reviewers in the English press, Cronin looks down on American Joyceans, describing them as "hermeneutical exegesists" whose "piety is off-putting." Ellmann, presumably, is excluded from this criticism, given his depiction of Joyce as sometimes weak and foolish; nevertheless, he is an American, "aided by the bounty of no fewer than five separate American organizations." The review ends: "It is a pity that while he was so busily putting so much in (and we should be grateful for it all) he appears also to have left something out."

Ellmann was angered by the review in the *Times Literary Supplement* (whether he knew Cronin had written it is uncertain, since *TLS* reviews were anonymous until 1974). He replied to it in the December 11 issue of the paper, in a letter directly following a letter from F. R. Leavis complaining about a different article. Most of Ellmann's letter addresses what he describes as the review's "errors" ("Your reviewer reproves me for discussing Joyce's drinking as if it were in any way notable, for, as he has observed independently, many people drink." "This is an agreeable theory, but it does not fit the facts, by which unfortunately a biographer must be limited.") As for the review's larger complaint that the book's depiction of Joyce is "confusing," Ellmann attributes it to an unwillingness to accept that "grandeur can live with human weaknesses."

A similar unwillingness marks the most important of the Irish reviews, that of Andrew Cass in the *Irish Times*. That Ellmann was "detached," Cass worries, jokingly, "might lead one to suspect that more is to come." Hence his hope that the book's bulk will result in its being called "definitive," as a result "discouraging others from out-inching Ellmann." The rest of the review is devoted to minor mistakes: the name of Mr. Seamus Wilmot is written 'Sean Wilmot,'" "There is no such office as 'Chief Justice of the High Court," "A mere Irishman would require further information as to the meaning of 'Irish Claddhagh or shawl.'"[24]

The unenthusiastic, at times caustic, reviews by Cronin and Cass were representative. In 1959, Irish literary attitudes to American Joyceans, according to Brooker's detailed account in *Joyce's Critics,* swung "between mockery and outright contempt." He cites Oliver Gogarty's "impatience with 'almost all literate North America,' showing 'genuine regard for every syllable of our bad boy from Belvedere'"; Niall Montgomery is quoted on Harry Levin, one of "the subtle overseas doctors in whom, under martial aid, are vested the exegetic rights in the Swiss master's work."[25] In *The Irish Writer and the World* (2005), Declan Kiberd recalls an anecdote Ellmann told him about meeting the poet Austin Clarke in the men's urinal by O'Connell Bridge. This was shortly after Clarke had savaged one of his books on Yeats in a review. "'Are you the man I think you are?' [Ellmann] asked tentatively. 'I'll wait until we're both completely finished before I answer your interesting question,' drawled the laconic Clarke, before adding the single word immortalised in a hundred cowboy films, 'pard'ner.'"[26] Ellmann suffered less of this treatment than more "pious" contemporaries, Kiberd believes, because he was "not in search of 'Irishness' but of the greatest modern artists who just happened to be Irish." Hence the friendships with Frank O'Connor and Sean O'Faolain, who had no time for "shamrockery" or "paddywhackery."[27] But to others, he remained an American, with his money and his file-card box, the prime target, he believed, of Patrick Kavanagh's poem "Who Killed James Joyce?"

Who killed James Joyce?
I, said the commentator,
I killed James Joyce
For my graduation

What weapon was used
To slay mighty Ulysses?
The weapon that was used
Was a Harvard thesis.

How did you bury Joyce?
In a broadcast Symposium.
That's how we buried Joyce
To a tuneful encomium.

. . .
Who killed Finnegan?
I said a Yale-man,
I was the man who made
The corpse for the wake man.

And did you get high marks,
The Ph.D.?
I got the B.Litt
And my master's degree.

Did you get money
For your Joycean knowledge?
I got a scholarship
To Trinity College.[28]

* * *

The acclaim *James Joyce* received in America was followed by the awarding of prizes. The first was the Carey-Thomas Award, "For a distinguished project of book publishing . . . as adjudged by a jury of five nominated by the office of *Publishers' Weekly*." The president of OUP in New York, John R. B. Brett-Smith, wrote to Ellmann on December 10, 1959, to say that though many people associated with the book deserved credit for the award, "the author on the one hand and Fon Boardman on the other should get the lion's share." Ellmann was invited to the award presentation at the Hotel Roosevelt in New York on January 7, 1960. Three weeks later, in an article in the January 29, 1960, issue of *Publishers' Weekly,* the reason *James Joyce* won was explained: "It grew from an anticipated book of 100,000 words to a fat tome containing about 300,000 words and sixteen pages of half-tones, necessitating a 'horrifying price of $12.50.' Fortunately, the venturesome publisher can report that the book received an acceptance by the trade unprecedented for a literary biography and went through a second printing before publication date, bringing the total number of copies in the trade edition to 15,000."

The prize that mattered most to the book's fortunes was the National Book Award for Nonfiction, which was presented for *James Joyce* on March 23, 1960, at five o'clock, in the Grand Ballroom of the Hotel Astor in New York. Ellmann and the other winners—Philip Roth for fiction

(*Good-Bye Columbus*) and Robert Lowell for poetry (*Life Studies*)—were presented with checks for $1,000. The award ceremony was attended by what the *New Yorker* described as "something like a thousand writers of books, publishers of books, reviewers of books, and thirsty skimmers of books." Before the ceremony there was an hour-long press conference at which journalists took photographs, asked questions, and were treated by the winners, again according to the *New Yorker,* "like well-intentioned ignorant children." Ellmann was congratulated on having "accumulated such a heavy mass of material on Joyce and asked, in effect, whether he had purposely refrained from interpreting it. With a charming smile, Dr. Ellmann said that he had been under the misapprehension that he *had* interpreted it." When the questioner later came up to Ellmann and hinted that she was going to use his book "as a source for a real study of Joyce, Ellmann went right on smiling."[29]

At the ceremony proper, before "the largest turnout the National Book Awards ever has known," the three winners were seated on stage with their judges behind them, like proud parents.[30] The winners then spoke in turn at the rostrum. Ellmann was introduced as the author of a biography that the nonfiction judges called "vital and monumentally complete . . . a shapely book written in an unobtrusively distinguished style." In an article about the ceremony in the *New Leader,* Leslie Fiedler, who had been a judge in 1957, described Ellmann's speech as quarreling "like a critic with other critics, defending the long biography." The other celebrities Fiedler spotted at the ceremony included John Barth, Amy Vanderbilt, and Ayn Rand, a finalist for the fiction award in 1958, looking around with "a mad glare." He also spotted Allen Drury, who would win the year's Pulitzer Prize for Fiction for *Advise and Consent.* Whether Samuel Eliot Morison was there, Fiedler does not say. Morison's *John Paul Jones,* a life of the naval commander, which was chosen after the National Book Award, beat *James Joyce* to the year's Pulitzer Prize in Biography.[31] A week after winning the National Book Award, Ellmann won a third prize: the Thormod Monsen Award, sponsored by the Society of Midland Authors, winning a check for $500.

In an article of March 29, 1960, in the *Daily Northwestern,* titled "Ellmann Gets More Awards," the happy biographer confessed to being "very pleased, particularly because the book is so big and heavy. . . . I suppose I'll use the money to buy a Citroen station wagon in Italy next year." He was going to Italy, taking his family with him, because Dean Simeon Leland had awarded him with a year's paid leave, part of a lucrative employment package to keep him at Northwestern. One impetus for the package, in addition to the success of *James Joyce,* was Ellmann's having informed the dean of job offers from the University of Chicago, the University of Virginia, and Emory University. "I'm delighted that you've decided to cast your lot with Northwestern," wrote Leland, in a letter of February 5, 1960:

> I hope this is a permanent decision and that you continue to have your career here among friends who know, love and appreciate you. . . . It makes me happy to tell you that your salary for the academic year will be $20,000.00 [roughly $208,000 today] . . . I am also recommending a leave of absence for you at full pay for the academic year 1960–61 and assume, as part of our obligation to you, a similar leave every third year, plus $2,000 each year "for such research needs as may occur in any given year."

In an addendum of February 12 to the terms of his employment, Ellmann was told, "The Dean has no objection to your using your year of absence for whatever you wish—even to teach elsewhere. You are such a productive scholar under any circumstances. . . . Besides it would do the University great good for you to accept the kind of honor you are likely to receive—the Beckman Lectureship, for example."

Ten days later Ellmann was invited to spend the second semester of the academic year 1960–1961 as the Beckman Professor of English Language and Literature at the University of California at Berkeley, following in the footsteps of Harry Levin, Stephen Spender, and Samuel Monk. He would be paid $10,000 to teach a single course and deliver several public lectures. This offer he declined. Later in 1960 he was made a member of the American Academy, an honorary society for US citizens in the creative arts. At Northwestern, more than one hundred students registered for "The Novel as a Literary Form" (C16), a discussion course with a planned enrollment of twenty-five. On April 1, 1960, the *Daily Northwestern* reported that Ellmann had compromised by excluding sixty-five applicants.[32] During the semester, he delivered lectures at Mount Holyoke, Smith, Amherst, Cornell, Michigan, Missouri, and Southern Illinois (where he visited with H. K. Croessmann in nearby Du Quoin). At Columbia, he spoke at the English

Institute; later, in 1962, he became chairman of that institute and joined the executive council of the Modern Language Association.[33]

The dean was not wrong about Ellmann's productivity. In the next ten years he published a second edition of *The Identity of Yeats* (1964); edited a new edition of *A Portrait of the Artist as a Young Man* (1964); edited, with Charles Feidelson, *The Modern Tradition: Backgrounds of Modern Literature* (1965); edited volumes 2 and 3 of *Letters of James Joyce* (1966); published a study of Yeats's influence, *Eminent Domain: Yeats among Wilde, Joyce, Pound, Eliot and Auden* (1967); and edited from manuscript Joyce's previously unpublished poetic fragment *Giacomo Joyce* (1968). During this period, in 1966, he also committed to a new full-length biographical project, a life of Oscar Wilde. In addition, he began reviewing for the *New Statesman, Encounter,* the *New York Times Book Review,* and the *New York Review of Books.*

* * *

Two of the books published in the decade after *James Joyce* deserve attention because of the evidence they provide of Ellmann's growing influence in academic English, an influence likely to draw readers to *James Joyce.* On American campuses in particular, *The Modern Tradition* became a staple of survey courses on modern and contemporary literature. In "Ellmann's Road to Xanadu," Ellsworth Mason describes it as "probably the most important book in exposing the kinds of ideas that underlie 20th century art, and beyond that the world of practical action and human culture." The topical headings under which the anthology's excerpts are grouped, Mason claims, provide "the groundwork for a general theory of modernism . . . demonstrating how wide is the range of ideas that must be taken into consideration in developing such a theory."[34]

The influence of *Eminent Domain* was more specialized. In addition to its accounts of Yeats and the individual writers he influenced, it offers an account of literary influence in general, one that predates Harold Bloom's *The Anxiety of Influence* (1970).[35] Bloom knew Ellmann and was working on a book on Yeats at the time when he was developing his own theories of influence. That book, also published in 1970 and titled *Yeats,* was dedicated to Ellmann and Martin Price, and frequently cites *Eminent Domain.* It is odd, therefore, that *The Anxiety of Influence* makes no mention of *Eminent Domain,* including of its opening paragraph, which reads as follows:

> "Influence" is a term which conceals and mitigates the guilty acquisitiveness of talent. That writers flow into each other like waves, gently rather than tidally, is one of those decorous myths we impose upon a high-handed, even brutal procedure. The behavior, while not invariably marked by bad temper, is less polite. Writers move upon other writers not as genial successors but as violent expropriators, knocking down established boundaries to seize by the force of youth, or of age, what they require. They do not borrow, they override.[36]

As the critic Neil Corcoran puts it: "Rewritten with energetic conviction and terminological brio, this is essentially the view of *The Anxiety of Influence*."[37] As previous chapters have shown, Ellmann was competitive as well as mild-mannered, fierce in protecting what he saw as his discoveries. According to his daughter Maud, what he thought of Harold Bloom was that he "had stolen his ideas from *Eminent Domain* and vulgarized them."[38] When Bloom died in 2019, he was the most famous literary critic in America, largely for attacks on what he called "resentnik" critics avid to point out canonical writers' failings (omissions, bias, naïveté). Bloom's fame began, though, with his theories of influence. *The Anxiety of Influence* was translated into fifty-five languages. Ellmann's feelings can be imagined when in 1983 Bloom was appointed Sterling Professor of Humanities at Yale, though by this date he himself was Goldsmiths' Professor of English Literature at Oxford. That he cared about prestige posts is suggested in the opening of an undated manuscript titled "New College Speech": "When I was a boy growing up in Detroit, Michigan, the two universities talked of in hushed tones were Yale and Harvard. Then when I got to Yale and Harvard, the two universities discussed in hush tones were Oxford and Cambridge. I suppose there must be some university in the sky beyond Oxbridge, but I'm not hurrying to that one."[39]

* * *

The standing of *James Joyce* among academic Joyceans could not have been higher in the decade after its publication. The *James Joyce Quarterly*, founded in 1963 by Thomas Staley, is the earliest and most influential of journals devoted to Joyce. Ellmann's *James Joyce* is the only text not written by Joyce to be referred to in the *Quarterly* by its own standard abbreviation, *JJ*. According to Joseph Brooker, "The word 'Ellmann' itself, like

'Bloom' [Leopold, that is, not Harold] or 'Weaver,' has an instant significance for anyone concerned with Joyce, usually functioning as shorthand for a reference to the 1959 biography."[40] Robert Scholes, the editor of the Cornell Joyce collection, thought "that Ellmann's presence as co-editor of the Viking Press *Portrait* was invoked 'ritualistically, for the sake of his prestige in matters Joycean.'"[41] "Other major writers," Bernard McGinley declares, "can have many biographers. Joyce, for historical reasons and because of the diverse skills of Ellmann, has only one that matters. 'It's in Ellmann' became epistemologically final—the last word."[42] In the *Hudson Review,* Robert M. Adams, its editor, the author of several books on Joyce, and a founding editor of the *Norton Anthology of English Literature,* called *James Joyce* "the best literary biography of our time."[43] Other Joyceans compared *James Joyce* to Boswell's *Life of Johnson.*[44]

In the twenty-three years separating the first and second editions of *James Joyce,* Ellmann continued to work on Joyce, publishing two books of interpretation, *Ulysses on the Liffey* (1972) and *The Consciousness of Joyce* (1977), editing the *Selected Letters* (1975) (in which the "dirty letters" of 1909 are printed in their entirety), authoring articles and essays in collections, writing reviews of books about Joyce, and speaking at conferences. In the second decade of this period, however, as critical fashion among academic Joyceans changed, the underlying principles of Ellmann's approach to Joyce's writings, both as a biographer and as a critic, were called into question. In the 1970s, scholars began to chafe under claims that the biography was "definitive." Such claims were voiced by reviewers, it should be recalled, not by its author, who made clear his opposition to the term. In "Literary Biography," for example, his 1971 inaugural lecture as Goldsmiths' Professor, he says flatly that "biographical possibilities cannot be exhausted; we cannot know completely the intricacies with which any mind negotiates with its surroundings to produce literature. . . . Whatever the [biographer's] method, it can give only incomplete satisfaction."[45] But the "definitive" label stuck, inciting rival scholars to scour *James Joyce* for faults and failings, at times with "resentnik" zeal.[46]

Chief among Ellmann's antagonists was Hugh Kenner, identified by Harold Bloom as "pope to the alternative tradition to that of Ellmann in Joyce studies."[47] Kenner was a critic of acute, if eccentric, insight (Beckett called his criticism "very brilliant and erudite but dementedly over-explicative")[48] and took against Ellmann's approach to Joyce from the start. He wrote his 1950 PhD on Joyce at Yale under Cleanth Brooks and, though hardly a New Critic, shared the New Critics' distrust of biography. In his first book, *Dublin's Joyce* (1956), he aligns himself with Ezra Pound's view of *Ulysses,* describing the novel as "an inferno whose apotheosis is the debris-crammed brain of hapless Leopold Bloom." In Brooker's words, for Kenner, "*Ulysses* emerges as an even more caustic book than Harry Levin had suspected."[49] Also at odds with Ellmann's reading is Kenner's much-anthologized account of Stephen Dedalus, which argues powerfully against identifying Stephen with Joyce. Kenner's account first appeared in an abridged form as "The *Portrait* in Perspective" in the *Kenyon Review* in 1947, then in Seon Givens's *Two Decades of Criticism* (1948); then, reedited, it became a chapter in Kenner's *Dublin's Joyce.*[50] Because Ellmann was unembarrassed about drawing connections between Stephen and Joyce, and saw *Ulysses* and Bloom so differently, he and Kenner were bound to clash.

Open hostilities began when Kenner reviewed *James Joyce* in the November 21, 1959, issue of William F. Buckley's *National Review,* which was in its fourth year at the time. In "Biography by the Ground Rules," Kenner criticizes Ellmann's focus on material matters: "The life of the mind, so far as Joyce himself led it, is allowed to amount to very little. Much energy has gone into chronicling the shillings various men lent him, how many, on what date, and whether they were repaid." He also objects to what he sees as Ellmann's tone: "It is legitimate to feel faintly superior to a man who could handle neither money nor wine, lived on the bounty of others, and was obsessed with the writing of books like that. He could never have held down an American professorship, it is clear."

Kenner was himself a professor, at the Santa Barbara College of the University of California (not yet the University of California, Santa Barbara), but as he wrote to his friend, the poet and critic Guy Davenport, in a letter of January 18, 1961, Harvard and Yale "wouldn't, I imagine, touch me with an 11-foot pole. I have been too impolitic for too long. One doesn't pan Ellmann and boycott the MLA and quarrel with Tate and write for *National Review* . . . and praise Wyndham Lewis and get away with it." On May 19, 1962, again to Davenport, Kenner says he is "hated by Levin and Ellmann . . . the object or subject [of] a conspiracy of scholars." On March 6, 1963, he complains of being "boycotted" by "the professional Irish who own James Joyce and whose branch office is R. Ellmann."[51]

Ellmann had read *Dublin's Joyce* when it came out in 1956 and had not been impressed. "He turns Joyce into an anti-Romantic and pro-Catholic," he tells H. K. Croessmann, in a letter of July 8, 1956, "and I think is wrong on both counts; but I'd rather you didn't mention this as I may someday review his book. His manner seems to me insufferable." It was not until 1975, however, in the *TLS,* that Ellmann hit back publicly, making fun of an essay Kenner had written in a collection of essays on *Ulysses.*[52] In his essay Kenner conjectures that Stephen Dedalus must have punched Buck Mulligan at Westland Road Station, sometime between the "Oxen of the Sun" and "Circe" episodes. Ellmann mocks this conjecture as "a new way of reading *Ulysses* by sparking up the plot," adding that Kenner has forgotten Joyce's distaste for violence, misreading "the ideology that informs the book." In the same review Ellmann takes a swipe at Kenner's *The Pound Era* (1971), the most influential of his books: "Mr. Kenner has been turning Joyce topsy-turvy for many years now, always asserting that Joyce was totally jaundiced towards the modern world."[53] The question of Joyce's attitude to "the modern world" is central to the differences between the two men. To quote Brooker: "Point for point, character by character, much of what Ellmann reads as sincere or affirmative is inverted by Kenner's work, interpreted as black comedy or ironic mockery on Joyce's part."[54]

A year after Ellmann's *TLS* review, Kenner hit back. In the *New York Times Book Review,* he panned Ellmann's *New Oxford Book of American Verse,* beginning with its introduction, which he thought too long and an attempt to compensate for "residence at Oxford among people who frown politely and frostily when Americans mention their poets."[55] He also complains about the absence of long poems. (In private, to Davenport, Kenner offered an explanation for the absence of poems by Louis Zukovsky, a poet known for his long poems. "He is omitted, by the by, not only from books on lit'ry NYC but also from Ellmann's New Oxford Bk of Am. Verse. Noting how many tastemakers are Jewish, I wonder if the explanation may not lie in some Jewish class struggle. Jews EXCLUDE other Jews for the subtlest reasons. And if you were an Ellmann, i.e. an on-the-make Sammy Glick, the kind of tribal totem you'd most like to kick in the stomach would be a rabbinical superego of the sort personified by LZ."[56]) Two years later, in a 1978 essay titled "Literary Biographies," Kenner upbraids Ellmann for getting details of Joyce's birth and baptism wrong, the sorts of mistakes "familiar to any grader of sophomore papers." He also attacks biography *per se,* as "finally" fiction. "If unlike the novelist the biographer can't invent fact, he can invent ways of covering its absence."[57]

Kenner's anti-biographical views are most fully and forcefully voiced in his *TLS* review of the 1982 second edition of *James Joyce,* published to coincide with the centennial of Joyce's birth. Titled "The Impertinence of Being Definitive," the review has three core complaints: that Ellmann makes factual errors; that he is too trusting of the tales he is told, often from biased or unreliable sources (for Ellmann, "the Irish fact [is] definable as anything they tell you in Ireland"); and that he draws on the fiction to interpret the life, often without acknowledgment. So seamless, or seamless-seeming, is Ellmann's narrative account of the interdependence of life and art that the reader is tempted to believe, in Kenner's words, that Joyce "put down little that he'd not actually seen and heard: indeed possessed so little imagination that 'imaginative' became a word of courtesy." That Joyce himself belittled his imaginative powers to Ezra Pound, Frank Budgen, and Jacques Mercanton does not mean he should be taken at his word. Doing so means that "testimony however shaky to an event that turns up in [Joyce's] writing acquires high plausibility."

The effect of Kenner's review was to dent the reputation of *James Joyce* among literary academics, a result younger Joyceans welcomed because it helped to clear space for further work—not just correcting errors, inevitable in so detailed a book, but attending to aspects of Joyce's life and writing that were overlooked, simplified, or elided by Ellmann. One scholar, Ronald Bush, went so far as to say that the effect of the second edition was to provide "an occasion to think about how the 1959 original, for all its virtues, might have hindered the processes of coming to terms with Joyce." Another scholar, Ira B. Nadel, described *James Joyce* as having contributed to "a critical and methodological paralysis" in Joyce studies that "has obstructed as much as it has defined aspects of Joyce's life."[58] Morris Beja, author of *James Joyce: A Literary Life* (1992), a book of 168 pages, thought that "a new, full length detailed biography would, if done well, be of immense service to Joyce scholarship. After all, every year, it seems, the world is given another full-length biography of D. H. Lawrence, or Joseph Conrad, or Ernest Hemingway, or William Faulkner—and one about Virginia Woolf just about every month, or so it sometimes seems. Why isn't there a similar degree of activity in the realm of Joyce biography? Of course a major element of any informed answer to that question would center on the massive influence and presence of Richard Ellmann's *James Joyce*, published in 1959."[59]

In contrast to reactions like these, the reception accorded the second edition by non-Joyceans, including academic non-Joyceans, was mostly celebratory. In Britain, *James Joyce* was awarded the 1983 James Tait Black Prize and the 1983 Duff Cooper Prize. In the States it was lauded once again on the front page of the *New York Times Book Review.* The bibliographer Philip Gaskell, librarian of Trinity College, Cambridge, reviewed the second edition in *Essays in Criticism,* calling it "not so much revised as added to, rather as Joyce himself had developed the text of *Ulysses.*" "Practically the whole of *JJI* is reprinted in *JJII* and the new material is silently slipped in. As Ellmann says in his prefatory note, 'more pages have been altered than not, by insertions ranging from a line to a page or more'; and he adds 'Many corrections (besides those entered on two occasions in earlier printings) have also been made." As for critics of the edition, as Gaskell puts it, "Those who were dissatisfied with major features of his account (such as Hugh Kenner . . .) are not going to find that Ellmann has changed his position. Neither has Ellmann intended to change his position." What is new, "besides the very large number of minor details added throughout the book," are Ellmann's "richly comical" accounts of Joyce's "unconsummated affairs" with Marthe Fleischmann and Gertrude Kaempffer. Chief among the materials that might have been included and are not, Gaskell notes, are the 1909 erotic letters, despite having been printed in full and discussed in the 1975 *Selected Letters.* Gaskell's review concludes: "Despite this carping—for my complaints are small ones in the context of the work as a whole—Ellmann's *Joyce* remains a magnificent and unrepeatable accumulation of the facts of Joyce's life, a truly great biography which leaves the reader who is disposed to disagree with any of the author's interpretations of the facts at liberty to do so."[60]

Christopher Ricks, an editor of *Essays in Criticism,* reviewed the second edition in the American periodical *Grand Street.* His review begins by reminding readers that Ellmann was "the man who did most to establish that a great feat of twentieth-century literary scholarship could take as its subject a twentieth-century figure. Today it is obvious enough; in 1959 it was either not obvious or not acknowledged." Ricks then lists five "niggling" criticisms, the last of which concerns the book's illustrations. Although these "have been quadrupled (from thirty to one hundred and seventeen), their quality in reproduction has been quartered (not Ellmann's fault, but still), as sometimes their size has been." That Ricks offers only minor criticisms, he readily admits, "others will find wide-eyed," especially those who have read what he calls Hugh Kenner's "wittily elaborated interrogation" in the *TLS.* When Ricks turns to the Joyce of *Finnegans Wake,* however, by way of a comparison of Joyce with Beckett, the extremity of his rejection of the work contains an implicit (inadvertent?) rebuke to Ellmann's seeming caution:

> Beckett, who wrote one of the earliest and one of the very best appreciations of *Finnegans Wake* (*Work in Progress,* as it then was), has nevertheless since created in his own art an achievement which cannot but expose as tragically wasteful the linguistic and literary theories that hurried Joyce from life and that enslaved him to his preposterous and bankrupting pet, *Finnegans Wake.* Ulysses was in no doubt that you should fear the gifts of such givers as he; the author of *Ulysses* came to forget that the one gift more ruinous than a wooden horse is a white elephant.[61]

This view, from a champion of *James Joyce,* was very much out of favor among younger Joyceans by the early 1980s, and Kenner challenges it implicitly in the last sentence of "The Impertinence of Being Definitive." In the preface to the second edition ("Mark II" in Kenner's review), Ellmann describes Joyce as "this bizarre and wonderful creature who turned literature and language on end," to which Kenner replies: "That seems insufficient, as regrettably, does Mark II." In contrast, from the start of his career Kenner had foregrounded the ways Joyce turns literature and language on end, not just in the later episodes of *Ulysses* and in *Finnegans Wake* but in all his writings. His affinities to younger Joyce scholars influenced by French theory (Derrida, Lacan, Kristeva, and Cixous all wrote on Joyce) are clear.[62]

One such scholar, Derek Attridge, traces the rise of post-structuralist approaches to Joyce to two gatherings in 1982, the year of both Joyce's centennial and the second edition of *James Joyce.* The first of these gatherings, a colloquium in Paris, was attended by French as well as English speakers and served as a sort of trial run for the second, a panel at the International Centennial James Joyce Symposium in Dublin, to be held on and around Bloomsday.[63] In the "mainly autobiographical" section of the introduction to his book *Joyce Effects: On Language, Theory, and History* (2000), Attridge describes the Dublin panel as "a thin wedge of 'French theory' in the Joycean critical discourse." Two years later, at the International James Joyce Symposium in Frankfurt, it had become "the dominant approach to

Joyce's writing." One of the speakers at the 1984 symposium was Jacques Derrida, who spoke on "Deconstructive Criticism of Joyce." In *Joyce Effects,* Attridge describes Derrida's talk as "memorable, among other things, for its brilliance, its humour, its extreme length, and for the fact that a large part of the audience could not follow, since it was in French with only brief English summaries interpolated by a heroic translator."[64] Ellmann was also at the Frankfurt symposium, though whether he attended Derrida's lecture is not clear. He was present, though, when Stephen Joyce attacked him in public for printing the 1909 "dirty letters." "I condemn and deplore this intolerable shameless invasion of privacy," he said, looking directly at Ellmann, "as would my grandparents, were they standing beside me today."[65] Ellmann also faced the indignity of seeing Kenner awarded the first Thomas Gear Gold Medal for outstanding services to Joyce scholarship.

If the 1984 symposium had unpleasant moments for Ellmann, the 1982 Dublin Centennial Symposium had been a triumph. Ellmann came to it having previously lectured on Joyce in France, Portugal, Lebanon, Spain, England, and the United States. In addition to delivering the opening speech at the symposium, he agreed to be on a panel on Joyce and Yeats (usually he delivered only keynote addresses). The other panelists were A. Walton Litz of Princeton and Giorgio Melchiori of the University of Rome, and the session was so popular that it had to be moved from a classroom in Newman House, University College Dublin, to the Aula Maxima, or great hall, now home to the Museum of Literature Ireland. "All the seats were filled," recalls Ellen Carol Jones, the graduate student who organized the panel, "and the overflow crowd stood arrayed against the back and side walls of the theater." Ellmann, she noticed, spoke from notes scribbled on stationary from the Shelbourne Hotel, the city's grandest.

Also speaking at the Dublin symposium, on the panel Attridge and others had prepared for in Paris, was Ellmann's daughter Maud, which was a source of pride for Ellmann, presumably. Maud does not remember if her father attended the panel.[66] (What she remembers is sitting with her parents in the lounge of the Shelbourne Hotel when her father nudged her and said: "'That's Borges!' And indeed it was.") Ellmann sometimes argued with Maud about her interest in critical theory, he admitted to Henry Hart, a student of his at Oxford. He also seems to have had reservations about Maud's often indirect approaches to Joyce's writing, characterizing them to Hart as lacking "meat and potatoes; it's all cranberry sauce." Hart "knew what it was like to have theoretical discussions categorically censured by Ellmann" and "sympathized with Maud."[67] What Maud's fellow panelists—if not Maud herself—thought of Ellmann and his "tradition" is suggested by Attridge, who describes *James Joyce* as "stressing the humanity and precision of [Joyce's] portrayals of human life and minimizing his games with the medium of representation—which usually meant dismissing *Finnegans Wake* and giving short shrift to *Ulysses* from 'Sirens' on." For Attridge, to properly weigh both Joyce's games with representation and his later works requires more than "an academic interest in the writing and life of James Joyce." It requires "a certain attitude to literature and to experience, a certain capacity to relish, without feeling threatened or becoming defensive, the imperfect world in all its multiplicity and messiness."[68]

* * *

Ellmann's decision not to engage with critical theory in the second edition of *James Joyce* or to add much about issues of language and representation can be variously explained. One answer is suggested by what Philip Gaskell in his review in *Essays in Criticism* calls "a minor irritant" of the second edition: "Ellmann's (deliberate) repetition of 'now' from *JJI* even when what was true in 1959 is no longer true in 1982." As Ellmann explains in the brief preface to the second edition: "Since this biography has to some degree the character of the year, 1959, when it first appeared, I have kept references to 'now' though they must be understood as referring to 'then.'" Whether he would have accepted the limiting terms in which some younger Joyceans chose to describe the book's "then" is another question. To John McCourt, who has done much to enrich and complicate the account Ellmann gives of Joyce's years in Trieste, the 1982 edition remains largely what it was: "a wonderful product of a particular time—post-war, conservative, 1950s America." The "typical" reader it sought to address, McCourt suggests, was "much like [Ellmann's] father, much like himself, an American liberal humanist."[69] In 2002, when these words were published in McCourt's essay "Reading Ellmann Reading Joyce," the phrase "liberal American humanist" was vaguely pejorative as well as patronizing, and in some circles still is.

A less charitable explanation for Ellmann's not engaging with new approaches to Joyce is offered by McCourt earlier in the essay. The failure of the 1982 edition "to take on board so much that was new, the fruits of the labours of so many other scholars," was only in part because Ellmann wished it to retain "to some degree the character of the year, 1959." It also derived from the fact that "he believed in his own Joyce, disliked competitors entering his field, and bristled at criticism which threatened his version and its so-called definitiveness."[70] As we have seen, Ellmann was certainly wary of competitors, especially in the run-up to the publication of *James Joyce,* and bristled at criticism (hardly a unique trait). But whether he bristled at criticism because he thought his work definitive is another question. He bristled at Kenner because Kenner's criticism was so aggressive, its manner "insufferable." Kenner belittled not just *his* biography but biography *per se,* characterizing it in the *TLS* review as "not a science but a modest sub-genre of fiction." Kenner also, of course, was in diametric opposition to Ellmann in his interpretation of *Ulysses,* a key to Ellmann's sense of Joyce's achievement. Anyone would have bristled under Kenner's persistent attacks. When Fritz Senn tried to bring the two men together, Ellmann declined "with unusual bitterness. He felt he had been 'hurt too much.'"[71] In 1984 Henry Hart "made the mistake of mentioning Kenner's name." "'I know some people respect Kenner in the States,' Ellmann said in an angry voice. 'But I don't see anything in him.'"[72]

With younger or less formidable critics, even very aggressive ones, Ellmann was more composed. One of the most influential of the up-and-coming English post-structuralists in the early 1970s was Colin MacCabe, who, as a graduate student at Cambridge, wrote what he now calls "a very unpleasant review—a nasty young man's review" of Ellmann's critical study *Ulysses on the Liffey* (1972). In MacCabe's review, in the June 1972 issue of the *Cambridge Review,* he accuses Ellmann of "once again" (as in *James Joyce,* presumably) assuming a "naïve" notion of the "author-subject" (a term from Michel Foucault). According to this naive notion, language is seen merely as an "instrument" used "to convey [the author's] message," a message thought to be "located in Joyce's head." For MacCabe and his fellow theorists, in contrast, Joyce's novels "refuse any reduction to some authorial point of view." The proper approach to Joyce, according to MacCabe, is to abandon any search for "an instrumental giving of sense to a fixed 'world'" and to focus instead on "the processes of the production of sense."[73] In a later review of Jonathan Culler's *Structuralist Poetics* (1975), MacCabe identifies critics like Ellmann with "traditional bourgeois culture." Such critics "refused to try to read modernism on its own terms but had attempted to explain and praise it from early nineteenth century positions."[74]

These views MacCabe elaborated in his first book, *James Joyce and the Revolution of the Word* (1979), the merits of which were heatedly debated two years later by the Cambridge English faculty when he was a candidate for tenure. Those who opposed him, notably Christopher Ricks, claimed that they did so because his book was "bad"; those who supported him claimed he was opposed because he was a theorist and taught post-structuralism to undergraduates. The "MacCabe affair" became a topic of dispute in the newspapers, and almost as soon as he was denied tenure by the Cambridge English faculty, the University of Strathclyde appointed him to a professorship, making him head of its English Department at the age of thirty-two. Twenty-two years later, in the 2003 second edition of *James Joyce and the Revolution of the Word,* MacCabe described his 1972 review of *Ulysses on the Liffey* as "compassionless," and praised Ellmann for the way he reacted to the review. It "in no way deflected his politeness and fairness in my subsequent dealings with him, a lesson that I endeavour to ensure governs all my dealings with the unwashed young."[75] In an interview, MacCabe recalled that when Ellmann was asked to comment on his tenure case ("a perfect opportunity to take revenge") he wrote "very warmly" on his behalf. That Maud Ellmann had been supervised by MacCabe at Cambridge, and thought very highly of him, may have played a part in Ellmann's warmth.[76]

Although Ellmann never engaged in print in the so-called wars of theory, his feelings about individual theorists were clear to his students at Oxford. Hart, an American, had written his undergraduate thesis at Dartmouth on *Finnegans Wake,* but when he approached Ellmann in 1976 to supervise a DPhil on Joyce, Ellmann told him he was "tired of the Joyce industry." When, eventually, Ellmann agreed to supervise a DPhil on Geoffrey Hill, Hart was taken aback not only by his lack of interest in theory but by "his insistence that I delete all references to literary theorists from my thesis." This insistence worried Hart; given academic fashion, he thought the absence of quotations from figures such as Derrida and Bloom "would hurt my chances of getting a degree." (As he got to know Ellmann better, Hart "assumed that in some cases he was reacting against specific scholars who had attacked him.")[77] When another of Ellmann's American DPhil students, Terence Diggory, was at work on a dissertation on Yeats and American poetry, Ellmann reacted to his references to theory by saying: "I'm glad someone knows about these things," a comment that led Diggory to feel "they were clearly things that he was not interested in."[78]

For the most part, Ellmann's personal interactions with theorists were polite and cordial. Jonathan Culler, whose parents knew the Ellmanns at Yale, was treated "very hospitably" by Ellmann and Mary, despite his influential status as a theoretician. Similarly, when Ellmann began teaching at Emory University in Atlanta (for six weeks each spring, between Hilary and Trinity terms at Oxford), he and Mary struck up a friendship with Gayatri Spivak, a self-described "radical" theorist at what she calls "an excellent but somewhat conservative department." Spivak recalls "a good deal" of talk with Ellmann about theory, but no acrimony. So emollient a presence was Ellmann at Emory, according to the Yeats scholar Ronald Schuchard, "that in controversial meetings of the English Department no one could dare to speak impatiently, dismissively, or discourteously to other colleagues in front of him." Spivak remembers learning from him, "often successfully, how to present points of view that might not be necessarily welcome."[79]

* * *

Theoretical approaches to Joyce's life and work were not the only ones Ellmann has been accused of overlooking or slighting in the second edition of *James Joyce.* Chief among these other approaches were new accounts of Joyce's politics; his years in Trieste (of particular importance not only to the creation of *Ulysses,* as McCourt has shown, but to the language of *Finnegans Wake*); the manner in which his works came into existence as revealed in drafts and versions (what today is known as genetic criticism); and his relation to Irish literary culture. In at least two of these areas, Ellmann actively encouraged research. One of his DPhil students, Dominic Manganiello, published a revised version of his thesis, partly biographical, called *Joyce's Politics* (1980), which went some way to answering the strictures of Empson and others; and another of his students, Declan Kiberd, in *Inventing Ireland: The Literature of the Modern Nation* (1995), pioneered the study of "Irish" modernism, as distinct from English or continental modernism. In a 1999 essay, "Joyce's Ellmann, Ellmann's Joyce," Kiberd describes Ellmann as having "held many of the keys to the distinctive features which set Irish modernism apart from other modernisms, but . . . for his own reasons, he chose not to turn them." These reasons, Kiberd suggests, had to do with a larger "reluctance to develop ideas of national identity," a product of "his background in a mid-western Jewish family."[80]

Ellmann's silence about new approaches to Joyce in the second edition of *James Joyce* can be explained in yet another way, apart from the explanations offered by McCourt, Kiberd, and Ellmann himself: He was very busy. In 1966 he had embarked on a new full-length biographical project, the life of Oscar Wilde, a book that would occupy him for the rest of his life. The idea of writing the biography came about through a request from Charles Ryskamp, a professor of English at Princeton and later the director of both the Morgan Library and the Frick Museum. In 1966 Ryskamp and several colleagues at Princeton put on an exhibition titled "Wilde and the Nineties," and Ryskamp asked Ellmann to write an essay for the exhibition catalog. Ellmann's essay, "The Critic as Artist as Wilde," led him to the decision to write a full-length life.[81] In the course of writing the life, just as he had done while at work on *James Joyce,* he published ancillary works: an edition of Wilde's critical writings, a collection of critical essays, and a new edition of *The Picture of Dorian Gray.* Although the claims and character of *Oscar Wilde,* like those of Ellmann's other publications written after *James Joyce,* are beyond the remit of this book, it is worth noting that the Wilde book was written on the scale of the Joyce biography, was published a year after Ellmann's death, and won both the Pulitzer Prize and the National Book Critics Circle Award.

Hugh Kenner.

Coda: Last Years

ELLMANN'S LIFE AWAY from the desk in the years after 1959 was full of incident. Northwestern held on to him until 1966, when he accepted a professorship at Yale, to be taken up in the academic year 1968–1969. Part of the reason for staying at Northwestern until that point, in addition to its willingness to better all offers, was concern for family. With the children at school full-time, Mary returned to teaching, first at Kendall College in Evanston, then at Roosevelt University in Chicago. She also began writing the articles and reviews that led to *Thinking about Women*, published in 1968, the year Stephen Ellmann finished high school and entered Harvard. With Mary coming into her own and Stephen off to university, the family was portable.

Professional pride and ambition also played a part in the move. On April 11, 1963, after learning that his Northwestern salary was to be raised "only slightly next year because I shall be on leave," Ellmann wrote in protest to Dean Simeon Leland. The decision slightly "bewildered" him, as did a minor alteration in the leave arrangement that had been agreed to in 1960:

> Another point which we then discussed was [the] special professorship which Illinois had offered me, but when I was told that Northwestern did not wish to set up chairs of this kind, I did not press the point.
>
> Subsequent events have been hard for me to reconcile with the spirit of those discussions. A year later a chair in English was in fact created, and then given to someone else! The salary level for the upper positions in the humanities, which in the past three years has risen from $20,000 by four or five thousand dollars at places like Berkeley and Chicago, has been much more modestly adjusted in my case. The prevailing attitude

was perhaps epitomized three months ago, when in your introduction to my public lecture you belittled the subjects of my scholarship and the places at which I had lectured. With due allowance for high spirits, the object seemed to be to cut me down to size.

What I feel compelled to ask is how long I am to be begrudged the arrangements made three years ago? In other words, how long shall I be punished for staying at Northwestern?

It is not clear if this letter was sent, but on September 1,1963, Ellmann was appointed Franklyn Bliss Snyder Professor of English at Northwestern, succeeding Arthur H. Nethercot, the first possessor of the chair. Three years later, when Yale made its offer, Leland more than matched it, writing to Ellmann on June 2, 1966, that "all of us have deep affection for you and Mary—as do all your friends and colleagues—and will deem it a deep personal loss should you decide to go to Yale or anywhere else. Indeed, we feel you belong to Northwestern and want you to continue your brilliant career here. No one will ever do better by you than we will."[1] Ellmann was not persuaded. He accepted Yale's offer and somehow negotiated with Northwestern to defer his departure for two years, the second year on paid leave. Lucy Ellmann, who was ten at the time, remembers her mother liking the idea "of being back in New England and fairly near her sister and other friends." Maud describes herself at the time as "miserable in Evanston as an adolescent" and perfectly happy to leave.[2]

For Mary and the children, the move was a success. The house the Ellmanns rented in New Haven was much loved. Maud remembers its sleeping porch and the "Chinese tea-paper" on the dining room walls. "It was a beautiful place," Lucy remembers, the open porch looking out onto the garden, a fine kitchen, her mother "cooking great meals in that kitchen with an opera playing on the record player. She was blossoming there, I think, with the book publication and all." The girls liked their new school; Stephen, at Harvard, was nearer the family than he would have been had they stayed in Evanston. Shortly after arrival in New Haven, however, Ellmann received a phone call from Isaiah Berlin. Would he, asked Berlin, be interested in succeeding Lord David Cecil as Goldsmiths' Professor of English Literature at Oxford? Would he, moreover, be willing to come to Oxford to discuss the position? He would have two weeks to decide. With Mary's approval Ellmann traveled to England, returning to New Haven laden with presents ("He was good with presents," Lucy recalls) and announcing that he had accepted the offer. What Maud remembers is that when Ellmann received the call from Berlin, "he did ask us if we'd be willing to move to England and we said yes. At that time, I for one didn't realize how much I would like New Haven and by the time we left . . . I would have done anything to stay put."

At the end of their first year in New Haven, neither Mary nor the girls wanted to leave. To do so meant abandoning the beautiful house, separating from Stephen in New England, and, in effect, abandoning Pepito (the current Ellmann poodle) for a year, given Britain's punitive quarantine rules.[3] Only Ellmann was keen on the move. At Yale, he had quickly realized, there would be altogether too much administration. "It took up all his time," Lucy recalled, "and exhausted him. He could never have written a biography in New Haven." John Kelly, who was Ellmann's friend, a Yeats scholar, and a fellow of St. John's College, Oxford, recalled that "established at Yale, [Ellmann] could predict easily which meetings he would be attending on any given day in the foreseeable future. Oxford offered no such predictability." With his mind increasingly bent on Wilde's life and works, Oxford offered "the chance to be within easy striking distance of the places where Wilde had spent so much of his life, besides the archival and library resources."

What happened next was terrible. On November 4, 1969, at home in New Haven, Mary suffered a ruptured blood vessel in her brain, an aneurysm, and nearly died. She then had neurosurgery, which went wrong and left her bedridden for several months, with slurred and labored speech, and permanently paralyzed down the left side. When she came out of hospital, she was wheelchair-bound. In the course of researching potential treatments, Ellmann met with a second neurosurgeon, supposedly the best brain surgeon in New York, who was willing to offer Mary a second operation, with what he calculated as a 2 percent chance of success. Ellmann declined the offer. It is sometimes said that stress can bring on an aneurysm, and Mary, like her daughters, had grown to resent the prospect of a move to Oxford. Ellmann was angry about the failed operation, guilty and sorrowful about Mary's condition, but more determined than ever to move to England. Oxford meant a cut in salary, but it also meant that Mary could be treated on the National Health Service. He worried that if he stayed at Yale, he would not be able to afford the extensive medical care and rehabilitation Mary required.

When the family made the move to England, on July 1, 1970, Mary was still largely bedridden. As Maud remembers it, for a year "she just wasn't there." When gradually she came to consciousness, "she was furious. . . . She hated Oxford really, really hated the sexism."[4] Maud describes her father in their first year at Oxford as "out of his mind" with worry and responsibility. He organized Mary's health care, tended to the needs and education of his unhappy teenage daughters, kept up correspondence with Stephen, bought and cooked meals, paid the bills, did household chores, and performed his duties as Goldsmiths' Professor of English Literature and Fellow of New College. When Mary's condition improved, he organized the couple's social life, with drinks and snacks most nights for friends and students in their house at 39 St. Giles, near New College.[5] Although he complained a lot ("to us," Lucy adds, "not to her"), he took no leave. "*Nothing* fell off," Maud recalls. In the remaining seventeen years of his life, he also produced eight new books, including the second edition of *James Joyce* and the Oscar Wilde biography, as well as several dozen book reviews, and over forty articles, introductions, and essays in collections.

Mary recovered something of her wit and toughness after the first year in Oxford. She and Ellmann bickered a lot, particularly after the illness, but when Maud was asked to describe her parents' marriage, she replied: "They were *there,* they were a rock." Once when the poet Craig Raine tried to draw Ellmann into saying something indiscreet, "Dick hesitated, began, stumbled, began again, was painfully euphemistic and long-winded. Suddenly, Mary said, using her speech to great comic purpose—she was slow in her delivery—'Dick every day you get to sound more and more . . . like . . . your *mother.*'" Another time Raine visited Mary in the hospital where she'd been taken after an emergency. He found her "asleep in a cot, her face a Union Jack of tape holding in oxygen and feeding tubes. I stayed for ten minutes, but just as I was leaving, she opened an eye, saw me, and said, 'Craig, can I get you a drink?'"[6] For the most part, in the first few years Mary's paralysis kept her confined to the house on St. Giles. As Henry Hart remembers it, "The simplest trips around Oxford were often painful and embarrassing odysseys. Many places in the ancient city were not easily accessible to the handicapped. Stories circulated about how Mary had to crawl on her rear-end upstairs when nobody could lift her in her wheelchair."[7] These humiliations Mary bore stoically. Kelly describes her as "a woman who knew suffering . . . sardonic, ironic, even pessimistic, with a totally unsentimental view of life."[8] In Lucy's novel *Ducks, Newburyport,* the narrator's mother has similarities to Mary, while also being different from her in important respects (the similarities, Lucy stresses, are "haphazard," "my focus was not on my real family"). "Shy, sick, and stuck in her wheelchair," the fictional mother could be sociable "with the people she really liked."[9] But she also "really did scare some of her visitors" (p. 765). John Kelly and his wife Christine remember keeping one friend away from Mary, "who would have cut him in half." "After Mommy got sick we just dwindled as a family," recalls the narrator of Lucy's novel: "We were all a mess" (p. 172). The narrator's father "really *tried* to keep things normal, get a normal life going for her, and Mommy went along with it all . . . but she didn't really have much fun. . . . She never liked going out in her wheelchair, or even being seen with her walker . . . that was a big problem for her, because she was shy and hated people staring at her" (p. 771).

Part of what sustained Ellmann in the Oxford years, in both his public life and his private life, was another life he kept secret from his family. Shortly after arriving in England he embarked on an affair that would last the rest of his life. The woman was Barbara Hardy, professor of English at Birkbeck College in London and an authority on Victorian writing. When Maud learned of the affair years after her father's death, her reaction was complicated. On the one hand, she was hurt that others knew about it when she and her family had not. On the other hand, she was grateful that it was kept secret from her mother. Had her father not had some relief from the stress of taking care of Mary, she believes, he would have been driven mad or have put her in a home. "There's a limit to what you can stand." Lucy, too, was hurt not to have known. "I wish he'd the courage to tell me about it, to trust me." But she too understood: "He was wholly determined to keep his love life secret, so as not to humiliate or hurt my mother." Did he feel guilty about the affair? Lucy believes he did: "He was prone to guilt at the best of times, and this was a big betrayal of my mother, whom I think he always loved deeply."[10]

In the preface to *Golden Codgers: Biographical Speculations* (1973), written a year after his own secret life began, Ellmann writes about the reasons for secrecy, among them "reasons of fondness or embarrassment," adding that for many writers "the urge to divulge is almost as strong as that to withhold."[11] Mary Ellmann died in 1989, two years after Ellmann. In 1996 Barbara Hardy published a novel about her affair with Ellmann,

Barbara Hardy.

titled *London Lovers*. It suggests Lucy might have been right about her father's guilt. "After we'd been away together" (on a rare three-day holiday), recalls Hardy's narrator, her lover "Mick" Solomon (like "Dick" Ellmann) "was no longer driven by desire, and relapsed into worry and guilt."[12] Hardy suggests that her lover's wife had given up sex after her illness. Ellmann's daughters believe this was true also of their mother. Ellmann was fifty-one when Mary had her aneurysm.

It was 2005 when the Ellmann children learned about their father's affair with Barbara Hardy. Before Hardy died, in 2016, the daughters had established contact with her. Maud even asked Hardy to contribute to a book of essays she was editing. Lucy remembers liking her "very much," despite "what she wrote about my mother in her tell-all novel." The affair in the novel begins at the end of a party. Florence, the narrator, is "genuinely startled" when Solomon voices "his delicately phrased proposition. 'Would it amuse you to meet me unprofessionally?'" Sometime later, she asks her lover if he had decided what to say in advance, and he says: "Yes, I'm afraid I did. Is that bad?" (p. 50). As their affair progresses, Solomon remains "an uxorious husband, despite having a wife less keen on sex than he was. . . . He remained an uxorious husband to an invalid, taking great care never to let gossips catch wind of our affair" (p. 46). How Ellmann managed to keep the affair secret can be related to habits or episodes of secrecy evident earlier in his life, as recounted in chapters of this book dealing with his war service in the OSS and his recovery of Joyce's correspondence and manuscripts.[13]

In 1984, the year of the Frankfurt Joyce Symposium, Ellmann, at the age of sixty-six, retired from the Goldsmiths' Professorship and became an Extraordinary Fellow at Wolfson College, Oxford. He would continue teaching at Emory, in Atlanta, for another three springs, in part because he and Mary missed what he called the "intimacy" of American life. "I think one has [such intimacy] in England," he told Henry Hart, "only if you've met people in childhood, forming life-long friendships. If you go at the age of 50 or so [as I did], you never feel quite so much a part of the situation." Ellmann mentioned other reasons for feeling estranged at Oxford. Modernist authors were still not fully accepted there, he warned Hart. Also, he had experienced both anti-American and antisemitic sentiments in Oxford.[14] (A joke Ellmann liked telling at Oxford—Ellmann liked telling jokes—concerned a new theory of Shakespearean authorship: that Shakespeare was an American. When asked the origin of this theory, he replied: "The talent warrants the presumption.") Spending time in Emory was also attractive because they could be near their son Stephen, who was now a lawyer. In 1976 he was a clerk in Atlanta's US Court of Appeals; during 1977–1983 he was staff attorney at the Southern Poverty Law Center in Montgomery, Alabama.[15] Another attraction was that Emory was rich enough, thanks to Coca-Cola money, to cover Mary's Blue Cross/Blue Shield insurance costs.

A year after Ellmann retired as Goldsmiths' Professor, he twice fell while jogging, and that winter "his voice was unaccountably hoarse." In June 1986, when traveling to Montreal to receive an honorary degree from McGill, "he experienced difficulty standing or sitting upright and his speech was now slurred."[16] When he returned from Canada, Christine Kelly noticed something was wrong with him: he was tired, slurring his words. She first noticed this at a party and thought he might have drunk too much (something she had never known him to do). Then she began to worry. She had read about David Niven's decline and death from motor neuron disease, known in the United States as Lou Gehrig's disease (also as ALS, amyotrophic lateral sclerosis), and guessed that this was what Ellmann had. In September 1986, when Ronald Schuchard arrived in Oxford from Emory as a visiting fellow at Wolfson College, he, too, noticed that Ellmann's speech was slurred. Ellmann "announced [it] as a symptom of what he thought was ALS. He had researched his symptoms."[17] "I'm going to beat it," he told the Kellys, though he knew the condition was fatal.

In October 1986 a specialist in London confirmed Ellmann's diagnosis. Schuchard was at the St. Giles house the day Ellmann returned from London, dripping wet, to announce: "Well I've got it. . . . Stage four. I'll be the shame of my family, living only to sixty-nine." As Schuchard remembers it, Mary took a drag on her cigarette—she smoked till the very end of her life—and a sip of her drink "and said in her sardonic deadpan way: 'Well you didn't expect to live forever, did you?' Dick didn't say anything."[18] Mary's deadpan response, Lucy believes, was due to Schuchard being in the room: "She put on a brave front with outsiders, which may have made her seem tougher than she was. She also was very depressed by her own illness (so much so that it could never be discussed) and shamed by her dependence on my father. She must have been terrified of what the future now held for her. So, quite a moment for the pair of them."[19] Soon Ellmann became an invalid, like Mary. "He struggled to walk. His speech was slurred. He often remained silent. Making the final corrections to the Wilde biography was an ordeal," writes Nicholas Barker. "Ultimately, a simple keyboard with roll printer became his sole means of communication; even so his words showed that the mind within was undiminished."[20]

In the final months of his life, Ellmann was helped in the preparation of the Wilde manuscript and proofs by Maud, Lucy, Mary, and the Wilde scholar Owen Dudley Edwards, "who came to wait on him hand and foot and eye."[21] At the end of the acknowledgments section of the Wilde book, Ellmann typed: "R.E., St. Giles, Oxford, Ides of March, 1987." This was in October. Later in the autumn, the president of Emory University, James T. Laney, flew to Oxford to tell Ellmann personally that Emory had agreed to establish the Richard Ellmann Lectures in Modern Literature. When Laney asked Ellmann who should deliver the inaugural lecture, "Dick replied softly, 'Seamus.'"[22]

On May 12 Ellmann was admitted to the John Radcliffe Hospital on Woodstock Road, where he died on the morning of May 13.[23] In the Ellmann

Richard Ellmann in April 1987,
a month before his death.

Papers there is a note written by Lucy after her father's death, addressed "To Whom It May Concern," in which she writes that "before he died a nurse asked him what religion he had, if any. I volunteered 'Jewish,' but my father vetoed this and said to me 'none.'"[24] He was not a religious Jew. A funeral service was held at New College, Oxford. There was an open wooden coffin and at the end of the service two members of staff placed the lid on the coffin and fastened it down with large screws and screwdrivers "in a dramatic physical show of finality."[25] Ellmann was buried just outside the Jewish section of Wolvercote Cemetery at the outskirts of Oxford (he was not allowed inside the Jewish section because he had not attended the synagogue). At the graveside service, the coffin was lowered into the ground by John Kelly, the poet and critic Jon Stallworthy, Ronald Schuchard, and Stephen Ellmann, who had arrived from the United States on the Concorde, too late to say goodbye to his father. The four pallbearers offered shovels to the few men and women present at the graveside who wished to place a shovel of dirt on the coffin, and then, in Schuchard's words, "we four packed him in, filling the grave and shaping the mound, sweating profusely in a hot sun, each of us moved and determined to honor his legacy as best we could thenceforth."[26]

* * *

When he was interviewed in 1982 by a reporter from the *International Herald Tribune,* for an article aptly titled "Portrait of the Artist as a Biographer," Ellmann was asked what he intended to write after the Wilde biography. He answered jocoseriously. "Well I'd like to try a series of short essays explaining how long books ought to be written—by other people."[27] This book has been an attempt to show how and why long biographies ought to be written, in the process honoring both *James Joyce* and the admirable scholar/artist who was its author.

NOTE ON SOURCES

ABBREVIATIONS

NOTES

ACKNOWLEDGMENTS

ILLUSTRATION CREDITS

INDEX

NOTE ON SOURCES

Unless otherwise specified, the source for all unpublished letters by and to Richard Ellmann, and all unpublished manuscript material, is Richard Ellmann Papers, Department of Special Collections and University Archives, McFarlin Library, University of Tulsa (cited in the notes as Ellmann Papers). On the advice of Special Collections, most letters are identified by author and date only, without reference to box or folder numbers. The Ellmann Papers are not yet fully processed, the collection continues to grow, and box and folder numbers may change. Box and folder numbers are provided, however, for grouped manuscript materials such as typed drafts of Ellmann's unpublished, undated talks.

ABBREVIATIONS

Ellmann Papers	Richard Ellmann Papers, Department of Special Collections and University Archives, McFarlin Library, University of Tulsa
JJ	Richard Ellmann, *James Joyce* (New York: Oxford University Press, 1959)
JJII	Richard Ellmann, *James Joyce: New and Revised Edition* (New York: Oxford University Press, 1982)
OUP	Oxford University Press
RE	Richard Ellmann

NOTES

INTRODUCTION

1. Anthony Burgess, "Creator of Oolisseez," review of second edition of Richard Ellmann, *James Joyce,* in the *Observer,* October 24, 1982. In the notes, Ellmann is referred to as "RE," the first edition of *James Joyce* as "*JJ,*" and the second edition as "*JJII.*"

2. Sheldon Meyer to RE, October 1, 1959.

3. The review of *JJ* in the *New York Times Book Review,* "All Life Was Grist for the Artist," October 25, 1959, was written by Stephen Spender; Frank Kermode's review, "Puzzles and Epiphanies," appeared in the *Spectator,* November 13, 1959.

4. Joseph Brooker, "Post-war Joyce," in *James Joyce in Context,* ed. John McCourt (Cambridge: Cambridge University Press, 2009), p. 57. Brooker's survey of the reception of Joyce's writings is *Joyce's Critics: Transitions in Reading and Culture* (Madison: University of Wisconsin Press, 2004).

5. Amanda Sigler, "Joyce's Ellmann: The Beginnings of *James Joyce,*" *Joyce Studies Annual* (2010); John McCourt, "Reading Ellmann Reading Joyce," *European Joyce Studies* 14 (2016). See also, among others, Joseph Kelly, "Stanislaus Joyce, Ellsworth Mason, and Richard Ellmann: The Making of *James Joyce,*" *Joyce Studies Annual* (1992); Phillip F. Herring, "Richard Ellmann's *James Joyce,*" in *The Biographer's Art,* ed. Jeffrey Meyers (London: Macmillan, 1988); and Ira B. Nadel, "The Incomplete Joyce," *Joyce Studies Annual* (1991).

6. W. B. Yeats's poem "The Choice" (1932) begins: "The intellect of man is forced to choose/Perfection of the life, or of the work,/And if it take the second must refuse/A heavenly mansion, raging in the dark."

7. Or so Marquez warned his biographer, as the biographer, Gerald Martin, recounts in *Gabriel Garcia Marquez: A Life* (New York: Vintage, 2010), p. 205.

8. The Montherlant quotation is a well-known abbreviated form of a line from his play *Don Juan* (1958): "Le bonheur écrit à l'encre blanche sur des pages blanches" (act 2, scene 4, line 1048).

9. See Philip Larkin, "A Neglected Responsibility: Contemporary Literary Manuscripts" (1979), in *Required Writing: Miscellaneous Pieces, 1955–1982* (London: Faber and Faber, 1983).

10. Nicholas Barker, "Richard Ellmann, 1918–1987," in *Biographical Memoirs of Fellows of the British Academy,* vol. 13 (London: British Academy), p. 186.

11. Ellsworth Mason to RE, October 6, 1978.

12. Lucy Ellmann, email, July 13, 2019.

13. Interview with Maud Ellmann, July 5, 2019.

14. See Zachary Leader, *The Life of Saul Bellow: To Fame and Fortune, 1915–1964* (New York: Knopf, 2015), p. 11. The quotation beginning "The fact is a wire" comes from "Chicago and American Culture: One Writer's View," a talk delivered by Bellow on October 10, 1972, at the Centennial Celebration of the Chicago Public Library. A typescript of the talk is among Bellow's papers in the Regenstein Library at the University of Chicago. When Bellow's friend Dave Peltz complained about his using material Peltz had been saving for his own memoirs, Bellow wrote to him on July 14, 1974, to apologize but also to defend himself. "The name of the game is Give All. You are welcome to all my facts. You know them. I give them to you. If you have the strength to pick them up, take them with my blessing. Touch them with your imagination and I will kiss your hands."

15. See Zachary Leader, ed., *On Life-Writing* (Oxford: Oxford University Press, 2019), p. 6.

16. See Zachary Leader, *The Life of Kingsley Amis* (London: Jonathan Cape, 2006), p. 2, for the Andrew Davies anecdote, and also for the quote about the restaurant, which comes from Amis, "Real and Made-Up People," *Times Literary Supplement,* July 27, 1973.The novel in which the restaurant appears is *The Biographer's Moustache.* Amis's comment about having already written an account of himself in his novels comes from his *Memoirs* (London: Century Hutchinson, 1991), p. xv.

17. In *JJ,* p. 375, RE introduces the relevant passage from *Finnegans Wake,* in which Shem "like a spider, produces 'from his unheavenly body a no uncertain quantity of obscene matter' and 'with this double dye . . . wrote over every square inch of the only foolscap available, his own body.'" The full passage from *Finnegans Wake* is found on pp. 185–86.

18. C. G. Bowen to RE, June 24, 1955.

19. RE to C. G. Bowen, July 4, 1955.

20. Hermione Lee, *Biography: A Very Short Introduction* (Oxford: Oxford University Press, 2009), pp. 88–89.

21. "Literary Biography," RE's 1971 inaugural lecture at Oxford, is reprinted in Richard Ellmann, *Golden Codgers: Biographical Speculations* (London: Oxford University Press, 1973); for discussion of Edel and Painter, see pp. 11–13.

22. RE, *JJ,* p. 1. (Hereafter cited in the text by page number.)

1. FAMILY

1. RE, *JJ,* p. vii.

2. Quoted in Amanda Sigler, "Joyce's Ellmann: The Beginnings of *James Joyce,*" *Joyce Studies Annual* (2010): 24–25. Sigler's own endnote to the quotation, giving her source, reads: "Notes based on interview with Jolas, July 22, 1953. REC [her abbreviation for Richard Ellmann Papers, Department of Special Collections and University Archives, McFarlin Library, University of Tulsa]. In Lucie Noel, *James*

Joyce and Paul L. Leon: The Story of a Friendship (New York: The Gotham Book Mart), 1950, Paul Leon's widow Lucie emphasizes Joyce's formality but also adds: 'He was very much a family man, a devoted husband, a good father, and a loyal son' (12)." (Lucie Noel was Lucie Leon's nom de plume.) As for the views of Joyce's children, Sigler quotes his son Giorgio, interviewed by RE in Trieste in July and August 1953 (while the family was based in Paris): "Ellmann asked Giorgio 'what he thought of the general feeling that Joyce is aloof and cold' [RE's notes on interview of August 7, 1953]. As if guessing Ellmann's theory, Giorgio replied that this was a completely erroneous characterization. Debunking the previous image of his father, he stressed the family's intimacy and Joyce's devotion to his children" (p. 23).

3. This is not to say that there were no moments when money was tight. At one such moment, sometime in the 1930s, James Ellmann was worried enough about money to tell his son William that he was considering selling the Connecticut Avenue house and having the family live year-round in the lakeside cottage (according to an email of February 6, 2021, from William's son Douglas). In a letter of thanks of July 15, 1936, to Walter G. Shotwell, whose scholarship RE had been awarded, RE writes that "the increasing demands on the family income by two of my brothers who are going to school, and my own inability to earn in a factory this summer more than a part of my expenses, have made the question of financing my second year most perplexing."

4. At the request of his grandson Christopher, in 1997, when he was eighty-two, Erwin Ellmann wrote a five-page single-spaced "memoir," a copy of which was provided to me by Erwin's son Michael. The title Michael gave to the memoir was "Fragment of EBE's Autobiographical Memoir" (hereafter cited as "Memoir"). The description of Samuel Ellmann comes from its first page.

5. In his youth, Malcolm X was convinced that his father had been murdered by the Black Legion. See Malcolm X and Alex Haley, *The Autobiography of Malcolm X* (New York: Grove Press, 1966), pp. 10, 15. As an adult he was less certain, according to Manning Marabele, *Malcolm X: A Life of Reinvention* (New York: Viking, 2011), p. 29. Les Payne and Tamara Payne, in *The Dead Are Arising: The Life of Malcolm X* (New York: Liveright, 2020), argue at the beginning of chapter 4 ("Pulling the Family Apart") that the Black Legion was not involved in Earl Little's death.

6. Quoted from an undated letter written in 1935 in Erwin's freshman year at USC.

7. This phrase is from Lucy Ellmann in an interview. The poems of an unlovable, possibly Jean-inspired, grandmother in Lucy's novel *Ducks, Newburyport* (Norwich, UK: Galley Beggar Press, 2019), p. 106, are described as "terrible."

8. William Ellmann's birth certificate lists his date of birth as March 23, 1921, and Jean's age "at last birthday" as thirty-one, which means she was born in 1889. But an obituary of July 27, 1979, in the *Detroit Jewish News* reports that she died on July 25, 1979, at age ninety-two, which would make her year of birth 1887.

9. Jean Ellmann, from her unpublished memoir "From Door to Door," p. 140. (Hereafter cited in the text by page number.)

10. The "family of gypsies" remark is reported in a letter to RE of April 29, 1939.

11. Erwin Ellmann, "Memoir," p. 2.

12. There was no synagogue in Highland Park, and Erwin remembers only one other Jewish family in the neighborhood ("Memoir," p. 5).

13. The speech was given at an annual reunion of the Websterian Oratorical Society, discussed later in this chapter.

14. What James had to say about socialism is not reported; forty years later, though, in a letter of August 25, 1939, written two days after the signing of the Hitler-Stalin Pact and quoted later in this chapter, James teases son Dick about "your good friends the communists."

15. Erwin Ellmann, "Memoir," p. 2.

16. Erwin Ellmann, "Memoir," p. 5.

17. I have taken a liberty here: Jean spells "important" as the child Dick pronounced it: "impoitant."

18. Erwin Ellmann to RE, November 23, 1933.

19. Jean Ellmann to RE, November 3, 1938.

20. Jean Ellmann to RE, October 7, 1935.

21. According to grandson Victor Rostow, Eugene Rostow's son, in an email of November 9, 2020. Both Rostows were socialists.

22. Or so she several times told her granddaughter; Victoria Rostow, daughter of Ralph Rostow, email to author, November 12, 2020.

23. See "Yale's Perfect Freshman," *New York Times,* September 15, 1929.

24. Ralph Rostow, born in 1920, was still in high school. He went to Antioch College, as progressive then as it is now, and had a career in business. Walt Rostow became an economics professor and political theorist. From 1966 to 1969 he served as national security advisor to Lyndon Johnson and was a key figure in shaping US foreign policy in Southeast Asia. Eugene Rostow became dean of the Yale Law School, served as under secretary of state for political affairs under Lyndon Johnson and later as director of the Arms Control and Disarmament Agency under Ronald Reagan. Both brothers were staunch and combative anti-Communists.

25. Victor Rostow, in an email of November 11, 2020.

26. Erwin Ellmann to RE, May 11, 1938.

27. Jean Ellmann to RE, May 24, 1938.

28. All three sons had estates, but Erwin, who was finishing two years of law school at the University of Michigan, had drawn on his, according to his letter to RE of May 22, 1938: "I think I took about a thousand dollars from the account—which would leave $200 liquid remaining. . . . I suspect Dad is getting fatigued with my support—a perfectly legitimate reaction, and there is no sense to burden him more."

29. At the end of the trip they would board the SS *Volendam* at Boulogne-sur-Mer on August 13, 1938, arriving in New York on August 23.

30. RE, "Overtures to 'Salome'" (1968), reprinted in *Golden Codgers: Biographical Speculations* (1973; Oxford: Oxford University Press, 1976), pp. 52–53.

31. The Thomas Hardy quotation is taken from Philip Larkin, "It Could Only Happen in England: A Study of John Betjeman's Poems for American Readers," in *Required Reading: Miscellaneous Pieces, 1955–1982* (London: Faber and Faber, 1982), p. 111. Larkin took it from Florence Emily Hardy, *The Life of Thomas Hardy, 1840–1928* (1928, 1930; rpt. London: Macmillan, 1962), p. 116.

32. Nothing is said of this incident in Bill's surviving letters. In a letter of July 11, however, sent from Olden in Norway, he writes of wandering "into a room

from which I heard melodious piano playing. . . . There was a sailor playing. He spoke only a little English. After a while several of his friends came in. Then he asked me to play, so I tried my one piece. Then I said goodbye and went out on the porch. I then looked at the breast of one of the sailors and saw a small Swastika. What a let down. Hitler seems to have them manoeuvering in the fyords."

33. RE to "Dears," January 29, 1936.

34. Ellsworth Mason, "Ellmann's Road to Xanadu," in *Omnium Gatherum: Essays for Richard Ellmann,* ed. Susan Dick, Declan Kiberd, Dougald McMillan, and Joseph Ronsley (Gerrards Cross, UK: Colin Smythe, 1989), p. 7.

35. The experiences did not produce a book, but they may have produced a story. In a letter of November 30, 1939, Jean Ellmann writes: "That was an interesting and illusive story about that ship, Dick. Maybe the day for miracles is not past after all."

36. According to an interview of February 12, 2020, with Michael Ellmann.

37. For George Cooke, see Erwin to RE, February 13, 1940: "A couple of weeks ago Steff sent me an essay on Yeats by George Cooke, a friend of Dave Fredenthal's who lives in Grosse Point, and who gives her occasional typing. . . . The best part consisted in a few interesting observations that Yeats made when Cooke visited him in Ireland in 1935. On the whole, the appraisal was pretty crappy, a cross between no criticism at all, and a Halliburtian novella of the Gaelic countryside. . . . George has used this thing to pass off as a writer; I doubt if it can be published save at his own expense. It should give courage to us all."

38. The date of Erwin's letter is unclear. In it he writes, "In another week I am going to Washington to see if I can take the first step in the process"—that is, the process of getting a job in the New Deal. "I have one promising prospect perhaps." The case for dating the letter in late 1939 (as opposed to late 1938)—that is, after Dick's tough letter—may be bolstered by the remark "how decently and effectively" the father presents his feelings, suggesting that he was influenced by Dick's criticisms in the letter of "abt 12/1/39." If so, it also suggests that Dick never told Erwin of the letter, a sign of his discretion.

39. The earliest reference to the letter comes in Erwin to RE, February 13, 1940: "I am in hearty accord with what you say about Bill and sluicing him into the law."

40. Quoted in Mason, "Ellmann's Road to Xanadu," p. 9. In a letter of February 25, 1940, Erwin comments on a poem Dick has sent him. The subject of the poem seems to be the relations between Olympians and Titans, the struggle of fathers and sons. No title of the poem is given, and all that is quoted from it is a line Erwin does not understand: "if it were not that your mightiest marrow is immured in me," a reference perhaps to Dick's sense of how much he has internalized of the father whose influence he means to challenge, if not to overthrow. A letter of March 12, 1940, from James Ellmann to RE offers another example of how the relations between fathers and sons or parents and children preoccupied RE and his father at this time. The letter concerns one of RE's friends and contemporaries. James Ellmann writes: "Fountain's analysis of Art as furtive is probably pretty good. I believe that your interpretation of it as being the result of henpeckery is also reasonably correct. He certainly is not being given any opportunity to stand on his own feet, to have a single thought of his own or anything of that sort. And the oddest part of it all is that neither of the parties are perhaps aware of the cause and effect."

41. According to his son Douglas, Bill was the first Jewish president of the Michigan Bar. He was president during the Detroit riots in 1967, when more than 7,200 people were arrested. In an article of August 4, 1967, the *Jewish News* reported: "William Ellmann, president of the State Bar of Michigan, played a leading role last week in the mobilization of lawyers who have been asked to volunteer their services free in behalf of the many hundreds of arrested who need assistance in the courts."

42. See also RE's accounts in *JJ* of Joyce's profligacy or prodigality, depicted in part as an inheritance from his (Joyce's) father. These accounts, again both witty and admiring, derive from RE's own quite different attitudes to money, also inherited. As for RE's treatment of the influence of family in Joyce's works, see the account in *JJ* of Stephen Dedalus's attempts to escape the "net" of family in *Ulysses* (as mentioned earlier), in particular to escape the influence of his several "fathers" (Bloom, Simon).

2. YALE

1. Among the Ellmann Papers are completed application forms to Harvard University, the University of Chicago, and Columbia University, as well as a letter of acceptance from Harvard. If he applied to the University of Michigan, the application form has been lost. His letter to Brown suggests that it had offered him a scholarship, though presumably not as generous as the scholarship he had received from Yale. He was admitted to Yale on the basis of his school record alone, without examination—an unusual occurrence described by Charles Seymour, the president of Yale, as "an act of faith abundantly justified, since he is graduated today a member of Phi Beta Kappa and with honors in English with exceptional distinction" (*Yale Alumni Magazine,* July 7, 1939, p. 21).

2. RE to "Dears," September 1935.

3. See Dan Oren, *Joining the Club: A History of Jews at Yale* (New Haven, CT: Yale University Press, 1985), chap. 3,"The Limitation of Numbers: Undergraduate Admissions between the World Wars."

4. The ceremony ratifying his election to Chi Delta Theta was to be held at Mory's, a private club adjacent to the Yale campus. On the morning of the ceremony, RE received an undated letter on society stationery instructing, "Wear a dark suit and bring with you a candle and Candleholder. In addition you are requested to bring a three to five hundred word thesis on 'Reprehensive neologies in Undergraduate Apparel.'"

5. RE to parents, September 26, 1935. The next day he described his English honors class as "my most interesting class, as well as most difficult. I never learned so much at one time in my life as I do in there." That RE was at least as smart as his fellow students is attested to by the number of prizes he won: the McLaughlin Memorial Prize as a freshman, the C. Wyllys Betts Prize in English Prose as a sophomore, the John W. Corwith Memorial Scholarship Prize (as well as a Lucius F. Robinson Prize) as a junior, and the Henry H. Strong Prize in American Literature as a senior. These prizes were in addition to tuition scholarships for all four years ("Plan B" in freshman year, then Walter G. Shotwell scholarships). RE also took out tuition loans from the university from sophomore year onward and earned

money from term-time employment provided by the Board of Appointments. RE's friend Ellsworth Mason describes him as having the money to purchase copies of Yeats's books "from an ample allowance." Ellsworth Mason, "Ellmann's Road to Xanadu," in *Omnium Gatherum: Essays for Richard Ellmann,* ed. Susan Dick, Declan Kiberd, Dougald McMillan, and Joseph Ronsley (Gerrards Cross, UK: Colin Smythe, 199), p. 6. But the book purchases may also have been made possible by scholarships and term-time jobs.

6. The by-line for "Yale's English" is "The Editors," but on the issue's masthead RE is identified as the issue's sole "associate editor." The "chairman" at the time—that is, the editor—was Roger Starr, also class of '39 and also Jewish, who would go on to serve for twenty-five years on the editorial board of the *New York Times* and later, controversially, as an urban planner for the City of New York. Starr was a philosophy major, not an English major, which is part of the reason I assume that RE was the author of the editorial. In 1941, when RE was in his second year as a grad student in English, Starr, a Trotskyist and staunch supporter of civil rights, offered to enlist in an African American regiment. The army declined his offer. It was Starr who had asked RE what his politics were and who urged him to read Mike Gold's novel *Jews without Money* (1930). Starr grew up in New York, in an apartment on Park Avenue. Although chairman of the *Lit,* and a wealthy graduate of Lawrenceville School, he, too, was never "tapped." In RE's words, Starr "could have been expected to be elected to a senior society. . . . I remember being with him on Tap Day when he was overlooked. With a part of one's mind one despised the senior societies, but there was of course another part, longing for acceptance and recognition. In general, Jewish students at Yale did not feel at home" (quoted in Jim Sleeper, "The Apple Polisher," a review of Roger Starr's *The Rise and Fall of New York City,* in *The Nation,* June 15, 1985).

7. *Yale Literary Magazine,* March 1938, p. 5. (Hereafter cited in the text by page number.)

8. According to Paul H. Fry, a professor of English at Yale and author of "History of the Department: A Very Brief History of the Yale English Department" (available on the departmental website).

9. See, for example, Ransom's claim in *The World's Body* (New York: Charles Scribner's Sons, 1938), p. 330, that an English Department has so little to say about "literature, an art," that it "might almost as well announce that it does not regard itself as entirely autonomous, but as a branch of the department of history, with the option of declaring itself occasionally a branch of ethics."

10. Mason, "Ellmann's Road to Xanadu," p. 7. (Hereafter cited in the text by page number.)

11. Charles J. Feidelson, *Symbolism and American Literature* (Chicago: University of Chicago Press, 1953), p. 5.

12. That Ellmann was thrashing around at this time is suggested by a paragraph in an article titled "Publications" in the September 1938 issue of the *Yale Lit.* The article was written by Starr. "Ellmann, on the ground floor [that is, before the *Lit* office was moved to a new basement location at the beginning of term in RE's senior year], was given to shy hesitant smiling and epigrams, and a rather boyish admiration for classical obscenity. Ellmann in the cellar became a twisted man, with violent attachments and a rather sallow interest in jazz."

13. The Editor, "Voluntary Action," *Mind* 5, no. 19 (1896): 354–56.

14. RE to "Dears," January 29, 1937.

15. As for Jews joining Yale's social clubs, Tinker found the idea "repulsive" (see Oren, *Joining the Club,* pp. 121, 283). George Pierson wrote a history of Yale University and was called "Father Yale" by his friends and colleagues in the later years of his life. He was a descendant of Yale's first rector, Abraham Pierson; his obituary appeared in the *New York Times,* October 5, 1993. Pierson's remark about Tinker and the incompatibility of Jews and the English literary tradition is quoted in Oren, *Joining the Club,* at p. 121, from a letter Pierson wrote to the plant biologist Arthur Galston on January 26, 1971.

16. Kathryn Feidelson, "Memories of Dick Ellmann," an attachment dated August 2020, in an email sent by her son John Feidelson, August 18, 2020.

17. *Yale College Undergraduate Courses of Study (1935–1940),* p. 84. In the undated letter RE wrote home before his trip to Scandinavia with Bill in the summer of 1939, he talks of the honors exam: "It comes on two successive days, 4 hours each day, on the 25th and 26th of May. Though I am not specially worried about passing it, I should prefer to pass well and get honors, though I haven't started working yet as most of the guys have."

18. The most daring of RE's *Lit* essays imagines the humiliations of the biblical Joseph (December 1939); the most autobiographical essay, titled "The Social Disadvantages of Yale" (February 1938), details the irritations and embarrassments of conversing with one's parents' friends at parties during Christmas vacation.

19. The anecdote about RE being "dragged" to Wanning's seminar comes from Henry V. Jaffa, "Strauss at 100," in *Leo Strauss, the Straussians, and the American Regime,* ed. Kenneth L. Deutsch and John A. Murley (Lanham, MD: Rowman and Littlefield, 1999), p. 42. The connection between modern poetry and New Critical practice was inevitable given the prominence of poets among the New Critics and their sources (Eliot, Empson, Ransom, Penn Warren). On April 17, 1939, Wanning sent Ellmann a note about the next week's seminar: "There will be a discussion of W. Empson for Wed. Of the poems (to be found on Reserve) I shd like you to analyze with special care *To an Old Lady* (14), *Arachne* (21), *Sleeping Out in College Cloister,* and the *Villanelle,* which is stuck in on a loose sheet. They are tough. Don't neglect notes on first 3 at end of the book."

20. In the November 4 letter, Feidelson wrote of planning an essay "on Richards and his critics," which he hoped to submit to the *Southern Review* (edited by Brooks and Penn Warren).

21. RE to "Dears," in an undated letter, ca. January 1941. In another undated letter from this period (box 9, folder 6, item 2) RE writes to his parents: "I am working out Carlyle's ideas of economics, which are closely related to his notions of politics; his worship of the hero or great man is very close to fascism, and he is continually advising the lower classes to obey, and the wise men to rule paternalistically. His hatred of democracy is as bitter as Hitler's."

22. According to Mason, "Ellmann's Road to Xanadu," p. 5, "Ellmann's dissertation on Yeats in 1947 was the first ever accepted on a 20th century subject. . . . Ellmann had no formal instruction in 20th century literature during his study for three degrees in literature at Yale, but he was working on it by himself."

23. Bruce Redford, "Frederick Albert Pottle," *Yale University Library Gazette* 66, no. 1–2 (October 1991): 64.

24. Pottle studied science as an undergraduate at Colby College in Maine (Tinker was also a Maine native). For lucid descriptions not only of Einstein's theory of relativity but also of what Einstein thought of the 1887 Michelson-Morley experiment, one of its starting points, see Frederick Pottle, *The Idiom of Poetry* (1941; Ithaca, NY: Cornell University Press, 1946), pp. 4–6. Here is how Pottle introduces his "relativist" literary theory in *The Idiom of Poetry* (p. 5):

> When Messrs. Brooks and Warren say that Shelley's *Indian Serenade* is a bad poem, how do they know? Poe calls it "exquisite," Browning thought it "divine." When T. S. Eliot and Paul Elmer More disagree about the value of Joyce's *Ulysses*, what is the cause of the disagreement? When Matthew Arnold and A. E. Housman pass judgments on Dryden diametrically opposed to those of Johnson and Gray, how shall we account for it? The history of criticism is a tangle of such conflicts. . . . Messrs. Brooks and Warren applied some kind of standard to Shelley's poem and found the poem wanting. Eliot and More each applied a measure to *Ulysses*. Arnold and Housman remeasured Dryden after he had been measured by Johnson and Gray. . . . I shall maintain that all critical judgments are relative to the age producing them, since the measure or standard varies unpredictably from one age to another. By this system, Johnson and Housman were wrong only in asserting absolute judgments. Each was right so far as he reported honestly the result of the application of his measure.

25. See Pottle, *The Idiom of Poetry*, pp. 4–6. For Pottle on the formation of his own taste I have relied on an email of March 31, 2021, from David Bromwich. For the New Critics' anti-Romantic bias, see Gerald Graff, *Professing Literature: An Institutional History* (Chicago: University of Chicago Press, 1987), p. 198: "The critics reinterpreted and re-evaluated earlier literature in the light of a modernist poetics that said poetry is neither rhetorical persuasion nor self-expression but an autonomous discourse that cannot be reduced to its constituent concepts or emotions. . . . More often than not, [their] conception of art caused poets like Spenser, Milton, Wordsworth, and Shelley to be rejected for philosophical or emotional discursiveness, while it elevated the metaphysical poets, who allegedly most resembled the moderns in their imagistic complexity." According to Frank Lentriccia, *After the New Criticism* (London: Athlone Press, 1980), p. 12, John Crowe Ransom once rhymed "Shelley" with "lemon jelly."

26. Pottle, *The Idiom of Poetry*, p. viii.

27. Pottle had been RE's teacher the year before *The Idiom of Poetry* appeared, and the book discusses issues that Pottle had written about. In a note dated February 23 in his 1942 "Composition Book," RE reports on a conversation with his fellow graduate student Norman Pearson about Pottle's book. Pearson "agreed with me that relativism is irrelevant, because it still remains for an age, once it has been granted that Donne was unknown 100 years ago and will perhaps be reviled 100 years from now. We have still the responsibility for [illegible] him for our time, under the *illusion of absolutism*. He applied this to war, to show that the feeling that 100 years from now this war will seem silly does not absolve us from the necessity of taking sides in it."

28. Frederick A. Pottle, *Pride and Negligence: The History of the Boswell Papers* (New York: McGraw-Hill, 1982), pp. 89–90. Pottle's tolerance of his subjects' failings and frailties is especially noteworthy given his religious convictions. According to Gordon Turnbull, a successor as general editor of the Yale Boswell Editions, Pottle was "sympathetic, tolerant, and humane. As a very devout Episcopalian (in the American sense) Christian, he needed to be those things, since the object of his whole career was James Boswell!" (email, May 3, 2021). Pottle is kind and respectful about Tinker, unlike others who knew or were taught by him. Tinker had a glass eye, and according to Martin Price, another Sterling Professor of English, it was "easy to pick out: the warm one" (as recounted by Lars Engle, a junior colleague of Price's at the time, in an email of April 30, 2021). There is, however, evidence to support Pottle's more tolerant view. When Ellmann was up for a job at Northwestern in 1950, Jean Hagstrum, of the university's English Department, who had been a student of Tinker's at Yale, was asked to sound Tinker out about Ellmann. "Top drawer," Tinker reported, "absolutely first rate" (Jean Hagstrum, "Richard Ellmann: A Memoir in Appreciation," fall 1987 issue of the Northwestern magazine *Arts and Sciences*). Nor did Tinker's opposition to modern poetry as a field of academic study prevent him from collecting it for the rare book department at Yale. After a Yale librarian rudely responded to Ellmann's offer of copies of some Yeats manuscripts, Ellmann's friend Ellsworth Mason remarked in a letter of August 12, 1946: "I surmise that if Tinker knew the status of the business and the Library's offer, he would be considerably annoyed, since he is very proud of our (i.e. *his*) Yeats collection, and has an admiration for WB."

29. See Frederick Albert Pottle, *The Literary Career of James Boswell Esq.: Being the Bibliographical Materials for a Life of Johnson* (Oxford: Clarendon Press, 1929), pp. xix–xxii.

30. Frederick A. Pottle, *Stretchers: The Story of a Hospital Unit on the Western Front* (New Haven, CT: Yale University Press, 1929), p. i. See also Redford, "Frederick Albert Pottle," pp. 64, 68.

31. Redford, "Frederick Albert Pottle," p. 67. Bromwich's description comes from an email of March 31, 2021.

32. Alvin Kernan, *In Plato's Cave* (New Haven, CT: Yale University Press, 1999), p. 75.

33. Pottle shared nothing of Tinker's feelings about Jews. According to Bromwich, reporting what Harold Bloom told him, when Bloom's tenure review was questioned, despite his having published three important books, Pottle supported it so strenuously "that the department couldn't say no." Bromwich was Bloom's pupil and reports that "Pottle was one of the few people he [Bloom] spoke about with unswerving respect—never the slightest trace of reservation or competitive irony. . . . [W]hat I used to hear from Bloom tallies with everything I heard about Pottle over the years from others, too." On January 5, 1950, "Fred" wrote to "Dick" for "advice" about a piece he was writing on literary biography: "Would you be willing to read the enclosed draft and make some suggestions for revision in the margin?" On February 3, 1950, he thanks RE "for your paragraphs on the aims of literary biography" and agrees with him about the dangers of an "explicit commitment to contemporary psychological theory," while admitting "I got a lot of help from Freud."

34. Although Wimsatt provided a meeting place for Ellmann's group, and wrote poems himself, winning the Cook Prize for Poetry in 1938, he had little interest in contemporary verse, according to Andrew Rosenheim, who worked as his Bursary assistant for some years (email of February 4, 2021). Norman Pearson, however, as a beginning instructor at Yale, seems at times to have allowed discussion of contemporary verse in his classes. See RE to Pearson, October 22, 1961: "It seems a long time ago (and I fear it is!) since you kindly allowed me to discuss the Byzantium poems in your class."

35. See Erwin Ellmann to RE, January 12, 1940: "From the little I can understand of the title, I like your poem. I don't know what [Botticelli] has to do with it; does he have a centaur picture?" See also February 25, 1940, in which Erwin admits that he does not understand lines about Kronus and Uranus in an unnamed poem. Erwin, too, cultivated difficulty. "Following are my two most recent attempts, for your critical delectation," he writes on October 6, 1940. "I bet you don't understand either; the ambiguities abound like dandelions."

36. Michael Ferber, an assistant professor of English at Yale from 1975 to 1982, reads "The Simplified Future" as implicitly sexual: "Maybe my mind is dirtier than yours, but I wonder if the first poem isn't about imagined intercourse or masturbation: crisis = orgasm, denouement = detumescence, 'that gun' = penis, etc. And what else but masturbation do priests concern themselves with in the confessional?" Possible support for this reading comes from a letter of October 3, 1955, from RE to Ellsworth Mason: "About expense of spirit—you probably know that spirit was an Elizabethan word for sperm. The waist [from Sonnet 129's "waste"] still seems to me rather remote from the vital spot."

37. Pottle, *The Idiom of Poetry*, pp. 99–100.

38. There is a possible thematic as well as formal connection between "Mr. Eliot's Sunday Morning Service" and "The Simplified Future," in that both concern themselves with changes in religious and/or moral outlook. According to one critic, Eliot's poem begins with a buried allusion to the Jewish philosopher Philo of Alexandria, whose disciple was Origen, the early church father; according to another, the "sapient sutlers" are Jewish, a people known for being "fond of their children" (one meaning of "philoprogenitive," in addition to "desiring many children"). To another critic, Hyam Maccoby, in "An Interpretation of 'Mr. Eliot's Sunday Morning Service,'" *European Judaism: A Journal for the New Europe* 17, no. 2 (Winter 1983/1984): 3, God is called the "Lord" (Jewish) in the first quatrain; "*τo ἐv*" (Greek) in the second; and "the Baptized God" (Christian) in the third. By the end of the poem we have moved to a debased present.

39. Craig Raine's comments on Ellmann's *Furioso* poems come in emails of April 15 and 16, 2021. Michael Ferber points out the commonplace nature of the trochaic tetrameter catalectic: "Twinkle twinkle little star," "Jack and Jill went up the hill," "Tyger tyger burning bright" (email of May 25, 2021).

40. Here, for completists, are a few comments on "Your Loveliness, I Say," a poem of ten lines that mixes sex with philosophy in the manner of Eliot's "Whispers of Immortality," a quatrain poem first collected in *Poems* (1919). In the Eliot poem the bosom of an "uncorseted" Russian temptress, Grishkin, promises "pneumatic bliss," though fleeting given the inevitable triumph of the physical over the metaphysical, of age and decay. Its closing quatrain reads:

And even the Abstract Entities
Circumambulate her charm;
But our lot crawls between dry ribs
To keep our metaphysics warm.

The inadequacy of what is left for "our lot" is like the implicit inadequacy at the end of "Your Loveliness, I Say." In Ellmann's poem, the beloved is described as "the Real . . . the Ding an Sich, / The Form, the Essence of each man's desire." The poem ends in direct address:

Lady, you are too final to be you,
Are an abstraction. I, distracted one,
Feel my hands in metaphysic as
I lightly pass them over what might be your hair.

"What might be your hair" is a poor substitute for the real thing, which, like all physical features, "dwells with Beauty—Beauty that must die" (Keats, "Ode on Melancholy"). It is an equivalent of the "dry ribs" in Eliot's poem, which take the place of the "pneumatic bliss" of Grishkin's "friendly bust." That there is an antique cast to metaphysical or idealized conceptions of love is suggested in RE's poem by the beloved being addressed as "Lady," a courtly love touch borrowed from Pound, whose own short poems are strewn with ladies: "The House of Splendour" ("And I have seen my Lady in the sun"), "Au Jardin" ("Well, there's no use your loving me / That way, Lady"), "The Bath-Tub" ("O my much praised but-not-altogether-satisfactory lady"), "A Virginal" ("As white their bark, so white the lady's hours").

41. T. S. Eliot, in "Dante" (1929), in *Selected Essays: 1917–1932* (New York: Harcourt, Brace, 1932), p. 210.

42. Left isolationists also tended to distrust reporting on the war. In a letter to Erwin of January 6, 1943, James Ellmann is cheered by Hitler's problems with Russia, adding: "Yes, I know you will discount seventy-five percent of what the press is saying, but even so."

43. Leon Trotsky, "War and the Fourth International," a pamphlet of June 1934, reprinted in *Writings of Leon Trotsky, 1933–34,* vol. 6 of *Writings of Leon Trotsky,* ed. George Breitman and Sarah Lovell, 14 vols. (New York: Pathfinder, 1947–1978), pp. 306–7.

44. Robin Winks, *Cloak and Gown: Scholars in America's Secret War* (London: Collins Harvill, 1987), p. 30. For a wider study of the "America first" movement, see Sarah Churchwell, *Behold, America: A History of America First and the American Dream* (London: Bloomsbury, 2018).

45. Quotations, statistics, and lists of activities taken from *Middlebury College Bulletin: December 1940: Bread Loaf School of English,* December 1940.

46. The paper opens: "It is only within the last fifty years that obscurity has become for English literature a major critical problem." There is a section on materialism, acquisitiveness, and the increasing specialization of knowledge as impediments to poetic understanding, as well as a definition of obscurity as "an obstruction" to the reader's "experience of the poem," which "is removable through closer reading and / or the acquisition of additional information" (p. 4). Gerard Manley Hopkins is quoted on the benefits of obscurity: "When the poem is

finally understood it explodes." On the same page RE distinguishes between "precision" and "clarity," a "type of precision" and "the true opposite of obscurity" (p. 7) (series 3, box 47).

47. In book 3, chapter 6, of an unpublished memoir titled "Wicked . . . and Spotless as the Lamb," Lyle Glazier, who became a professor of English at SUNY–Buffalo, wrote about the summer session of 1941 at Bread Loaf, which he attended expressly to meet and be taught by John Crowe Ransom. In the memoir he recalls RE introducing himself at the beginning of the session in terms like those of his July 1 letter to his parents. When asked what he was doing at the school, RE replied: "loafing . . . I don't need credits so the deal is I can move around as I please" (p. 63). When RE discovered that Glazier knew several Yeats poems by heart, however, he immediately asked him to room with him. He had a big room all to himself, with a second cot. Glazier liked and was impressed with RE but declined the invitation. Still, "Dick and I often stop on the north lawn for a gab in a pair of the wide-armed wooden chairs on the croquet ground west of the tennis courts" (p. 67). The manuscript can be consulted at Middlebury College, Archives and Special Collections.

48. Jean Douglas to RE, February 13, 1942.

3. THE WAR YEARS

1. These details come from RE's "Statement of Experiences and Qualifications," produced after he was eventually drafted into the Navy on January 22, 1943, to be transferred to "European Shore Duty" (box 44, series 3).

2. From an undated letter of June 1942 to his parents.

3. See Robin W. Winks, *Cloak and Gown: Scholars in the Secret War, 1939–1961* (1987; New Haven, CT: Yale University Press, 1996). p. 25.

4. For Hall's firing, see undated letter from Paul Pickerel; for O'Donnell's firing, see his letter of September 4, 1942. O'Donnell went on to teach English at Massachusetts State College (later the University of Massachusetts Amherst).

5. Winks, *Cloak and Gown,* p. 35.

6. Ellsworth Mason, "Ellmann's Road to Xanadu," in *Omnium Gatherum: Essays for Richard Ellmann,* ed. Susan Dick, Declan Kiberd, Dougald McMillan, and Joseph Ronsley (Gerrards Cross, UK: Colin Smythe, 1989), p. 8. (Hereafter cited in the text by page number.)

7. Here is Jean Douglas's poem from her letter of April 15, 1942: "I need not think to hear from you, you say,/Till you have filed a memorandum;/Tho what is memorable I would not say/Yet twixt the deed and doing, still you may/Set forth a penny postal, love, my way."

8. According to an undated postcard to his parents.

9. The quotation from Alice Silberstein comes from a letter to James Ellmann, excerpted in James Ellmann to RE, September 14, 1942.

10. This exchange with the Radcliffe girl is reported in a May 10, 1943, entry in RE's own journal.

11. Courtney Borden to RE, January 15, 1943.

12. Baudelaire's challenge appears in a letter prefacing *Le Spleen de Paris: Petits poèmes en prose* (1869). The challenge, in translation, opens the introduction to

Catherine Flynn's *James Joyce and the Matter of Paris* (Cambridge: Cambridge University Press, 2019): "Which of us has not, in his moments of ambition, dreamed of the miracle of a poetic prose, musical, without rhythm and without rhyme, supple enough and rugged enough to adapt itself to the lyrical movements of the soul, the undulations of reverie, the sudden starts of consciousness? It was, above all, out of the exploration of huge cities, out of the intersection of the innumerable interrelations, that this obsessive ideal was found." See Flynn's book for the influence Baudelaire's challenge had on Joyce.

13. RE to parents, December 29, 1942.

14. The postcard, from New Haven, dated October 21, 1942, describes the weekend get-together for the Harvard-Yale game as a "virtual reunion." The signature on the postcard is indecipherable. The Fran Anderson letter is dated November 28, 1942.

15. The letter is undated. Feidelson was the first of RE's Yale friends to be drafted.

16. See also RE to parents, January 17, 1943: "I'm continuing my Spanish intensively and Portuguese a little less so. With Spanish I am just beginning to know enough words to express myself. On the whole the Berlitz method costs more than it should, and I don't think I'll go on with it even if I do remain for awhile."

17. RE's spelling was "Democlecian" in an undated letter of May 1943. Mason, in "Ellmann's Road to Xanadu," p. 8, also quotes the phrase, spelling it "Democletian."

18. James Ellmann to RE, in undated letter from the first week of March 1943.

19. RE to James Ellmann, undated postcard, late July.

20. Mason, "Ellmann's Road to Xanadu," p. 8.

21. Mason, "Ellmann's Road to Xanadu," p. 8.

22. See RE to parents, September 17 and October 11, 1943. The only relief from the tedium of their office work for RE and his fellow yeomen came on the weekends when they hitched rides into Williamsburg, six miles away. There RE made contact with a Yale classmate, Joseph Bottkol, who taught English at William and Mary College. Bottkol introduced Ellmann to several colleagues, among them the head of the English Department, "a very jovial guy," reported RE, who "took a fancy for me, so that Bottkol said I could probably get a job there after the war." The Bottkols and their friends aside, there was "nothing to do" in Williamsburg. In October, Bottkol left for Washington, where he was to take a job with the OSS, the sort of job Ellmann himself sought. After the war Bottkol would teach for many years at Mount Holyoke.

23. See RE to parents, November 1, 1943.

24. The first lectures he was assigned were on Navy traditions and laws, "including articles of government, military courtesy, betrayal (not a navy custom), sentry duty, and interior guard" (RE to parents, November 4, 1943). "They're the dullest lectures to give, but it will be a change. And something may yet come from Washington" (RE to William Ellmann, November 5, 1943). After a few days of lecturing, RE was surprised to have found the experience "very pleasant. One falls into a dictatorial tone so that the discipline problem is not too bad even though you are talking to 250 to 600 tired men" (RE to parents, November 15, 1943).

"Two things I've discovered," he reports later in the same week, "one is how easy it is to be tough; the other is what a difference there is between one group and another; one group will listen attentively . . . another has to be threatened continually with being forced to stand to attention, or some such thing." He was soon given new subjects to teach: "on scouting and patrolling, which includes map-making, and on Offensive Combat Tactics; your little son Dick, mind you, who has never held a Springfield rifle in his life. But it's all in the books so I shall struggle through" (RE to parents, November 18, 1943).

25. RE says of Joyce that "he decided to make Bloom amiable and even noble in a humdrum sort of way, but to save him from sentimentality by making him also somewhat absurd as a convert, a drifter, a cuckold" (*JJ*, p. 373).

26. RE to parents, in an undated letter of January 1944.

27. Helen Manning to RE, February 24, 1944.

28. RE to Erwin Ellmann, undated letter February 1944.

29. James Ellmann to RE and Erwin Ellmann, February 27, 1944.

30. RE to James Ellmann, February 29, 1944.

31. Helen Manning to RE, March 2, 1944.

32. James Ellmann to RE, March 25, 1944: "To them you are a pariah. I rather think you were made to feel that from your first meeting with her dad, though I can well be mistaken about this."

33. RE to James Ellmann, March 29, 1944.

34. James Ellmann to RE, April 11, 1944.

35. From an email of January 12, 2022.

36. Reported in RE to parents, January 24, 1944.

37. The move involved a brief spell in the Stevedore Pool in Camp Peary, described in a letter to Mason as "hell" (RE to Ellsworth Mason, February 15, 1944). Mason explained to Ellmann, in a letter of March 21, 1944, what Stevedore Pools do: mostly "traveling around loading and unloading convoy cargo. . . . They contain a godawful number of storekeepers, as hatch-checkers, but how they utilize the yeomen, I do not know."

38. RE to parents, July 6, 1944.

39. James Ellmann to RE, May 13, 1944.

40. RE to parents, May 14 and 19, 1944.

41. RE to parents, May 21, 1944.

42. RE to parents, June 6, 1944.

43. Frank Trager (1906–1984) was program director of the American Jewish Committee from 1938 to 1943 and of the Anti-Defamation League of B'nai B'rith from 1943 to 1945. In the early 1930s he had been a supporter of Norman Thomas and secretary and treasurer of the New York State Socialist Party. After the war he moved to the right and was an outspoken anti-Communist and supporter of the Vietnam War. He was to teach at MIT, Yale, NYU, and Johns Hopkins.

44. James Ellmann to RE, June 13, 1944.

45. RE to William Ellmann, June 25, 1944.

46. RE to an unnamed "My Dear," June 16, 1944.

47. RE to William O'Donnell, June 23, 1944.

48. RE to Ellsworth Mason, August 18, 1944.

49. RE to parents, in undated letter of August 1944. The letter he wrote to the Bureau of Naval Personnel, on July 4, 1944, was to Lt. Martin Bickford, the Yale graduate who had interviewed him at Camp Peary. It was written "with the temerity fostered by attendance at the same university, and more in desperation than in hope." In it, RE reminds Bickford of his experience and that he was barred from a commission because of his myopia, and requests "assignment to European shore duty in view of my language qualifications, travel in Europe, intelligence work in the OSS, and Special Assignment status."

50. RE to William Ellmann, August 25, 1944.

51. RE to Frank Trager, January 7, 1945.

52. RE to Andrews Wanning, December 3, 1944.

53. RE to Frank Trager, January 7, 1945.

54. Winks, *Cloak and Gown,* p. 349.

55. James Ellmann to RE, October 5, 1944.

56. RE to Andrews Wanning, December 3, 1944.

57. RE to Ellsworth Mason, December 5, 1944; RE to parents, January 18, 1945.

58. RE to parents, January 12, 1945.

59. RE to "Mel," a fellow Seabee from Charleston, March 9, 1945.

60. RE to unidentified "Victor," March 10, 1945.

61. RE to parents, September 29, 1944.

62. RE to parents, October 22, 1944.

63. RE to parents, October 3, 1944; the parenthetical remark about the war being "too serious to write about" comes from a letter to parents, December 23, 1944.

64. RE to Julie Smith, January 22, 1945: "Since we have known each other almost six months now, I presume upon your love by sending you the above [a poem] in its rather undigested form. My next will be more Apollonian."

65. From Auden's "In Memory of W. B. Yeats (d. Jan. 1939)." Andrew Rosenheim points out: "The 'we' RE quotes in 'And we will pardon Paul Claudel' needs a *sic* since it's not in the poem—it's Time that pardons Paul Claudel not us" (email of December 18, 2021). These lines, from the original 1939 published version, were excised in later reprintings.

66. RE to parents, October 22, 1944.

67. RE to parents, October 25, 1944.

68. RE to parents, October 29, 1944.

69. RE to parents, November 13, 1944.

70. RE to "Bert," a friend from New York, now in Calcutta, October 30, 1944.

71. RE incorrectly refers to her throughout his Paris correspondence as "Mme. Mande." She was Proust's literary executor and later referred to herself as "Mante-Proust" or "Mante Proust."

72. RE to Helen Manning, November 5, 1944.

73. Helen Manning to RE, November 9, 1944.

74. RE to parents, November 11, 1944.

75. From the second page of a four-page draft of "Down Under with Michaux" ("Aux antipodes avec Michaux," in Thérèse Lauriol's translation). RE's contribution appears in *Henri Michaux,* a volume of essays on Michaux edited by Raymond

Bellour (Paris: Cahiers du l'Herne, 1966), pp. 272–73. Other contributors to the volume include Paul Celan, Jorge-Luis Borges, Jacques Prévert, Allen Ginsberg, and Maurice Blanchot.

76. RE to parents, November 24, 1944.

77. *Confluences* was founded in Lyon by René Tavernier during the Occupation and subsequently edited in Paris by Bertelé.

78. RE to parents, December 3, 1944. The article appeared as "Lettre de New York: Mars et les Muses américaines," *Confluences* (January/February 1945): 6–99. Its opening sentences read: "En Am é érique la réaction contre l'isolationisme nous a font nous poser périodiquement la question de savoir ai nous a nous été suffisamment 'troublés' par la guerre. Nos écrivans n'ont échappé à cette interrogation." The article was translated by Jacques Calmy.

79. RE to parents, December 4, 1944.

80. RE to Henry Wells, April 15, 1945; also RE to Ellsworth Mason, December 5, 1944, for Gide's role in gaining for Michaux "official recognition" and recognition as "the favorite of the French literary avant-garde."

81. Richard Ellmann, trans. and ed., *Selected Writings of Henri Michaux: The Space Within* (New York: New Directions, 1951), p. viii. When a second edition of *Selected Writings* was printed in 1968, RE added several paragraphs to his introduction. This revised introduction was reprinted in a posthumous collection of RE's essays titled *a long the riverrun: Selected Essays.* It was published in 1988 in London by Hamish Hamilton.

82. RE to Ellsworth Mason, December 5, 1944; then RE, introduction to *Selected Writings of Henri Michaux,* p. viii.

83. Quoted in the introduction to RE, *Selected Writings of Henri Michaux,* pp. xx–xxi.

84. The quotation about the "big adult" comes from David Ball, trans., *Darkness Moves: An Henri Michaux Anthology, 1927–1984* (Berkeley: University of California Press, 1994), p. x. RE's quotations from Michaux about the self's instability come from a Michaux passage he does not translate in *Selected Writings*—the "Afterword" to *Plume précédé de lointain intérior* (1938), translated by Ball as *Plume Preceded by Far Off Inside,* p. 77. Here is a fuller excerpt from the passage RE quotes and translates, in Ball's translation:

> Perhaps we are not made for just one self. We are wrong to cling to it. The prejudice in favor of unity. (Here as elsewhere, the will: impoverishing and sacrificing. . . .) The greatest fatigue of the day and of a life may be caused by the effort, by the tension necessary to keep the same self through the continual temptations to change it.
>
> We want too much to be someone.
>
> There is not one self. *There are not ten selves. There is no self. ME is only a position in equilibrium.*

85. Malcolm Bowie, *Henri Michaux: A Study of His Literary Works* (Oxford: Clarendon Press, 1973), p. 2.

86. RE to Julie Smith, March 15, 1945.

87. RE, "Down Under with Michaux," p. 1.

88. See RE to Julie Smith, November 19, 1944, and RE to Helen Manning, November 15, 1944.

89. RE to Mason, December 5, 1944.

90. On January 23, 1945, in a letter to Andrews Wanning, RE says of his article that it "started from Macleish's 'Irresponsibles' [an essay in the *Nation,* May 18, 1940, criticizing American intellectuals for failing to defend liberal and democratic ideals], pointed out a lot of specifically anti-fascist books and then a lot of reform novels, discussed the exchange of citizenship by Eliot and Auden, a little on our critic-ridden age, and a word or two on popular novels." To Connie Dimock Ellis, in a letter of May 22, 1945, he describes the article as "workmanlike."

91. In a letter of February 2, 1955, to Harriet Weaver, Beach recalled that she "met Ellmann during the war when he was in the navy, a young fellow in a sailor suit and very much interested in poetry. He translated a great deal of Michaux's and did a very good job of it I think." Keri Walsh, ed., *The Letters of Sylvia Beach* (New York: Columbia University Press, 2010), p. 235.

92. James Laughlin, "Richard Ellmann's Michaux: A Publisher's Recollections," in Dick et al., *Omnium Gatherum,* p. 23. Two years before Ellmann's volume appeared, Laughlin published Sylvia Beach's translation of Michaux's *A Barbarian in Asia.*

93. The first Stage Door Canteen was a nightclub for American and Allied servicemen in the Broadway theater district. It was founded in 1942 by the American Theatre Wing (ATW), with entertainers who volunteered their services by way of buoying up the morale of American troops during World War II. Its popularity led to the establishment of other canteens throughout the United States as well as in London and Paris. There is a brief film clip of couples dancing on opening night of the canteen in Paris, though I was unable to pick out RE, nor is there any footage of Noel Coward, Maurice Chevalier, or Marlene Dietrich. See: https://www.bridgemanimages.com/en/noartistknown/the-opening-of-stage-door-canteen-a-military-recreational-club-in-paris-france-in-1945/footage/asset/779452.

94. RE's account of the opening and his dance with Dietrich comes from a letter to his parents of March 10, 1945.

4. YEATS

1. The letter is addressed to an unidentified "John," and ends "I envy you working with Craig, whom I respect. Chapel Hill even in wartime must be pleasant. I'm sorry not to be in a position to drop in on you for a weekend. I hope this finds Clarice and you very well."

2. RE to parents, March 1, 1945.

3. That "TD" is an abbreviation for "Tradevman," a type of naval petty officer, is of little help. Lucy Ellmann suggests "Temporary Duty," citing https://en.wikipedia.org/wiki/Temporary_duty_assignment, which offers the military abbreviations "TDY" (temporary duty travel) and "TAD" (temporary additional travel).

4. RE to parents, May 5, 1945, which includes RE's recounting of what he had written to Pearson.

5. See Marla Strassberger, "The Spy Who Made Good in Dublin," *Daily Northwestern,* January 20, 1967.

6. Elliot Weinberger, "Tinker, Tailor, Poet, Spy: Tales of Literary Espionage," *New York Times,* October 4, 1992; Erwin Ellmann's letter was published in the *Times* on November 22, 1992.

7. Robin Winks, *Cloak and Gown: Scholars in the Secret War, 1939–1961* (1987; New Haven, CT: Yale University Press, 1996), p. 299.

8. RE to Charles Feidelson, July 17, 1945; RE to William Ellmann, June 26, 1945.

9. RE to parents, undated letter; Arthur Krock, "In the Nation; The OSS Gets It Coming and Going: The Key Men the Joint Chiefs Take Over," *New York Times,* July 31, 1945.

10. RE to Julie Smith, August 22, 1945; the description of the citation RE wrote for himself comes from a letter to his parents of October 29, 1945; the quotation from Winks comes from *Cloak and Gown,* p. 299.

11. See also RE to parents, September 7, 1945: "I shall always regret not being made an officer, but I can hardly complain of my last 3 stations—Washington, Paris, London, and my present work is pretty interesting and responsible."

12. RE to Ellsworth Mason, June 8, 1946.

13. Ellsworth Mason to RE, June 9, 1956.

14. RE to Ellsworth Mason, June 10, 1956.

15. RE to Ellsworth Mason, December 7, 1953.

16. RE to Oxford University Press, May 24, 1956.

17. RE to Julie Smith, August 28, 1945.

18. RE to parents, July 20, 1945.

19. RE to Julie Smith, August 22, 1945.

20. RE to parents, undated letter, early August 1945.

21. Angleton had been recruited by Pearson in 1942. In March 1945, shortly before Ellmann's arrival in London, Angleton was made "Chief of X-2 for all Italy, at twenty-seven the youngest X-2 branch chief anywhere" (Winks, *Cloak and Gown,* p. 352). Although born in Idaho, Angleton had spent his boyhood in Milan, where his father owned the Italian franchise of National Cash Register Corporation and was head of the American Chamber of Commerce. He had boarded at Malvern College in Worcestershire from 1933 to 1936 before entering Yale. As head of the Italian desk, he was a busy man, often working late into the night at 14 Ryder Street. According to Michael Holzman, one of his biographers, he was basically "living in his office." When he did go out, two of the places he frequented were the Connaught Hotel and Quaglino's. Holzman, *James Jesus Angleton: The CIA, and the Craft of Counterintelligence* (Amherst: University of Massachusetts Press, 2008), pp. 49–50.

22. Pound's visit to New Haven was a side trip. His main aim in the United States was to lobby in Washington against American intervention in the European war. He was not the only celebrated poet to advise *Furioso.* So did E. E. Cummings and William Carlos Williams. While at Yale, Angleton had offered to bring out an Italian edition of T. S. Eliot's poems, an offer Eliot took seriously. The two men corresponded frequently both before and after Angleton's service in X-2.

23. RE to parents, August 19, 1945.

24. RE's guess about why Mrs. Yeats answered his letter comes from a four-page unpublished manuscript titled "Visit to Mrs. Yeats." The point about Mrs. Yeats being English comes from an unpublished two-and-a-half-page manuscript titled "In Pursuit of Joyce and Others." Both manuscripts found in box 61, folder 10, Ellmann Papers. Folder 10 is titled "Misc. Joyce, German essay on Joyce."

25. RE, "Visit to Mrs. Yeats."

26. From the thirty-two-page 1979 preface to Richard Ellmann, *Yeats: The Man and the Masks* (1948; Oxford: Oxford University Press, 1979), p. xi. (Hereafter the preface cited in the text by page number.)

27. RE, "Visit to Mrs. Yeats."

28. RE to parents, September 28, 1945.

29. RE to Douglas Hyde, August 22, 1945; RE to Richard Hayes, September 6, 1945.

30. RE to parents, September 6, 1945.

31. RE to Julie Smith, October 6, 1945.

32. See RE to parents, October 11, 1945: "I'm excited over my Dublin researches and have managed to buy several books in London that will prove very useful in substantiating my thesis and so far as I know have never been used with regards to Yeats before; they're on his secret society of the Golden Dawn."

33. RE to parents, October 11, 1945.

34. These quotations come from an unpublished and untitled manuscript in box 61, folder 10, Ellmann Papers. In both *The Identity of Yeats* (London: Macmillan, 1954), pp. 86–88, and *James Joyce,* pp. 106–8, RE publishes the account of the meeting Yeats had given in his unpublished preface to *Ideas of Good and Evil.* The relevant exchange reads: "Presently he got up to go, and, as he was going out, he said, 'I am twenty. How old are you?' I told him, but I am afraid I said I was a year younger than I am. He said with a sigh, 'I thought as much. I have met you too late. You are too old.'" Roy Foster, in *W. B. Yeats: A Life, 1865–1914,* vol. 1 (Oxford: Oxford University Press, 1997), p. 585n90, recounts the following anecdote, from W. R. Rodgers's "Notes for the Radio": "John McCormick once repeated the story to Dulanty, the Irish ambassador in London, and Dulanty asked if it were true. Joyce was very cross about it, cross with Gogarty. 'Why,' said Joyce to Dulanty, 'even if I'd *thought* it I wouldn't have *said* it to Yeats. It would have been unmannerly.'"

35. Leslie Cross, book editor for the *Milwaukee Journal,* in a profile for September 11, 1960.

36. Henry Hart, "Richard Ellmann's Oxford Blues," *Sewanee Review* 117, no. 2 (Spring 2009): 280.

37. The episode took place in 1965 at Northwestern University. The newly appointed junior colleague was the poet, novelist, and essayist Michael Anania, who recounted it to me in an email of July 22, 2020.

38. Ellsworth Mason recalled that Ellmann "felt demeaned by his non-officer status throughout the war. I first realized this one evening as we were walking in his barracks area and a fellow yeoman approached us with Ensign Bubenick, from Oregon he said, and Ellmann did something extraordinary to avoid saluting that officer. He pulled off his sailor's hat! While an enlisted man does not have to salute an officer when he is not wearing a hat (to avoid popping salutes continually

indoors), the fact of not wearing a hat outdoors constitutes being out of uniform, a condition punishable under the regulations of the Navy, but this Ellmann risked to avoid the salute." Ellsworth Mason, "Ellmann's Road to Xanadu," in *Omnium Gatherum: Essays for Richard Ellmann,* ed. Susan Dick, Declan Kiberd, Dougald McMillan, and Joseph Ronsley (Gerrards Cross, UK: Colin Smythe, 1989), pp. 8–9. (Hereafter cited in the text by page number.)

39. RE to Julie Smith, October, 1945.

40. In an undated letter from this period (box 9, folder 3, item 1, Ellmann Papers), RE's father writes after hearing of an initial offer from Yale: "Congratulations on the possibility you describe today in the matter of an association with Yale. . . . French has come through like a gentleman for you."

41. See, for example, Richard Ellmann, *Yeats: The Man and the Masks,* pp. 75–76, 273–75, 288. (Hereafter cited in the text by page number.)

42. The Frank O'Connor anecdote of June 30, 1946, recorded by RE, is in "'Gasping on the Strand': Richard Ellmann's W. B. Yeats Notebooks," ed. Warwick Gould, *Poems and Contexts: Yeats Annual 16* (2005): 279–361, quoted at pp. 295–96. (Hereafter cited in the text by page number.)

43. Second paragraph of one-and-a-half-page untitled manuscript (box 61, folder 10, Ellmann Papers). The manuscript begins: "Yeats's father was always trying to reduce his metaphysics to humanistic proportions while Yeats was always trying to raise his father's humanism to metaphysical dimensions." The quotations within square brackets about the Pollexfens and Yeatses come from RE, *Yeats: The Man and the Masks,* p. 10.

44. RE to parents, September 28, 1945; Norman Pearson as "guardian angel" comes from RE to his parents, September 30, 1945.

45. Unpublished four-page manuscript "Visit to Maud Gonne" (box 61, folder 10, p. 1, Ellmann Papers). See also RE to mother, December 2, 1945: Hayes "is the guy to whom I promised the melon seeds (Michigan musk melon would be allright); he also likes cigars and tea. Please don't send quite so much as you did to the others; 3 pounds of tea, a few cigars, and some seeds would be very adequate."

46. RE's anxieties about the Dublin Irish are voiced in an undated letter to his parents probably written during his visit of 1946–1947 (box 9, folder 4, item 19, Ellmann Papers): "DeVane wrote very complementarily about the first eleven chapters, but as usual made almost no comments except about punctuation. He is an amiable, intelligent man who knows nothing about the subject—but don't quote me. I find as I get older that I can't speak out about anything, and that is especially true here in Dublin, where everything I say is likely to be transmitted to the wrong people."

47. RE to parents, December 28, 1945.

48. RE to parents, December 23, 1945.

49. RE to parents, October 11, 1945.

50. RE to parents, November 17, 1945.

51. On December 1, 1945, in a letter of reference to Donald Goodchild of the Rockefeller Foundation, Robert Menner wrote of RE: "Like many men of a literary turn of mind, he is quite sure of his own literary taste, and dislikes some kinds of literature as heartily as he likes other. I don't believe that this characteristic would prevent him from achieving distinction. What might prevent it is no fault of his own, the fact that Jews do not have a fair chance in our profession today. I

should personally hope that this would be another reason for helping a man of first-rate ability."

52. RE to parents, November 24, 1945. See also RE to parents, December 2, 1945: "I'm now planning to return to Ireland as soon as I'm discharged, rather than waiting for a year during which others may grab at the same material; also I now feel that I am severely handicapped by my lack of a degree."

53. See RE to parents, undated, early October 1946: "I find that my proposed single chapters generally proliferate into two or three before I'm done."

54. RE to parents, in an undated letter. In December 1947 RE applied to the Rockefeller Foundation for a six-month extension of his fellowship, which was granted, taking him through June 1947.

55. Strassberger, "The Spy Who Made Good in Dublin."

56. John Kelleher, "With Dick in Dublin," in Dick et al., *Omnium Gatherum*, p. 17. (Hereafter cited in the text by page number.)

57. Details about John Kelleher are from an obituary in the *Harvard Gazette*, January 22, 2004; details about junior fellows at Harvard come from the Society of Fellows website: https://socfell.fas.harvard.edu/about.

58. RE to parents, undated letter, fall 1947.

59. Roy Foster, *W. B. Yeats: A Life*, vol. 2, *The Arch-Poet, 1915–1939* (Oxford: Oxford University Press, 2003), p. 468. Foster lists his sources as two letters by Maud Gonne, one of July 24, 1946, to Ethel Mannin, the other an undated letter of the later 1940s.

60. See Ann Saddlemyer, *Becoming George: The Life of Mrs. W. B. Yeats* (Oxford: Oxford University Press, 2002), p. 623.

61. Saddlemyer, *Becoming George*, p. 622.

62. This quote and the preceding details about gifts and favors come from Saddlemyer, *Becoming George*, pp. 622–23, 788.

63. See Saddlemyer's account of this remark in *Becoming George*, p. 326: "George's memories of these happy times were overshadowed by one particular incident that she frequently recalled: 'When Michael was about three or even four, WBY had taken Anne [Michael's sister] to the postbox to post letters. Michael had not been taken and was very jealous; one or two mornings later, when I was bringing him downstairs, he saw WB going to the bath, he just looked over his shoulder and said, "who is that man?"'" (p. 326). In James Stephens's version of the story, quoted by Saddlemyer, when passing Michael on the stairs, Yeats, "thinking he ought to say something to his own baby, murmured a couple of lines from John Donne. . . . The infant looked at him with no reference, and roared in a titanic voice: 'Go away, Man!' Yeats and I went abashed away" (p. 327).

64. James E. Cronin, *St. Louis Post-Dispatch*, April 3, 1949. In a mostly negative review, Cronin ends by saying "you will need to read this book." He says that RE "displays great skill" in bringing his scholarly knowledge to bear; and that "he has one of the freshest, most mature and sinuous styles ever to come unscathed through the fiery furnace of the Yale Graduate School." Earlier in the review he complains, "When one considers how important a place money has had in the lives of poets it is extraordinary how casual their biographers are on the subject."

65. It was also the view of RE's brother Erwin, who was perhaps his toughest critic, and yet was the dedicatee of *Yeats: The Man and the Masks*. Here are some

of his comments from a letter of March 5, 1948: "I don't know where you got your title, unless from me, but I don't care for it"; "Leave out Hegel and say it straight"; "Chapter 5 seems to throw an awful lot of theosophical material at the reader for a very slim harvest in terms of your man."

66. O'Connor's opinion of the dissertation was relayed by RE to his parents in a letter of June 28, 1947: "He thought it excellent down to the marriage but suggested the last five chapters should be expanded to a separate volume. This is probably true. He said it was the first time a great poet has been handled soon enough after his death so that one could tell how he happened to write what he did. In general he was very flattering."

67. Feidelson's description of the dissertation as "reactionary" in method comes from an undated letter written by RE to Mason, in reply to Mason's letter of January 27, 1948.

68. That RE had anxieties about Pottle-like "old-fashioned" examiners, as well as New Critical ones, is suggested by a letter to his parents of September 14, 1946: "I'm trying to mention as many names as I can," he writes, "to make it a literary history as well as an intellectual biography."

69. Quoted from the Yale website: https://gsas.yale.edu/academic-requirements/dissertations/field-porter-dissertation-prizes.

70. Ellsworth Mason to RE, January 27, 1946.

71. RE originally thought his extern was Seamus O'Sullivan, whose real name was James Starkey. In a letter to his parents, he described Starkey as "very well educated and I hope not too crotchety though he and Yeats got on very ill." (Yeats once said of him, "The trouble with O'Sullivan is that when he's not drunk he's sober," a crack Ellmann prudently kept out of the dissertation). Of Hone's disapproval (which RE thought was Starkey's), he told his parents: "I don't consider this criticism very serious because of its source, but I don't like it." The correct identification of RE's "extern" as Hone comes in a letter of April 27, 1947.

72. RE to parents, May 3, 1947.

73. RE to parents, September 17, 1947.

74. See RE to parents, July 13, 1947: "There are two Macmillans—I have been warned against the New York one."

75. RE to parents, undated postcard.

76. The letter's author is unnamed. It ends "Yours faithfully, Macmillan & Co., Ltd."

77. RE to parents, December 1, 1946.

78. Mary M. Colum, review of *Yeats: The Man and the Masks*, in *Tomorrow*, February 1949. (Of course, RE "dropped over" to Dublin just after the war, not at its beginning.) Warwick Gould's account of Jeffares's feelings about *Yeats: The Man and the Masks* and about RE himself come from an interview of March 13, 2020.

79. The review, by "M.A.R," appeared in the *Irish Independent* on December 31, 1949, under the title "American Professor's Study of Yeats and His Work." In an undated letter to his parents, probably written toward the end of his 1946–1947 stay in Dublin, RE recounts a visit to a meeting at the "National University, which Joyce attended as a young man." At this meeting, "some fellow said in a speech that he didn't understand how American Jews like Harry Levin could

dare to write about someone so Irish as and European as Joyce. There were no public questions, but afterwards I went up and asked him if he'd read Levin's book on Joyce, which he hadn't, and I pointed out to him that Joyce, when he read Levin's manuscript, said it was the book he had been waiting for. He seemed a little abashed" (box 9, folder 4, item 42, Ellmann Papers).

80. James J. Sweeney, "The Development of the Poet Yeats," review of Richard Ellmann, *Yeats: The Man and the Masks,* in *New York Times,* December 19, 1948.

81. Mason, "Ellmann's Road to Xanadu," p. 11.

82. Foster, *W. B. Yeats,* vol. 2, p. 285.

83. Foster, *W. B. Yeats,* vol. 2, p. 282.

84. See Saddlemyer, *Becoming George,* p. 623.

85. Maud Ellmann's remarks come from a contribution to a panel at the virtual James Joyce International Conference of June 16, 2021. The panel commemorated the life and work of the Joyce scholar Michael Groden, who had died that year.

86. RE to parents, January 1, 1947. In an undated letter from this period (box 9, folder 3, item 1, Ellmann Papers), RE's father writes after hearing of an initial offer from Yale: "Congratulations on the possibility you describe today in the matter of an association with Yale. . . . French has come through like a gentleman for you." In a later, undated letter (item 13 in the same folder) RE's father advises regarding Harvard: "Some other university may offer you some juicy opportunity. I know you are not deceived by the cash, nor the title. Both have value; but they must [be] balanced by the . . . advantage of being connected with Harvard—with its magical name."

5. MARY / NORTHWESTERN

1. Sherburn's letter was dated November 4, 1946. RE answered it on November 19, 1946: "I'm very sorry to have occasioned even a good-natured rebuke. In the Times note you mention I found it hard to describe briefly my tenuous connection with Harvard. . . . After consulting with another wandering scholar I let myself believe that I was oversimplifying rather than perverting the truth. The distinction between faculty and staff is one which would not have occurred to me, though it doubtless should have. . . . Needless to say I shall give Harvard no further cause for complaint."

2. RE to Ellsworth Mason, February 13, 1948.

3. The course RE eventually proposed was "Blake and Yeats," described in a letter of April 22, 1948, to B. J. Whiting, chair of the English Department, as "a comparative study, with emphasis on their poetic 'systems' as attempts to cope with the literary, religious, and political problems of their time." In a second paragraph, RE elaborates: "I would try to deal with such matters as the effect on the poets of contemporary events (the French Revolution and the Irish Revolution, for example); their use of Christian and non-Christian symbols and of the mystical tradition; their efforts to resist contemporary philosophy and science (the theories of Newton and Locke, [Herbert] Spencer and Darwin); their efforts to impress intellectual coherence upon their experiences; their stylistic developments; the influence of Blake on Yeats)."

4. RE to parents, December 16, 1947.

5. Bentley's PhD dissertation was published in 1944 as *A Century of Hero Worship* (reissued in 1969 as *The Cult of the Superman*).

6. Coe College in Cedar Rapids, Iowa, a private liberal arts college, was founded in 1851.

7. James Ellmann to RE in an undated letter.

8. RE to Ellsworth Mason, November 1, 1947.

9. Her mother's quoted words are as Lucy Ellmann recalls them, in an email of April 15, 2022. In addition, she complained about the Minnesota winter, which she found too cold, too harsh, too snowy, and too long. Hivnor's daughter Margaret LaBarbera, in an email of May 16, 1922, reported that she thought it "unlikely that [her father] had an 'affair'; he was cautious, anxious, loyal, and shy." Hivnor had come to Minnesota from the Yale School of Drama rather than the Yale English Department. In January 1948 his three-act play *Too Many Thumbs* was produced at the Minneapolis Theater. He went on to write plays produced off-Broadway, and with his wife, Mary Otis, along with Robert Lowell, Lionel Abel, and Eric Bentley, he was associated in New York with the Theater of Living Ideas, which showcased new drama through Sunday afternoon play readings.

10. Had she stayed at Minnesota a second year, her pay would have been $2,800; her pay at Wellesley was $2,600.

11. A copy of "The Sisters" is in the Ellmann Papers. The fate of the novel, as well as the dates of its composition, are unclear from correspondence. On January 13, 1952, a friend of Mary's named Rosalyn, who was living in New York and working at the US-owned international radio broadcaster Voice of America, asked, "Have you been able to work on your novel?" On May 2, 1953, Mary wrote to her parents-in-law: "Books are always a great nuisance. I sent mine, as you know, to our friend Jane Lawson at Little, Brown and Co. But almost a month later I discover, in a letter from her, that she's no longer with Little, Brown—a new job, not publishing at all, at M.I.T. She offered to read the MS though and write me what publisher it would be best to try it on. But I was disappointed—to find out it really hadn't gone anywhere at all yet. So now more waiting."

12. This quotation from "The Sisters" comes from pp. 7–8 of the manuscript. (Hereafter cited in the text by page number.)

13. Lucy Ellmann, email, April 15, 2022.

14. Craig Raine, email, April 22, 2019.

15. Mary Poovey, "Recent Studies of Gender," *Modern Philology* 88, no. 4 (May 1991): 415.

16. Lucy Ellmann, email, March 24, 2022. Maud Ellmann does not recall hearing this story about the effect her father's legs had on her mother. "My mother was rather prudish," Maud writes in an email of July 12, 2022, "and I can't imagine her talking to us about my father's legs."

17. The *Tithonus* thing is probably "Tennyson's *Hail, Briton!* and *Tithon* in the Heath Manuscript," *PMLA* 64 (June 1949): 385–416, the third of three articles on Tennyson that Mary published under her maiden name, Donahue. As Mary Ellmann she published two more Tennyson articles: "Tennyson: Revision of *In Memoriam,* Section 85," *MLN* (January 1950): 22–30, and "Tennyson Unpublished Letters, 1833–36," *MLN* (April 1950): 223–38.

18. Mary Ellmann to RE, August 6, 1948.

19. Lucy believes her mother was married in a dark navy suit, which she remembers seeing in her closet.

20. Lucy Ellmann, email, May 10, 2022.

21. Lucy Ellmann, email, March 24, 2022.

22. The telegram is not in the Ellmann Papers. Both Maud and Lucy were told that it contained the phrase "We forgive you," but also, wrongly, that it was sent when Stephen was born.

23. Maud's remark about Mary hating the name Joan comes from an email of June 29, 2022. That Ellmann himself did not object to his parents calling Mary "Joan," or found an excuse not to object, might partly be explained by Erwin's habit of addressing him as "Dave" in correspondence (David was Ellmann's middle name). It is hard, though, to see their parents' use of Mary's middle name as similarly playful or affectionate.

24. The quotation from "Joan" is cited in a later letter from James Ellmann to RE, August 24, 1949.

25. What James Ellmann has to say in the letter of August 17 about the girl his son is in love with (the decision to call her Joan has not yet been agreed to, but it is noteworthy that he does not call her Mary) is that "if she is already your wife, we are her friend, of course, but I must confess, a grudging friend for the time being. We shall try hard to be her friend from the bottom of our hearts, if life permits it, and if she desires to earn our friendship."

26. Lucy Ellmann, email, July 13, 2019. According to Special Collections and Archives at Georgia Tech University, where Esta Klein taught English for twenty-eight years (1965–1993), Klein's papers contain no correspondence. Klein died on March 28, 2011, predeceased by her husband. They had no children. To Sylvia Berkman, Mary wrote cards and a letter disclosing their plan to be married, and on August 16, 1949, Sylvia wrote to congratulate them, but also to dread the prospect that "Mary will no longer be among us at Wellesley."

27. Mary Ellmann to RE, July 7, 1949.

28. Mary Ellmann to RE, July 2, 1949.

29. Mary Ellmann to RE, July 4, 1949.

30. Mary Ellmann to RE, July 7, 1949.

31. RE to Mrs. W. B. Yeats, October 8, 1949.

32. The remark about Mary teaching again "at least this year" comes from RE to parents, August 20, 1949, in which Mary is "Joan." The account of shipboard activities comes from RE to Mrs. W. B. Yeats, October 8, 1949.

33. In addition to freshman composition, Mary taught an introductory course titled "The Interpretation of Literature," described as a study of the theory and practice of poetry, fiction, and drama (the poets assigned were Donne, Pope, and Eliot).

34. Mary Ellmann, *Thinking about Women* (New York: Harcourt Brace Jovanovich, 1968), p. 88. (Hereafter cited in the text by page number.)

35. Email from Michael Anania, one of RE's younger colleagues at Northwestern, July 31, 2020.

36. Ellsworth Mason, "Ellmann's Road to Xanadu," in *Omnium Gatherum: Essays for Richard Ellmann,* ed. Susan Dick, Declan Kiberd, Dougald McMillan, and Joseph Ronsley (Gerrards Cross, UK: Colin Smythe, 1989), p. 12.

37. Simeon Leland to RE, July 10, 1950.

38. Frederic E. Faverty to Simeon Leland, July 10, 1951.

39. A claim made by RE to Ellsworth Mason, letter of November 2, 1956.

40. Mary Ellmann to RE, May 26, 1950.

41. James Ellmann to RE, September 17, 1951.

42. The date of Mary Ellmann's reassuring note is uncertain. It is a handwritten addition to a typed letter dated September 15, 1951. The addition begins "Dear Dick—I had your letter just before I was going to mail this."

43. RE took pride in his efforts as house painter, decorator, and handyman. In an undated letter to his parents written shortly after Adlai Stevenson's presidential nomination on July 26, 1952, he informs them that "next week I'm putting a wire fence around the grassy part of the back yard" so that Stevie can "be outside without getting onto the street." On August 15, 1952, he writes to Ellsworth Mason: "I've painted the kitchen and built a fence and am now painting some bedroom furniture and hope to do the upstairs rooms before school starts." In a letter of September 28, 1952, to his parents he reports that he has been "painting storm windows and I also did the front porch, which looks much improved. The painting of the study I shall have to put off till near Christmas." On January 4, 1953, he writes of not having been able to do much academic work over the Christmas holiday "partly because of making a record and radio cabinet, and partly because of painting my study."

44. Maud Ellmann, email of September 21, 2022, on the Jewish upbringing of the Ellmann children: "Our Jewish upbringing was pretty casual. I remember when we were quite young that we attended Sabbath services at a suburban school which was turned over to a reformed synagogue on Saturdays (or maybe it was Sundays! It certainly wasn't orthodox). After that our synagogue attendance lapsed until I was 12 years old and went to a music camp called Interlochen, which was largely Jewish, where I was deeply shamed by not knowing what a bar mitzvah was. So I asked my parents if I could go back to synagogue—it might have been Beth Emet—and they decided to send Lucy too. I don't think Steve joined in. I got a better education in sabbath school than I was getting at Haven Junior High School in Evanston—a dreadful place. But our Jewish adventure lasted only two years and ended when we moved to New Haven in 1968."

Here is Lucy on the same question, in an email of September 20, 2022: "The somewhat cowardly deal my father made with his parents was perhaps not his finest hour. It was an unfortunate instance of shilly-shallying—but this type of thing is awfully common in many families, no? Families in which the pull of religiosity is lessening but the parents still expect to be placated. Though it's hypocritical to force religion on children, when you no longer believe in it yourself, it sure happens a lot. In our case, the offence was quite limited. No insistence on bar or bat mitzvahs, for instance. . . . We also received Chanukah presents from my grandmother until we reached 13 (we were unimpressed when this present stream dried up). This was kind of her, if also a little demanding and interfering. We possessed a menorah and candles, which we duly lit up every night in order to justify pouncing on the presents. And that was about it. We ate pork and shellfish, celebrated a secular form of Xmas and Easter, had very little awareness of Jewish history (apart from the Holocaust), customs or holidays, and did not identify as being (half) Jewish except in the secular sense. (The influence of my mother's lapsed

Catholicism was meanwhile nil—so, to that extent, my grandparents won.) We never belonged to a synagogue."

45. James Ellmann to RE, undated brief note: "I have not had time to answer fully your reassuring letter."

46. Maud Ellmann, email, June 29, 2022.

47. Emer Nolan, "*Ulysses* at 100," *Times Literary Supplement*, June 3, 2022. Something of RE's "mild liberalism" is suggested in an undated letter to his parents written shortly after Adlai Stevenson's presidential nomination speech of July 26, 1952:

> The Stevenson nomination was most exciting; I stayed up to hear his acceptance speech, and was not disappointed; he promises to bring an eloquence and wit into American public life that we've not had for a long time; he's wittier than Wilson and probably just as intelligent. I don't know what his policies are, but I expect to vote for him. His acceptance speech had a gift for phrasing that promises to make very clear the contrasts between him and Eisenhower, who can't speak in generalities. Although he said that the party should choose a position rather than a man, I'm afraid that like the Republicans they've chosen a man rather than a position.

48. There are over a dozen substantive references to Blake in *James Joyce*. In his memoir, *My Brother's Keeper* (London: Faber and Faber, 1958), edited and introduced by RE, Stanislaus Joyce writes of his brother that "in early youth . . . his gods were Blake and Dante" (p. 53).

49. Maud Ellmann, email, July 12, 2022.

50. Michael Anania, email, July 22, 2020.

51. According to Kevin B. Leonard, university archivist, Northwestern "was founded in 1850 and chartered by the State of Illinois in 1851. 1851 is the date which appears on Northwestern's seal and is considered its legal date of establishment. Strictly speaking, the founding occurred in 1850. For what it is worth, Northwestern first opened its doors to students in 1855" (email, May 16, 2024).

52. Maud Ellmann on the choice of names for the Ellmann children: "Stephen is for Stephen Dedalus. Maud is Tennyson's Maud: my mother wrote her PhD thesis on Tennyson. Lucy is indeed Wordsworthian" (Mary's remarks about Wordsworth's "Lucy" poems in *Thinking about Women* notwithstanding). Maud Ellmann, email, September 21, 2022.

53. Kendall College, a private junior college founded in 1934 by Methodists, attracted students who wanted a work-study program that would lead to decent full-time jobs. At Kendall many of those jobs were at the Evanston Insurance Company, which funded the college. Roosevelt University, founded in 1945 and named after the late Franklin Delano Roosevelt and Eleanor Roosevelt, drew its students from African American, Jewish, and immigrant communities. The students Mary taught at both Kendall and Roosevelt came from poorer backgrounds than RE's students at Northwestern, who in the 1950s were mostly white, Protestant, and privileged. In 1937, when Saul Bellow—Jewish, politically radical, and a would-be writer—transferred to Northwestern from the University of Chicago, he described its students as destined "for bond houses, insurance companies, Dad's business."

Bellow wanted to stand out, he explained, when asked his motives for moving from Hyde Park to Evanston: "I wanted attention." Zachary Leader, *The Life of Saul Bellow: To Fame and Fortune, 1915–1964* (New York: Knopf, 2018), p. 187.

54. Ellsworth Mason's recollections of RE's view, from Mason, "Ellmann's Road to Xanadu," p. 12.

55. Lucy Ellmann, email, July 13, 2019.

56. Interview with Maud Ellmann, July 5, 2019.

57. RE to Mary Ellmann, undated letter, mid-May 1951.

58. Gerald Graff, preface to Walter Scott, *Parodies, Etcetera and So Forth*, ed. Gerald Graff and Barbara Heldt Monter (1978; Evanston, IL: Northwestern University Press, 1985), p. viii.

59. Ellmann's description of Scott's coterie audience is from the introductory pages of the Walter Bernard Scott Papers, Charles Deering McCormick Library of Special Collections and University Archives, Northwestern University (hereafter cited as Scott Papers). The exchange between Nabokov and Wilson is quoted in Graff, preface to Scott, *Parodies*, p. vii.

60. Nabokov's praise of Scott's "Letter for a Festschrift" comes from "Nabokov, Near 71, Gets Gift for 70th," an interview with Alden Whitman, *New York Times*, March 18, 1970. The Festschrift itself was *Vladimir Nabokov on His Seventieth Birthday*, ed. Alfred Appel Jr. and Charles Newman, special issue, *TriQuarterly* 17 (Winter 1970). Katharine White of the *New Yorker* wrote to Scott on February 1, 1950, after reading Scott's "Letter from Chicago"—a parody of what Dwight Macdonald called "the more precious and insider-oriented snobberies of our Little Magazines; I think he must have had some of *Partisan Review*'s foreign correspondents in mind" (quoted in Graff, preface to Scott, *Parodies*, p. vii). Barbara Epstein wrote to Scott on June 26, 1963, shortly after publication of the first two issues of the *New York Review of Books*.

61. Walter B. Scott to RE, December 10, 1975, in which Scott described himself as having been "flattered" that RE had once asked him to collaborate in an editing project.

62. RE, quoted in Scott Papers, introductory pages.

63. Quoted in Roy V. Wood, "Walter Scott Memorial Remarks," Scott Papers. Wood was appointed dean of the School of Speech in 1972.

64. Michael Anania, email, July 23, 2020.

65. Walter Scott to RE, February 2, 1978.

66. Quotations about the Michelini's lunches are from Michael Anania, email, July 22, 2020.

67. Walter B. Scott, undated diary entry, Scott Papers. Both anecdotes, of course, are made up, as Graff hopes will be clear (email, July 20, 2022).

68. Walter B. Scott to Mary Ellmann, June 25, 1960.

69. For the relation between Scott and those of his bosses who were his friends, see the following exchange with Lyn Shanley, who at the time was associate dean of the College of Liberal Arts and James H. McBurney, dean of the School of Speech. On the morning of January 22, 1958, the Office of the Dean of Liberal Arts received a letter from "Mr. Akos Ludasy" (a creation of Scott's). Shanley forwarded the letter to Dean McBurney, accompanied by the following note:

> Since it [the letter] is an enquiry related to the work of Professor Walter Scott, I thought you should handle the question.
>
> I know you as well as we, are always happy to find deep interest in the University in far-flung spots, particularly when that interest has been aroused by people knowing members of the faculty. Furthermore, it is conceivable that considerable renown might accrue to the University were Mr. Ludasy's "Space Cruiser Romance" to be successfully produced after he had benefited from Professor Scott's tutelage.
>
> In view of Mr. Ludasy's interest in oil painting, it is conceivable that Professor Scott might work out some combination of work in playwriting and oil-painting for Mr. Ludasy.
>
> I have not had time to check with our rocket engineering professor as to Mr. Ludasy's statement about his mode of travel, but perhaps Professor Scott will do this before getting in touch with Mr. Ludasy.

Dean McBurney then wrote to Scott: "Since Mr. Ludasy appears to be one of your protégés, I should appreciate your advice in replying to him," at which point, Scott does, indeed, write a letter to the supposed Mr. Ludasy, dated January 30, 1958. After saying how delighted he was "to learn that you have persevered in your endeavors as a journalist," Scott had a complaint to make:

> Frankly, I think it too bad that you addressed your letter simply to the "Deans Office, NW-ern Univ," because all such "open" communications are sent directly to "Dean" J. Lyndon Shanley. "Dean" Shanley is a pleasant chap, as all of us here at Northwestern are I think agreed, and we wish him well. But he is hardly the person to handle such intricate requests as yours. It may be indiscreet of me to mention these facts to someone who is not a member of the Northwestern "family," but the thing is, "Dean" Shanley is a sort of ward of the University, if not legally at least morally and physically.

The letter goes on in some detail to explain how Dean Shanley ended up in his present state, the result of being struck on the head by a blackboard. Presumably Scott forwarded copies of these letter to both deans, as he circulated the diary entries about Graff and Hayford to their friends.

70. Jean Hagstrum to RE, March 9, 1964.

71. RE to Jean Hagstrum, March 24, 1964, and May 21, 1964.

72. Mason, "Ellmann's Road to Xanadu," p. 12.

73. Mason, "Ellmann's Road to Xanadu," p. 12. See also RE to Ellsworth Mason, June 20, 1956, from Bloomington, Indiana, where RE was a fellow in the School of Letters at Indiana University: "Did you know that W. R. Parker of MLA is coming here next fall as professor at a salary of $18,000? This must be highest in the business. It seems an ambitious and energetic place. They're also getting H. J. Muller from Purdue, I presume for less. The chairman here is reputed to get $16,500 [$160,000 in today's money]. Ah for a state university." Four years later, RE's Northwestern salary would be $20,000. Just before Gerald Graff joined the English Department at Northwestern, he was told that RE's salary was $40,000, "astonishing for 1965" (email of July 20, 2022).

74. In 1953 Robert Mayo founded a department periodical, the *Analyst,* with RE's help. It was published "at intervals," and its aim, as announced at the head of its

first issue, was "annotating difficult texts in modern British and American literature." The first issue was devoted to "A Guide to Ezra Pound's *Cantos (I–IV),*" by E. M. Glenn, an instructor in the Department of English at Northwestern. At the end of his "Guide," Glenn thanks RE. Although originally intended mostly for colleagues, *The Analyst* soon widened its readership, while narrowing its focus, eventually becoming a forum focused on two writers, Pound and Joyce. In its mimeographed pages, contributors from Europe as well as North America wrestled with the most difficult passages in Pound's *Cantos* or Joyce's *Finnegans Wake* or the "Oxen of the Sun" episode of *Ulysses.* The first issue appeared in March 1953, after RE had begun work on Joyce; the last appeared in 1971, three years after RE left for Yale. Mayo, its editor, a scholar of eighteenth-century and Romantic periodical culture, published several books on Pound in the 1950s. Many of the Joyce contributors were or became friends of RE. Often their contributions spawned lengthy responses in the "Commentary" section. These contributors included Ellsworth Mason, John Kelleher, Hugh Kenner, Fritz Senn, Vivien Mercier, Adaline Glasheen, and Gerald O'Flaherty. For the most part the exchanges in "Commentary" were collegial, in the spirit of the *Finnegans Wake* reading group. By publishing pioneering scholarship, the *Analyst* could be said to have forwarded the department's scholarly reputation, in the process extending RE's network of contacts. Although RE's name is not on the masthead, he was Mayo's advisor when it came to editorial matters, as indicated in an undated note in his papers at Northwestern in which he warns Mayo that "Jean Hagstrum is I think to try to persuade you to publish some papers he got on the ode in the Analyst. This may well be quite reasonable—if a little regressive to the old type Analyst. My only thought is that we should consider carefully—after all, one arrives at a character by exclusion. We must keep our character above all else. Huzzah." Ellmann Papers.

Scott has a wicked parody of the sort of correspondence published in *The Analyst,* a detailed refutation, written in the style of the University of Chicago critic R. S. Crane, of a recent contribution "on the *Chicago Telephone Directory, September 1948,* as well as the articles on this work by your associates, Douglas Minor and Shanley Minor." Scott, "The Problem of Tragedy," in *Parodies,* pp. 13–16.

75. Jean Hagstrum, "Richard Ellmann: A Memoir in Appreciation," in *Arts and Sciences, Magazine of the College of Arts and Sciences, Northwestern University,* fall 1987, p. 19.

76. Hagstrum, "Richard Ellmann," p. 19. RE also served a three-year term on the Budget Committee of the College of Liberal Arts. After finishing his second year on the committee, RE wrote to his parents on April 13, 1957, that "the dean made decisions about the members of the committee's salaries, since it would have been too embarrassing otherwise, and I came out better than I expected. There is something to being a big fish in a small pond. I felt I had had some effect as a committee member too in protecting the interests of my dept, and of other related depts, that I was supposed to be representing."

77. For an account of the Condit committee, see *Daily Northwestern,* March 29, 1966.

78. From the introduction to Dick et al., *Omnium Gatherum,* p. xv.

79. This phrase comes from Gerald Graff, interview, June 10, 2021. Graff had in mind "Fredson Bowers and some of the other big names at Southern universities at my first convention in December 1961" (Graff, email, July 20, 2022).

80. Joseph Epstein, interview, June 9, 2021.

81. According to Jane Lidderdale, a close friend of RE's and the author of a 1970 biography of her godmother, Harriet Weaver, who was Joyce's benefactor and literary executor. Quoted in the introduction to Dick et al., *Omnium Gatherum,* p. xi.

82. According to Laurence Senelick, interview, February 12, 2020.

83. That the name of the town appears only once, at the end of the novel, made the question an especially good one, as the point of the quizzes was to make sure the students had done the reading. Details concerning RE's European Novel course come from the Senelick interview, February 12, 2020. Senelick remembered RE's teaching assistants on the course as "in awe of him, he was a star." He also remembered that RE treated them well.

84. Henry Hart, "Richard Ellmann's Oxford Blues," *Sewanee Review* 117, no. 2 (Spring 2009), p. 279. On the same page Hart then quotes from Lucy Ellmann's 1988 novel, *Sweet Desserts,* in which the heroine, Suzy Schwarz, who in some ways resembles Lucy, shows her scholar father a section of her thesis: "Daddy returned my essay to me with so many corrections all over it that I could hardly bring myself to look at it, except for the bits where he'd written, 'good.'"

85. John Sutherland, email, January 25, 2020. In June 1983, RE and an external examiner failed outright an Oxford PhD dissertation on Hart Crane by a candidate who went on to become a professor of American literature at Oxford. As in the case Sutherland recounts, RE and the external examiner were prevailed upon to refer the dissertation—that is, allow it to be extensively rewritten.

86. Justin O'Brien, "Poetry of the Mind," review of Henri Michaux, *Selected Writings: The Space Within,* translated with an introduction by Richard Ellmann, in the *Saturday Review of Literature,* December 29, 1951.

87. In addition to the Yeats and Michaux books, RE also edited and introduced Stanislaus Joyce's memoir *My Brother's Keeper* and, with Ellsworth Mason, *The Critical Writings of James Joyce* (London: Faber and Faber, 1959).

88. RE, *The Identity of Yeats* (1954; New York: Oxford University Press, 1964), pp. v, vi. The preface is dated June 13, 1963. (Hereafter cited in the text by page number.)

6. CHOOSING JOYCE

1. Mason's thesis advisors were Eugene M. Waith, whom RE had known from the London office of the OSS, and Robert Menner. In a letter of January 16, 1947, Mason wrote to RE to explain his aims in his dissertation: "I am trying to show what Joyce took from Vico and how he used it in the Ulysses. The cyclical theory seems to be basic to the structure of the novel, and my study will be largely an explication of the structure." On January 21, 1947, RE writes with lots of suggestions about cyclical theory and other sources aside from Vico that EM should consider. Nothing oracular or condescending about these suggestions.

2. For "gibes and violence of speech," see James Joyce, *A Portrait of the Artist as a Young Man* (1916; New York: Viking Press, 1966), p. 78.

3. RE to Mason, undated letter, November or December 1946.

4. Mason to RE, December 20, 1946.

5. For Mason's comments on RE's work, see Mason to RE, January 27, 1948, in which he praises RE's dissertation and his abilities, while also pointing out "many places where I am sure a mature reflection would make you throw out what you had said as invalid, as it obviously is." These places are mostly masked "by the positive tone of the book, and by your charming style which would let you get away with a lot of crap if you wanted to." Mason then objects to Ellmann's readings of "Sailing to Byzantium" and "Byzantium," which end his dissertation (and the book it became), rounding off its main themes. RE's response to Mason's letter of November 11 had been contrite. In a letter of January 9, 1947, he wrote from Dublin: "Dear Ellsworth, you must be right about my letter to you, which I think I wrote as I was coming down with flu, and so sorry if you found its tone so oracular as to conceal the fact that I was trying to be helpful. I gather you have embarked on Joyce—is it Joyce and Vico?—and I'm sure Kelleher will be glad to make suggestions if you are resolved on it. . . . If you'll let me know exactly what you are writing about and the sort of stuff you need, I'll keep it in mind on my local peregrinations. Would you for example want a huge map of Dublin?"

6. Padraic Colum (1881–1972), poet and critic, and his wife, Mary, literary critic and author, feature in Chapters 2 and 4 of this book; Eugene Jolas (1894–1952), friend and publisher of Joyce, cofounder, with his wife, Maria, of the literary magazine *transition;* Roger MacHugh (1908–1987), the first professor of Anglo-Irish literature at University College Dublin; Robert N. Kastor, brother of Helen Joyce, Giorgio Joyce's wife, a New York stockbroker who had been instrumental in securing a contract in 1932 for the publication of *Ulysses* by Random House.

7. Ellsworth Mason, "Ellmann's Road to Xanadu," in *Omnium Gatherum: Essays for Richard Ellmann,* ed. Susan Dick, Declan Kiberd, Dougald McMillan, and Joseph Ronsley (Gerrards Cross, UK: Colin Smythe, 199), p. 9. (Hereafter cited in the text by page number.)

8. RE to Mason, undated.

9. In an undated letter of spring or early summer 1952, RE offered detailed advice about obtaining the fellowship: "Tell them something to this effect; Stanislaus is in Trieste, apparently available, knows more about Joyce's development as a young man than anyone else—you know the field thoroughly, have written a brilliant thesis on Ulysses, talked at MLA, know Italian and translated Stan's book, expect you can solve the following puzzles: to what extent did he foresee his development; what was his real relation to fellow students, Yeats, etc. (mention here Stan's probable possession of such things as Yeats's letter to Joyce about his early work). These are just suggestions, but they must be made as impressive as possible, with much on the fact that Stan knew him best." The advice continues for three more paragraphs, in one of which RE says, "I think you should probably say you are writing a biography—that is probably what it would come to if you got much—but you will know whether this is accurate or not. You might indicate your divergence from Gorman, or how you would do a different sort of, say, intellectual biography." Later in the letter he advises Mason, "Ask your dept. head to write a number of colleges explaining that he, expecting you to get a Fulbright, with your

consent filled your job and now has nothing to offer; that he thinks you a very good man, etc."

10. For the delivery date of *The Identity of Yeats* to Macmillan, see the August 15, 1952, letter from Fred Faverty, chair of English, to Simeon Leland, dean of the College of Liberal Arts.

11. The relevant passage from the Yeats poem "To a Friend Whose Work Has Come to Nothing" begins "turn away/And like a laughing string/Whereon mad fingers play,/Around a place of stone,/Be secret and exult."

12. Richard Ellmann, "Joyce and Yeats," *Kenyon Review* 12, no. 4 (Autumn 1950): 618–38, reprinted as "The Hawklike Man" in Ellmann, *Eminent Domain: Yeats among Wilde, Joyce, Pound, Eliot and Auden* (New York: Oxford University Press, 1967), p. 29 (further quotations from this reprint are cited in the text by page number). Later in the article RE quotes Joyce's preference for "the footprint seen on the sand by Robinson Crusoe to the eternal city envisioned by John. The fallen world was his natural habitat" (p. 54). In "Adventures and Misadventures of a Biographer," RE uses differences between Yeats and Joyce to introduce other features of Joyce's writing:

> On the whole he [Joyce] was suspicious of that metaphysical world which so attracted Yeats. He liked to assert his attachment to Aristotle and Hume rather than to Plato and Berkeley. . . . Joyce was less willing to see life as a dualistic battle between dream and reality. He saw it as a single substance; he liked circumstances and trivia. So instead of celebrating the victory of mental imaginings over physical shortcomings, he was inclined to see what was physical as mental too, and what was mental as also physical. As a result there is a good deal of emphasis in Joyce on physical processes—bodiliness in all its aspects, including phenomena such as sneezing, gastric noises, urinating, defecating, masturbating, menstruating, copulating. He treated most of these things with humor, and yet he was seriously determined to include them as things important to think about as well as do. He often used four-letter words to describe them, words that Yeats, as his widow told me, could never bring himself to use. I am not urging that either was more right than the other, only that they were different. Joyce took an interest not only in such processes but in related details of the physical world.

13. Later in the article, Ellmann quotes Yeats on Joyce's connection to Rabelais, "one of the greatest masters of the past," whose works have also been labeled "obscene." After calling *Ulysses* "more indubitably a work of genius than any prose written by an Irishman since the death of Synge," Yeats is still not sure it is "a great work of literature. . . . All I will say is that it is the work of a heroic mind" (p. 53).

14. Quoted from publicity material for the Northwestern University Library exhibition. Especially noteworthy items in the collection were all three states of the first edition of *Ulysses* as well as a copy of the first edition of *Ulysses* in French (*Ulysse,* 1926), signed by Stuart Gilbert and inscribed by Joyce to his daughter Lucia on the date of issue.

15. The quotations from RE in this paragraph come from two sources: William K. Robinson, "A Portrait of James Joyce's Biographer," *Miami Herald,* March 21, 1982, reprinted in Dick et al., *Omnium Gatherum,* p. 44; and the typed

manuscript of an unfinished talk titled "In Pursuit of Joyce and Others," Ellmann Papers.

16. Hugh Kenner, *Ulysses* (1980; Baltimore: Johns Hopkins University Press, 1987), p. 171; Brenda Maddox, *Nora* (London: Hamish Hamilton, 1988), p. 510.

17. See Bernard McGinley, *Joyce's Lives: Uses and Abuses of the Biografiend* (London: University of North London Press, 1996), p. 13, quoting from Stuart Gilbert, *Reflections on James Joyce: Stuart Gilbert's Paris Journal,* ed. Thomas F. Staley and Randolph Lewis (Austin: University of Texas Press, 1993), p. 68.

18. Quoted in McGinley, *Joyce's Lives,* p. 7. For a catalog of failings that leads McGinley to conclude that Gorman's biography is "inadequate to its task" (p. 12), see pp. 10–14. RE instances distortions and evasions forced upon Gorman by Joyce. *JJ,* pp. 631–32.

19. See McGinley, *Joyce's Lives,* p. 13, quoting from Stuart Gilbert, *Reflections on James Joyce,* p. 68.

20. Quoted in *JJ,* p. 719.

21. The American university libraries with the most important Joyce holdings are at Buffalo, Texas, Yale, Cornell, and Tulsa.

22. In the 1940s Slocum helped to run a small literary agency whose authors included Ezra Pound, whom he had met in 1935 (he testified at Pound's treason trial), and Wyndham Lewis, Henry Miller, and Anaïs Nin. In 1949 he mounted an unsuccessful attempt to have Joyce's remains repatriated to Ireland, as Yeats's had been.

23. Slocum's success in accumulating more disparate materials in Ireland is described by Brenda Maddox, Nora Joyce's biographer: "When word reached the press that this young and wealthy Joyce enthusiast from the U.S. State Department had paid Nora's sister Kathleen forty-five pounds for some of Michael Healy's letters and some pictures [Healy was Nora's uncle], Slocum found himself deluged with letters from people all over Ireland with battered copies of Joyce's works to sell" (*Nora,* p. 506). In a letter of June 6, 1956, to the book collector H. K. Croessmann, RE writes of meeting "Jake" Schwartz, whom he describes as "a picturesque type."

24. RE to Mason, August 15, 1952, in which he promises Mason that he will write to Slocum "in a few days."

25. RE to Mason, December 5, 1952.

26. Mason to RE, November 29, 1952.

27. These quotations are from an unpublished and unfinished manuscript found in box 61, folder 10, Ellmann Papers.

28. RE was originally put in touch with Hayes through Norman Pearson, with whom he worked in intelligence during the war. Hayes had been recruited for Ireland's G2 intelligence service and became one of the most important code breakers of the war, working closely with MI5 and Bletchley Park, thus with the OSS. Hence his friendship with Pearson.

29. On January 7, 1952, Hayes had warned Ellmann that "Yeats is now being overdone, about three books on him per annum. Why not become another of the Joyce specialists. You only need imagination and nerve."

30. Hayes to RE, August 2, 1952.

31. RE to parents, April 13, 1953.

32. RE to parents, April 13, 1953.

33. Niall Montgomery (1915–1987) was an architect and early champion of Joyce; his father James Montgomery had been a friend of Oliver St. John Gogarty and Arthur Griffith, both of whom his son remembered meeting. Niall Sheridan (1912–1998), a writer and broadcaster, was a friend of Flann O'Brien (Brian O'Nolan) and is thinly fictionalized in O'Brien's *At Swim-Two-Birds,* a copy of which he brought to Paris to give to Joyce, who informed him that he had already read it.

34. The Skeffingtons deserve further description. Roy Foster, in an email of October 15, 2023, explains: "Owen's father Francis, Joyce's friend, was a well known pacifist, suffragist, journalist who was murdered by an English officer in 1916. His wife Hanna was one of a formidable sisterhood, to whom Joyce was much attached, especially to her sister Mary. Hanna was a pioneering socialist, radical feminist, and campaigner against British imperialism. Their son Owen a much-loved Trinity academic and Senator."

35. RE's account of his meeting with Best is in a letter to Herbert Cahoon, April 16, 1953. But Amanda Sigler points out that "there is a dating conflict with this letter and the Best interview, since Ellmann writes on April 16 that Best made his comments 'yesterday,' but these comments occur in the interview which Ellmann labels as having taken place on April 16." Sigler, "Joyce's Ellmann: The Beginnings of *James Joyce,*" *Joyce Studies Annual* (2010): 9.

36. See RE to parents, April 13, 1953

37. Constantine Curran was a lawyer and a historian of eighteenth-century Dublin architecture, culture, and plasterwork. His book on Joyce, *James Joyce Remembered,* was not published until 1968.

38. Amanda Sigler, "Joyce's Ellmann," p. 10.

39. RE to father, April 23, 1953.

40. RE to Frank Budgen, May 1, 1953.

41. Quoted in *James Joyce,* p. 349, from Joyce to Grant Richards, March 4, 1914, in Stuart Gilbert, ed., *Letters of James Joyce* (New York: Viking Press, 1957), p. 75. In addition to threatening to sue Maunsel and Company, Joyce wrote an open letter to the press attacking it for its treatment of *Dubliners.* Only two Irish papers published the letter, the *Northern Whig* in August 1911 and *Sinn Fein* in September 1911. Almost three years later, in the January 15, 1914, issue of Harriet Weaver's *The Egoist,* it was published under the title "A Curious History." RE quotes the last paragraph of the letter in *JJ,* p. 353.

42. For a recent account of Joyce's problems getting *Dubliners* published, see Frank McNally, "Poison Ivy: On How the Death of Two Monarchs Caused Legal Issues for Joyce," *Irish Times,* October 6, 2022.

43. Mary Ellmann to RE's parents, May 10, 1953.

44. RE to C. G. Bowen, July 13, 1953.

45. RE to John Slocum, May 24, 1953.

46. RE to C. G. Bowen, July 13, 1953.

47. See May Monaghan to RE, January 12, 1959: "Her influence on her family was very strong—as is evident from both Jim's and Stannie's writings and it was she who took a practical interest in their welfare and studies. Any confidence the boys gave—was to her. Certainly my father was not a man to confide in." It is pos-

sible that if the letter had been written earlier, RE might have given more attention to Joyce's mother in *James Joyce,* which has been criticized for undervaluing her influence. As Sigler points out, "Joyce's mother had passed away when he was still a young man, and hence there were comparatively few sources still living in the 1950s who had known her" ("Ellmann's Joyce," p. 16). The "complete frankness" of Joyce's sister Eileen Schaurek, in her interview with RE, of June 6, 1953, is exemplified by her having suggested that Roberto Prezioso, editor of the Trieste newspaper *Il Piccolo della Sera,* had had an affair with Nora, also that he was homosexual and attracted to Joyce as well, and that Joyce not only encouraged the affair with Nora but dramatized the relationship between Prezioso and the Joyces in his play *Exiles.* For RE's treatment of these matters, see *James Joyce,* pp. 326–28, in which Joyce is described as breaking with Prezioso when he "endeavored to become Nora's lover rather than her admirer" (p. 327). When RE began work on *JJ,* four of Joyce's sisters were still living. In addition to Eileen and May there was Eva, to whom he also talked, and Florence, who alone was unwilling to talk to anyone but apparently once said: "We're an extraordinary family and I wish to God we weren't" (quoted in an unpublished, unfinished, and undated—though post-1982—talk by RE titled "Adventures and Misadventures of a Biographer").

48. How Belvedere learned that Joyce was a promising student is explained on p. 35 of *JJ:* "Just now John Joyce, walking in Mountjoy Square one day, had a fortunate encounter with Father John Conmee, who had left the position of rector of Clongowes to become prefect of studies at Belvedere College. He was not yet Provincial of the Jesuit Order in Ireland; he became so in 1906, but he was already influential. Hearing that his former pupil was obliged to attend the Christian Brothers' school, and remembering his ability, Conmee kindly offered to arrange for James, and his brothers too, to attend the fine Jesuit day-school, Belvedere College, without fees." In a note to this anecdote RE cites "information from the rector of Belvedere" (p. 761).

49. RE to Bowen, May 31, 1953.

50. In a note to RE's account of his visit to Clongowes (in the letter to Budgen of May 31, 1953), Amanda Sigler quotes Herbert Cahoon to RE (July 21, 1953) responding to a similar account of the visit: "Herbert Gorman once told me that when he visited representatives of Clongowes and University College he had to pretend he was interested in doing a history of education in Ireland (or some such dodge) in order to get any cooperation at all."

51. These quotations come from *JJII,* p. 661n, which is an addition to a footnote in *JJ,* p. 673. Of course not all the models for Joyce's characters are "real-life"; some are "literary," a product of a lifetime of voracious reading.

52. On October 1, 1951, Daniela wrote Ellmann, urging him to come for a visit: "It would be nice to see you again without having to wait for another liberation." The reference presumably is to the liberation of Paris in autumn 1944. Although it is possible that they met earlier, in the summer of 1938 or 1939, when Ellmann spent time in France, first with brother Erwin and then with brother Bill.

53. Daniela herself had musical connections, being a descendant of Franz Liszt. The festival Edme presided over—Festival des musicales de l'Abbaye de Lessay—was held every summer. See Chapter 3 for reference to Liszt's ancestor.

54. Recent residents of the Villa Montmorency have included Isabelle Adjani, Gerard Depardieu, and Nicolas Sarkozy. In her letter of October 1, 1951, Daniela wondered, jokingly, how the Ellmanns were bringing up Stephen, having heard "the wildest tales of American children throwing vases out of windows or spilling them over costly carpets." The weekly $100 rent might have been a form of damage insurance.

55. RE to Ellsworth Mason, February 12, 1947.

56. Sigler, "Joyce's Ellmann," p. 22.

57. RE to Sylvia Beach, undated letter.

58. Sylvia Beach to Harriet Weaver, February 2, 1955, in *The Letters of Sylvia Beach*, ed. Keri Walsh (New York: Columbia University Press, 2010), pp. 233–35. For tensions with RE over Michaux, see Chapter 3, this volume. Just before recounting RE's visit in the summer of 1953, Beach asks Weaver, "How is Richard Ellmann getting on with his book on Joyce?" Beach knew Weaver approved of RE and recounts with some regret the reception she gave him ("I fear I wasn't helpful"). She also explains, "I met Ellmann during the war when he was in the navy, a young fellow in a sailor suit and very much interested in poetry. He translated a great deal of Michaux's and did a very good job of it I think." At other times she sees him as another "rag-picker," as in a letter to Weaver of December 15, 1955 (*Letters of Sylvia Beach*, pp. 240–43), in which she writes that Joseph Prescott was coming to visit "and I suppose in the spring he will be found most any day sitting at one of those big tables in my dusty room, with all the Joyce material spread out, and Joseph burying himself in it. If, however, I happen to be in the United States where I expect to go on business with my publishers, his will have to wait. Then there is Dick (Ellman) [*sic*] who is threatening to look us up soon. I hope you will keep them busy in England."

59. Bernard McGinley, *Joyce's Lives: Uses and Abuses of the Biografiend* (London: University of North London Press, 1996), p. 19. In a footnote, McGinley cites Noel Riley Finch, *Sylvia Beach and the Lost Generation* (1983), p. 43, adding in a note that "Joseph Prescott was similarly treated."

60. $25,000 in 1931 was roughly the equivalent of $450,000 today (calculations range from $487,000 to $432,000); £1,000 in 1931 was roughly the equivalent of £75,000 today.

61. Although Joyce is the "diver" here as opposed to the one "falling," Jung also described him to RE as "a latent schizoid who used drinking to control his schizoid tendencies" (p. 693).

62. In a second interview, of June 21, 1954, Beckett told RE that he suspected that Lucia might have been bulimic; in an interview in July 1953, Philippe Soupault told RE he suspected that Lucia might have suffered from anorexia.

63. Lucie Leon's memoir, written under her maiden name, Lucie Noel, was *James Joyce and Paul L. Leon: The Story of a Friendship* (New York: Gotham Book Mart, 1950), p. 12.

64. According to Maria Jolas to RE, undated letter, 1953.

65. For an account of the "museyroom" episode in *Finnegans Wake*, see Joseph Valente, "Joyce and Sexuality," in *The Cambridge Companion to James Joyce*, ed. Derek Attridge (1990; Cambridge: Cambridge University Press, 2004), pp. 219–23. The fullest account of rumors and intimations of father/daughter (also brother/sister)

incest in the Joyce family is found in Carol Loeb Shloss, *Lucia Joyce: To Dance in the Wake* (New York: Farrar, Straus and Giroux, 2003). Much of the "evidence" Shloss adduces comes from *Finnegans Wake.* Joyce scholar Luca Crispi, in an email of October 17, 2022, commented, "The fact that Maria and Lucie were concerned about such rumours cannot be dismissed. . . . But I wonder whether it wasn't just paranoia and a tremendous desire to protect Joyce's legacy, especially when questions about syphilis contracted from prostitutes in Dublin or Trieste were also circulating in the same way." What perplexes Crispi about the worries of Lucie Leon and Maria Jolas (that RE was digging "too deep for discretion") is whether they "were based on actual knowledge from the family or other sources [that is, members of the circle around Joyce]." Much of Shloss's speculation is based on the relation between Joyce's remarks about his children in his notebooks from the time he was at work on *Finnegans Wake* and the work itself. Crispi comments, "One could say all of Book II, Chapter 2 is about incest between the brothers and the sister, and father and daughter."

66. RE to parents, April 5, 1953.

67. C. G. Bowen to RE, February 26, 1952.

68. RE to Bowen, February 29, 1952.

69. C. G. Bowen to RE, March 12, 1952.

70. RE to Fred Faverty, May 23, 1953.

71. From the speech RE gave in acceptance of the 1982 Duff Cooper Prize, awarded for the second edition of *James Joyce.*

72. See RE's Duff Cooper Prize speech: "What became increasingly clear to me was that the man I was dealing with had at least the usual number of kinks and frailties, but that his tenacity of purpose, his brilliant imagination which enabled him to turn events and people into words, and his sense of himself as an artist overrode faults and pettinesses."

7. PEOPLE AND PAPERS

1. See RE to H. K. Croessmann, November 13, 1954: "Ransom, the editor of the Kenyon Review, offered me a Kenyon Review fellowship in criticism, an award which is sponsored by the Rockefeller Foundation; but I needed to get this increased by Northwestern if I was really to have the year off. . . . I had to bring special pressure to bear. And I am glad to say that it has all worked out satisfactorily." H. K. Croessmann, an important Joyce collector, is discussed in Chapter 8.

2. RE's letter to Thomas F. Staley, January 25, 1960, quoted in Staley, "A Life with Joyce," *Joyce Studies Annual* (2008): 6–7. Alessandro Francini Bruni, one of Joyce's friends, was deputy director of the Scuola Berlitz in Pola and later taught with Joyce in the Scuola Berlitz in Trieste. Roberto Prezioso, editor of the main newspaper in Trieste, *Il Piccolo della Sera,* was one of Joyce's pupils and an ardent, overly ardent, admirer of Nora Joyce, as we shall see. Italo Svevo was the pen name of another of Joyce's pupils, Ettore Schmitz, who was a businessman as well as a novelist. Dr. Sinigaglia, also one of Joyce's pupils, was the doctor who delivered Giorgio. Signora Moise Canarutto was briefly the Joyces' landlady in Trieste.

3. Ellsworth Mason, "Ellmann's Road to Xanadu," in *Omnium Gatherum: Essays for Richard Ellmann,* ed. Susan Dick, Declan Kiberd, Dougald McMillan, and Joseph Ronsley (Gerrards Cross, UK: Colin Smythe, 1989), p. 19.

4. See Phillip F. Herring, "Richard Ellmann's *James Joyce,*" in *The Biographer's Art: New Essays,* ed. Jeffrey Meyers (Basingstoke: Macmillan, 1989), p. 126; Bernard McGinley, *Joyce's Lives: Uses and Abuses of the Biografiend* (London: North London University Press, 1996), p. 37; Hugh Kenner, "The Impertinence of Being Definitive," *Times Literary Supplement,* December 17, 1982, p. 1384. These quotations (there are others in the same vein) are taken from Joseph Brooker, *Joyce's Critics: Transitions in Reading and Culture* (Madison: University of Wisconsin Press, 2004), p. 101.

5. The unpublished manuscript for the talk, "Writing Joyce's Biography," is found in Ellmann Papers, box 61, folder 10. It is unfinished and erratically paginated. For other accounts of RE's visit to Pola, see Leslie Cross, "Joyce's 'Detective' Is Ready for Some New Cases," *Milwaukee Journal,* September 11, 1960 (the source of the "society of Yugoslav authors" quote); RE to C. G. Bowen of OUP, August 8, 1954; Amanda Sigler, "Joyce's Ellmann: The Beginnings of *James Joyce,*" *Joyce Studies Annual* (2010): 37–38; and an unfinished manuscript for RE's speech accepting the 1982 Duff Cooper Prize for *JJII.*

6. See also John McCourt, *The Years of Bloom: James Joyce in Trieste, 1904–1920* (Dublin: Lilliput Press, 2000), pp. 192–93, who writes of Roberto Prezioso's "overzealous interest in Nora," mentioned earlier; at the time Prezioso was acting editor of the Trieste newspaper *Il Piccolo della Sera* and political editor of *Il Piccolo:* "Prezioso made a number of afternoon visits to Nora. All proceeded well until the Italian made an explicit declaration to her, saying, 'Il solo se'e levato per Lei'—the sun has risen for you (*JJ,* p. 316). Nora instantly called a halt to his advances and told Joyce what had happened. Joyce rapidly sought out the offender and gave him such a virulent public dressing down that Prezioso burst into tears." In addition to having Bloom say to Molly, "The sun shines for you," Joyce exploited the material more thoroughly in *Exiles,* where Brigid, the old servant, says to Bertha regarding Robert Hand, the friend who is trying to seduce her: "Sure he thinks the sun shines out of your face, ma-am" (McCourt, *The Years of Bloom,* p. 194).

7. The quotations about Eileen Vance Harris come from pp. 10–11 of the unpublished and unfinished manuscript of RE's talk "Adventures and Misadventures of a Biographer," box 61, folder 10, Ellmann Papers.

8. Straumann says in a prefatory note to "Four Letters to Martha Fleischmann," in Richard Ellmann, ed., *Selected Letters of James Joyce,* vol. 2 (New York: Viking Press, 1966), p. 428, that Marthe told him she first met Joyce when she was about to enter her house and "he happened to pass by her door. . . . Joyce then apologized in German and said that she very strongly reminded him of a girl he once had seen standing on the beach in his home country ('*Sie erinnern mich an ein Mädchen, das ich einmal in meinem Heimatland am Strand stehen sah*'). . . . Fraulein Fleischmann could not remember if in later conversations Joyce again referred to the girl on the beach."

9. See RE, *Selected Letters of James Joyce,* vol. 2, p. 428.

10. RE, "Writing Joyce's Biography."

11. See *JJ*, p. 353: "One of his girl students [in Trieste] . . . was Amalia Popper, the daughter of a Jewish businessman whose first name was Leopoldo. She was to serve as one of the models for the character and Southern European looks of Molly Bloom." Joyce's relations with Amalia, and her purported fictional incarnations—in *Giacomo Joyce* "he envisions her as a Jewess come out of the dark East to hold his western blood in thrall" (p. 353)—are discussed on pp. 353–60. See also Brenda Maddox, *Nora: A Biography of Nora Joyce* (London: Hamish Hamilton, 1988), pp. 215–17.

12. See RE, ed., *Letters of James Joyce,* vol. 2, p. 433. In a letter to Maria Jolas, December 16, 1954, RE describes the style of the letters as "romantic but certainly not contemptible." He sees "the aesthetic objection got up by Stephen and probably George as a more convenient pretext than the moral objection or the objection in the name of family pride."

13. On June 22, 1954, when RE interviewed Budgen in London, Budgen told him of Joyce's affair with Marthe. RE's notes mention only the date of the meeting (February 2), the candlestick, Budgen's dimly lit studio, and Marthe's limp. Ten years later, on June 5, 1964, after publication of the biography, RE interviewed Budgen again. The notes from this interview contain some but not all of the details that were to appear in Budgen's memoir, *Myselves when Young* (London: Oxford University Press, 1970), and subsequently in *JJII.*

14. Budgen, *Myselves when Young,* pp. 192–93, 194.

15. Budgen, *Myselves when Young,* pp. 187–88.

16. Maddox, *Nora,* p. 216. As Ellmann puts it in the first edition of *JJ,* which makes no reference to the sighting in the bathroom, Joyce was "more onlooker than lover," "a looker with pathetically blurred vision" (p. 464).

17. Budgen, *Myselves when Young,* p. 191.

18. Budgen, *Myselves when Young,* p. 194.

19. This is a quotation from Budgen, who made the remark to J. S. Atherton. See Atherton's "Facts, Fictions and Fadographs," *Times Literary Supplement,* December 12, 1975, p. 1483.

20. See *JJII,* pp. 418–19.

21. Budgen, *Myselves when Young,* p. 189. Wells's term "cloacal obsession" appeared in his review of *A Portrait of the Artist as a Young Man* in the *New Republic,* March 9, 1917.

22. See RE to Erwin Ellmann, April 7, 1954: "It is a big job trying to maintain my world operation—I've got people working for me in Dublin, Zurich, and Trieste, with more or less success. But the correspondence alone is harrying."

23. RE to Alfred Dutli, August 8, 1953.

24. Evelyn Cotton became a close friend of Nora Joyce and took care of her in Zurich after Joyce's death, often answering correspondence on Nora's behalf.

25. When Joyce confronted the actor at the consulate, it was in front of two other employees. "With measured tactlessness," writes Ellmann, Joyce asked him for money owing on tickets. So provoking was Joyce's manner, that the actor, whose name was Henry Carr, shouted, "You're a cad. You've cheated me and pocketed the proceeds. You're a swindler. If you don't get out I'll throw you down stairs. Next time I catch you outside I'll wring your neck" (*JJ,* p. 440).

26. There is no mention in either edition of *JJ* of a resemblance between Joyce the litigant and Denis Breen the litigant. The "Lestrygonians" episode was completed on October 25, 1918, according to a chart dating the completion and publication dates of the episodes of *Ulysses* in *JJ*, p. 456. A character named Carr is introduced at the beginning of the "Circe" episode: "*(Private Carr and Private Compton, swaggersticks tight in their oxters as they march unsteadily rightabout-face and burst together from their mouths a volleying fart)*" (lines 48–51), and at the end Private Carr strikes Stephen, who falls to the ground unconscious (lines 4747–50).

27. RE to Alfred Dutli, October 10, 1953.

28. RE was open about the element of calculation in his favors. To his parents, on July 2, 1955, he writes of having "helped two Joyce people, Slocum and Cahoon, with an introduction to some newly discovered pages of Stephen Hero, which was an early version of the Portrait of the Artist. They have both been nice to me, and I was able to give them some important new facts for their introduction. I think they are going to make fairly vigorous acknowledgment of my help, so it should help in giving me some authority in the field. Likewise my introduction to a census of Finnegans Wake which Northwestern is going to publish—and the chronology of Joyce's life that I did for Gilbert. But after these I must do my own work."

29. In *JJ*, RE describes Byrne at University College as "handsome, athletic and clever. . . . [I]n a world of foppishness, Byrne had the courage to be plain. But it was his manner that attracted: he moved about with the air of a man who knows all the secrets but disinclines to exercise the power he thereby possesses. . . . His power over Joyce came from his habit of refraining from comment: Joyce's admissions about his feelings towards family, friends, and church, about his overweening ambitions, struck like waves against Byrne's cryptic taciturnity. . . . Joyce needed no other friend as he did Byrne . . . [a] receptive but neutral ear for new disclosures" (p. 66).

30. Byrne's upset is explained more fully in *JJ*. The postcard he received had a photo of Joyce on one side and space for a message on the other side, on which Joyce had copied one of his poems. The postcard "pleased Byrne very much. He showed it to Cosgrave and said proudly that no man in Dublin knew more about Joyce than he did. Cosgrave, making the retort irresistible, slyly took a similar photograph from his pocket and showed it to Byrne saying, 'Perhaps that's something you didn't know.' Byrne read Joyce's description in dog-Latin of Paris whoredom with consternation: he had explicitly warned Joyce not to confide in Cosgrave, and the details were evidently shocking to him. He handed both postcards to Cosgrave saying, 'You can have this one, too'" (p. 120).

31. RE's notes from an interview with J. F. Byrne, March 22, 1957.

32. J. F. Byrne, *Silent Years: An Autobiography with Memoirs of James Joyce and Our Ireland* (New York: Farrar, Straus and Young, 1953), p. 156.

33. J. F. Byrne to Joyce, August 19, 1909, in RE, *Letters of James Joyce*, vol. 2, p. 235. In *Nora*, Brenda Maddox throws doubt on Byrne's conspiracy theory, which she describes as "emotional first aid, spoken to calm a friend":

> It required him [Joyce] to believe that Gogarty, a successful surgeon with a busy practice, met Cosgrave after Joyce's unexpected return and plotted to break Joyce's

trust in Nora. It required him to believe that both men wanted revenge against him—Gogarty for the imbroglio over the tower and Cosgrave for the pseudonym of Lynch. It required Joyce to believe that Gogarty had been lying when, as he and Joyce parted during their meeting the previous week, he had shaken Joyce's hand and said, 'I don't care a damn what you say of me as long as it is literature'" (p. 125).

34. Maddox, *Nora,* p. 125.

35. RE to J. F. Byrne, February 2, 1957.

36. See RE to C. G. Bowen of OUP, January 12, 1954, for rivalry with Tindall.

37. J. F. Byrne to RE, March 31, 1954.

38. As we shall see in Chapter 8, what spurred RE to publish these essays was his fear of rivals.

39. Byrne to RE, January 29, 1954.

40. Sigler, "Joyce's Ellmann," p. 32.

41. Ira B. Nadel, "'Unriddling the Writing': The 'Letters of James Joyce,' Volume 1," *Joyce Studies Annual* (Summer 1992): 86. My account of Gilbert's editing of the first volume of *Letters of James Joyce* is drawn from Nadel's essay.

42. Stuart Gilbert to Harriet Weaver, May 8, 1950, quoted in Jane Lidderdale and Mary Nicholson, eds., *Dear Miss Weaver* (New York: Viking, 1970), p. 419.

43. Nadel, "'Unriddling the Writing," p. 88; the earlier Harriet Weaver reference is from a detailed memorandum of July 5, 1954, quoted at p. 95.

44. The idea of a second volume of Joyce's letters had been clear to Gilbert from at least as early as 1955. "There are still many hundreds of letters worth publishing," he wrote to Benjamin W. Huebsch of Viking on March 21, 1955, "and a second selection, handled by an expert editor, might be worth considering."

45. See Nadel, "Understanding the Writing," p. 96; also Stuart Gilbert to Harriet Weaver, May 8, 1950.

46. See RE to OUP, November 27, 1956: "Biographically the most important part of the Stanislaus Joyce papers are the letters from James to Stanislaus, and by editing them I might pre-empt their use."

47. Stanislaus Joyce and Ellsworth Mason, eds., *The Early Joyce: The Book Reviews, 1902–1903* (Colorado Springs: Mamalujo Press, 1955).

48. Mason to Stanislaus Joyce, August 23, 1953, quoted in Joseph Kelly, "Stanislaus Joyce, Ellsworth Mason, and Richard Ellmann: The Making of 'James Joyce,'" *Joyce Studies Annual* (Summer 1992): 107. See also Mason to RE, March 10, 1956:

> I have mentioned you twice in my letters to Ms. Joyce, most recently as follows:
>
> "About your husband's papers, a good friend of mine named Richard Ellmann, who has been helping me to promote our little book [his and Stanislaus's edition of *The Early Joyce: The Book Reviews, 1902–1903* (1955)], is to be in Zurich, Trieste, and Pola later in this spring, finishing off his research for a biography of Joyce, and I have asked him to stop in to pay his respects to you. . . . Mr. Ellmann may be able to give you advice about the significance and value of your husband's papers."

49. RE to Mason, December 7, 1953.

50. RE to Bowen of OUP, October 10, 1953.

51. Oliver St. John Gogarty (1878–1957), an author and poet, as well as a surgeon, politician, and athlete, was the inspiration for Buck Mulligan in *Ulysses.* RE's remark about Stanislaus's "eloquent attack" comes from a letter of November 22, 1953, to Mary Monaghan, a Joyce sister. For Gogarty's attack on Joyce, see Oliver Gogarty, "They Think They Know Joyce," *Saturday Review of Literature,* March 18, 1950. Mason himself had been enlisted by Stanislaus in an attempt to counter Gogarty's unflattering portrait. See Kelly, "Stanislaus Joyce, Ellsworth Mason, and Richard Ellmann," p. 100. Kelly's article details other instances of Mason's support for Stanislaus. It also provides an account of Mason's relations with RE, including his criticisms as well as his support of RE's methods as biographer.

52. RE to May Monaghan, November 22, 1953.

53. RE to Bowen of OUP, August 30, 1953.

54. RE to Bowen of OUP, August 8, 1954.

55. RE to Harriet Weaver, August 17, 1954.

56. RE to Harriet Weaver, July 16, 1955.

57. RE to parents, July 2, 1955.

58. RE to Mason, May 17, 1956.

59. RE to Harriet Weaver, July 5, 1956.

60. Mason to RE, September 26, 1955. Prior to his visit to Nelly, RE wrote to Mason on March 6, 1956: "I expect to be in Trieste the last week of April, and should be grateful if you will pave the way with Mrs. S. Joyce. I don't know exactly what approach to recommend—you will know better than I—but I suppose the main thing is to give her confidence, in so far as you feel you can without perjuring yourself, in my general probity. Should I also write her now, do you think? I'll be glad to have your advice. I expect to leave here two or three days before end of March."

61. RE to Bowen of OUP, September 30, 1956.

62. RE to Harriet Weaver, November 27, 1956. See also RE to Mason, June 8, 1956: "I can't tell you how exhilarating it was to be the first that ever burst into that silent sea. I suspect even Stan didn't know, or had forgotten, what a lot of the stuff was. It was mostly in the cellar, and she didn't know what most of it was." Both sides of the correspondence, along with the so-called dirty letters of 1909, were found in the cellar, because Joyce left them in Trieste.

63. T. S. Eliot, introduction to Stanislaus Joyce, *My Brother's Keeper* (London: Faber and Faber, 1958), pp. 12–13. (Hereafter cited in the text by page number.)

64. William Empson, "The Joyce Saga: Before Bloomsday and After," *New Statesman,* October 31, 1959.

65. During RE's earlier 1954 research trip, Mary writes on July 15 of a brief visit of RE's father to Evanston: "Your mother chose not to be so hurried—evidently to follow by herself sometime this month. She sent me by your father four handkerchiefs all enormously monogrammed with 'J.' The combination of your absence and her presence—blow upon blow—sent me to bed the other night in one of my old great floods of weeping."

8. RIVALS AND RESTRICTIONS

1. RE to H. K. (Harley) Croessmann, July 8, 1956.

2. RE to Harriet Weaver, July 5, 1956.

3. RE to parents, November 26, 1956.

4. Erwin Ellmann was a tough critic, as can be seen in the undated letter he wrote when he received ER's "The Backgrounds of *Ulysses*": "The Kenyon article seemed nicely to accomplish the purpose intended for it. While I will still need a bit of persuading of their legitimacy, the anecdotes are rather fun. Do the new discoveries of the identity of Bloom require you to alter and trim or is this a vindication of the method which permits you to fit any facts into the conclusion?"

5. RE, "The Backgrounds of *Ulysses*," *Kenyon Review* 16, no. 3 (Summer 1954): 345. (Hereafter cited in the text by page number.)

6. Even when real-life detail seems extraneous, it serves a purpose, according to RE. "[Joyce's] naturalism in *Ulysses* has many intricate supports, and one of the most interesting is the blurred margin. He introduces much material which he does not intend to explain, so that his book, like life, gives the impression of having many threads that one cannot follow. For example, on the way to the funeral [of Dignam], the mourners catch sight of Reuben J. Dodd, and Mr. Dedalus says, 'The devil break the hasp of his back.' This reaction seems a little excessive unless we know that Dodd had lent money to Joyce's father, and that the subsequent exactions were the efficient cause of Mr. Dedalus's irritation" (RE, "The Backgrounds of *Ulysses*," p. 360).

7. RE to C. G. Bowen, July 13, 1953.

8. Joyce especially valued the "Circe" episode. As RE puts it in *JJ:* "After having rewritten the episode from start to finish six or seven or eight or nine times (the count varied), he pronounced it done. In a rare moment of appraisal he commented to Francini Bruni, 'I think it is the best thing I have ever written'" (p. 511).

9. Attempts by Joyce scholars to find the phrase "Come in" in a passage of *Finnegans Wake* that Joyce might have dictated to Beckett have failed. See Nathan Halper, "On an Anecdote of Beckett's," *A Wake Newsletter,* June 1966, pp. 54–56; Sam Slote, "The Joyce Circle," in *Samuel Beckett in Context,* ed. Anthony Uhlmann (Cambridge: Cambridge University Press, 2013), p. 151: "The phrase, even allowing for Wakean distortion—has not been located in any of the manuscripts that Beckett worked on or could have worked on." Neither Halper nor Slote disputes the truth of the anecdote (which Beckett told in identical terms to the Beckett scholar James Knowlson), and both offer possible explanations for its non-appearance.

10. Luca Crispi points out that there is no evidence that Nora fed Joyce seedcake on Howth. Crispi, *Joyce's Creative Process and the Creation of Characters in Ulysses: Becoming the Blooms* (Oxford: Oxford University Press, 2015), pp. 168–69. Crispi thinks the likely source of this story is Oliver St. John Gogarty, who spent a day on Howth in 1904 with a young woman while he and Joyce were staying together at the Martello Tower. Gogarty wrote about the encounter in letters and is likely to have recounted it to Joyce.

11. See RE, *Ulysses on the Liffey* (1972; London: Faber and Faber, 1974), pp. 168–69. The odd phrase "gave the man a bit out of the apple" (one expects "bite" not "bit") is not found in *Ulysses on the Liffey,* and may or may not be a misprint. Here is how apple and seedcake are brought together in the book: "If we remember that *Finnegans Wake* speaks of the apple in the Garden of Eden as seed-fruit, there is a momentary connection with the apple which Eve passed to Adam as Molly to Bloom." Perhaps "bit," in the essay, derives from Molly's monologue at the end of *Ulysses:* "first I gave him the bit of seedcake out of my mouth" (1574). According to its preface, *Ulysses on the Liffey* was "largely developed in the course of preparing the T. S. Eliot Memorial Lectures at the University of Kent" (p. xvii).

12. "What happened?" asked the seven-year-old son of a friend of mine, on first seeing the Forum from the Palatine Hill.

13. RE published two other essays on Joyce while at work on the biography, both of which preview themes that will feature in the finished work. The first of these essays, "A Portrait of the Artist as Friend," *Kenyon Review* 18, no. 1 (Winter 1956), concerns Joyce's complex sense of himself as exile. Joyce "was neither bidden to leave nor forbidden to return," Ellmann writes at the beginning of the essay, "but whenever his relations with his native land seemed in danger of improving, he found a new incident to solidify his intransigence and reaffirm the rightness of his voluntary exile" (p. 53). This pattern is seen also in the behavior of the heroes of his books, "who seek freedom, which is also exile, voluntarily and by compulsion" (p. 54). Friendship was therefore problematic for Joyce and his heroes, for "it impugns the quality of exile and of lonely heroism. . . . Joyce allows his hero to sample friendship before discovering its flaws, and then with the theme of broken friendship represents his hero's broken ties with Ireland and the world" (p. 55). The flaws of friendship often take the form of supposed treachery or betrayal, in Joyce's life as well as his fiction. A prominent example in the essay involves Joyce's friendship with Ottocaro Weiss, as we shall see later in this chapter.

One other essay, "Ulysses the Divine Nobody," *Yale Review* 47 (September 1947), argues a central theme of *JJ*—that Joyce, like Stephen in *A Portrait,* is post-Christian rather than anti-Christian, "in that he finds new secular meanings to fill the husks of religious words he regards as dead" (p. 58). His temperament "retained a faculty of adoration . . . [although] it was turned not toward God but toward all creation. . . . 'Welcome, O life,' cries Stephen Dedalus at the end of 'Portrait' in a conclusion as decisive as Molly's 'yes' at the end of 'Ulysses'" (p. 60). Thus, "the illuminations of life exist within life, not above it, and are inseparable from the dirt in which they are imbedded. . . . Eliot uses the same technique of paralleling contemporaneity and antiquity that is implicit in the title of 'Ulysses.'" Eliot's example "had made it difficult to read Joyce without reading into his books something of Eliot's scorn of the modern world and of the world in general. There is no evidence that Joyce scorned either" (p. 62). Hence the essay's interpretation of Bloom "as a modern personification of the Ulyssean spirit, and not a parody of Ulysses" (p. 67). Ellmann quotes Aldous Huxley, who said that Joyce "used to insist upon a 'medieval' etymology for the Greek form of Ulysses' name, *Odysseus;* he said it was a combination of *Outis*—nobody, and *Zeus*—God. The etymology is merely fanciful, but it is a controlled fancy which helps to reinforce Joyce's picture of the modern

Ulysses. For Bloom is a nobody—an advertisement canvasser who, apart from his family, has virtually no effect upon the life around him—yet there is God in him" (pp. 66–67).

14. This phrase is Maria Jolas's from "Notes re RE biography of JJ," September 26, 1959, Ellmann Papers. It is cited by Carol Loeb Shloss, *Lucia Joyce: To Dance in the Wake* (London: Bloomsbury, 2004), p. 11. My account of the trunk, its contents, and their fate draws heavily on the introduction to Shloss's book.

15. William Brockman, "Learning to Be Joyce's Contemporary? Richard Ellmann's Discovery and Transformation of Joyce's Letters and Manuscripts," *Journal of Modern Literature* 22, no. 2 (Winter 1998–1999): 254.

16. Shloss, *Lucia Joyce,* p. 12.

17. See Jolas to RE, February 22, 1959. Joyce's "dirty letters" were not among the papers Paul L. Leon retrieved from the Joyces' Paris apartment after they had fled the city. They were among Stanislaus's papers in Trieste and ended up at Cornell. The letters Leon retrieved "were given by [him] to the Irish legation in France for safekeeping, with a request that they be sealed for 50 years [i.e., until 1992]" (William Brockman, "Letters," in *James Joyce in Context,* ed. John McCourt (Cambridge: Cambridge University Press, 1909), p. 27.

18. Brenda Maddox, *Nora: A Biography of Nora Joyce* (1998; Harmondsworth: Penguin Books, 2000), p. 524, quotes the Joyce biographer Peter Costello ("The Trieste Letters," *Irish Times,* July 2, 1976), for whom the absence of Nora's side of the correspondence "meant that a very one-sided view of the Joyce marriage has emerged and that the personality of Nora Joyce has been overshadowed by her husband."

19. Maddox, *Nora,* p. 524. For Maddox's reconstruction of Nora's obscenities, see pp. 139–45. RE did what he could to publish Joyce's side of the 1909 letters, arguing forcefully with the publishers of volumes 2 and 3 of the *Letters of James Joyce* for their inclusion, telling Peter du Sautoy of Faber and Faber, "Every one of Joyce's books in his lifetime, except *Chamber Music,* temporarily outraged or offended some people, and there is something appropriate about his continuing to outrage (but ultimately to awaken respect) from outre-tomb. He felt—as he said in 'The Holy Office'—that his mission as an artist was to tell the truth about the body when his contemporaries were off in soul-country. I think we are keeping faith with him if we publish his letters as he wrote them." When the letters were finally published in their entirety in RE's edited volume *Selected Letters of James Joyce* (London: Faber and Faber, 1975), RE explained their character, and defended their inclusion, in a lengthy preface:

> [Joyce's] first letters were filled with remorse [for having accused Nora of being unfaithful]. . . . But gradually he tried to turn the incident to advantage by ushering her into a greater intimacy. His letters became a turbulent mixture of erotic imagery and apologies for it, the apologies being accompanied by equally extreme flights of adoration. His relationship with her had to counterbalance all his rifts with other people. Having become partners in spiritual love, they must now share an onanistic complicity, agitating each other to sexual climax by means of their letters. In this way J renewed the conspiratorial and passionate understanding that they had when they first left Ireland together.

> These letters of 1909 and 1912 present Joyce with more intensity than any others. . . . [H]e mixes his pleas with tender rebuke, scolding her for scolding him. She is rude to him, ruder than he deserves. To vary the note, he sometimes delights in acknowledging his faults, including his infidelities with prostitutes, in imagining her as even more merciless to him, whipping him like the ladies of Sacher-Masoch, and with furs on to complete the picture. . . . Then, to renew his innocence and hers, he leans upon her as if she were a mother, and longs to be her child or even her unborn infant: 'take me into the dark sanctuary of your womb. Shelter me, dear, from harm!'
>
> He feels compelled to set images of purity against images of impurity. He dwells upon the association of the sexual and excretory organs, then fears she will consider him corrupt, although he has found learned sanction in Spinoza. At moments they fasten intently on peculiarities of sexual behaviour, some of which might technically be called perverse. They display traces of fetishism, anality, paranoia, and masochism, but before quartering Joyce into these categories and consigning him to their tyranny we must remember that he was capable, in his work, of ridiculing them all as Circean beguilements, of turning them into vaudeville routines. (pp. xxiv–xxv)

20. Jolas to RE, October 4, 1957.

21. Brockman, "Learning to Be Joyce's Contemporary?," p. 258.

22. See RE to Herbert Cahoon, November 4, 1954.

23. Croessmann to RE, April 1, 1956.

24. Croessmann to RE, November 20, 1957.

25. Herbert Cahoon to RE, December 7, 1957.

26. RE to Marshall Best, December 11, 1957, and January 3, 1958.

27. Brockman, "Learning to Be James Joyce's Contemporary?," p. 257. In a footnote on the same page Brockman cites Eileen MacCarvill to Herbert Cahoon, December 16, 1957, and January 11, 1958.

28. Mason was also unworried by the MacCarvill book, writing reassuringly to RE on February 4, 1958.

29. According to Lucy Ellmann, RE's daughter, in an email of August 20, 2023, her father "was not above being crafty, if he deemed it necessary, but he would not have taken it to immoral lengths. For example, I bet he was appalled that MacCarvill gave up completely due to pressure from him and his supporters. I can imagine him obsessed with the race to the finish line, and finishing his own book; not in scuppering someone else's."

30. Amanda Sigler, "Joyce's Ellmann: The Beginnings of *James Joyce*," *Joyce Studies Annual* (2010): 47. But see also RE to Ottocaro Weiss, November 2, 1946: "The whole sense of Joyce as a member of a family, with father, mother, brothers, and sisters comes out very strongly [in the letters in the Stanislaus collection] and in a way that it does not emerge anywhere else. In fact, the picture of his personality is remarkably complex. Most of the letters are long and detailed, and deal both with his external life and his intellectual history."

31. See RE to Frederic Faverty, January 9, 1957, which relates OUP's reaction.

32. See RE to Croessmann, May 3, 1957; also RE to parents, April 13, 1957, describing his last meeting as a member of the Budget Committee of the College of Liberal Arts.

33. Maddox, *Nora,* p. 219.

34. Maddox, *Nora,* p. 220.

35. RE to Gilbert, May 4, 1956. Weiss himself suggested that RE cut certain risqué passages, though for linguistic reasons. See RE to parents, September 25, 1955: "Weiss agreed with Dad about some of the off-color anecdotes, and I think I'll remove most of them since they don't fit in very well. Weiss's point was that Joyce liked them as much for their dialect as for the obscenity, and the dialect doesn't carry into English."

36. The collection was exhibited in the Librairie La Haine's *Exposition en hommage à James Joyce,* and consisted of over 10,000 pages of manuscript, correspondence, notebooks, and so on, as well as Joyce's library.

37. Maddox, *Nora,* pp. 517–18.

38. RE to Weiss, May 27, 1956.

39. The president told Mennen what Weiss had told McCarthy: that Cornell could obtain the "basic collection" for $30,000, and that including an additional group of letters in the sale (among them the erotic letters of 1909) would cost another $6,000—for a total of almost $500,000 in today's money. Previously, Northwestern, Yale, and Harvard had declined to bid—Northwestern and Yale for monetary reasons, Harvard, as mentioned earlier, "for administrative reasons" (a cover, perhaps, for monetary reasons).

40. For Cornell's purchase of the Stanislaus Joyce collection, see M. H. Abrams, "An Unlikely History: How Cornell Got Its Joyce Collection" (https://rmc.library.cornell.edu/joyce/unlikelystory.pdf), a talk given on June 9, 2005, at the opening of an exhibition of Cornell's Joyce Collection, which was timed to coincide with the 2005 North American James Joyce Convention, "Return to Ithaca," hosted at Cornell on June 14–18. See Maddox, *Nora,* p. 517, for the dean's comparison of the Stanislaus Joyce collection to a cyclotron.

41. Mason to RE, telegram, December 27, 1956.

42. RE to parents, December 1956 (no day given, though probably written on December 30, three days after Mason's telegram). In the letter RE described Mason as "very noncommittal," unable to admit that he was "in a mess." RE suspected that Mason might have "written to Kansas to find out if they'll support him if he is sued for libel." This suspicion RE gained when he called Mason three days after receiving his cable, despite having been told there was no need to call and that Mason was writing. Mason's manner on the phone was conciliatory. He was "very well disposed toward me personally, and carefully avoided getting angry or unpleasant." But RE remained pessimistic, fearing Mason was "quite capable of deciding that this is a matter of integrity, that he cannot give way an inch in spite of all the pressure, and so forth." Mary Ellmann, listening on another line, felt there was "a good chance he will yield."

43. Was RE not troubled, Mason asks in the same New Year's Eve letter, by the fact that Spoerri had concluded, "not once, but twice," that Weiss had committed himself to sell the collection to Kansas? As for the letter to Cornell, "it was not an attempt to squelch the transaction. . . . There is not a librarian in the world that would have cut off a transaction because of my letter."

44. Mason to RE, December 31, 1956.

45. RE to parents, December 1956 (no day given).

9. WRITING

1. The chapters in parts 1–3 (1882–1920) are twelve to twenty-five pages long; some chapters in parts 4–5 (1920–1941), in which Joyce gains a degree of fame, are five to ten pages longer. The chapters on the publication of *Portrait of the Artist* and *Ulysses* are longer than those on *Finnegans Wake,* partly because RE did not have access to the Paul L. Leon Archive.

2. See RE to Maria Jolas, December 26, 1953: "I'm glad to report that I've [begun] to write the book in preliminary form, beginning with a chapter on *Ulysses,* in which I try to show that all Joyce's experiences and a good many of his friends are in the book."

3. See RE to Mason, January 7, 1959. For OUP's thoughts on a two-volume edition, see Lee E. Grove (who replaced C. G. Bowen as trade editor) to RE, October 10, 1958.

4. RE to parents, January 21, 1959.

5. For the O'Mordha quote, see his essay "Richard Ellmann and Film Collaboration," in *Omnium Gatherum: Essays for Richard Ellmann,* ed. Susan Dick, Declan Kiberd, Dougald McMillan, and Joseph Ronsley (Gerrards Cross, UK: Colin Smythe, 199), p. 29; RE to Georg Goyert, May 14, 1955.

6. For the decision to bring Eileen to Trieste, see *JJ:* "Stanislaus objected that one sister [Eva] was enough, but Joyce insisted on bringing her. The 'dreadful house' at 44 Fontenoy Street was no place for her, and they must try to manage" (p. 318). At Fontenoy Street lived John Joyce and five of his daughters: May, Eileen, Eva, Florence, and Mabel. A sixth daughter, Margaret, who was about to leave to become a Sister of Mercy in a New Zealand convent, had run the house for six years. A brother, Charles, had left the year before. "Joyce felt a burst of pity for them and resolved to do something about it" (p. 293).

7. See William K. Robertson, "A Portrait of James Joyce's Biographer," in Dick et al., *Omnium Gatherum,* p. 44; originally published in the *Miami Herald,* March 21, 1982.

8. The quote about Stephen Dedalus's lice and Bloom's broken cup comes from the unfinished manuscript for a talk, "Writing Joyce's Biography," box 61, folder 10, Ellmann Papers. For Joyce and the body's everyday functions, see Cheryl Temple Herr, "Being in Joyce's World," in *James Joyce in Context,* ed. John McCourt (Cambridge: Cambridge University Press, 2009), p. 165. RE would later make amends for omitting references to bodily functions: in May 1971 he delivered the first T. S. Eliot Lecture at the University of Kent: "Why Does Stephen Dedalus Pick His Nose?" (reprinted in the *Times Literary Supplement,* May 21, 1971); a year later, *Ulysses on the Liffey* closes with a chapter titled "Why Molly Bloom Menstruates" (reprinted in the *New York Review of Books,* March 23, 1972). Times had changed, and Harriet Weaver, Joyce's patron and executor, had died (in 1961, two years after the publication of *JJ*). RE was indebted to and admired Miss Weaver and had been careful of her sensitivities. In the 1982 edition of *JJ,* he recounts an anecdote about her last illness. "When she had to submit to physical examination, she insisted that Joyce, Pound, Eliot, and Wyndham Lewis, whose photographed faces lined her bedroom, be turned to the wall so that her frail body would not be subjected to their scrutiny" (p. 352n).

9. Robertson, "A Portrait of James Joyce's Biographer," p. 43.

10. For "burrowing," not "ferreting," see p. 3 of "Adventures and Misadventures of a Biographer," box 61, folder 10, Ellmann Papers. RE's inaugural lecture at Oxford, "Literary Biography," is reprinted in Richard Ellmann, *Golden Codgers: Biographical Speculations* (London: Oxford University Press, 1973), p. 15. For the quotation from "Freud and Literary Biography," reprinted in Ellmann, *a long the riverrun: Selected Essays* (London: Hamish Hamilton, 1988), see p. 264. Joyce himself was skeptical about both Freud and Jung. In *JJ,* RE quotes a letter of June 24, 1921, from Joyce to Harriet Weaver: "A batch of people in Zurich persuaded themselves that I was gradually going mad and actually endeavoured to induce me to enter a sanitorium where a certain Dr. Jung (the Swiss Tweedledum who is not to be confused with the Viennese Tweedledee, Dr. Freud) amuses himself at the expense (in every sense of the word) of ladies and gentlemen who are troubled with bees in their bonnets" (p. 525).

11. RE, "Freud and Literary Biography," p. 256.

12. Joyce's quotation about wishing to "nestle in your womb" comes from a letter to Nora of September 2, 1909.

13. Here is another example, from the opening of chapter 16, "1907–1909": "During Joyce's early years on the continent he demonstrated a remarkable capacity to fall from every slight foothold, to teeter over every available precipice. Stanislaus, like Joyce's friends in Dublin, may be pardoned for supposing that each debacle was the beginning of the end. No artist ever inspired gloomier predictions from his associates than Joyce did. The wonder was that each time he contrived, with little effort, to fall on his feet" (p. 264). A footnote to this passage reads: "The predominant characteristic of Stephen Dedalus, as Bloom notes, is 'Confidence in himself, and equal and opposite power of abandonment and recuperation'" *Ulysses* (p. 657 [634]). (On p. xi of the preface to *JJ,* RE explains that the dual page references following quotations from *Ulysses* come from "Random House Inc., and Modern Library, 1942, and John Lane The Bodley Head, 1937.") In this example, the suggested connection between character and creator, Stephen and Joyce, is corroborating, but there is no suggestion that Stephen *is* Joyce. There are, however, instances in *JJ* in which the two are confused, as in the instance cited in Chapter 8, in which "The Dead" is said to have "dealt mainly with" Joyce's family as opposed to "drawn upon" it.

14. Quotes from Donoghue come from "Joyce's Many Lives," an omnibus review of Joyce biographies in the *New York Review of Books,* October 21, 1993. Ellmann was no more squeamish than Joyce about masturbation, referring to it elsewhere in the biography, but in this instance he judges that it is best, as well as more prudent, to neither go into detail (that is, make up detail, however plausible), nor cite, let alone quote, the passage Costello quotes from *Ulysses.*

15. Donoghue's reply appeared in the *New York Review of Books,* May 12, 1994.

16. The Seamus Heaney quote comes Heaney, Inaugural Richard Ellmann Lecture on Modern Literature, *The Place of Writing* (Atlanta, GA: Scholar Press for Emory University, 1989), p. 18.

17. Another Johnsonian example is Joyce's account of the opera singer John Sullivan. RE quotes from a letter Joyce wrote to Harriet Weaver: "In temperament he is intractable, quarrelsome, disconnected, contemptuous, inclined to bullying,

and undiplomatic; but on the other hand good humoured, sociable, unaffected, amusing and well informed." The quote is introduced by RE's description of a photograph taken of Sullivan, Joyce, and the writer James Stephens: "Joyce suggested the picture be captioned, 'Three Irish Beauties.' Sullivan had, as Joyce noted, the body of a member of the Dublin Metropolitan Police and looked like someone who had 'escaped from a boarding-school at the age of forty-nine'" (p. 633).

18. Patrick Hayes, *Postwar to Contemporary, 1945–2020,* vol. 7 of *The Oxford History of Life-Writing* (Oxford: Oxford University Press, 2022), p. 298.

19. These quotes are from W. J. Bate, *Samuel Johnson* (New York: Harcourt Brace Jovanovich, 1975), p. 542.

20. RE's attraction to a Johnsonian or Joycean wit, with its unexpected or paradoxical joining of things "remote from each other," owed something not only to Joyce and Johnson but to the New Criticism, a key driver of Joyce studies. Like RE, the New Critics were attracted to difficulty, in poetry as well as prose. Hence their interest in the Metaphysical poets, an interest inherited from T. S. Eliot. In "The Metaphysical Poets" (1921) Eliot defends the Metaphysicals against Johnson's claim that they sacrifice the "natural" for the sake of the "new." But in doing so he takes over Johnson's definition of metaphysical "wit," as "a kind of *Discordia concors;* a combination of dissimilar images, or discovery of occult resemblances in things apparently unlike." As Eliot puts it, in Metaphysical poetry "the most heterogeneous ideas are yoked by violence together." T. S. Eliot, *Selected Essays, 1917–1932* (New York: Harcourt Brace, 1932), p. 243. For the New Critics as a driver of Joyce studies in the United States, see Jeffrey Segall, *Joyce and America: Cultural Politics and the Trials of Ulysses* (Berkeley: University of California Press, 1993), pp. 135, 136: "In many respects, the New Critics were the ideal readers of Joyce." Ransom, Brooks, Tate, and Warren all wrote about Joyce, "[setting] the substance and tone for much of the Joyce criticism that followed. What today has become a Joyce industry consists almost entirely of exegetical analyses of the sort pioneered by the New Critics."

21. RE to Erwin and Steffani Ellmann, January 9, 1958.

22. Harry Levin to RE, October 14, 1958; RE's mother's disapproval of "The Hawk-Like Man" comes in a letter of November 13, 1958.

23. Amanda Sigler, "Joyce's Ellmann: The Beginnings of *James Joyce,*" *Joyce Studies Annual* (2010): 33.

24. Declan Kiberd, *The Irish Writer and the World* (Cambridge: Cambridge University Press, 2005), p. 244.

25. "See also *JJ*, p. 447: "Joyce, mindful of Father Daly's pandying which he had endured at Clongowes, never punished either child at all, and said. 'Children must be educated by love, not punishment.'"

26. These examples come from chapters 10 ("1904"), 26 ("1918"), and 23 ("1914–1915").

27. Finn Fordham, "Biography," in McCourt, *James Joyce in Context,* p. 22. In Joyce's case, blank periods could last "days or weeks on end, or, artistically, the years 1928–31." *JJ* devotes forty-five pages to the years 1918–1931.

28. Fordham, "Biography," p. 17. See also Joseph Brooker, *Joyce's Critics: Transitions in Reading and Culture* (Madison: University of Madison Press, 2004),

p. 110: "There is wisdom in Ellmann's view of Joyce. His eye for the ridiculous is matched by the grace of his sentences, in which the subject's disorderly life is brought into shape. If the heroic mode exalts the artist, the ironic note makes the man's life a more cheerful spectacle, however grim the evidence."

29. Hugh Kenner, "Inventing Literary Lives: The Biographical Fallacy," *Harper's,* October 1978.

30. John McCourt, "Reading Ellmann Reading Joyce," *European Joyce Studies* 14 (2002): 51.

31. Quoted in Laura Marcus, *Auto/biographical Discourses: Theory, Criticism, Practice* (Manchester: Manchester University Press, 1995), p. 92.

32. See Margot Norris, *The Decentered Universe of "Finnegans Wake"* (Baltimore: Johns Hopkins University Press), p. 11, for whom Joyce's book "fails to support . . . novelistic premises and, indeed, there is ample evidence to suggest that the work is designed precisely to refute the realist epistemology that has dominated prose fiction since the eighteenth century. The narrative technique of *Finnegans Wake* challenges the primacy of subjective individual experience in several ways. The singularity of individual experience—its uniqueness—is undermined by the replication of events and the instability of characters. The causal relationship of events in novelistic narration is replaced in *Finnegans Wake* by contiguous associations on the order of psychoanalytic free associations."

33. Kiberd, *The Irish Writer,* p. 246.

34. McCourt, "Reading Ellmann Reading Joyce," p. 42.

35. "Folly" here may well have a double meaning.

36. Quoted in Robertson, "A Portrait of James Joyce's Biographer," p. 43.

37. Elizabeth Cameron, the book's line editor at OUP, approved the epigraphs in a letter to RE, February 18, 1959: "Your epigraphs—and how did you ever choose them so well—make me think that at last I can read FW and relate it to something firm; a side-effect of your contribution for readers."

38. Hayes, *Postwar to Contemporary,* p. 298.

39. For different accounts of the trajectory of Joyce's writing career, see Brooker, *Joyce's Critics,* esp. chaps. 1, 3 and 4.

40. Harry Levin, *James Joyce: A Critical Introduction* (1941; London: Faber and Faber, 1960), pp. 101, 102.

10. RECEPTION / AFTERLIFE

1. RE to Harriet Weaver, September 30, 1958.

2. In October 1958 Meyer had taken over as trade editor from Lee Grove, who had in turn taken over from C. G. Bowen.

3. RE to parents, January 21, 1959.

4. Levin's undated report can be found in series 1, box 180, Ellmann Papers.

5. Harry Levin, *James Joyce: A Critical Introduction* (New York: New Directions, 1941), p. 42: "The final paragraph, in slow, spectral sentences, cadenced with alliteration and repetition, takes a receding view of the book itself [*Dubliners*]. It sets up, like most departures, a disturbing tension between the warm and familiar and the cold and remote."

6. Levin, *James Joyce,* p. 42.
7. RE to Elizabeth Cameron, March 1, 1959.
8. RE to parents, September 22, 1959.
9. RE to Weaver, November 1, 1959.
10. Two of the other friends of Joyce who attended the launch were James John Sweeney, an art critic and museum director who had helped Joyce in the writing of *Finnegans Wake,* and Arthur Laubenstein, a young American musician who for a period in Paris met with Joyce three evenings a week.
11. The title of Schorer's review was "A Cartoon Was Changed into a Life-Size Portrait." At the time of the review, Schorer was at work on what would become a comparably voluminous and fact-filled biography of Sherwood Anderson, published in 1961 to mixed reviews.
12. Stephen Spender's review, "All Life Was Grist for the Artist," appeared in the Sunday edition of the *New York Times,* October 25, 1959.
13. See Horace Reynolds, "The Complex Joyce in Ellmann Biography," *Christian Science Monitor,* October 22, 1959.
14. Anonymous review, "Dublin's Prodigal Son," *Time,* November 9, 1959.
15. William York Tindall, "The Full, Complex Life of a Modern Literary Titan," review of *JJ, New York Herald Tribune,* October 25, 1959.
16. Stuart Gilbert, "In the Wake of His Life Flowed His Art," *Saturday Review,* October 24, 1959. It is perhaps worth quoting Gilbert's implicit defense of having omitted some of the letters from his edition of the *Letters:* "Whatever the Rabelaisianism of his writing, there was no trace of it in his speech. Indeed he was something of a stickler for decorum and he would certainly have been horrified by the thought that one day his intimate letters to his wife were to be exposed to the public gaze."
17. Frank Kermode, "Puzzles and Epiphanies," *Spectator,* November 13, 1959.
18. F. R. Leavis, "James Joyce and the Revolution of the Word," *Scrutiny* 2, no. 2 (September 1933): 194, 197.
19. Joseph Brooker, *Joyce's Critics: Transitions in Reading and Culture* (Madison: University of Wisconsin Press, 2004), p. 78.
20. William Empson, "The Joyce Saga: Before Bloomsday and After," *New Statesman,* October 31, 1959.
21. Cyril Connolly, "A Long Look at the Tragedy of James Joyce," review of *JJ, Sunday Times,* November 1, 1959.
22. Anthony Powell, "The Pressures on Joyce," review of *JJ, Daily Telegraph,* October 30, 1959.
23. Matthew Hodgart, "Joyce's Boswell," review of *JJ, Guardian,* October 30, 1959.
24. Andrew Cass, "Portrait of the Artist as a Sick Man," review of *JJ, Irish Times,* November 6, 1959.
25. Brooker, *Joyce's Critics,* p. 201. The Montgomery quote is from his essay "Joyeux Quicum Ulysses . . . Swissairis Dubelllay Gadelice," in *A Bash in the Tunnel: James Joyce by the Irish,* ed. John Ryan (Brighton, UK: Clifton Books, 1970), pp. 61–72.
26. Declan Kiberd, *The Irish Writer and the World* (Cambridge: Cambridge University Press, 2005), p. 236, in a chapter titled "Joyce's Ellmann, Ellmann's

Joyce," dated 1999, derived from a talk delivered in Rome (La Sapienza) in 1998, on Bloomsday.

27. See Declan Kiberd, "The Giant Who Had a Gentle Touch," *Irish Times*, May 19, 1987, an article in praise of RE written on the day he was buried. "Paddywhackery" is a coinage of Myles na Gopaleen (Flann O'Brien).

28. Patrick Kavanagh, *Collected Poems* (London: Martin Brian and O'Keefe), 1972. Brooker, *Joyce's Critics*, p. 201, suggests that the poem also aims at Levin and Kenner. In recent years, Ireland having produced its own academic Joyceans, Ellmann's account of "the Swiss master" has been criticized for undervaluing the Irishness of his writing. This undervaluing, Kiberd thinks, derives from the fact that though "he loved Irish people as individuals, the plain truth was that he did not particularly like Ireland": "'It's a lovely country to visit,' Ellmann remarked during our first conversation in 1973, 'but I don't know how you manage to live there'" (Kiberd, *The Irish Writer*, p. 240). This attitude, Kiberd believes, derived from an outdated notion of Ireland, countered in lines from John Montague: "Puritan Ireland's dead and gone,/A myth of O'Connor and O'Faolain" (*The Irish Writer*, p. 240). One of the tasks of Irish Joyceans, therefore, was "a discrimination of modernisms, a recognition that Irish modernism is not at all the same thing as English modernism . . . that one doesn't need to turn only to Europe to explain his modernism, for it was already inherent in the formal demands placed on artists by the Irish situation" (p. 248).

29. The unsigned article in the April 2, 1960, issue of the *New Yorker*, in "Talk of the Town," was written by Brendan Gill and titled "Words, Words."

30. The comment about the judges sitting behind the winners like proud parents comes from Blake Bailey, *Philp Roth: The Biography* (New York: Vintage Books, 2021), p. 191.

31. Leslie Fiedler's article, "The 1960 National Book Awards," appeared in the *New Leader*, May 16, 1960.

32. Dick Steele, "Ellmann Drops 65 from Class to Preserve Discussion Plan," *Daily Northwestern*. April 1, 1960.

33. The English Institute was founded in 1939 and held yearly conferences at Columbia until 1972, after which Harvard, Yale, and a few other universities took turns hosting conferences. Ellmann organized the 1972 conference, "A Reconsideration of Romanticism," with talks by Lionel Trilling, Northrop Frye, M. H. Abrams, and René Wellek. "The talks were later published," recalled Jean Hagstrum in his tribute to RE in the Fall 1987 issue of Northwestern's *Arts and Sciences* magazine, "and may be the finest collection of essays produced by that intellectually elitist organization."

34. Ellsworth Mason, "Ellmann's Road to Xanadu," in *Omnium Gatherum: Essays for Richard Ellmann*, ed. Susan Dick, Declan Kiberd, Dougald McMillan, and Joseph Ronsley (Gerrards Cross, UK: Colin Smythe, 1989), p. 11.

35. *Eminent Domain* also predates W. J. Bate's *The Burden of the Past and the English Poet* (1970), which Bloom acknowledges as an influence, along with T. S. Eliot's essay "Tradition and the Individual Talent" (1920).

36. RE, *Eminent Domain: Yeats among Wilde, Joyce, Pound, Eliot and Auden* (Oxford: Oxford University Press, 1970), p. 3.

37. Neil Corcoran, *Shakespeare and the Modern Poet* (Cambridge: Cambridge University Press, 2010), p. 1.

38. Interview with Maud Ellmann, July 5, 2019.

39. Harold Bloom died on October 14, 2019. His obituary in the *New York Times,* "Harold Bloom: A Prolific Giant and Perhaps the Last of His Kind," appeared the next day, written by Dwight Garner.

40. Brooker, *Joyce's Critics,* p. 100.

41. Robert Scholes, *In Search of James Joyce* (Urbana: University of Illinois Press, 1992), p. 54, quoted in Brooker, *Joyce's Critics,* p. 100.

42. Bernard McGinley, *Joyce's Lives: Uses and Abuses of the Biografiend* (London: North London University Press, 1996), p. 31. Also quoted in Brooker, *Joyce's Critics,* p. 100.

43. Robert M. Adams, "In Joyce's Wake," *Hudson Review* (Winter 1959–1960), p. 502.

44. See McGinley, *Joyce's Lives,* p. 23; Joseph Ronsley, "Richard Ellmann, 1918–1987," *Irish Literary Supplement,* September 1, 1987; and Hodgart, "Joyce's Boswell."

45. RE, "Literary Biography," reprinted in *Golden Codgers: Biographical Speculations* (Oxford: Oxford University Press, 1973), p. 16. However, the passage goes on to say that "at moments, in glimpses, biographers seem to be close to it, and the effort to come close, to make out of apparently haphazard circumstances a plotted circle, to know another person who has lived as well as we know a character in fiction, and better than we know ourselves, is not frivolous."

46. In addition to McGinley's *Joyce's Lives,* see, for example, Ira B. Nadel, "The Incomplete Joyce," *Joyce Studies Annual* (Summer 1991): 86–100; Joseph Kelley, "Stanislaus Joyce, Ellsworth Mason, and Richard Ellmann: The Making of 'James Joyce,'" *Joyce Studies Annual* (Summer 1992); and John McCourt, "Reading Ellmann Reading Joyce," *European Joyce Studies* 2, no. 14 (2002): 41–58.

47. Harold Bloom, ed., *James Joyce: Modern Critical Views* (New York: Chelsea House, 1986), p. ix, quoted in Brooker, *Joyce's Critics,* p. 98.

48. James Knowlson, *Damned to Fame: The Life of Samuel Beckett* (London: Bloomsbury, 1966), p. 454, quoted in Brooker, *Joyce's Critics,* p. 98.

49. Quoted in Brooker, *Joyce's Critics,* p. 116, from Hugh Kenner, *Dublin's Joyce* (1956; New York: Columbia University Press, 1987), p. 230.

50. In the summer of 1968, at a conference in Buffalo, New York, Kenner was fiercely attacked by William Empson for his interpretation of *A Portrait.* Fritz Senn, a speaker at the conference, recalls that Empson mounted a "personal attack on Kenner, who, by unmasking many features of the *Portrait* as ironic that had once been taken straight, 'had destroyed the *Portrait* for a generation of readers.' Empson was visibly upset and even questioned Kenner's morals. The audience was taken aback by the unexpected violence of the debate." As for "exactly how Kenner responded," Senn does not recall. He was too busy preparing his own remarks. See *Joycean Murmoirs: Fritz Senn on James Joyce,* ed. Christine O'Neill (Dublin: Lilliput Press, 2007), p. 30.

51. Edward M. Burns, ed., *Questioning Minds: The Letters of Guy Davenport and Hugh Kenner,* 2 vols. (New York: Counterpoint Press, 2018), vol. 1, pp. 29, 123, 274.

52. Hugh Kenner, "Circe," in *James Joyce's "Ulysses": Critical Essays,* ed. Clive Hart and David Hayman (Berkeley: University of California Press, 1974).

53. RE, "Pieces of Ulysses," review of *James Joyce's 'Ulysses': Critical Essays,* ed. Hart and Hayman, *Times Literary Supplement,* October 3, 1975.

54. Brooker, *Joyce's Critics,* p. 115.

55. The introduction to RE's edition of the *New Oxford Book of American Verse* (Oxford: Oxford University Press, 1976) begins: "American poetry, once an offshoot, now appears to be a particular stem. Speculative, daring, and sometimes melodious, it has become the register of some of the most independent minds [in modern literature]."

56. Kenner to Davenport, October 8, 1976, in Burns, *Questioning Minds,* vol. 2, p. 1621.

57. Hugh Kenner, "Literary Biographies" (1978), reprinted in *Historical Fictions* (1990; Athens, GA: University of Georgia Press, 1995), pp. 46–53.

58. Ronald Bush, "James Joyce: The Way He Lives Now," *James Joyce Quarterly* (Summer 1996): 523; Ira B. Nadel, "The Incomplete Joyce," *Joyce Studies Annual* (1991): 89; both articles quoted in Brooker, *Joyce's Critics,* pp. 105–6.

59. Morris Beja, "Citizen Joyce, or My Quest for Rosebud," *Journal of Modern Literature* 22 (Winter 1998–1999): 208.

60. Philip Gaskell, "Joyce Again," review of *JJII, Essays in Criticism* 33, no. 3 (July 1983): 252–55. In "Ellmann Rejoycing," *New York Times Book Review,* September 19, 1982, RE explains the genesis of the second edition: "Soon after the publication of 'James Joyce,' there drifted in letters, reminiscences and other records of which I had known nothing. Corrections could be made in subsequent printings, but larger changes would have to await a second edition. The Oxford University Press took an indulgent view of the prospect, and now after 23 years, it has been realized. Although the character of the book is undisturbed, perhaps a 100 pages have been added and many of the old pages altered. I have been moved and amused by fresh instances of Joyce's originality and bizarreness."

61. Christopher Ricks, "Ellmann Re-Joyces," *Grand Street,* Spring 1983, pp. 89, 96.

62. For a summary of Kenner on Joyce's use of language and what it implies about representation, from *Dublin's Joyce* onward, see Brooker, *Joyce's Critics,* pp. 127–30, in which parallels are drawn with "contemporary theory" (p. 130). Kenner's partial disavowal of these parallels is also discussed.

63. The Centennial Symposium in Dublin was the eighth such international symposium. The first was held in 1967, twenty-six years after Joyce's death, and had some 80 participants. By 1969 more than 230 participants convened in Dublin for an entire week. The numbers only increased over the 1970s. A year was skipped to meet the Centennial Symposium of 1982, for which 550 people registered, 250 of whom participated in the program. Patrick Hillery, the president of Ireland, welcomed the assembled Joyceans.

64. Derek Attridge, *Joyce Effects: On Language, Theory, and History* (Cambridge: Cambridge University Press, 2000), pp. 8, 9.

65. Brenda Maddox, *Nora* (London: Hamish Hamilton, 1988), p. 532.

66. This was Maud's second International James Joyce Symposium. In 1979 she delivered a paper on a panel alongside Colin MacCabe and the novelist and critic David Lodge.

67. Henry Hart, "Richard Ellmann's Oxford Blues," *Sewanee Review* 17, no. 2 (Spring 2009): 283.

68. Attridge, *Joyce Effects,* p. 3. In a later book, *Forms of Modernist Fiction: Reading the Novel from James Joyce to Tom McCarthy* (Edinburgh: Edinburgh University Press, 2023), pp. 50–51, Attridge makes clear the possible compatibility of differing approaches: "Many of the literary practices that we rather inadequately label 'postmodernist' have accustomed us to operations of contingency and chance in our texts, and although the realist narrative thrives as much as it has ever done, we have come to understand that convincing representation can quite happily go hand-in-hand with exposure of the means of representation. *Ulysses,* therefore, becomes even more central to our account of the literary revolution of this period, and contemporary writers are encouraged to explore formal techniques whose function is more than the enhancement of content."

69. McCourt, "Reading Ellmann Reading Joyce," p. 57. RE was in some ways a conservative. But he eloquently defended Henry Miller's *Tropic of Cancer* at trial, January 10–12, 1962 ("He was the very best and most impressive witness in that case," wrote Elmer Gertz, the defending attorney, to Jean Hagstrum, in a letter of January 11, 1988). He testified in support of James Baldwin's *Another Country* in January 1965, when there was a move to ban it from assignment in Chicago Public Schools. On February 7, 1968, at a symposium on university-military relations, he spoke against recruiters from Dow Chemical, makers of napalm, being allowed on campus. And on May 7, 1968, he was one of three Northwestern faculty members who circulated a statement—a statement he wrote—in support of the demands of Black students for more recruitment and financial aid for Black students, desegregation of the university's real estate holdings, and creation of a Department of African American Studies; these demands were made in the wake of an occupation of the Bursar's Office on May 3.

70. McCourt, "Reading Ellmann Reading Joyce," p. 52.

71. Senn, *Joycean Murmoirs,* p. 180. Senn recounts seeing two other meetings—one involving "polite handshakes," the other "courteous nods in passing" (p. 179).

72. Hart, "Richard Ellmann's Oxford Blues," p. 282.

73. Colin MacCabe, "Uneasiness in Culture: Joyce Studies," review of *Ulysses on the Liffey* by Richard Ellmann, *Cambridge Review* 93, no. 2208 (1972): 174–77. The comment about its being a "nasty young man's review" is from an interview MacCabe gave on November 27, 2023.

74. Colin MacCabe, review of *Structuralist Poetics* by Jonathan Culler, *Cambridge Review* 96 (1975): 186.

75. Colin MacCabe, *James Joyce and the Revolution of the Word* (1979; London: Palgrave, 2003), p. xxxii.

76. Interview with MacCabe, November 27, 2023. Maud Ellmann described her sessions with MacCabe on Freud, Marx, and Nietzsche (for the "Moralists" paper of the English Tripos examination) as "a life-changing experience," one for which she said she would be grateful "for the rest of my life" (email, December 2, 2023).

77. Hart, "Richard Ellmann's Oxford Blues," pp. 279, 280.

78. Terence Diggory, email, May 28, 2020.

79. Gayatri Spivak, email, July 31, 2020; Ronald Schuchard, "Richard Ellmann at Emory," in *Where Courageous Inquiry Leads: The Emerging Life of Emory University,* ed. Gary S. Hauk and Sally Wolff (Atlanta: Emory University, 2010), p. 339.

80. Kiberd, "Joyce's Ellmann, Ellmann's Joyce," reprinted as chap. 15 in Kiberd, *The Irish Writer,* p. 245.

81. The exhibition lasted from February to April 1966, so RE must have been asked to contribute to its catalog in 1965.

CODA: LAST YEARS

1. Yale had been trying to lure RE for several years. In 1966 it offered him a $25,000 salary, a two-thirds teaching load, and one semester leave every three years, their normal sabbatical plan. Leland countered with $26,000 in salary for 1966–1967, $28,000 for 1967–1968, and $30,000 thereafter, plus $2,000 a year research grant, a reduced teaching load of two courses for the first two quarters and no courses for the third (the fourth being summer), or a continuation of his current deal, with the same teaching load and every third year off with full pay.

2. Lucy Ellmann, email, November 13, 2023; Maud Ellmann, email, December 2, 2023. Subsequent quotations from Maud Ellmann come from interview of July 5, 2019.

3. When the quarantine period was reduced from a year to six months, Pepito was removed from the commune in Maine where he had been staying, survived the reduced quarantine, and joined the family in Oxford.

4. This is not how Nicholas Barker described Mary's feelings, in his obituary for the British Academy, "Richard Ellmann 1918–1987," in *Biographical Memoirs of Fellows of the British Academy,* vol. 13 (London: British Academy), p. 187: "Mary was adamant that the planned move should go ahead, and Dick was duly elected to the chair; and the fellowship [at New College] that went with it."

5. For a characteristically acid account of drinks and snacks at 39 St. Giles, see Roger Lewis, *Anthony Burgess* (London: Faber and Faber, 2002): RE taught Lewis at Oxford in the mid-1980s, and in the prologue to the Burgess biography Lewis describes Ellmann as "making a meal of fetching gin and tonics. . . . No bottles were left conveniently at hand. A plastic tub of what might have been called guacamole made a brief appearance. Ellmann may have held several honorary doctorates and written masterpieces of twentieth-century biography, but as a host he needed to stay and see the teacher after class" (p. 14). As Lewis sees it, RE "wholly lacked the Oxford way of people being interested in each other only for their own advantage"; but then, "He didn't seem interested in people at all" (p. 5n). When Lewis describes Burgess as "a genuine fake," RE laughs, then offers an "unusually forthright" warning:

> I worry about your tone—outsmarting its subject. I feel sure that you regard Burgess as an extraordinary phenomenon, without whom literature would be poorer. If he writes a lot, that's because writing comes so naturally to him, even though he loves artifice. I can't think of anyone in the history of literature who provides us with so many books, none of them simple-minded, all vastly ambitious, much

more ambitious than necessary (or advisable) for a popular success. Of course you know all this and to some extent say it, but I'd like to feel that you were not above patting him on the back. I realise that you have somewhat striated feelings about your subject. Still, in the hierarchy of virtues, kindness ranks above unkindness. (pp. 383–84).

6. Craig Raine, email, April 22, 2019.

7. Hart, "Richard Ellmann's Oxford Blues," p. 278.

8. John Kelly, interview, March 11, 2022. Subsequent quotations from Kelly, also from his wife Christine, come from this interview.

9. Lucy Ellmann, *Ducks, Newburyport* (Norwich, UK: Galley Beggar Press, 2019), p. 812. (Hereafter cited in the text by page number.)

10. Lucy Ellmann, email, July 13, 2019.

11. RE, *Golden Codgers: Biographical Speculations* (Oxford: Oxford University Press, 1973), p. ix.

12. Barbara Hardy, *London Lovers* (London: Peter Owen, 1996), pp.135–36. (Hereafter cited in the text by page number.)

13. Less secret, and looked at askance by Mary, was a platonic dalliance RE had with a wealthy woman he met in Monte Carlo at a Joyce conference organized by the Princess Grace Library. This woman, Rosita Fanto, wrote a roman à clef about their relationship titled *Lady of the Cards: A Memoir in the Form of a Novel* (Bloomington, IN: Xlibris, 2010). She also involved RE in a project related to the Wilde biography: a set of Oscar Wilde playing cards, which was published before the biography and celebrated at a launch RE attended at the Cadogan Hotel. The writer Andrew Rosenheim tells of a party given by Arthur and Ann Friedman at which he and his parents and the Ellmanns were present. Arthur Friedman, a professor of English at the University of Chicago, had been Rosenheim's father's "dissertation adviser, colleague, and closest faculty friend." The Italian writer Gaia Servadio was also there, wearing a posy of flowers in her hair. "She was a great beauty and fawned on Dick at length, sitting on the floor next to his chair. Mary was spitting by the end of the do" (email, December 22, 2023).

14. Hart, "Richard Ellmann's Oxford Blues," pp. 275, 274.

15. From 1983 to 1992 Stephen J. Ellmann was an associate professor of law at Columbia University, and from 1992 until his death from cancer on March 8, 2019, he taught at New York Law School. He wrote on the ethics and skills of legal work, on interviewing and counseling clients, and on human rights in South Africa under apartheid. According to his sister Maud, Stephen "really did idealize" his father, and at the end of his life followed in his footsteps by writing a biography of the South African lawyer Arthur Chaskalson, titled *Justice for All: Arthur Chaskalson and the Struggle for Equality in South Africa,* published posthumously in 2020.

16. Barker, "Richard Ellmann, 1918–1987," p. 190.

17. Ronald Schuchard, email, July 30, 2020.

18. Ronald Schuchard, email, July 15, 2020.

19. Lucy Ellmann, email, December 24, 2023. In an email of January 4, 2024, Lucy adds: "She cared about my father deeply, devoted her life to him, and was lost without him after he died."

20. Barker, "Richard Ellmann, 1918–1987," p. 190.

21. Barker, "Richard Ellmann, 1918–1987," p. 190.

22. Schuchard, "Richard Ellmann at Emory," p. 341. Seamus was RE's friend, the poet Seamus Heaney.

23. On May 11, Catherine Carver, the editor, was in Oxford to deliver proof corrections for the Wilde biography. She seems to have remained on for a day or two. She and Ron Schuchard were in the hospital to see RE on May 13, the day he died, but had not been allowed into the room. According to a story told to Schuchard ("by someone, maybe even a nurse"), after Catherine Carver had gone over the proofs with RE—this was in the hospital—and had left the room, RE sat up in bed and pulled "all the wires and tubes out very dramatically before his death." This story was heard also by Gigi Schendler, widow of Sylvan Schendler, a student of Ellmann's at Northwestern. Neither Lucy nor Maud had heard the story before I brought it to their attention, nor do they believe it. They were present at their father's deathbed, and he pulled out no tubes or wires. As Maud puts it: "He wanted to live. Right up to the end." In Lucy's words, "He wanted to live to see his book come out. He wanted to see the book in the flesh. . . . He was *not the least bit interested in dying.*"

24. Lucy Ellmann's handwritten note and material from RE's doctor in Oxford are in Ellmann Papers.

25. Ronald Schuchard, email, July 15, 2020.

26. Ronald Schuchard, email, July 15, 2020.

27. Bob Reilly, "Portrait of the Artist as a Biographer, *New York Times Book Review,* September 19, 1982.

ACKNOWLEDGMENTS

My first debt is to Ellmann's daughters, Maud and Lucy, who approved the idea of this book. Their brother, Stephen Ellmann, a law professor, died in 2019, before we could meet. Other family members to whom I am indebted are Michael Ellmann, the son of Richard Ellmann's older brother Erwin; Michael's son Christopher; and Douglas Ellmann and Robert Ellmann, sons of Ellmann's younger brother William. Lucy Ellmann's husband, Todd McEwan, and Stephen Ellmann's widow, Teresa M. Delcorso, provided helpful suggestions. Soon after I began work on the book I was put in touch with Amanda Sigler, author of "Joyce's Ellmann: The Beginnings of *James Joyce*," published in *Joyce Studies Annual* (2010). Sigler's brilliant essay, which began life as an undergraduate thesis, was my work's starting point. When we met early in 2020 in Tulsa, Oklahoma, she welcomed the prospect of a book-length study.

I am grateful to the administration and staff of Special Collections and University Archives at the McFarlin Library at the University of Tulsa, where Ellmann's papers are housed. I want especially to thank Milissa Burkart, Melissa Kunz, Jessica Castaño, and the late Marc Carlson. I am also grateful for the support of Adrian Alexander, at the time dean of the Library. When my wife's illness cut short our stay in Tulsa, the many papers I had still to see were scanned and sent to me by Nathan Blue and Cooper Casale, graduate students in English to whom I am deeply indebted. I am indebted also to the encouragement of two Joyceans at Tulsa, Sean Latham and Robert Spoo, as well as to the extraordinary generosity and hospitality of Lars Engle and Joli Jenson of the English Department, and of Jeni Halliday, a Tulsa native and friend.

At the Beinecke and Sterling Memorial Libraries at Yale University I was helped by Casey Thomas, Michael Frost, Katy Darr, and Jessica Becker. I also benefited from the advice of David Bromwich and Paul Fry of the English Department. Yuka Saji, a resourceful undergraduate research assistant, helped to answer queries and locate and scan documents. At Middlebury College, Kaitlin Buerge, the college archivist, provided information about the Bread Loaf School of English. At Harvard University, I was helped by Nicholas Watson of the English Department and by reference staff at the Houghton Library and at Harvard Archives, particularly James Capobianco and Megan Sniffen-Marinoff, university archivist. For information about Mary Donahue Ellmann at the University of Minnesota, I was helped by Rebecca Toov, collections archivist, University Archives. For information about Mary's time teaching at Wellesley College, I am grateful to Katie Lamontagne and Rebecca Goldman, of Wellesley College Archives. For Helen Taft Manning at Bryn Mawr, I am grateful to Alison Mills, college archivist, Special Collections. At the National Library of Ireland, I was helped by Mary B. Broderick. At the Library of Trinity College Dublin, I was helped by Jane Maxwell. At Northwestern University, during COVID, all libraries and archives were closed to outside scholars. Kevin B. Leonard, university archivist, not only sought out and scanned the materials I wanted, but for several days allowed me to see papers he had brought back to his house in Evanston. These papers I studied in a quiet den off the living room, interrupted only when Kevin and his wife served me lunch in their kitchen.

At the Wylie Agency I owe thanks to Andrew Wylie and Jeff Posternak. At Harvard University Press special thanks to Sharmila Sen, who commissioned the book, and to Samantha Mateo, Stephanie Vyce, Katrina Vassallo, Kate Brick, Colleen Lanick, and Rebekah White. Also thanks to copy editor Wendy Nelson. Riley Moore, the most able of research assistants, provided crucial help in obtaining photographs and permissions. I am indebted to the British Academy for a BA/Leverhulme Small Research Grant, especially to its administrators Eve Waller and Charles Hamilton, models of patience and sympathy. The book's last chapter and the Coda and Introduction were written outside Genoa at the Liguria Study Center for the Arts and Humanities, on a fellowship from the Bogliasco Foundation. Portions of the book were presented as talks at the Oxford Centre for Life-Writing (thanks to Hermione Lee, Kate Kennedy, and Elleke Boehmer); the University College Dublin James Joyce Research Centre (thanks to Luca Crispi and Anne Fogarty); and the Trieste Joyce School (thanks to Ronan Crowley and Laura Pelaschiar). On each of these occasions I benefited from questions and comments from audience members.

For careful reading of the entire manuscript, I am once again indebted to Lindsay Duguid, who improved the book at every stage of its composition. Lucy Ellmann, Luca Crispi, Andrew Rosenheim, and Roy Foster also read and improved the whole manuscript. I am grateful to the following individuals for information, advice, and hospitality: Sabrina Alonso, Michael Anania, Alison Armstrong, Isobel Armstrong, Susan Arnold, Morris Beja, Joachim Beug, Austin Briggs, Martine Bromley, Kate Carl, Paul Cohen, Judith Miller Conlin, Jonathan Culler, Terence Diggory, Maud Ellmann, Joseph Epstein, John Feidelson, Warwick Gould, Gerald Graff, Liz Grasty, Nicholas Grene, Selina Hastings, Richard Holmes, Jacob Howland, Vivien Igoe, Ellen Carol Jones, John and Christine Kelly, Declan Kiberd, Colin MacCabe, Jim Maddox, Lauro Martines, John McCourt, Linda and Mike Mewshaw, Doris Palca, Robert Potts, Ed Mulhall, Brian Ostrander, Patrick Parrinder, Paul Psilos, Craig Raine, Alison Reynolds, Christopher Ricks, Nancy Rosenbloom, Nicholas Rostow, Victoria Rostow, Gigi Schendler, Erik Schneider, Ronald W. Schuchard, Laurence Senelick, Fritz Senn, Maggie Simmons, Milan Singh, Philip E. Smith, William Smith, Gayatri Spivak, Thomas F. Staley, Laura Stevens, John Sutherland, Gordon Turnbull, and David Willis. Thanks also to Mary Ellen Ellis, who compiled the book's index.

Finally, I thank my family: my sons Nick and Max Leader, and my daughter-in-law Nicole Jackson. My wife, always my first reader, was able to comment on drafts of the first two-thirds of the book. That she had been taught by Ellmann at Northwestern (I met him there just once, briefly) gave extra weight to her suggestions and observations.

ILLUSTRATION CREDITS

page 7 Robert Lowell, Richard Ellmann, Philip Roth. *Source:* Bettmann/ Getty Images.

12 Four generations of the Joyce family. *Source:* © IMEC, Fonds MCC, Dist. RMN-Grand Palais/Art Resource, NY.

14 Ellmann family in 1926. *Source:* Courtesy of Lucy Ellmann.

30 Erwin Ellmann, early 1940s. *Source:* Courtesy of Christopher Ellmann.

34 William Ellmann, mid-1940s. *Source:* Courtesy of Douglas Ellmann.

43 Erwin and Steffani Ellmann. *Source:* Courtesy of Christopher Ellmann.

48 Ellmann's parents, Jean and James Ellmann. *Source:* Courtesy of Lucy Ellmann.

50 Executive editorial board, *Yale Literary Magazine. Source:* Yale College, Class History of 1939, Manuscripts and Archives, Yale University Library.

57 Ellmann, class photo. *Source:* Yale College, Class History of 1939, Manuscripts and Archives, Yale University Library.

71 Bread Loaf Writers, Conference, summer 1941. *Source:* Middlebury College Special Collections, Middlebury, Vermont.

78 Jean Douglas, early 1940s. *Source:* The University of Tulsa, McFarlin Library, Department of Special Collections. Used by permission of Liz Miller Grasty.

103 Ellmann in naval uniform, 1945. *Source:* Courtesy of Lucy Ellmann.

112 Henri Michaux. *Source:* Digital image © CNAC/MNAM, Dist. RMN-Grand Palais/Art Resource, NY.

118 Stage Door Canteen, Paris, March 9, 1945. *Source:* Courtesy of Lucy Ellmann.

127 Mrs. W. B. Yeats. *Source:* Reproduced from Ann Saddlemyer, *Becoming George: The Life of Mrs. W. B. Yeats* (Oxford University Press, 2002), illustration 29.

153 Cover of the *Saturday Review* picturing Yeats and Ellmann. *Source: The Saturday Review,* November 13, 1948.

182 The beach at Northwestern University. *Source:* Northwestern University Archives.

184 Walter B. Scott. *Source:* Northwestern University Archives.

189 Mary Ellmann, early 1960s. *Source:* Courtesy of Lucy Ellmann.

206 Stanislaus and Nelly Joyce, 1926. *Source:* Reproduced from Richard Ellmann, *James Joyce: New and Revised Edition* (Oxford: Oxford University Press, 1983), insert XXXVIII, top right.

226 Sylvia Beach and Harriet Weaver. *Source:* Carlton Lake Collection of Maurice Saillet, Harry Ransom Center.

236 Marthe Fleischmann and Rudolf Hiltpold. *Source:* Reproduced from Richard Ellmann, *James Joyce: New and Revised Edition* (Oxford: Oxford University Press, 1983), insert XXX, right.

246 J. F. Byrne. *Source:* Image courtesy of University College Dublin Digital Library produced from an original held in the Curran-Laird Collection, UCD Special Collections.

252 The cellar where Nelly Joyce showed Ellmann Stanislaus's papers. *Source:* Courtesy of Erik Schneider.

257 Pierre the poodle. *Source:* The University of Tulsa, McFarlin Library, Department of Special Collections.

270 Richard Ellmann and his children. *Source:* The University of Tulsa, McFarlin Library, Department of Special Collections.

282 Ottocaro Weiss. *Source:* Reproduced from Marili Cammarata, ed., *Trieste Raccolta: Il Fondo Ottocaro Weiss presso le Assicurazioni Generali* (Trieste: Editrice la Compangna, 1996).

287 Ellsworth Mason. *Source:* Hofstra University Special Collections Department.

290 Ellmann early manuscript drafts. *Source:* The University of Tulsa, McFarlin Library, Department of Special Collections.

317 Ellmann at the typewriter. *Source:* Courtesy of Lucy Ellmann.

320 Harry Levin. *Source:* Schlesinger Library, Harvard Radcliffe Institute.

323 Mary Ellmann, Richard Ellmann, John R. B. Brett-Smith, and Frances Steloff. *Source:* The University of Tulsa, McFarlin Library, Department of Special Collections.

347 Hugh Kenner. *Source:* Courtesy of Walter Baumann.

354 Barbara Hardy. *Source:* © National Portrait Gallery, London.

357 Richard Ellmann in April 1987. *Source:* Courtesy of Gigi Schendler.

INDEX

Page numbers in italics refer to illustrations.